Inside the Windows 95 File System

Inside the Windows 95 File System

Stan Mitchell

O'REILLY™

Cambridge · Köln · Paris · Sebastopol · Tokyo

Inside the Windows 95 File System
by Stan Mitchell

Copyright © 1997 O'Reilly & Associates, Inc. All rights reserved.
Printed in the United States of America.

Published by O'Reilly & Associates, Inc., 101 Morris Street, Sebastopol, CA 95472.

Editor: Andrew Schulman

Production Editor: David Futato

Printing History:

> May 1997:   First Edition

This book is printed on acid-free paper with 85% recycled content, 15% post-consumer waste. O'Reilly & Associates is committed to using paper with the highest recycled content available consistent with high quality.

ISBN: 1-56592-200-X

Table of Contents

Preface

This book will walk you through the inner workings of the Windows 95 file system. The standard file systems which ship with Windows 95 include: VFAT, the virtual FAT file system; VREDIR, the Microsoft Networks client; and NWREDIR, the Microsoft Netware client. These and other file systems supplied by third party developers register with the Installable File System Manager, or IFSMgr, to make their services available to the system. IFSMgr manages the resources which are currently in use by each file system and routes client requests to the intended file system.

This book anticipates some of the changes to the file system which will appear in the successor to Windows 95 (code-named Memphis). These new features include FAT32, support for volumes up to 2 terabytes in size, and WDM (the Win32 Driver Model). The Microsoft Networks file and printer sharing protocol—the SMB (Server Message Block) protocol—is also undergoing some changes to make it suitable for accessing the Internet. SMB's future extension to the Internet as CIFS (the Common Internet File System) is also examined.

The core of this book is based on the flow of execution through the layers of the file system (stopping short of the disk system, managed by IOS, the I/O Supervisor). Requests are made of the file system through the application programming interfaces (APIs) that are appropriate for the operating environment (interrupt 21h, Win16, or Win32). These requests ultimately arrive at IFSMgr, which must find a file system driver to relay the request to. Although three different Windows 95 operating environments generate these requests, IFSMgr relays them to the file system drivers using a common I/O request packet structure. A file system driver doesn't know and doesn't care if the request originated in a DOS application or in a Win32 program.

As file system requests pass through IFSMgr on their way to file system drivers, a file system monitor may intercept the I/O request packets. These monitors may simply report the file system requests and pass them on, or they may change the operation or direct it to a different driver. This capability provides some interesting possibilities for developers.

Of the three Windows 95 programming environments, special attention is given to the new Win32 environment. The focus will be on the mapping between the Win32 APIs and the lower level file system functions which are used to implement them. This will also lead us to explore KERNEL32 objects, especially the file object.

The structure of file system drivers (FSDs) is examined and two sample FSDs are implemented. One is for a character device which acts as an interface to a monochrome display adapter; the other implements a "file system within a file" by using some of IFSMgr's ring-0 services. The VFAT and VREDIR file system drivers are also scrutinized.

Our coverage will stray a little from IFSMgr and FSDs by examining paging and cache services. The paging file in Windows 95 is implemented as a VFAT file; page-ins and page-outs to this file are done using the system *pagers*, routines which control the lifecycle of pages. FSDs rely upon VCACHE's services to keep the most recently used disk blocks in memory, thereby minimizing disk "hits." Chapter 11, on VCACHE, will explain how these services work.

Since much of this material is new, you are probably wondering: "What is the source for this information? Do you have access to IFSMgr source code, or do you have a good connection at Microsoft?" Recently, Geoff Chappell (author of *DOS Internals*) was asked a similar question in an Internet newsgroup. His answer says it all:

Q: *So have you gotten your hands on IFSMgr code somehow, or are you just hacking through it with SoftICE?*

A: I have my hands on IFSMgr code. So have you. Source code, of course, is another matter—but why should I want that? I may be the only person on the planet who works primarily with VxDs but who doesn't use SoftICE (and indeed never have), but yes, if I talk of looking over code, I mean the code that the machine sees. I prefer to think of this as high-quality documentation written in a language that happens not to be English. It is, however, the only authoritative, reliable documentation that Microsoft releases.

Versions

Unless otherwise stated, code fragments shown in the book are from Windows 95 build 950. This is the retail release of the product. Some material is specific to OEM Service Release 2, also known as Windows 95 build 950B. References to this material are flagged with the abbreviation "OSR2".

Intended Audience

This book is geared to engineers and managers who wish to tap into the new capabilities of Windows 95. IFSMgr, file system drivers, and file system monitors are all implemented as kernel mode or ring-0 components. In the Windows 95 environment this means they are implemented as virtual device drivers, or VxDs. First-hand experience with VxDs is *not* a requirement for reading this book. However, I do not attempt to provide a tutorial on VxDs.

MultiMon—a Windows 95 internals snooping tool—and the other utilities and samples on the companion disk can be used for exploration as is. However, if you intend to write your own drivers and use some of the development aids which accompany this book, you will need to have a copy of the Windows 95 device driver kit (DDK) as well as a compatible version of Visual C++.

The book takes a hands-on approach and where appropriate demonstrates an idea with example code. Several working programs are developed over the course of the book and these are included on the accompanying diskette. Thus, this book also provides examples that can serve as starting points for your own projects.

Chapter Summary

This book contains fourteen chapters and four appendixes:

Chapter 1, *From IFSMgr to the Internet*, introduces and provides an overview of IFSMgr. MultiMon is used to watch the Netscape web browser load and surf the Internet.

Chapter 2, *Where Do Filenames Go?* traces the path of filenames, UNC names, and device names as they pass through the file system.

Chapter 3, *Pathways to the File System*, examines the mechanisms that the kernel (VMM) uses to allow DOS, Windows 3.x, and Win32 programs access to IFSMgr.

Chapter 4, *File System API Mapping*, reveals how the Win32 APIs create Kernel32 file objects and how file object services ultimately become Interrupt 21h requests.

Chapter 5, *The "New" MS-DOS File System*, shows that the MS-DOS interrupt interfaces are still supported but now they are mostly implemented in IFSMgr's ring-0 code.

Chapter 6, *Dispatching File System Requests*, looks at the how I/O request packets are routed to file system drivers. Three key IFSMgr data structures are introduced: the `ifsreq` structure, the shell resource, and the `fhandle` structure. These data structures allow IFSMgr to call into the appropriate file system driver entry points.

Chapter 7, *Monitoring File Activity*, examines the use of file system hooks and looks at several example programs. **IFSMgr_NetFunction** and path hooks are also discussed.

Chapter 8, *Anatomy of a File System Driver*, looks at the details of the linkage between file system drivers and IFSMgr. It examines in detail how each type of FSD handles the mounting and dismounting operations. Two sample FSDs are described: MONOCFSD, a character FSD, and FSINFILE, a remote FSD.

Chapter 9, *VFAT: The Virtual FAT File System Driver*, reviews the FAT16 file structure and contrasts it with that of FAT32. Some implementation details of VFAT are examined, including initialization and registration, mounting a volume, opening a file, and locating a directory. Some basic IOS data structures and services are introduced.

Chapter 10, *Virtual Memory, the Paging File, and Pagers*, shows how the paging file is accessed via IFSMgr. The use of each of the system pagers is also explored.

Chapter 11, *VCACHE: Caches Big and Small*, describes the VCache services and data structures. Many undocumented features are described here.

Chapter 12, *A Survey of IFSMgr Services*, categorizes and enumerates all IFSMgr services. It provides undocumented details on heap management, event management, and path-parsing services.

Chapter 13, *VREDIR: The Microsoft Networks Client*, looks at how the redirector interfaces with other network components. The NetBIOS and SMB protocols are introduced and these protocols are traced with MultiMon to see how remote file system requests are handled. The CIFS protocol is contrasted with the SMB protocol.

Chapter 14, *Looking Ahead*, explores the differences between the Windows NT and Windows 95 file systems. The impact of WDM is also assessed.

Appendix A, *MultiMon: Setup, Usage, and Extensions*, describes how to install and use MultiMon, a Windows 95 internals snooping tool. A sample extension driver is also described.

Appendix B, *MultiMon: Monitor Reference*, is a reference for the set of monitor drivers which accompany the book. These include file system, Winsock, DeviceIo-Control, NetBIOS, SMB, and other monitors.

Appendix C, *IFSMgr Data Structures*, provides typedefs and descriptions of some key (and undocumented) IFSMgr data structures.

Appendix D, *IFS Development Aids*, describes four tools for VxD writers using the DDK, including IFSWRAPS, a library of all IFSMgr services, and DEBIFS, a debugger "dot" command for examining IFSMgr data structures.

What's on the Diskette?

All of the programs and drivers on the companion disk come with complete source code. These include:

MultiMon and monitor drivers
> A Windows 95 internals snooping tool

Sr
> A utility that dumps IFSMgr's local and remote volume data structures

Fh
> A utility that dumps IFSMgr's data structures for a volume's open files

Sample file system hook VxDs
> Sample VxDs which show techniques for calling into FSDs from a file system hook

MonoCFSD
> A character file system driver for a monochrome display adapter

FSinFile
> A remote file system driver that implements a file system within a file

DumpDisk
> A utility that displays important FAT16 and FAT32 structures

Pagers
> A utility that displays the system pagers

Chentry
> A utility for removing leading underscore on VxD's export name

Header Files for File System Development
> Supplements to the DDK headers

IFSWraps
> A C-callable library of all IFSMgr services

DebIFS
> A debug command for use with WDEB386 or SoftICE

Typographical Conventions

Throughout this book, we have used the following typographic conventions:

Bold
> Indicates the name of a Windows API or a VxD service name, functions, monitors, and commands. Bold is also used to indicate menus, buttons, dialogs, and other parts of the Windows 95 GUI.

Italic
> Indicates filenames, variables, and is used for emphasis. Manifest constants are represented by uppercased italicized names, e.g., *MAXFUNC*.

`Constant width`
> Indicates a language construct such as a data type, a data structure, a macro, or a code example.

Comments and Corrections

Every effort has been made to verify the accuracy of this book's contents. Please report any errors and corrections to the author at *stanm@sourcequest.com*. An errata sheet will be posted to the web site listed below. We would also like to hear comments and suggestions you have for improving future editions of this book.

Getting Updates

Updates to the source code on the companion diskette can be found at:

> *http://www.sourcequest.com/win95ifs*

From time to time, new utilities will be posted there for download.

Acknowledgments

Thanks are due to the many people who have helped make this book possible.

Andrew Schulman, my editor, who saw the significance of the Windows 95 file system and encouraged me to expose it in a Nutshell series book. This book would not have been attempted without his encouragement. Although he sparks controversy by his writings, he has won the admiration and respect of the developer community with his classic books on undocumented DOS and Windows. His suggestions and comments helped immensely.

Ron Burk, the editor at *Windows/DOS Developer's Journal.* When he published my article "Monitoring Windows 95 File Activity in Ring 0," in July 1995, I had no idea it would be the seed for a new book.

Andy Cohen, for technical review.

Geoff Chappell, for sharing some of his intimate knowledge of IFSMgr. Material that he has generously provided is duly noted.

Rajeev Nagar, author of the forthcoming *Windows NT File System Internals,* for making suggestions about the content of the "Looking Ahead" chapter.

Mark Russinovich, for supplying me with an advance copy of his *Dr. Dobb's Journal* article, "Examining the Windows NT Filesystem" (February 1997), written with Bryce Cogswell.

Ed Stitt, Steve Farrell, and Gary Schoolcraft, my co-workers at Xerox/XSoft. Our discussions on the Windows 95 architecture helped me expose the gaps in my knowledge.

Russ Arun at Microsoft for prying the "IFS Specification" loose and getting it into developers' hands during the Chicago beta.

The many developers who post file-system related questions in the Internet newsgroups and CompuServe forums. Some of these questions became the basis for a book topic or sample program.

The crew at O'Reilly who helped this novice bookwriter learn the ropes. Special thanks to Troy Mott, my "O'Reilly connection," who helped resolve many issues that arose during the course of the project. Thanks also to Edie Freedman for her excellent cover design. Frank Willison, Editor in Chief, who made many suggestions for improvement. David Futato, for producing an attractive addition to our bookshelves.

And last, but not least, Maggie, my wife, for enduring yet another project. Her support kept me sane during the long haul. She also kept an eye on my schedule and kept me moving towards the final goal.

1

From IFSMgr to the Internet

The file system in Windows 95 resides in a component named the *Installable File System Manager,* or IFSMgr. As its name suggests, IFSMgr is responsible for routing file system requests to the installed file systems. Multiple file systems are implemented as independent drivers underneath IFSMgr. Thus, it is hard to get a complete picture of the file system without examining file system drivers (FSDs) too. Later chapters will focus on the underpinnings of IFSMgr and file system drivers, but for now let's get a feel for why the file system is so important.

Long Filenames

One of the most touted features of Windows 95 is its support for long filenames. This support is brought to you through the Win32 API (application programming interface) and also through the clunky, old Int 21h interface. These two interfaces cover three of the Windows 95 operating modes: Win32, Win16, and DOS box. But what about MS-DOS mode, the real-mode DOS version 7.0? Does it support long filenames?

To find out, let's build the simple DOS application in Example 1-1, which uses one of the new long filename APIs (the source and executable for this example are in the *DOSVOL* directory of the companion disk).

For brevity, Example 1-1 does not display the implementations of several support routines such as **GetStartupDrive()**, **GetVolInfo()**, etc. These are small C functions that contain inline assembler Int 21h calls.

This little application prints the MS-DOS version and, if Windows is detected, the Windows version as well. The function **GetVolInfo** moves its function arguments into appropriate registers and then invokes interrupt 21h function 71a0h. This Int 21h service returns volume information for the drive specified by a root path string, e.g., *C:*. If successful, this service returns the file system name, the maximum length for a filename component, and the maximum length for a fully qualified filename for the specified volume. This is essentially the DOS equivalent of the Win32 function **GetVolumeInformation**

Example 1-1. DOSVOL: Test Application Using Long Filename API

```
void main(void) {
    unsigned short flags, maxfn, maxpath;
    char szFS[32], szRootName[4];

    printf( "MSDOS Version %d.%02d", GetDosMajorVersion(),
            GetDosMinorVersion() );

    if ( WinCheck() == 0 )
        printf( " - Windows Version %d.%02d\n", GetWinMajorVersion(),
                GetWinMinorVersion() );
    else printf( "\n" );

    strcpy( szRootName, "@:\\" ); /* volume string */
    szRootName[0] += GetStartupDrive();

    printf( "Get Volume Information, Int 21h Function 71A0h.\n" );
    if ( !GetVolInfo( szRootName, szFS, sizeof( szFS ),
                      &maxfn, &maxpath, &flags ) )
        printf( " Drive %c - FAILED.\n\n", szRootName[0] );
    else
        printf( " Drive %c - File system: %s  MaxFileName: %d "
                MaxPathName: %d\n\n", szRootName[0], szFS, maxfn,
                maxpath );
}
```

Executing DOSVOL in a Win95 DOS box yields this output:

```
MSDOS Version 7.00 - Windows Version 4.00
Get Volume Information, Int 21h Function 71A0h.
 Drive C - File system: FAT  MaxFileName: 255  MaxPathName: 260
```

Now let's take the same DOS application and execute it in MS-DOS mode. You reach that mode by selecting "Restart windows in MS-DOS mode" from the **Shut Down Windows** dialog. This time you get these results:

```
MSDOS Version 7.00
Get Volume Information, Int 21h Function 71A0h.
 Drive C - FAILED.
```

Hmm... long filename support is not available from real-mode DOS! Well, where is it coming from then? Function 71a0h and the other long filename (71xxh) functions are supplied by IFSMgr. IFSMgr defines the APIs that a file system can support, but it in turn needs an installed file system driver to fulfill the requests. This simple example illustrates that the DOS long filename APIs are only available if VxDs, like IFSMgr, are present to provide them.

It might appear that IFSMgr is adding features to an MS-DOS base. Actually, the change is more fundamental than that. Most of the DOS-like functionality that you enjoy in a Windows 95 DOS box, at least as far as the file system goes, is brought to you by IFSMgr. It is more accurate to think of IFSMgr as a replacement for the DOS file system. The MS-DOS code base is still used for some functions, but in a subservient role.*

We've just looked at a single API here, one of many that are documented in "Part 5: Using Microsoft MS-DOS Extensions," of *Programmer's Guide to Microsoft Windows 95*. Microsoft calls these new APIs MS-DOS extensions. The name is significant: they look like good old MS-DOS but they are *not* a part of a new MS-DOS version. Rather, they are part of IFSMgr, extending it from the baseline implementation that came with Windows 3.11.

Windows 3.11 Had an IFSMgr?

Yes, IFSMgr quietly debuted in Windows for Workgroups version 3.11. That version of IFSMgr had already implemented a substantial portion of the MS-DOS interrupt 21h interface. However, where it lacked a complete implementation, it "gracefully degraded" to using 16-bit file access through MS-DOS.

A good example of this is provided by the DOS **subst** command. The **subst** command, you'll recall, is used to map a drive letter to a local directory. If you have a Windows 3.11 configuration available, you might want to try this. First you should make sure that you are currently using 32-bit file access. You do this with the 386 virtual memory settings from the Control Panel. Once you have 32-bit file access set up, insert a command like this into *autoexec.bat*:

```
subst d: c:\windows\system
```

where d: is whatever the next available drive letter might be for the system.

Now shut down Windows and reboot the system so that the new line added to *autoexec.bat* will execute. After the initial Windows logo screen is displayed, a blue character mode "pop up" will appear with the following message:

```
                  32-bit File System
The 32-bit file system is incompatible with the SUBST utility.
 To use 32-bit file access, do not use the SUBST utility before
              starting Windows for Workgroups.
                 Press any key to continue
```

---

* This topic is discussed in great detail in *Unauthorized Windows 95* by Andrew Schulman (especially Chapter 8, appropriately entitled "The Case of the Gradually Disappearing DOS"). Also see *http://www.sonic.net/~undoc/*.

If you press Return, Windows continues to start up. But if you check the 386 virtual memory settings in the Control Panel, you will find that you are using 16-bit file access, even though the checkbox for 32-bit file access is checked. What is happening here? If IFSMgr detects that you have **subst** drives in the system during its initialization, it will not support 32-bit file access on any drive, and drops back into 16-bit file access using MS-DOS.

subst is only one example where the Windows 3.11 IFSMgr gracefully degrades back to 16-bit file access; other examples include the presence of a DOS 6.0 DoubleSpace drive, the presence of some other types of compressed drives, and the existence of open files on a drive when IFSMgr initializes. In contrast, Windows 95 fully supports **subst** drives and DoubleSpace drives.

Peering "Under the Hood"

By now you should have a feel for the hands-on approach I will take in this book. By "hands-on," I mean exploring with tools like MultiMon—a general purpose monitor for examining Windows internals, looking at source code or pseudo-code of portions of Windows 95, and stepping through that code with a debugger. We'll also be writing some code, including small sample applications and drivers. (Source and executables for these are provided on the companion disk.)

MultiMon is an exciting new tool, which you get with this book. It is described in detail in Appendix A, *MultiMon: Setup, Usage, and Extensions*, and you also get complete source code for it. Unlike a lot of other "snooping tools," MultiMon reveals what is going on at ring-0. It doesn't tell you which Win32 API is being called; instead, it may reveal a sequence of ring-0 APIs and events that correspond to a single Win32 API.

The experiments we conducted at the beginning of this chapter give you first-hand knowledge about the role IFSMgr plays in Windows 95. Tools like MultiMon will take you much further and allow you to ferret out many other secrets about IFSMgr and other Windows 95 internals. Before we put MultiMon to work, let's digress a bit to get an overview of IFSMgr. The next section may be a little abstract, but having this conceptual framework will prepare you for what's to come.

An Overview of IFSMgr

To reiterate, the Installable File System Manager is responsible for routing file system requests to the installed file systems, and file systems are implemented as independent drivers under IFSMgr. The target file system for a request depends upon the format of the filename by which the file is initially opened or created. The forms that a filename may take are discussed in Chapter 2, *Where Do File-names Go?*

The system components to which IFSMgr interfaces are shown in Figure 1-1. The arrows leading in to IFSMgr are from clients that make requests upon a file system. The arrows leading out from IFSMgr are to file system drivers (FSDs). All of the components shown here execute in one of the Intel x86 processor's protected modes. The dark grey boxes indicate components with the least privilege level (ring-3) whereas the pale boxes are virtual device drivers with the highest privilege level (ring-0).

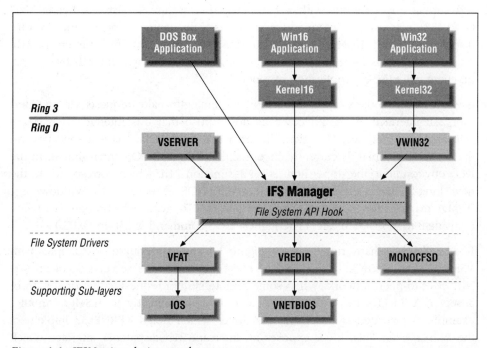

Figure 1-1. *IFSMgr in relation to other system components*

IFSMgr's Client Interface

There are many ways in which IFSMgr is called upon to provide services. The most common request mechanism is for an application to call a published API. In the Windows 95 environment, there are three operating modes that are the source of such file system requests. The first of these is MS-DOS executing in a special Intel x86 processor mode known as *virtual-86 mode*. Here, file system requests are made via software interrupt 21h, with CPU registers loaded with command parameters. This mode is available in a "DOS box," a window into a virtual 8086 machine executing some DOS application.

The second mode corresponds to a 16-bit Windows application. In this protected mode, the processor addresses memory using 16-bit selectors and offsets. The Win16 API supplies the commonly used file system services. Ultimately these functions are implemented as calls to software interrupt 21h. Inasmuch as the processor is in protected mode as opposed to virtual-86 mode, the ring-0 handler for interrupt 21h is different from that used by "DOS box" applications.

The third mode corresponds to a 32-bit Windows application. In this protected mode, the processor addresses memory using 32-bit linear addresses. The Win32 API supplies applications with a rich set of file system services. A helper VxD (VWIN32) acts as an intermediary; it takes calls from Kernel32 and in turn dispatches them to IFSMgr using the ring-0 service Exec_PM_Int for interrupt 21h. An intermediary is necessary because issuing a software interrupt 21h from a 32-bit client will raise an application exception.

Given that all of these application modes ultimately make requests via an interrupt 21h interface, it should come as no surprise that this interface is IFSMgr's primary client interface. However, this interrupt 21h interface is extended beyond the range of commands currently encountered in the MS-DOS environment. In the DOS environment, the upper limit is set at function 71h, which corresponds to the new long-filename commands added as MS-DOS extensions to Windows 95. IFSMgr maps commands over the range 00h to E7h, with 00h through 71h being equivalent to MS-DOS usage. (The highest DOS command is 73h in OSR2.)

IFSMgr also has many ring-0 clients. Figure 1-1 shows a couple of examples with VSERVER and VWIN32. VSERVER provides support for the server side of an MS-NET peer-to-peer network. When some remote system requests a file operation of a server, VSERVER fields the request and routes it directly to IFSMgr. Another example is provided by VWIN32, the driver which helps KERNEL32 implement the Win32 APIs. This driver exposes an interrupt 21h dispatcher interface which ultimately calls into IFSMgr when it executes interrupt 21h requests on behalf of Win32 applications. Yet another example is provided by DYNAPAGE, the driver which supports the dynamic paging file. When the memory manager needs to page-out or page-in some part of virtual memory, it uses IFSMgr to do the reads and writes via the DYNAPAGE driver.

IFSMgr's Management of Resources and Handles

IFSMgr's job is to field these requests and pass them on to a file system driver (FSD). It isn't sufficient to just identify the target FSD; it must also specify one of perhaps several resources the FSD owns. This information and other parameters which are required by the service request are combined in an `ifsreq` data structure. IFSMgr uses this common `ifsreq` structure to send commands to all FSDs. The FSD also uses the `ifsreq` structure to return the command results.

IFSMgr must keep track of registered resources and the FSDs that registered them. Resources can include local disk drives, network connections, network drives, and character devices. When a resource is added to the system, it is registered with IFSMgr through a "mount" operation. This operation also binds a resource to a particular FSD. Resources may also be removed from the system through a "dismount" operation.

Similarly, IFSMgr tracks open file handles and the resources with which they are associated. A file handle may refer to a mapping between a filename and a disk allocation, or it can refer to a search context, as in the Win32 functions **FindFirstFile** and **FindNextFile**. A file handle may also be used for tracking clients which are accessing a character device.

Resources and file handles each have their own sets of operations. These operations are exposed by each FSD through two separate function tables: a table of functions for accessing a resource's services and a table of functions for accessing services requiring an open file handle. The functions which make up these tables are defined by the FSD interface; each function expects specific usage of fields in the `ifsreq` structure for passing arguments and returning results.

When IFSMgr receives a request, it must convert it into one or more calls to an FSD's function table. It uses the information in the request to pair up with a particular FSD. In the case of local drives, the volume number provides this association; in the case of remote drives and connections, the server name and share name are used; in the case of character devices, the device name is used.

File Systems and Their Drivers

FSDs come in three different flavors: local, remote, and character. Each type has its own characteristics.

Local drive FSDs (e.g., VFAT) are responsible for implementing the semantics of a particular file system. They know about things like disk layout, disk storage allocation, and file and directory naming. These FSDs call upon IFSMgr for help with name parsing but rely upon IOS (I/O Supervisor) for accessing the physical disk.

A local file system is created to provide user-friendly names to chunks of disk storage and to shield the programmer from the intricacies of hardware. Fixed disks and disk controllers come in an endless variety. It is the purpose of the IOS to provide low level services that allow physical locations on a disk to be read and written. A physical location is identified by head, cylinder, and sector coordinates. Local file systems are used to partition the fixed disks and to provide hardware-independent coordinates for locations on the disk (e.g., volume C, logical sector 234). The I/O Supervisor is only briefly discussed in this book.

Remonte or network FSDs (e.g., VREDIR) typically package a file system request in one or more packets and ship it across a network. The request is translated into a file-sharing protocol (such as SMB) and transferred using a transport protocol (such as NETBEUI). These FSDs call upon IFSMgr for help with name parsing, setting up, and tearing down connections, but rely upon the transport layer for accessing the remote system.

In terms of the layers of the Open System Interconnect (OSI) Reference Model, a network FSD or redirector occupies the application and presentation layers and interfaces at its lower boundary with the session layer (e.g., VNETBIOS).

Character FSDs (e.g., MONOCFSD) model devices that send and receive data one byte at a time, in a serial fashion.

All FSDs use the same function table structure to interface with IFSMgr. The functions that each type of driver exposes can be quite different. If an FSD does not need to support a particular function, it returns an error if a client should happen to call it. This is necessary because there is no means of determining in advance which functions a particular FSD has implemented.

To finish up this introduction, I'll introduce MultiMon by putting it to work, examining the popular web browser Netscape Navigator 3.0. Let's start by looking at how Netscape utilizes the file system to load as a new process.

Loading Netscape Navigator

From the point of view of the file system, creating a process consists of loading its image into memory. What starts out as a **ShellExecute**, **WinExec**, or **CreateProcess** function call for a particular EXE can expand into implicit loads of multiple DLLs. As a real world example, Figure 1-2 shows a filtered trace that was collected by MultiMon when loading Netscape Navigator (*netscape.exe*). Only file opens (**FS_OpenFile**) and file closes (**FS_CloseFile**) were sampled.

The Function column in Figure 1-2 displays the names **FS_OpenFile and FS_Close-File**. These are the names of entry points provided by a file system driver. The Device column tells us which file system driver is being used. In this case, all of the file opens are completed by VFAT, the Virtual FAT file system. The Handle column contains the numeric value of the handle returned by the open. Two ranges of numeric handles will be seen in this column: DOS handles, which are less than 200h, and extended handles, which are 200h and greater. The Args column contains the pathname of the file. It is followed by a Flags2 column

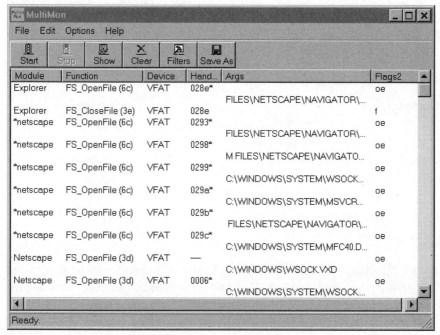

Figure 1-2. MultiMon trace from loading Netscape Navigator

which contains "oe" for each of the opens, which indicates *open-existing*, meaning the open will fail if the file does not already exist.

In Figure 1-2, we see the span of time which starts with Explorer calling **ShellExecute** until Netscape is an independent process. We are narrowing our focus to those components that are loaded by the operating system *before* control is actually passed to the newly-formed Netscape process. During this intermediate stage, the address space for Netscape is being prepared. It's not quite a complete process yet, so its module name is flagged with a * prefix. You can see this in the column labeled Module, where the name changes from "Explorer" to "*netscape" to "Netscape".

Table 1-1 contains a list of the files that we see being opened in Figure 1-2. At the bottom of the table, there is an entry for the VxD WSOCK. This is a helper VxD that *wsock32.dll* opens when its entry point is called with the DLL_PROCESS_ ATTACH flag. This is *after* the Netscape process is created, so we will ignore it for now.

You may feel a little uneasy about what is missing in this Table 1-1. Where are KERNEL32, USER32, and GDI32? Surely, Netscape uses these ubiquitous system DLLs. Actually, a better way to get a list of required modules is to look at the import list for Netscape using a utility like Quick View. Doing this yields the following, more complete list of import modules: KERNEL32, USE32, GDI32, SHELL32, OLE32, OLEAUT32, COMDLG32, ADVAPI32, MFC40, MSVCRT40, RPCRT4, VERSION, JRT3230, and PR3230. JRT3230 and PR3230 both use imports from WSOCK32. Why don't we see opens for all of these DLLs?

Table 1-1. Files Opened During Netscape Load

Files Opened	File Handle
..\NETSCAPE\NAVIGATOR\PROGRAM\NETSCAPE.EXE	0293h
..\NETSCAPE\NAVIGATOR\PROGRAM\PR3230.DLL	0298h
\WINDOWS\SYSTEM\WSOCK32.DLL	0299h
\WINDOWS\SYSTEM\MSVCRT40.DLL	029Ah
..\NETSCAPE\NAVIGATOR\PROGRAM\JRT3230.DLL	029Bh
\WINDOWS\SYSTEM\MFC40.DLL	029Ch
\WINDOWS\SYSTEM\WSOCK.VXD	0006h

You may be thinking that these DLLs reside in shared memory and so there is no need to load them for each process. That answer is *partially* correct. To see why, let's look at the image base addresses for each of Netscape's imported modules. The image base address is the preferred address at which a module wishes to be loaded. If it gets that address, its memory image does not have to be relocated, so this provides a load-time optimization. (Image base addresses can also be determined using Quick View.)

Table 1-2 shows the modules and their image base addresses in descending order. The linear address of an application is divided into four regions or *arenas*: DOS (0–003fffffh), private (00400000–7fffffffh), shared (80000000–bfffffffh), and system (c0000000–ffbfffffh). The first five modules in Table 1-1 are loaded to the shared memory arena. To quote the DDK documentation, "This arena is used for ring-3 shared code and data." Thus, once one of these DLLs is loaded it will be visible to all other code and data, such as 16-bit Windows applications and DLLs, DPMI memory, and 32-bit system DLLs.

Table 1-2. Netscape Import Modules

Module Name	Image Base
ADVAPI32	bfef0000h
VERSION	bfee0000h
KERNEL32	bff70000h
USER32	bff60000h
GDI32	bff30000h
OLE32	7ff60000h
COMDLG32	7fed0000h

Table 1-2. Netscape Import Modules (continued)

Module Name	Image Base
SHELL32	7fe00000h
RPCRT4	7fd00000h
WSOCK32	7e2e0000h
OLEAUT32	76de0000h
MFC40	5f800000h
MSVCRT40	10200000h
JRT3230	10050000h
PR3230	10000000h

The remaining ten modules in Table 1-2 are destined to be loaded into Netscape's private arena. The private arena is used for code and data that is private to a Win32 process. Private means that the page table entries corresponding to the linear address range are kept separately for each process. Each Win32 process has its own mapping of pages in its private arena; this mapping is called a *memory context*. This is why all applications can load at the same linear address of 400000h.

At this point you are probably comfortable with the idea of sharing DLL code and data as long as it is in the shared arena. But what if modules are loaded into a process's private arena—can they still be shared with other processes? We need more information to answer this. Let's try another MultiMon trace. This time we'll continue to look at only file opens (**FS_OpenFile**) and file closes (**FS_CloseFile**) but we'll start sampling from the time the system boots and continue until we have launched Netscape. This, in effect, will give us a list of open modules at the time we start Netscape.

This experiment produces a lot of output, over 1800 lines for this particular configuration. Many files go through an open and close cycle; we are not interested in these. Once we filter out this noise, we are left with files which are opened and remain opened. Further condensing this list to just the modules which Netscape is dependent on, we arrive at Table 1-3.

Table 1-3. Modules Opened Before Netscape Is Launched

Module Name	Open File Handle
KERNEL32	201h
GDI32	215h
ADVAPI32	216h
USER32	21Dh
SHELL32	252h

Table 1-3. Modules Opened Before Netscape Is Launched (continued)

Module Name	Open File Handle
OLE32	2CCh
RPCRT4	2CEh
COMDLG32	2F1h
OLEAUT32	2F2h

In this experiment, we get a slightly different list of modules which are opened and loaded along with *netscape.exe*. This list is given in Table 1-4.

Table 1-4. Modules Loaded Along with netscape.exe

Module Name	Open File Handle
PR3230	280h
WSOCK32	281h
MSVCRT40	282h
JRT3230	283h
VERSION	284h
MFC40	285h

What we see here is that any module that has already been loaded won't be loaded again. It makes no difference whether the module is loaded into a private arena; it can still be shared.

How does Windows 95 do this? It turns out that there is an obscure function, called **_PageAttach**, made just for this purpose. For example, if I know that the memory context for *explorer.exe* contains an image of the module OLE32, I can map all or some of the pages of that image into my process's memory context. Selective mapping is necessary because some pages of the image, such as data, may have to be loaded directly from the source file and not be shared with other memory contexts.

MultiMon shows us the gory details of OLE32's attachment to the Netscape process in Figure 1-3. The **PageReserve**, **PageCommit**, and **PageAttach** functions are Win32 services provided by VMM, the Virtual Machine Manager. The handle 02cch used by the **FS_ReadFile** calls corresponds to *ole32.dll* (see Table 1-3).

Here is an interpretation of this trace. Netscape requests that 134 pages of memory be reserved starting at the linear address 7ff60000h, the image base of OLE32. The first page is committed and thus is private to Netscape. The next 102 pages starting at linear address 7ff61000h (the `.text` section) are mapped to the same set of pages in the memory context whose handle is c10a0e20h (Explorer). Similarly, the 5 pages starting at linear address 7ffc7000h (the `.orpc` section) are

Module	Function	Hand...	Args
*netscape	FS_ReadFile (3f)	02f7	cnt=1000H ofs=6a400H ptr=c135f000H
*netscape	PageReserve		0007ff60 00000086 00000010
*netscape	PageCommit		0007ff60 00000001 09 00b20000 60040000
*netscape	PageAttach		7ff61 c10a0e20 7ff61 66
*netscape	PageAttach		7ffc7 c10a0e20 7ffc7 5
*netscape	PageCommit		0007ffcc 00000001 01 00b00000 60060000
*netscape	PageCommit		0007ffcd 00000001 01 00b50001 60060000
*netscape	PageAttach		7ffce c10a0e20 7ffce 1
*netscape	PageAttach		7ffcf c10a0e20 7ffcf 6
*netscape	PageCommit		0007ffd5 00000003 08 a0b00070 60060000
*netscape	PageCommit		0007ffd8 00000001 08 a0b10073 60060000
*netscape	PageCommit		0007ffd9 00000002 08 c0b00073 60060000
*netscape	PageCommit		0007ffdb 00000001 08 c0b30075 60060000
*netscape	PageAttach		7ffdc c10a0e20 7ffdc 2
*netscape	PageAttach		7ffde c10a0e20 7ffde 2
*netscape	PageAttach		7ffe0 c10a0e20 7ffe0 6
*netscape	FS_ReadFile (3f)	02cc	cnt=1000H ofs=73c00H ptr=c135f000H
*netscape	FS_ReadFile (3f)	02cc	cnt=1000H ofs=74c00H ptr=c135f000H
*netscape	FS_ReadFile (3f)	02cc	cnt=600H ofs=75c00H ptr=c135f000H
*netscape	PageCommit		0007ffd9 00000001 08 c0b00073 60060000
*netscape	FS_ReadFile (3f)	02cc	cnt=1000H ofs=73c00H ptr=c135f000H
*netscape	FS_ReadFile (3f)	02f7	cnt=1000H ofs=6b400H ptr=c135f000H

Figure 1-3. Netscape "attaches" to OLE32

also mapped to the same set of pages in Explorer's memory context. You get the idea: attached pages are mapped and thus shared whereas committed pages are private. The three **FS_ReadFile** calls load a private copy of the .idata section, the module's import table. A summary of how the page ranges are treated is given in Table 1-5.

Table 1-5. Attachment of OLE32 to Netscape (all values are in HEX)

Base Addr	Pages	Section	Treatment	Properties
7ff60000	1		commit	
7ff61000	66	.text	attach	code
7ffc7000	5	.orpc	attach	code
7ffcc000	2	.bss	commit	uninitialized data
7ffce000	1	.sdata	attach	initialized, shared data
7ffcf000	6	.rdata	attach	initialized, read-only data
7ffd5000	3	.data	commit	initialized, writeable data
7ffd9000	3	.idata	commit	imports, read from disk
7ffdc000	2	.edata	attach	export table
7ffde000	2	.rsrc	attach	resources
7ffe0000	6	.reloc	attach	relocation table

What we have seen in our first example is how the file system intermingles with operating system internals. Now let's turn our attention to an example from the application realm.

Going to www.ora.com

Now that we have Netscape loaded, it's time to do some web surfing. We're going to look at a typical surfing operation, connecting to a server and displaying its home page. Today's web applications, like Netscape, utilize Windows Sockets for establishing connections and transferring data "over the wire." If we can monitor Netscape's socket calls, we can get a much clearer picture about how this application works.

A glance back at Table 1-1 will remind you that Netscape loads *wsock32.dll* and then *wsock.vxd* is opened by WSOCK32. The relationship between these two components is that of a client and a service provider. WSOCK provides an interface to socket services, and WSOCK32 exports the Windows Sockets APIs and makes calls into WSOCK to implement the APIs. WSOCK32 accesses these ring-0 socket services via the **DeviceIoControl** Win32 API.

It just so happens that we have a MultiMon extension for monitoring **DeviceIoControl** calls (see Chapter 3, *Pathways to the File System*). Each **DeviceIoControl** call targets a specific device; it specifies a command code and buffers for input and output arguments. To report on WSOCK calls, we just need to interpret the arguments which are passing through the monitor. A little bit of work leads to the mapping shown in Table 1-6.

Table 1-6. DeviceIoControl Command Codes for Winsock APIs

WSOCK32 API	WSOCK ControlCode	Argument Length
accept	100h	1Ch
bind	101h	14h
closesocket	102h	04h
connect	103h	14h
getpeername	104h	0ch
getsockname	105h	0ch
getsockopt	106h	18h
ioctlsocket	107h	0ch
listen	108h	08h
recv	109h	28h
recvfrom	109h	28h
select	10ah	20h

Table 1-6. DeviceIoControl Command Codes for Winsock APIs (continued)

WSOCK32 API	WSOCK ControlCode	Argument Length
*select	10bh	18h
WSAAsyncSelect	10ch	10h
send	10dh	28h
sendto	10dh	28h
setsockopt	10eh	18h
shutdown	10fh	08h
socket	110h	14h
?	111h	
?	112h	
?	113h	
?	114h	
?	115h	
?	116h	
?	117h	
WsControl	118h	18h
SetPostMsgAddr	119h	04h
Arecv	11ah	14h
Asend	11bh	14h

Armed with our primitive Winsock monitor we can now see web browser operations in terms of socket calls. For the results which I show here, the Netscape disk cache was cleared and a connection to my Internet service provider was already established. To minimize extraneous noise, the display of the default home page which you connect to should be finished as well. MultiMon is then started and monitors are enabled for "VWIN32 DeviceIoControl" and "IFSMgr Filehook" (with **FS_OpenFile, FS_CloseFile, FS_ReadFile**, and **FS_WriteFile** APIs selected). Then go back to Netscape and at the **Go to:** prompt enter `http://www.ora.com/` and press **Return**. This will take you to the O'Reilly & Associates, Inc. home page. Once the status message says "Document Done", you can stop MultiMon.

The output that I got for this experiment is spread over several examples, starting with Example 1-2. The output has been "cleaned up" by removing traces of swap-file I/O, extra *select calls, and file I/O for non–web-page files.

Example 1-2 shows the steps that are taken just to get connected to *www.ora.com*. To establish a connection a socket is opened with the **socket** API. Sockets have handles just like files do, but they also have a "handle context," which is like a file descriptor structure. The first socket opened returns a handle of 42h, but is referenced in subsequent calls with the handle context of c0f10e50h.

Next we see several calls setting up the properties and event handlers on this socket. For instance, the **WSAAsyncSelect** call requests that notifications for read, write, connect, accept, etc. be sent as Windows messages to the window with handle 408h. A single registered message (`cffeh`) is used with the socket handle in the *wparam* and the event in the *lparam*. The **setsockopt** API requests that the socket linger a certain amount of time when it is closed if unsent data is present. The **ioctlsocket** call requests that the socket operate in non-blocking mode.

Example 1-2. Resolving the IP Address

```
        Function Device    Handle Args
        (socket) WSOCK         42 AF_INET, SOCK_STREAM, IPPROTO_TCP
(WSAAsyncSelect) WSOCK   c0f10e50 hWnd=408, wMsg=cffe, 3f
    (setsockopt) WSOCK   c0f10e50 SOL_SOCKET, SO_LINGER, buf=0090f214 len=8
   (ioctlsocket) WSOCK   c0f10e50 FIONBIO, parm=1
        (select) WSOCK            Rd=1 Wr=1 Err=1
        (select) WSOCK            Rd=1 Wr=1 Err=1
 FS_OpenFile (6c) VFAT      2cd*C:\WINDOWS\HOSTS                          oe
 FS_ReadFile (d6) VFAT      2cd cnt=19H ofs=0H ptr=6eec79H               ---
FS_CloseFile (3e) VFAT      2cd f
        (socket) WSOCK         62 AF_INET, SOCK_DGRAM, IPPROTO_IP
       (connect) WSOCK   c0f11ca8 AF_INET, 53, 204.156.128.1
  (send/sendto) WSOCK   c0f11ca8 buf=006eee80 len=1d flags=0
                                  0,3,1,0,0,1,0,0,0,0,0,3,
                                  "www",3,"ora",3,"com",
                                  0,0,1,0,1,0,0,0
        (select) WSOCK            Rd=1 Wr=0 Err=0
 (recv/recvfrom) WSOCK   c0f11ca8 buf=00d6ee38 len=400 flags=0
   (closesocket) WSOCK   c0f11ca8
       (connect) WSOCK   c0f10e50 AF_INET, 80, 204.148.40.9
        (select) WSOCK            Rd=1 Wr=1 Err=1
        (select) WSOCK            Rd=1 Wr=1 Err=1
       (connect) WSOCK   c0f10e50 AF_INET, 80, 204.148.40.9
```

Next we see a couple of **select** calls. A **select** is similar to a **WaitForMultipleObjects** call. It could block its thread until it is signaled or a timeout occurs, or (if the timeout value is 0) it will return immediately. A **select** call takes three lists of sockets: the first list is interested in whether the socket is readable, the second list is interested in whether the socket is writeable, and the third list is interested in any error conditions on the listed sockets. On return from **select**, each list is updated to indicate the status of each socket.

At this point socket 42h is poised to connect to *www.ora.com*, but before it can do so it needs to know the IP address (204.148.40.9) to connect to. The next few lines are involved with resolving this name. First, we see a read from the local *HOSTS* file to see if there is a matching entry. My *HOSTS* file only contains names of local machines so I know that will fail. So Netscape is forced to go to the Internet to find the IP address for the name. To do this it opens another socket, number 62h, and connects on that socket to 204.156.128.1, the IP address of my service provider's DNS (Domain Name System) name server. It connects on the well-known port 53 for DNS and sends a packet containing information about the name it is searching. The **select** call waits for the reply and the subsequent **recv** presumably gets a matching IP address back. Now that we have the IP address, we're done with socket 62h, so **closesocket** gets rid of it.

Now we're really ready to connect to *www.ora.com*. The **connect** call succeeds on the second try; socket 42h is now connected on the well-known port 80 for HTTP.

Continuing with the trace in Example 1-3, Netscape sends a packet containing the string "GET / HTTP/1.0...", which requests the server's home page from the root directory of the web server. Several **recv**'s are then made on socket 42h, but the actual amount read is uncertain since the requested amount is usually not the same as the returned amount. With some portion of the HTML home page read in, Netscape creates a file named *mop17ie0* in its *.\cache* directory in which to store it. As more data is received on socket 42h, it is appended to a local buffer. Finally, at the bottom of Example 1-4, the entire home page has been received—all 0a18h bytes—the socket handle is closed, the buffer is written to *mop17ie0*, and the file is closed.

Example 1-3. Retrieving the Home Page

```
       Function Device    Handle   Args
  (send/sendto)  WSOCK  c0f10e50   buf=012569e0 len=a5 flags=0
                                   "GET / HTTP/1.0",d,a,
                                   "Connection: Keep-Alive",d,a,
                                   "User-Age",0,
(recv/recvfrom)  WSOCK  c0f10e50   buf=0090f534 len=104 flags=0
(recv/recvfrom)  WSOCK  c0f10e50   buf=0090f534 len=104 flags=0
       (select)  WSOCK             Rd=1 Wr=0 Err=0
       (select)  WSOCK             Rd=1 Wr=0 Err=0
(recv/recvfrom)  WSOCK  c0f10e50   buf=0090f534 len=104 flags=0
(recv/recvfrom)  WSOCK  c0f10e50   buf=0092bc94 len=400 flags=0
FS_OpenFile (6c)  VFAT      20e*   ..\NETSCAPE\NAVIGATOR\CACHE\M0P17IE0   ca
```

While the home page is still being read in, sockets 63h, 64h, and 65h are created in Example 1-4. These sockets are created in the same fashion as socket 42h was. Note that as these new sockets are added, the socket lists passed to **select** appear to include them as well, since the list sizes increase by the same amount. Each of these sockets is going to handle the transfer of a referenced image in the HTML page.

The final bit of output that we'll look at, shown in Example 1-5, corresponds to socket 65h (handle context c0f29a3ch). The output for sockets 63h and 64h is essentially the same, so there is no need to show that too. After connecting to the IP address for *www.ora.com*, Netscape sends a packet containing the string "GET /

graphics/space.gif HTTP/1.0", which requests the server's *space.gif* file from the /
graphics directory of the web server. Several **recv**'s are then made on socket 65h.
Once the GIF file has been received, Netscape creates a file named *mop17IE3.gif*
in its *.\cache* directory and then closes socket 65h. At the bottom of Example 1-
5, the received buffer is written to *mop17IE3.gif*, and the file is closed.

Example 1-4. Create a Socket for Each Embedded GIF

```
         Function Device      Handle  Args
          (socket) WSOCK          63  AF_INET, SOCK_STREAM, IPPROTO_TCP
(WSAAsyncSelect) WSOCK c0f1bca8      hWnd=408, wMsg=cffe, 3f
    (setsockopt) WSOCK c0f1bca8      SOL_SOCKET, SO_LINGER, buf=0090efe8 len=8
    (ioctlsocket) WSOCK c0f1bca8     FIONBIO, parm=1
         (connect) WSOCK c0f1bca8    AF_INET, 80, 198.112.208.23

(recv/recvfrom) WSOCK c0f10e50       buf=0092bc94 len=7c00 flags=0

          (socket) WSOCK          64  AF_INET, SOCK_STREAM, IPPROTO_TCP
(WSAAsyncSelect) WSOCK c0f25e54      hWnd=408, wMsg=cffe, 3f
    (setsockopt) WSOCK c0f25e54      SOL_SOCKET, SO_LINGER, buf=0090f0f0 len=8
         Function Device      Handle  Args
    (ioctlsocket) WSOCK c0f25e54     FIONBIO, parm=1
         (connect) WSOCK c0f25e54    AF_INET, 80, 198.112.208.23

(recv/recvfrom) WSOCK c0f10e50       buf=0092bc94 len=7c00 flags=0
         (select) WSOCK             Rd=3 Wr=2 Err=2
         (select) WSOCK             Rd=3 Wr=2 Err=2
(recv/recvfrom) WSOCK c0f10e50       buf=0092bc94 len=7c00 flags=0

          (socket) WSOCK          65  AF_INET, SOCK_STREAM, IPPROTO_TCP
(WSAAsyncSelect) WSOCK c0f29a3c      hWnd=408, wMsg=cffe, 3f
    (setsockopt) WSOCK c0f29a3c      SOL_SOCKET, SO_LINGER, buf=0090f0f0 len=8
    (ioctlsocket) WSOCK c0f29a3c     FIONBIO, parm=1
         (connect) WSOCK c0f29a3c    AF_INET, 80, 198.112.208.23

(recv/recvfrom) WSOCK c0f10e50       buf=0092bc94 len=7c00 flags=0
    (closesocket) WSOCK c0f10e50
FS_WriteFile (d6) VFAT          20e  cnt=a18H ofs=0H ptr=12c6618H          ---
FS_CloseFile (3e) VFAT          20e  f
```

This example illustrates the limits of looking just at the file system. If all we saw
were the opens, writes, and closes, we would be unaware of the concurrency of
these operations. By combining some rudimentary information about Windows
sockets with a trace of file system activity, we see that a socket connection is
assigned to each file transfer, and when the transfer completes, the socket goes
away.

We have covered a lot of territory in this chapter, literally from IFSMgr to the
Internet. I hope it has impressed upon you how pervasive the file system is. In

the next chapter we'll continue our excursion with a look at the varieties of filenames supported by Windows 95.

Example 1-5. Retrieving a GIF file

```
         Function  Device     Handle   Args
         (select)  WSOCK               Rd=3 Wr=3 Err=3
         (select)  WSOCK               Rd=3 Wr=3 Err=3
        (connect)  WSOCK   c0f29a3c    AF_INET, 80, 198.112.208.23
    (send/sendto)  WSOCK   c0f29a3c    buf=012b50f0 len=d0 flags=0
                                       "GET /graphics/space.gif HTTP/1.0",d,a,
                                       "Referer: http:",0,8,0,0
  (recv/recvfrom)  WSOCK   c0f29a3c    buf=0090f534 len=104 flags=0
  (recv/recvfrom)  WSOCK   c0f29a3c    buf=0090f534 len=104 flags=0
         (select)  WSOCK               Rd=3 Wr=2 Err=2
         (select)  WSOCK               Rd=3 Wr=2 Err=2
  (recv/recvfrom)  WSOCK   c0f29a3c    buf=0090f534 len=104 flags=0
  (recv/recvfrom)  WSOCK   c0f29a3c    buf=0092bc94 len=400 flags=0
FS_OpenFile (6c)   VFAT        29b*    ..\NETSCAPE\N..R\CACHE\M0P17IE3.GIF    ca
    (closesocket)  WSOCK   c0f29a3c
FS_WriteFile (d6)  VFAT        29b     cnt=39H ofs=0H ptr=12c6618H            ---
FS_CloseFile (3e)  VFAT        29b     f
```

2

In this chapter:
- What's in a Name?
- Accessing Local Files
- Accessing Remote Files
- Accessing Devices

Where Do Filenames Go?

A file system is an abstract idea. What you deal with on a daily basis are the names of files that a file system stores and retrieves. Before Windows 95, DOS and Windows 3.x users learned to accept the limitations of their systems. Instead of a descriptive name like *FooTech Annual Report 97.doc*, they constructed a name like *foo_ar97.doc*. Much of the talk about the Windows 95 file system focuses on this transition from "short names" to "long names." While increasing a name's length is a long-awaited benefit, there are much more interesting aspects of a filename.

What's in a Name?

Most of us equate filenames with strings like *c:\foobar\foo.txt*. This example adheres to the "8.3" convention of limiting filename components to 8 characters with an optional dot followed by a three-character extension. Characters like \ (or /) and . serve as a form of punctuation that allows us to combine simple strings to represent a disk directory hierarchy. Another special character, the colon (:), delimits a leading character which stands for a physical or logical volume. The 8.3 naming convention also places the limit on the length of a fully-qualified filename, including the drive letter, at 64 characters. This kind of naming is used by the MS-DOS FAT filesystem.

Windows 95 has extended this file-naming convention to now allow filename components of up to 256 characters in length, including the null terminator. The length of a fully-qualified filename is limited to 260 characters. The dot character may now be used like any other character in composing a filename; it is not limited to marking the start of a three-character extension. Spaces and the + character are also valid path component and filename characters. While filenames are not case sensitive, case is preserved. This kind of naming is used by the Windows

95 VFAT file system. VFAT continues to support the 8.3 naming convention and provides for conversions between long and short forms of pathnames.

We won't delve into the detailed rules governing the construction of valid filenames in the FAT and VFAT systems. These topics have been addressed in other books and periodicals (see "Long Filenames" in *Programmer's Guide to Microsoft Windows 95*, Microsoft Press, 1995).

Another kind of naming that you will encounter follows the Universal Naming Convention (UNC). A UNC name consists of two leading backslashes followed by a machine name, a share name, and then directory and filename, as in *\\TOPDOG\DEVDISK\bin\nmake.exe*. These names are used primarily for referencing network resources, although a local share can be accessed with a full UNC name, as in *\\MYMACHINE\MYSHARE\foodir\foofile.txt*. The machine name is limited to 16 characters, including the null terminator, and the share name is limited to 13 characters, including the null terminator. The remaining portions of a UNC name follow the VFAT naming conventions.

Some special forms of UNC names are based on the use of a dot (.) for the server name. These names are used to refer to resources residing on the local machine. For example, a local mailslot is referenced as *\\.\MAILSLOT\fooslot*. Windows 95 also uses this form of UNC name for referencing some devices. To open a virtual device driver, you pass the name *\\.\VxDName* to the Win32 API **CreateFile**. *VxDName* can be either a VxD module name, a VxD file name, or an entry under the registry key *HKLM\System\CurrentControlSet\Control\SessionManager\KnownVxDs*. A filename is distinguished by having the name include an explicit extension.

Another type of device name is used to reference the "standard devices." Some of these are holdovers from MS-DOS: devices like CON, LPT1, and PRN. New standard device names can be added to the system by implementing a character file system driver and registering it with IFSMgr.

So we see that Windows 95 supports several kinds of names. Some are meant to access plain-vanilla disk files, others reach across the network to access a file at a remote location, and yet others point to a device. Let's look at how Windows 95 deals with these different varieties of names.

Accessing Local Files

Filenames can be introduced into the operating system through a variety of APIs. The Win32 functions **CreateFile**, **OpenFile**, **_lcreat**, and **_lopen** are perhaps the most common ones. The C run-time library offers the more portable wrappers for these APIs with **fopen**, **_creat**, and **_open**. The companion disk contains a sample application, called NT32, for testing names with the Win32 APIs. It attempts to open the filename entered on the command line with the **fopen**, **CreateFile**, and **OpenFile** functions. If the function is successful, the returned handle is immediately closed. This little application also emits tag strings at each step so that we may easily trace its execution with MultiMon. Here is the MultiMon trace that was logged when the command **nt32 c:\windows\system.ini** was executed:

```
Type     Function          Flags1    Dev  Hdl     Args             Flags2
tag  ======== fopen
w21  LFN(71)Ext.Open(6c)                             c:\windows\system.ini
p21  LFN(71)Ext.Open(6c)                             c:\windows\system.ini
fsh  FS_OpenFile (6c)      e_cLnu_s..VFAT 2da* C:\WINDOWS\SYSTEM.INI        oe
w21  IOCTL(44)GetDevData (00)           2da
p21  IOCTL(44)GetDevData (00)           2da
w21  Close(3e)                          2da
p21  Close(3e)                          2da
fsh  FS_CloseFile (3e)     e_cLnu_s..VFAT 2da                              f
tag  ======== CreateFile
w21  LFN(71)Ext.Open(6c)                             c:\windows\system.ini
p21  LFN(71)Ext.Open(6c)                             c:\windows\system.ini
fsh  FS_OpenFile (6c)      e_cLnu_s..VFAT 2e9* C:\WINDOWS\SYSTEM.INI        oe
w21  Close(3e)                          2e9
p21  Close(3e)                          2e9
fsh  FS_CloseFile (3e)     e_cLnu_s..VFAT 2e9                              f
tag  ======== OpenFile
w21  LFN(71)GetFileAttr(43)                          c:\windows\system.ini  Gt
p21  LFN(71)GetFileAttr(43)                          c:\windows\system.ini  Gt
fsh  FS_FileAttribs(43)    e_cLnu_s..VFAT      C:\WINDOWS\SYSTEM.INI        Gt
w21  LFN(71)Extended Open(6c)                        c:\windows\system.ini
p21  LFN(71)Extended Open(6c)                        c:\windows\system.ini
fsh  FS_OpenFile (6c)      e_cLnu_s..VFAT 2f9* C:\WINDOWS\SYSTEM.INI        oe
w21  IOCTL(44)RemDrvChk(09)             drive: C
p21  IOCTL(44)RemDrvChk(09)             drive: C
v21  IOCTL(44)RemDrvChk(09)             drive: C
w21  IOCTL(44)RemovMedChk(08)           drive: C
p21  IOCTL(44)RemovMedChk(08)           drive: C
v21  IOCTL(44)RemovMedChk(08)           drive: C
fsh  FS_Ioctl16Drive(4408) e_cLnu_s..VFAT     drive: C
w21  Get File Date/Time(5700)           2f9
fsh  FS_FileDateTime(57)   e_cLnu_s..VFAT 2f9                              Gm
w21  Close(3e)                          2f9
p21  Close(3e)                          2f9
fsh  FS_CloseFile (3e)     e_cLnu_s..VFAT 2f9                              f
tag  =======================
```

This output packs quite a bit of information. Let's start by getting familiar with what each column contains. The first column, Type, tells us which MultiMon monitor reported the line. This trace contains lines of output contributed by five different monitors: **tag** comes from TAGMON, **fsh** comes from FSHOOK, **w21** comes from WIN32CB, and **p21** and **v21** come from I21HELP1.

The next column, labeled Function, contains a description of the API or event which the line represents. Many of the lines identify functions of the interrupt 21h interface. Those whose names begin with "FS_" are functions in a file system driver like VFAT.

The Flags1 column looks like a pattern in a bowl of alphabet soup. All these odd-looking characters are described in detail in Appendix B, *MultiMon: Monitor Reference*. Each character represents a state flag that is either on—uppercase, or off—lowercase. For instance, the leading e indicates the function call succeeded whereas an E indicates the function failed. The next four flags indicate the kind of resource where a filename resides. In this example, every call into VFAT was accompanied by the flags cLnu; the capital L signifies local.

The Dev (or Device column) contains the module name of the device that is receiving the function request. For instance, in this listing, each "FS_" call is to the VFAT file system driver.

The Hdl (or Handle) column contains the system file number, if the call is handle-based. When a file is initially opened and the handle is first created, it is marked with an asterisk.

The Args column contains the filename or pathname that is an argument to the function. There is a limit to how many characters are stored, so you may see truncation at the beginning of the name.

Finally, we have another flags column, called Flags2. This column reports flags that are passed to a function as part of the calling parameters. Here, we have oe for open existing, f for final, Gt for get attributes, and Gm for get modification time and date.

Now that you are little more comfortable with the output, what does it mean? Start with the **fopen** call. In our test application, *nt32*, there are two program statements:

```
fh = fopen( argv[i],"r" );
if ( fh != NULL ) fclose( fh );
```

The first response we see to **fopen** is an interrupt 21h function 716ch, or extended file open (the 71h indicates that this is the long filename, or LFN, variant). We see this request in the **w21** for the Int21Dispatch in VWIN32. This is the result of a call from KERNEL32, via the Win32 API VxDCall, into VWIN32's ring-0 Win32 service for dispatching interrupt 21h requests. VWIN32 acts as a middle-man and just passes it to the protected-mode interrupt 21h interface, which is hooked by many VxDs, including IFSMgr. The I21HELP1 monitor hooks the protected-mode interrupt 21h interface just before requests are sent down to IFSMgr; this is where we get the type **p21** line for function 716ch. The next line that we see is an **FS_OpenFile** reported by the **fsh** monitor. This is where IFSMgr is making a call into the VFAT file system driver. This open succeeds and returns a handle of 0x2da. Note that this handle is not the same as the handle returned by **CreateFile**.

What we have seen so far corresponds to a **CreateFile** call within the **fopen** function. Before **fopen** returns, it also makes a call to the Win32 API **GetFileType**. This call appears in the log as two lines reporting the interrupt 21h function 4400h (get device data). As with the extended file open call, the **w21** monitor first picks it up as a KERNEL32 call into VWIN32. Then VWIN32 passes it to the protected-mode interrupt 21h interface which generates the **p21** monitor line. Since this call is not sent along any further, i.e., to the file system driver, it is presumably handled by IFSMgr.

To keep our little program tidy, we close the file descriptor returned by **fopen** as soon as **fopen** returns. The **fclose** call adds three lines to our trace. These entries follow the same pattern. We first see the close request in the **w21** monitor of VWIN32. VWIN32 passes the request down to the protected-mode interrupt 21h interface, which generates the **p21** monitor line. The next line that we see is an **FS_CloseFile** reported by the **fsh** monitor. Again, we see IFSMgr making a call into the VFAT file system driver.

I won't provide detailed descriptions of the **CreateFile** and **OpenFile** traces since they are very similar. It is interesting that **OpenFile** is the "busiest" of the three; apparently it has more work to do to fill in an OFSTRUCT. **OpenFile** also has some different sequences than we have seen before. For instance, the removable media check function 4408h goes from **w21** to **p21** to **v21** to **fsh**. The **v21** monitor is a virtual-86 mode interrupt 21h hook; it will see the interrupt before IFSMgr sees it on its V86 interrupt 21h hook. By absorbing this interrupt 21h request much later in the chain, IFSMgr is giving a wider range of drivers an opportunity to see it.

Before we move on to see how the system handles a UNC name, let's sketch a picture of the path we have followed. Tracing our path in Figure 1-1, we started in a Win32 application (**nt32**), then dropped down into the file system, passing through KERNEL32, VWIN32, IFSMgr, and finally ended up in VFAT.

Accessing Remote Files

Let's use **nt32** again, but this time we'll supply it with the name of a remote file, or, more accurately, a UNC name of a remote file. In this example, a second machine called WETSUIT shares its *c:* drive as C. The two machines are connected in a peer-to-peer Microsoft Network.

Here is a portion of the MultiMon trace that was logged when the command **nt32** **\\WETSUIT\C\windows\system.ini** was executed:

```
Type      Function        Flags1   Dev    Hdl      Args            Flags2
tag   ======== fopen
w21   LFN(71)Ext.Open(6c)                          \\WETSUIT\C\
                                                   windows\system.ini
p21   LFN(71)Ext.Open(6c)                          \\WETSUIT\C\
                                                   windows\system.ini
fsh   FS_OpenFile (6c)    e_clNU_s..VREDIR 2fa* \WINDOWS\SYSTEM.INI      oe
w21   IOCTL(44)GetDevData (00)           2fa
p21   IOCTL(44)GetDevData (00)           2fa
w21   Close(3e)                          2fa
p21   Close(3e)                          2fa
fsh   FS_CloseFile (3e)   e_clNU_s..VREDIR 2fa                           f
tag   ======== CreateFile
```

Here we only show the response to the **fopen** call. If you compare this with the function sequence for a local file system call, you'll see they are the same. However, if you compare the **FS_OpenFile** and **FS_CloseFile** calls you'll see that they reference different devices—in this case VREDIR instead of VFAT. VREDIR is a network file system driver, also known as a redirector. Note that the Flags1 field has also changed from **cLnu** for a local file system call to **clNU** for a remote file access. The "N" signifies a network resource is being accessed and the "U" indicates that the filename is a UNC name.

In the **FS_OpenFile** call to VREDIR, the server name and share name have been stripped off; only the directory and filename are supplied (for example, *\\WETSUIT\C\windows\system.ini* becomes *\windows\system.ini*). This truncated name is passed because there is an implicit connection established with the server called "WETSUIT" for the share named "C". Once the connection is made there is no need to keep passing around its name; a resource handle is used instead. This resource handle is a hidden argument to **FS_OpenFile**.

What we have been looking at is the client side of Microsoft Network. If you have configured your machine to share files (and printers, too), you can be a server like WETSUIT in the example above. If we run MultiMon on the server side, we get a log like this corresponding to the **fopen** call:

```
Type      Function        Flags1     Dev Hdl        Args          Flags2
fsh   FS_FindFirstFile(4e) e_cLnu_S.. VFAT 262* C:\WINDOWS\SYSTEM.INI
fsh   FS_FindClose(dc)     e_cLnu_S.. VFAT 262                          h
fsh   FS_OpenFile(6c)      e_cLnu_S.. VFAT 263* C:\WINDOWS\SYSTEM.INI   oe
fsh   FS_CloseFile(3e)     e_cLnu_S.. VFAT 263                          f
```

What is conspicuously absent is any interrupt 21h call; we only see calls into VFAT. First there is an attempt to locate the file using **FS_FindFirstFile**, and if that succeeds an open is attempted. If you have keen eyesight, you might have also noticed that the **S** flag is set in the Flags1 column. This flag is set if a file system request originates by a call to **IFSMgr_ServerDOSCall**. This is sort of a "back door" into IFSMgr that file servers use to service client requests.

Before we move on to see how the system handles a device name, let's refer back to Figure 1-1 to trace the the path we have just followed. On the client side, we started in a Win32 application (**nt32**) and then dropped down into the file system passing through KERNEL32, VWIN32, IFSMgr, and finally ending up in VREDIR and ultimately out onto the LAN. On the server side, packets come in and move up through the network layers to arrive at VSERVER; it passes the request directly to IFSMgr, who relays it on to the local file system driver, VFAT.

One type of naming that IFSMgr is unable to cope with is a Uniform Resource Locator (URL). For example, in Chapter 1, *From IFSMgr to the Internet*, we retrieved a graphics image from the O'Reilly & Associates home page using the URL *http://www.ora.com/graphics/space.gif.* In addition to the server's directory and filename, */graphics/space.gif,* this name specifies a protocol, *http,* and server location, *www.ora.com.* Currently, URLs are handled in the Explorer shell's namespace using OLE COM (Component Object Model).* But there is an effort underway to extend the SMB protocol, which is currently used as the LAN file sharing protocol, to also share files across the Internet. This new file sharing protocol is called CIFS, for Common Internet File System (see Chapter 13, *VREDIR: The Microsoft Networks Client).*

Accessing Devices

To complete our mini-tour of file system names, we'll look at the peculiarities of using device names. Let's use **nt32** again, but this time we'll supply it with the name of a "standard device." The standard device that we'll access is housed in the file system driver, MONOCFSD, which is presented in Chapter 8, *Anatomy of a File System Driver* (instructions are given there for installation). MONOCFSD adds a device called "mono" which stands for a monochrome TTL display (as opposed to a monochrome VGA display). This is a write-only device.

Here is a portion of the MultiMon trace that was logged when the command **nt32 mono** was executed:

```
Type      Function       Flags1    Dev     Hdl      Args        Flags2
tag   ======== fopen
w21   LFN(71)Ext.Open(6c)                           E:\ifsbook\
                                                     nt32\mono
p21   LFN(71)Ext.Open(6c)                           E:\ifsbook\
                                                     nt32\mono
```

---

* See the article "Sweeper," by Paul DiLascia and Victor Stone, in *Microsoft Interactive Developer*, available at *http://www.microsoft.com/mind/0396/sweeper.sweeper.htm.*

Type	Function	Flags1	Dev	Hdl	Args	Flags2
fsh	FS_MountVolume(00)	e_clnu_s..	MONOCFSD		drive: A	m
fsh	FS_OpenFile (6c)	e_Clnu_s..	MONOCFSD	2d8*	\IFSBOOK\NT32\MONO	oe
w21	IOCTL(44)GetDevData(00)			2d8		
p21	IOCTL(44)GetDevData(00)			2d8		
fsh	FS_Ioctl16Drive(4400)	e_Clnu_s..	MONOCFSD			
w21	Close(3e)			2d8		
p21	Close(3e)			2d8		
fsh	FS_CloseFile(3e)	e_Clnu_s..	MONOCFSD	2d8		f
tag	======== CreateFile					
w21	LFN(71)Ext.Open(6c)				E:\ifsbook\ nt32\mono	
p21	LFN(71)Ext.Open(6c)				E:\ifsbook\ nt32\mono	
fsh	FS_OpenFile(6c)	e_Clnu_s..	MONOCFSD	2eb*	\IFSBOOK\NT32\MONO	oe
w21	Close(3e)			2eb		
p21	Close(3e)			2eb		
fsh	FS_CloseFile (3e)	e_Clnu_s..	MONOCFSD	2eb		f
tag	======== OpenFile					

If you compare this with the function sequences for our previous examples, you'll see they are quite similar. One call that stands out here is **FS_MountVolume**. On the first call to open this device, IFSMgr calls MONOCFSD's mount entry point. This function establishes the linkage between the file system driver and IFSMgr. Since this is a character file system driver, subsequent calls into MONOCFSD have the C flag set in the Flags1 column, to indicate that this is a character resource.

Although we passed *mono* as the filename to **fopen** and **CreateFile**, notice that the argument that the interrupt 21h functions see—and that ultimately gets passed to **FS_OpenFile**—is *E:\ifsbook\nt32\mono*. The directory *E:\ifsbook\nt32* was the directory from which I executed **nt32**. IFSMgr doesn't care because when it comes to standard device names, it ignores the drive and path.

In the section "What's in a Name?" earlier in this chapter, I mentioned that another form of device name is used to reference virtual device drivers. Here is MultiMon trace that we get when we try the command **nt32 \\.\ifsmgr**:

Type	Function	Flags1	Dev	Hdl	Args	Flags2
tag	======== fopen					
tag	======== CreateFile					
tag	======== OpenFile					
w21	LFN(71)Get File Attr(43)				\\.\ifsmgr	Gt
p21	LFN(71)Get File Attr(43)				\\.\ifsmgr	Gt
tag	=====================					

In this case, IFSMgr doesn't see these requests. Instead this is a job that VWIN32 assumes as part of its support for the **DeviceIoControl** function. If we change

MultiMon's filters to include VWIN32's **DeviceIoControl** interface, we get a more informative trace log:

```
Type      Function          Flags1    Dev      Hdl     Args        Flags2
tag     ======== fopen
dev     Open Device                   IFSMGR
dev     Close Device                  IFSMGR
dev     (256)                         TAGMON
tag     ======== CreateFile
dev     Open Device                   IFSMGR
dev     Close Device                  IFSMGR
dev     (256)                         TAGMON
tag     ======== OpenFile
w21     LFN(71)Get File Attr(43)                       \\.\ifsmgr      Gt
p21     LFN(71)Get File Attr(43)                       \\.\ifsmgr    . Gt
dev     (256)                         TAGMON
tag     =====================
```

The new lines that we have added, of Type dev, originate in the WIN32CB monitor. One of the things this driver monitors is VWIN32's ring-0 Win32 service to support KERNEL32's **DeviceIoControl** interface. This interface is also "wired-up" to the Win32 functions **CreateFile** and **CloseHandle**, when these functions are referencing a VxD name. That is what we are seeing here, an "Open Device" for IFSMgr from **CreateFile** and a "Close Device" for IFSMgr from **CloseHandle**. The TAGMON driver, which spits out the tag strings in our trace, also uses **DeviceIo-Control** to receive tag strings. The private code that it assigns to this function is 256. This trace also shows us that the Win32 **OpenFile** API doesn't accept VxD device names.

To finish up our mini-tour of filenames, let's refer back to Figure 1-1 one last time. We have traced two different paths for device names. For a standard device name, we start in a Win32 application, then pass through KERNEL32, VWIN32, and IFSMgr before ultimately arriving at the character file system driver, MONOCFSD, in our example. On the other hand, for a VxD device name, only KERNEL32 and VWIN32 are involved.

Our exploration of filenames was based on a Win32 application. We could easily repeat these experiments using a Win16 or a DOS-box application. Figure 1-1 shows that a Win16 application interfaces with the 16-bit Kernel, which in turn issues protected-mode interrupt 21h requests to IFSMgr. A DOS-box application, on the other hand, issues virtual-86 mode interrupt 21h requests to IFSMgr.

This chapter has been a quick "once-over" to introduce you to some of the system components which play a role in the file system's operation. I have thrown out some terms like *Win32 services, protected-mode interrupts,* and *virtual-86 interrupts.* These system features are at the heart of what makes the file system tick. They are the focus of the next chapter.

In this chapter:
* *The Big Bang*
* *Accessing IFSMgr*
* *The Win32 Callback*

3

Pathways to the File System

In this chapter we will focus on file system plumbing—those mechanisms that are used to make file system services available to an array of operating system modes: DOS/V86, Win16, Win32, and ring-0. In the next chapter we'll look at what gets carried through this plumbing: the various APIs.

To carry the plumbing analogy further, when a building is finished the pipes are hidden from view. To see the plumbing you have to peer into crawl spaces with a flashlight, or remove wall panels. But, if you visit while the building is going up, before the floors and walls are erected, the plumbing is in clear view.

Well, we're not going to rebuild Windows 95 from the ground up; instead we're going to watch as Windows 95 starts up to get a clearer view of the file system. We'll be tracing through Windows 95 from the "Big Bang" to its quiescent state, kernel idle. Armed with this background, we'll come back to the Windows 95 operating system modes, and examine how the file system is accessed from each of them.

The Big Bang

By the time you type your password to log on as a Windows 95 user, an enormous amount of software has executed to prepare the system to do useful work. Out of this mountain of software, we will concentrate on the main Windows 95 kernel components: *vmm32.vxd*, *krnl386.exe*, and *kernel32.dll*. VMM32 is a compressed library of virtual device drivers along with a real mode loader. Each VxD in the library may execute real mode initialization before the processor is switched to protected mode. Upon entering protected mode, VMM issues system control messages to notify VxDs of each initialization stage. Here is a summary of these stages:

1. The first stage is *System Critical Init*. At this point, interrupts are still disabled, so it provides an opportunity for drivers to install hardware handlers and perform other critical initialization steps. During this phase there are restrictions on which services are available to VxDs. For instance, **Exec_Int**, a service for executing software interrupts, is not available.

2. *Device Init* stage follows System Critical Init. During this stage most services are available to drivers. This is the stage at which most drivers perform the bulk of their initialization.

3. *Init Complete* stage follows Device Init. After this stage, VMM discards the driver initialization code and data segments. Subsequent stages continue the preparation of the system virtual machine.

4. *System VM Init* marks the stage at which the system virtual machine has been created and initialized.

5. *Begin PM App* marks the execution of KRNL386 in the system VM.

6. *Kernel32 Init* indicates that KERNEL32 initialization in the system VM is complete.

These stages provide a timeline along which we can mark important and interesting events.

Within each stage, there is another timeline which is based on the initialization order of devices. Each device specifies a doubleword init order ranging from 0, the first, to FFFFFFFFh, the last. Each category of VxDs has a specific init order; for instance, IFSMgr has the value A0010000h, whereas file system drivers are assigned A0010100h. This assures that IFSMgr is initialized prior to the FSDs which rely upon it.

By the time the kernel components have initialized, many VxDs have hooked interrupts, installed callbacks, and in other ways have left their imprint on the final system configuration. MultiMon is an ideal tool for watching these initialization steps.

Sampling the Startup Timeline with MultiMon

To make the sequence of events easier to visualize, we'll be using MultiMon to log events of interest during system startup. For a detailed description of MultiMon and for instructions on installing it, see Appendix A, *MultiMon: Setup, Usage, and Extensions*. We will be making use of the BOOTMGR driver, which allows us to monitor and collect a log of events during the time the system is booting. More accurately, the log will collect events from System Critical Init until Kernel Idle.

MultiMon can be configured with a variety of drivers to collect information about different APIs and events. In this chapter, we are especially interested in looking at how the interrupt vector tables and callbacks get initialized. With this goal in mind, I've used the set of MultiMon drivers shown in Table 3-1 to collect the traces that we will be examining in the coming sections.

Table 3-1. MultiMon Configuration for Creating a Log file

MultiMon Driver	Monitor	API Selections
BOOTMGR		
VECTORS	Interrupts & Callbacks	
I21HELP1	Int21 PM (pre-IFSMgr)	Set Vect(25)
"	Int21 V86 (pre-IFSMgr)	Set Vect(25)
I2FMON1	Int2F PM (pre-IFSMgr)	Win/386 Multiplex(16)
"	Int2F V86 (pre-IFSMgr)	Win/386 Multiplex(16)
WIN32CB	VWIN32 DeviceIoControl	
"	VWIN32 Win32 Services	K32Init (36)
"	VWIN32 Win32 Services	ReplGlobalEnv (47)

If you want to repeat this on your own system, you need to follow these steps:

- Install the drivers listed in Table 3-1, using MultiMon's **Add/Remove Driver...** dialog from Options on the main menu.

- You must reboot your system to actually get the drivers loaded, since these are static VxDs.

- After rebooting, start MultiMon and bring up the **Filters** dialog to adjust your session logging options. Make sure the monitors in Table 3-1 are checked off and other monitors are disabled. Within in each monitor, select only the APIs listed in Table 3-1.

- After each monitor and its associated APIs are selected, press the dialog button **Save As Default**. (This button must be pressed once for each monitor.)

- Now reboot your system and this time, as it starts up, a log file will be created. Once the system has finished initialization, launch MultiMon; you will be greeted with a message box stating: "BOOTMGR has captured a log file. Do you wish to display it now?" Answer yes; you may also save the log file in text form using the **Save As...** button.

- To disable MultiMon's "boot-logging" mode later, remove the BOOTMGR driver using the **Add/Remove Driver...** dialog from Options on the main menu; you may also want to remove other drivers which you don't plan to use again.

Interpreting MultiMon Output: Pre-System VM

In this section we will examine a typical log file. The example shown here was collected from a Texas Instruments TM-4000M notebook with Microsoft Networks client and server installed.

The session log file is subdivided into the following sections:

> Initial V86 Interrupt Vectors
> Initial IDT Vectors
> Sys Critical Init
> Device Init
> Init Complete
> Sys VM Init
> Begin PM App
> Kernel32 Initialized

These sections mark easily recognizable stages during system startup and correspond to control messages that BOOTMGR receives from VMM. Within each section, each log entry is divided into columns. The first column is labeled Module. Generally, this column contains the name of a process that owns the thread from which the event was generated. In the case of descriptive messages, the monitor driver that generated the message will be entered here (e.g., BOOTMGR or VECTORS). The next column is labeled Type. This column contains a three-character abbreviation for the name of the monitor, e.g., **vec** for Interrupts & Callbacks. The third column is labeled Function. For the early portion of the log file, these entries will refer to virtual device driver services. The VxD services that will be seen here are:

> Get_PM_Int_Vector
> Get_V86_Int_Vector
> Allocate_PM_Call_Back
> Allocate_V86_Call_Back
> Set_PM_Int_Vector
> Set_V86_Int_Vector
> Hook_V86_Int_Chain
> Allocate_V86_Break_Point

With the exception of the first two services, all of these services are *hooked* by *vectors.vxd*. For these hooked services, VECTORS has installed a preamble and/or postamble which is executed whenever these services are called.

In the last two sections of the session logfile, Begin PM App and Kernel32 Initialized, we also see other types of entries in the Function column. In these cases, the line Type will be **p21**, **v21**, **p2f**, **v2f**, **vw32**, or **dev**. The first four refer to interrupts 21 and 2f, whereas **vw32** and **dev** refer to the Win32 callback. We have hooked these interfaces by installing an interrupt handler and chaining it to the previous handler. Hooking the Win32 callback is a little more involved and we'll get to the details later in this chapter.

The other columns you will see in the log are:

Flags1

    May contain "Entry" or "Return" to indicate which side of a call the line was reported from

Device

    May contain the name of the VxD which is being called into

Handle

    Used to store the interrupt number, as in "Int 21"

Args

    A string describing input arguments or return values

Flags2

    Not used

Let us examine the output section-by-section, starting with the first two tables, shown in Figure 3-1. These tables display the values of the V86 and protect mode interrupt vectors for the five software interrupts which IFSMgr monitors. The V86 vectors are segment:offset pairs that reference code that executes in V86 mode. The protect mode vectors all have the characteristic 003Bh selector which earmark it as a protected mode callback. The segment with this selector consists of an array of Int 30h instructions (interrupt gates) which change the execution ring level (see the sidebar "Breakpoints and Callbacks").

Module	Type	Function	Flags1	Handle	Args
BOOTMGR	txt	**** SysCritInit			
VECTORS	txt	Initial V86 Interrupt Vectors			
?	vec	Get_V86_Int_Vector	Entry	Int 17	V86 Vector=DEC:0A28
?	vec	Get_V86_Int_Vector	Entry	Int 21	V86 Vector=DEC:04A0
?	vec	Get_V86_Int_Vector	Entry	Int 25	V86 Vector=C9:0FBC
?	vec	Get_V86_Int_Vector	Entry	Int 26	V86 Vector=C9:0FC6
?	vec	Get_V86_Int_Vector	Entry	Int 2F	V86 Vector=159B:03CC
VECTORS	txt	Initial IDT Vectors			
?	vec	Get_PM_Int_Vector	Entry	Int 17	PM Vector=3B:2E
?	vec	Get_PM_Int_Vector	Entry	Int 21	PM Vector=3B:42
?	vec	Get_PM_Int_Vector	Entry	Int 25	PM Vector=3B:4A
?	vec	Get_PM_Int_Vector	Entry	Int 26	PM Vector=3B:4C
?	vec	Get_PM_Int_Vector	Entry	Int 2F	PM Vector=3B:208

Figure 3-1. Initial IVT and IDT Contents

Breakpoints and Callbacks

During VMM initialization, one or more pages are allocated in which system breakpoints and callbacks are stored. The amount of storage set aside depends on the value of the *MaxBPS* key in the [386Enh] section of *system.ini*. In Windows 95 Build 950, the default value for *MaxBPS* is 400. The *MaxBPS* value is rounded upwards to the actual number of breakpoints (*ActualBPS*) so the storage claimed is the nearest whole number of pages. This storage is divided into two portions.

The lower portion begins at the base address of the allocation and is *ActualBPS**8 in size. Each V86 callback or PM callback consumes 8 bytes of this region. A V86 breakpoint needs twice as much storage as a callback. To get the additional space, *ActualBPS* is reduced by one and the freed storage is used for the breakpoint.

For every callback and breakpoint two doublewords are stored, the Refdata value and the Callback address as they were passed as arguments to the corresponding services. Note that this table does not distinguish a V86 callback from a PM callback or a V86 breakpoint. This table grows towards higher addresses, limited only by *ActualBPS*.

The additional 8 bytes of storage required for a V86 breakpoint is also allocated from this same region but from the other end, i.e., from higher addresses towards lower. The first breakpoint would be stored at (*ActualBPS*–1)*8, the next at (*ActualBPS*–2)*8, and so on. Thus as breakpoints are added, the maximum number of breakpoints (and callbacks) is reduced by one. In the 8 bytes of additional storage, the first doubleword is the linear address of the V86 breakpoint, followed by a word index into the "Refdata/Callback" array, followed by the byte replaced with the **arpl** instruction, and then a byte of 0ffh for padding (and probably to assure a mismatch when scanning for a matching CS:EIP).

Immediately following the region just described is a region filled with Int 30h instructions, the interrupt gates for jumping from ring-3 to ring-0. The size of this region is defined by the equation (*ActualBPS*+100h)*2 bytes. A descriptor with selector 3Bh is defined just to reference this table. The additional 100h entries are included for default reflection of protect-mode interrupts to V86 mode.

When a V86 callback is called, an invalid opcode fault causes the program to enter VMM. VMM uses the CS:EIP in the client registers to determine if the caller came from the **arpl** byte location. If it did, the actual segment-offset encoding of the address is used to look up the entry in the "Refdata/Callback" array.

—Continued—

When a PM callback executes its matching Int 30h instruction, the interrupt gate transfers control to VMM. VMM uses the CS:EIP in the client registers to determine if the interrupt came from code executing with selector 3Bh. If so, EIP–2 is used to index into the "Refdata/Callback" array.

When a V86 breakpoint is "hit", an invalid opcode fault causes the program to enter VMM. In this case, the CS:EIP in the client registers does not point to the single callback **arpl** instruction; rather, it points to an **arpl** that has been inserted in the instruction stream. VMM uses the CS:EIP value to scan the breakpoint array to locate a matching CS:EIP. If found, the index value is used to look up the corresponding "Refdata/Callback" entry.

IDT stands for interrupt descriptor table. There isn't just one IDT; separate IDTs exist for virtual-86 and protected mode. What is more, each virtual machine has its own pair of V86 and PM IDTs. The current IDT is constantly changing, as VMM switches VMs and execution modes are changed within a VM. When **Set_PM_Int_Vector** is called it sets the protected mode IDT vector referenced by the current VM to the specified handler; the IDT for V86 mode is not affected. In V86 mode, it is the V86 IDT which is consulted when a hardware or software interrupt occurs, not the interrupt vector table (IVT) at 0:0 in the current VM. The IVT comes into play when no protected mode handler services the request. VMM then reflects the interrupt to "real mode" to the corresponding entry in the IVT. To assign a vector to the IVT for the current VM, **Set_V86_Int_Vector** is used. This service stuffs the vector into the currently mapped VM at 00000000+4*intnum.

Software interrupts or traps occurring in V86 mode are always going to be initially serviced at ring-0. In protected mode, the situation is a little more complicated. Each entry in the PM IDT is a gate with a specific privilege level. When a software interrupt occurs, the privilege level of the interrupting program is compared against the privilege level of the gate. The interruptor must be at least the same privilege level as the gate or a general protection fault is issued against the int *n* instruction. This will still force the program to enter VMM, but at the GP fault handler rather than at the intended interrupt handler.

This property of PM software interrupts also allows the PM IDT to contain addresses of handlers which reside in a ring-3 DLL. It is also for this reason that protected mode callbacks go through an interrupt gate which has a privilege level of 3.

Now we have seen that **Set_PM_Int_Vector** and **Set_V86_Int_Vector** apply to the current VM, but during System Critical Init, Device Init, etc. a VM does not yet exist, so what affect do they have at this early stage? The DDK reference tells us that if these services are called before the System VM Init control message is broadcast, the installed handler becomes part of the default IDT and IVT which are used for every VM which is subsequently created.

Another observation we can make from the protected mode vectors shown in Figure 3-1 is that each one is at an offset of 2*intnum in the Int 30h segment. The first 100h entries in this array are the default protected mode vectors that are used for each VM. Their corresponding addresses will be from 3b:0000 to 3b:01fe. Note that the address for the Int 2f handler lies outside this range. This is because VMM has already overidden the default entry by installing a callback at 3b:0208. The default protected mode vector which this handler should chain to would be at 3b:005e.

Continuing with the System Critical Init phase, Figure 3-2 shows a few of the entries from this stage. There are no entries made by IFSMgr, but DOSMGR does install protected mode handlers for Int 21h, 25h, and 26h, the same interrupts IFSMgr has an interest in. Note that for each protected mode handler installed, first a callback is allocated and then the protected mode vector is set to this call-back address. Each of the **Allocate_PM_Call_Back** calls associates a ring-0 procedure with the callback. For instance, in the case of Int 21h, the ring-0 procedure is c02201ac. VMM provides a handy service, **_GetVxDName**, that converts a ring-0 address into a device name, segment, and offset form. For example, the ring-0 address c02201ac is located in DOSMGR segment 0Ah at an offset of 1ACh from its origin (DOSMGR(0A) + 000001AC).

Type	Function	Flags1	Handle	Args
vec	Allocate_V86_Call_Back	Entry		Ring0 Function=c025a22c (DOSMGR(13) + 00000190)
vec	Allocate_V86_Call_Back	Return		V86 App Callback: fe65:18dd
vec	Hook_V86_Int_Chain	Entry	Int 2A	Ring0 Hook=c02943cc (DOSMGR(05) + 0000002C)
vec	Hook_V86_Int_Chain	Entry	Int 21	Ring0 Hook=c0220000 (DOSMGR(0A) + 00000000)
vec	Hook_V86_Int_Chain	Entry	Int 24	Ring0 Hook=c022b270 (DOSMGR(0B) + 000002A4)
vec	Hook_V86_Int_Chain	Entry	Int 23	Ring0 Hook=c025a237 (DOSMGR(13) + 0000019B)
vec	Hook_V86_Int_Chain	Entry	Int 1B	Ring0 Hook=c025a2d7 (DOSMGR(13) + 0000023B)
vec	Allocate_PM_Call_Back	Entry		Ring0 Function=c02201ac (DOSMGR(0A) + 000001AC)
vec	Allocate_PM_Call_Back	Return		PM App Callback: 3b:0330
vec	Set_PM_Int_Vector	Entry	Int 21	PM Vector=3B:330
vec	Allocate_PM_Call_Back	Entry		Ring0 Function=c022b77e (DOSMGR(0B) + 000007B2)
vec	Allocate_PM_Call_Back	Return		PM App Callback: 3b:0332
vec	Set_PM_Int_Vector	Entry	Int 25	PM Vector=3B:332
vec	Allocate_PM_Call_Back	Entry		Ring0 Function=c022b77e (DOSMGR(0B) + 000007B2)
vec	Allocate_PM_Call_Back	Return		PM App Callback: 3b:0334
vec	Set_PM_Int_Vector	Entry	Int 26	PM Vector=3B:334

Figure 3-2. MultiMon trace fragment from System Critical Init

Hook_V86_Int_Chain is used to install V86 interrupt handlers for 1Bh, 21h, 23h, 24h, and 2Ah. When VMM receives the interrupt via the V86 IDT, it will check to see if any handlers have been installed for the interrupt by the **Hook_V86_Int_**

Chain service, and if so, control is passed to the handler. This service may be used to install multiple V86 handlers for a particular interrupt. The last handler installed gets the first crack at handling the interrupt. Only if it doesn't handle the interrupt or wishes other handlers to see the interrupt too, it returns with carry set. If carry is cleared on return, then VMM does not pass the interrupt on any further. Only if all of the installed handlers fail to service the interrupt (or if no ring-0 handlers have been installed) VMM consults the IVT for this VM and pass the interrupt to the "real mode" components in the VM.

Device Init phase is the phase during which devices do most of their initialization. This is the phase where we see the first entries in the log file for IFSMgr. We see from the output in Figure 3-3 that IFSMgr is interested in interrupts 17h, 21h, 25h, 26h, and 2Fh. Of these, 21h, 25h, and 26h have protected mode vectors installed using the **Allocate_PM_Call_Back** service along with **Set_PM_Int_Vector**, as we saw with DOSMGR. For the V86 IDT, IFSMgr installs ring-0 handlers for interrupts 17h, 21h, 25h, 26h, and 2Fh. The only thing unaccounted for is the V86 call back. This callback is passed to the DOS device driver *ifshlp.sys*. It provides a way for it to enter IFSMgr (see the section "Bouncing Back from ifshlp.sys" in Chapter 5, *The "New" MS-DOS File System*).

Type	Function	Flags1	Handle	Args
vec	Allocate_V86_Call_Back	Entry		Ring0 Function=c00aae59 (IFSMGR(01) + 00000521)
vec	Allocate_V86_Call_Back	Return		V86 App Callback: feb0:142d
vec	Hook_V86_Int_Chain	Entry	Int 21	Ring0 Hook=c00abb22 (IFSMGR(01) + 000011EA)
vec	Allocate_PM_Call_Back	Entry		Ring0 Function=c00aba78 (IFSMGR(01) + 00001140)
vec	Allocate_PM_Call_Back	Return		PM App Callback: 3b:03c6
vec	Set_PM_Int_Vector	Entry	Int 21	PM Vector=3B:3C6
vec	Hook_V86_Int_Chain	Entry	Int 17	Ring0 Hook=c0276c1a (IFSMGR(03) + 000016DA)
vec	Hook_V86_Int_Chain	Entry	Int 25	Ring0 Hook=c0276bcc (IFSMGR(03) + 0000168C)
vec	Hook_V86_Int_Chain	Entry	Int 26	Ring0 Hook=c0276bcc (IFSMGR(03) + 0000168C)
vec	Allocate_PM_Call_Back	Entry		Ring0 Function=c0276b6f (IFSMGR(03) + 0000162F)
vec	Allocate_PM_Call_Back	Return		PM App Callback: 3b:03c8
vec	Set_PM_Int_Vector	Entry	Int 25	PM Vector=3B:3C8
vec	Allocate_PM_Call_Back	Entry		Ring0 Function=c0276b6f (IFSMGR(03) + 0000162F)
vec	Allocate_PM_Call_Back	Return		PM App Callback: 3b:03ca
vec	Set_PM_Int_Vector	Entry	Int 26	PM Vector=3B:3CA
vec	Hook_V86_Int_Chain	Entry	Int 2F	Ring0 Hook=c00ab81c (IFSMGR(01) + 00000EE4)

Figure 3-3. MultiMon trace fragment from Device Init

Figure 3-4 shows the entries for the final VMM initialization stage, Init Complete. Here, we see VMPOLL install both protected mode and V86 mode handlers for Interrupt 21h.

Interpreting MultiMon Output: Post-System VM

Once the System VM is created, VMM broadcasts the Sys VM Init message, to allow VxDs to perform any initialization needed for the new VM. The initial V86

Type	Function	Flags1	Handle	Args
txt	**** InitComplete			
vec	Hook_V86_Int_Chain	Entry	Int 21	Ring0 Hook=c0220310 (VMPOLL(05) + 00000068)
vec	Allocate_PM_Call_Back	Entry		Ring0 Function=c02202fc (VMPOLL(05) + 00000054)
vec	Allocate_PM_Call_Back	Return		PM App Callback: 3b:03d6
vec	Set_PM_Int_Vector	Entry	Int 21	PM Vector=3B:3D6

Figure 3-4. MultiMon trace fragment from Init Complete

IVT and protected mode IDT of the system VM are stored away as templates to be used for creating future VMs.

VMs begin life in V86 mode, and the System VM is no different. To switch the VM to protected mode requires launching an application in the VM that makes use of Window's DPMI services to make the change. The application that gets launched is *krnl386.exe*, a 16-bit protected mode application. When a protected mode application starts in a VM, VMM broadcasts the message "Begin PM App." Starting with this stage, we see ring-3 services added to the MultiMon trace in Figure 3-5.

Many of the services listed in the Function column in Figure 3-5 are ring-3, application level services. These include:

> **Win/386 Multiplex**, Get Device API (Int 2Fh, AX=1684h)
> **Win/386 Multiplex**, Get DPMI Extension (Int 2Fh, AX=168Ah)
> **Win/386 Multiplex**, Get Win32 API (Int 2Fh, AX=188Dh)
> **SetVect** (Int 21h, AH=25h)
> **ReplGlobalEnv** (VxDCall(002A0031h))
> **K32Init** (VxDCall(002A001Fh))

These are just a small fraction of the services that could be logged at this stage. There are numerous Int 21h and Win32 services that don't show up here. The services that were selected were chosen because they help to account for the ring-0, **Allocate_PM_Call_Back**, and **Set_PM_Int_Vector** calls.

The log shows us that KRNL386 at this stage is concerned with fault and exception handlers. We see it installing protected mode handlers for Interrupts 1 and 3, the Debug Exception and Debug Breakpoint. We also see several PM callbacks being allocated to the VMM address c023183bh. These are used to install exception handlers for interrupts 6, B, C, D, and E: the invalid opcode, segment not present, stack exception, general protection fault, and page fault, respectively. Presumably DPMI calls are used to set these exception handlers.

There are several Int 2Fh calls to retrieve the protected mode interfaces for devices. The devices that are interrogated on this system are: PAGEFILE, VWIN32, VMM, and VTDAPI. Note that the protected mode callback (which is used for the PM APIs for these VxDs) is not allocated until some client requests it from the device.

Type	Function	Flags1	Device	H...	Args
txt	**** Begin PM App				
vec	Allocate_PM_Call_Back	Entry			Ring0 Function=c00a9849 (VWIN32(01)
vec	Allocate_PM_Call_Back	Return			PM App Callback: 3b:03da
p2f	Win/386 Multiplex(16)DPMIExt(8a)				
p2f	Win/386 Multiplex(16)GetDevAPI(84)		PAGEFILE(21h)		
vec	Allocate_PM_Call_Back	Entry			Ring0 Function=c0006186 (VMM(01) + (
vec	Allocate_PM_Call_Back	Return			PM App Callback: 3b:03dc
p2f	Win/386 Multiplex(16)GetDevAPI(84)		VWIN32 (2Ah)		
vec	Allocate_PM_Call_Back	Entry			Ring0 Function=c0006186 (VMM(01) + (
vec	Allocate_PM_Call_Back	Return			PM App Callback: 3b:03de
p2f	Win/386 Multiplex(16)GetDevAPI(84)		VMM (1h)		
vec	Allocate_PM_Call_Back	Entry			Ring0 Function=c0006186 (VMM(01) + (
vec	Allocate_PM_Call_Back	Return			PM App Callback: 3b:03e0
vec	Allocate_PM_Call_Back	Entry			Ring0 Function=c023183b (VMM(0D) +
vec	Allocate_PM_Call_Back	Return			PM App Callback: 3b:03e2
p21	Set Vect(25)				
vec	Set_PM_Int_Vector	Entry		Int 1	PM Vector=117:ABA
p21	Set Vect(25)				
vec	Set_PM_Int_Vector	Entry		Int 3	PM Vector=117:AC4
vec	Allocate_PM_Call_Back	Entry			Ring0 Function=c023183b (VMM(0D) +
vec	Allocate_PM_Call_Back	Return			PM App Callback: 3b:03e4
vec	Allocate_PM_Call_Back	Entry			Ring0 Function=c023183b (VMM(0D) +
vec	Allocate_PM_Call_Back	Return			PM App Callback: 3b:03e6
vec	Allocate_PM_Call_Back	Entry			Ring0 Function=c023183b (VMM(0D) +
vec	Allocate_PM_Call_Back	Return			PM App Callback: 3b:03e8
vec	Allocate_PM_Call_Back	Entry			Ring0 Function=c023183b (VMM(0D) +
vec	Allocate_PM_Call_Back	Return			PM App Callback: 3b:03ea
p2f	Win/386 Multiplex(16)GetDevAPI(84)		VWIN32 (2Ah)		
p2f	Win/386 Multiplex(16)GetWin32Api...				
vec	Allocate_PM_Call_Back	Entry			Ring0 Function=c00dbcff (WIN32CB(01
vec	Allocate_PM_Call_Back	Return			PM App Callback: 3b:03ec
p2f	Win/386 Multiplex(16)GetDevAPI(84)		VTDAPI (442h)		
vec	Allocate_PM_Call_Back	Entry			Ring0 Function=c0006186 (VMM(01) + (
vec	Allocate_PM_Call_Back	Return			PM App Callback: 3b:03ee
vw32	ReplGlobalEnv(47)				
vec	Allocate_PM_Call_Back	Entry			Ring0 Function=c026f1ae (VWIN32(04)
vec	Allocate_PM_Call_Back	Return			PM App Callback: 3b:03f0
vw32	K32Init(36)				

Figure 3-5. MultiMon trace from Begin PM App

There are also a couple of rare Int 2Fh calls: 168Ah, which retrieves the protected mode callback to vendor specific DPMI extensions, and 168Dh, which retrieves the protected mode callback to Win32 services. It is KERNEL32 which actually uses this callback to implement the undocumented **VxDCall** function. At the time **Get Win32 API** is called, a protected mode callback is allocated and asssigned a ring-0 handler in VMM. In order to monitor **VxDCall** traffic we install our ring-0 handler in its place and then chain on to the original handler. This allows us to examine all **VxDCall** calls, but we only show two at the end of this section of the log. The first, **ReplaceGlobalEnv**, is a wrapper for the VMM function **VMM_Replace_Global_Environment**. **K32Init** is a wrapper for the VMM **System_Control** service. It is used to broadcast the control message "Kernel32 Init," which marks the beginning of the next stage.

After the Kernel32 Initialized message is broadcast, the kernel continues with its initialization and performs operations similar to what we saw in the previous stage. The log is much longer for this stage; a portion of it is shown in Figure 3-6. Again, there are several Int 2Fh calls to retrieve the protected mode interfaces for devices. The devices that are interrogated on this system include VDD, VTDAPI, VMOUSE, Device=37h, REBOOT, SHELL, VMM, VFLATD, CONFIGMG, MMDEVLDR(44ah), VDSPD, and VJOYD.

Type	Function	Flags1	Device	Han...	Args
p21	Set Vect(25)				
vec	Set_PM_Int_Vector	Entry		Int 2F	PM Vector=317:9C47
p21	Set Vect(25)				
vec	Set_PM_Int_Vector	Entry		Int 10	PM Vector=317:9C3E
p2f	Win/386 Multiplex(16)GetDevAPI(84)		VDD (Ah)		
p2f	Win/386 Multiplex(16)GetCurVMID(...				
p21	Set Vect(25)				
vec	Set_PM_Int_Vector	Entry		Int 9	PM Vector=247:44
p21	Set Vect(25)				
vec	Set_PM_Int_Vector	Entry		Int 2F	PM Vector=317:9C47
p21	Set Vect(25)				
vec	Set_PM_Int_Vector	Entry		Int 24	PM Vector=117:9094
vec	Set_PM_Int_Vector	Entry		Int 24	PM Vector=3B:386
p21	Set Vect(25)				
vec	Set_PM_Int_Vector	Entry		Int 0	PM Vector=117:9298
p21	Set Vect(25)				
vec	Set_PM_Int_Vector	Entry		Int 2	PM Vector=117:92BA
p21	Set Vect(25)				
vec	Set_PM_Int_Vector	Entry		Int 4	PM Vector=117:92C0
p21	Set Vect(25)				
vec	Set_PM_Int_Vector	Entry		Int 6	PM Vector=117:92C6
p21	Set Vect(25)				
vec	Set_PM_Int_Vector	Entry		Int 7	PM Vector=117:92CC
p21	Set Vect(25)				
vec	Set_PM_Int_Vector	Entry		Int 3E	PM Vector=117:92D2
p21	Set Vect(25)				
vec	Set_PM_Int_Vector	Entry		Int 75	PM Vector=117:92D8
p21	Set Vect(25)				
vec	Set_PM_Int_Vector	Entry		Int 31	PM Vector=117:8899
p21	Set Vect(25)				
vec	Set_PM_Int_Vector	Entry		Int 21	PM Vector=117:849A
p2f	Win/386 Multiplex(16)GetDevAPI(84)		VTDAPI (4...		
p2f	Win/386 Multiplex(16)TSRIdent(b)				
p2f	Win/386 Multiplex(16)GetDevAPI(84)		SHELL (1...		
p2f	Win/386 Multiplex(16)GetDevAPI(84)		(44Ah)		
dev	Open Device		IFSMGR		
dev	(IFS_IOCTL_21) - AX:5f8a		IFSMGR		
dev	(IFS_IOCTL_21) - AX:5f8a		IFSMGR		

Figure 3-6. MultiMon trace fragment after Kernel32 Init

The kernel also continues to toy with the protected mode IDT. In this stage we see handlers installed for interrupts 0, 2, 4, 6, 7, 9, D, 21, 24, 2f, 31, 3e, 71, and 75. The handlers that are getting installed are in ring-3; they are specific to the System VM. Recall that after System VM Init, **Set_PM_Int_Vector** applies to the current VM. So, the modification of the IDT we have seen here and in the previous stage only affects the System VM.

This trace shows us traces from the **dev** monitor for the first time. These lines come from the monitor for WIN32 **DeviceIoControl**. This isn't the Win32 **DeviceIo-Control** exactly; rather, it is the VWIN32 function that implements a large portion of it. We are seeing this function called through the Win32 callback on behalf of Win32 APIs: **DeviceIoControl**, **CreateFile**, and **CloseHandle**.

Up until now our trace has shown a lot of Int 2Fh calls to retrieve the protected mode interface for a variety of devices. These protected mode callbacks can only be used from Win16 programs that still allow Int 2Fh calls. Win32 programs are required to use a new mechanism for accessing VxDs.

This requirement is that the device be opened by **CreateFile**, exchanges data or commands using **DeviceIoControl**, and is closed with **CloseHandle**. All three of these functions go through the same VWIN32 function. If the *dwIoControlCode* is 0 we have an open on behalf of **CreateFile** (labeled as Open Device in the trace); if the *dwIoControlCode* is −1 we have a close on behalf of **CloseHandle**. Other *dwIoControlCode* values indicate specific **DeviceIoControl** commands that are private to the device, i.e., a value of 100 for IFSMgr does not mean the same as a value of 100 for VREDIR.

For IFSMgr, the *dwIoControlCode* of 100 is defined in *ifs.h* from the DDK as **IFS_IOCTL_21**. The comment with the equate states "These definitions are used by MSNET32 for making **DeviceIoControl** calls to IFSMgr." The last two lines in Figure 3-6 show two such calls with an AX value of 5f8ah, indicating a call to the DOS Int 21h function 5f8ah. There are three other *dwIoControlCodes* which IFSMgr recognizes: **IFS_IOCTL_2F**(101), **IFS_IOCTL_GET_RES**(102), and **IFS_IOCTL_GET_NETPRO_NAME_A**(103). In the next chapter we'll take a closer look at what these functions do.

Accessing IFSMgr

Figure 3-7 illustrates the IFSMgr entry paths from the four Windows 95 execution modes. IFSMgr is a virtual device driver that executes in ring-0; thus, three of the paths involve a ring transition from the application level, ring-3, to the kernel level, ring-0. To support DOS and Windows 3.x applications, we see continued support for the software interrupt interfaces, whereas for Win32 applications and ring-0, new interfaces have been introduced.

Accessing IFSMgr from DOS/V86 Mode

The bottom arrow in Figure 3-7 symbolizes pathways from Windows DOS boxes to IFSMgr.

Recall that in virtual-86 mode, interrupts are serviced by ring-0 handlers in VMM. Using MultiMon, we traced the installation of these handlers for all interrupts by hooking the VMM service **Hook_V86_Int_Chain**. Table 3-2 summarizes V86 interrupt handlers for interrupts 17h, 21h, 25h, 26h, and 2fh, the interrupts that IFSMgr

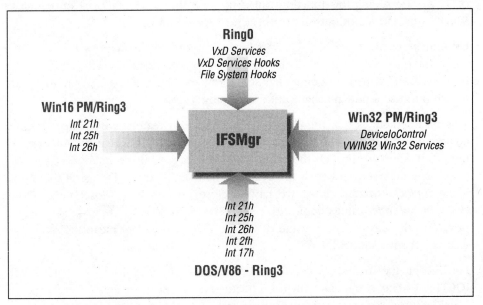

Figure 3-7. Pathways to IFSMgr

monitors. Each column shows the sequence of events for servicing that interrupt. For instance, interrupt 17h is initially handled by the service routine in the VM's V86 IDT. This will be a ring-0 interrupt handler in VMM that will check for installed V86 handlers. If handlers have been installed, then the last one installed is called first, then next most recent, etc., until one services the interrupt. If none of them service it, then the ring-3 V86 handler in DOS is used.

Table 3-2. Sequence of Events for V86 Interrupt Handlers

Int 17	Int 21	Int 25	Int 26	Int 2f
VM V86 IDT	VM V86 IDT	VM V86 IDT	VM V86 IDT	VM V86 IDT
Ring-0 Int Hdlr	Ring-0 Int Hdlr	Ring- Int Hdlr	Ring-0 Int Hdlr	Ring-0 Int Hdlr
IFSMGR(03) + 16DA	VMPOLL(05) + 68	IFSMGR(03) + 168C	IFSMGR(03) + 168C	IFSMGR(01) + EE4
VMPOLL(06) + 30	SHELL(0A) + 12C			DOSMGR(05) + F4
VPD(01) + 5C4	IFSMGR(01) + 11EA			VDD(01) + 37B
	DOSMGR(0A) + 0			VCDFSD(01) + 3A
				SHELL(01) + 47C

Table 3-2. Sequence of Events for V86 Interrupt Handlers (continued)

Int 17	Int 21	Int 25	Int 26	Int 2f
				VSHARE(01) + 29E
V86 hdlr 0c59:0a28	V86 hdlr 0c59:04a0	V86 Hdlr 00c9:0fbc	V86 hdlr 00c9:0fc6	V86 hdlr 10c0:03cc

A DOS box is a VM that contains an application running in V86 mode (unless it is using a DOS extender). This VM's V86 IDT is cloned from a template that had been created by the time the "System VM Init" message was broadcast. It doesn't have the customizations to the protected mode IDT like the System VM does, but if you are executing in V86 mode, a program wouldn't use those customizations anyway. What is important is that IFSMgr (as well as DOSMGR, etc.) are thoroughly hooked into the interrupt plumbing of a DOS box through the ring-0 V86 interrupt handlers. As we see in Table 3-2, DOS programs which invoke software interrupts 17h, 21h, 25h, 26h, and 2fh stand a good chance of executing some IFSMgr code. Whether that happens depends on which function request is being made and whether IFSMgr is interested in that function or whether a driver installed later handles it before it gets to IFSMgr.

IFSMgr does not export a V86 API.

Accessing IFSMgr from Win16/Protect Mode

The left arrow in Figure 3-7 symbolizes pathways from 16-bit Windows to IFSMgr. The same interrupts that we examined for DOS/V86 mode are shown in Table 3-3. Here, the interrupts are serviced in 16-bit protected mode, so the System VM's PM IDT determines the interrupt handler.

Table 3-3. Sequence of Events for PM Interrupt Handlers

Int 17	Int 21	Int 25	Int 26	Int 2f
VM PM IDT	VM PM IDT	VM PM IDT	VM PM IDT	VM PM IDT
	117:849a	3b:03be (IFSMGR)	3b:03c0 (IFSMGR)	30f:026c
	3b:03c4 (VMPOLL)	3b:0332 (DOSMGR)	3b:0334 (DOSMGR)	3b:03b8 (V86MMGR)
	3b:03bc (IFSMGR)			3b:0372 (VDD)
	3b:0330 (DOSMGR)			3b:0208 (VMM)
3b:002e	3b:0042	3b:004a	3b:004c	3b:005e

The handlers in the protected mode IDT may reside in 16-bit Windows DLLs or in ring-0 VxDs. In Table 3-3, the first handlers to get a shot at Int 21h and Int 2fh reside in DLLs. All of the other handlers in this table are the addresses of protected mode callbacks. Each of these callbacks corresponds to an Int 30h interrupt gate which maps the callback to a ring-0 handler. The VxDs which own these handlers are shown in parentheses in the table.

As we saw in our trace of MultiMon events, KRNL386 has further customized the System VM by installing ring-3 protected mode interrupt handlers. This gives KRNL386 an opportunity to look at some of the interrupt requests before they are passed down to ring-0 drivers. The kernel has a chance to "skim off" some Int 21h requests and handle them internally so they never reach the lower interrupt chain, or perhaps arrive there in a different form.

At the bottom of each column is the address of the default PM callback. If none of the PM handlers service the interrupt request, then when VMM sees a default PM callback it reflects the interrupt to V86 mode. This means the interrupt chain continues in the corresponding column of Table 3-2.

One exceptional case is Int 17h. It does not have a protected mode interrupt handler installed for it in the PM IDT. So whatever handler is found here was installed by VMM during system initialization. If you examine the PM IDT (using WDEB386 or WinIce) you will find a ring-0 interrupt gate in the Int 17h slot. Gates are like selectors in that they have descriptors which provide details about their address, type, and privilege level. When issuing a software interrupt from a protected mode application, the interrupt gate or trap gate must have a privilege level no higher than that of the application.

In the case of Int 17h, the interrupt gate has a privilge level of 0, but it is being called by an application with a privilege level of 3; the result is a General Protection fault (Int 0Dh). The fault handler in VMM looks at which instruction caused the fault; if it was an **Int** *n*, it reflects the interrupt to V86 mode as if VMM had encountered the default PM callback for that interrupt number.

IFSMgr does not export a PM API.

Accessing IFSMgr from Win32/Protect Mode

The previous two sections describe features that are carried over from Windows 3.x to support legacy DOS and Windows applications. In this and the next section, we'll be describing new interfaces that have been introduced with Windows 95. We first turn our attention to the right arrow in Figure 3-7, the arrow which represents the interfaces between Win32 applications and IFSMgr.

Although we have entered the brave new world of 32-bit Windows development, maintaining compatibility with 16-bit applications puts some serious constraints on the Windows 95 architecture. One such constraint is the "bitness" of VMs.

Recall that VMs begin life in virtual-86 mode. If DPMI services are subsequently used to switch the VM into protected mode, either a 16- or 32-bit mode is selected as one of the arguments. Thereafter, that VM is marked as either a 16-bit or 32-bit protected mode VM.

Since the System VM is created to load KRNL386 (a 16-bit protected mode application), the System VM is marked as a 16-bit protected mode VM. The offshoot of this is that if Win32 apps were to call into VMM through PM callbacks, VMM would still perceive them as having a 16-bit stack. This breaks routines like **Simulate_Iret** when it manipulates the stack using the contents of the **Client_Register** structure.

For these reasons, Microsoft is endorsing the **DeviceIoControl** interface as the way to go. Protected mode callbacks are out. Here is a quote from the introductory chapter of the DDK reference on VMM:

> ...Win32 programs will appear as 16-bit applications from VMM's point of view. In other words, Win32 programs will not be recognized by VMM as 32-bit applications. This should not be a problem because Win32 programs should be using the **DeviceIoControl** interface to communicate with VxDs. *This is merely a warning not even to try it any other way because it won't work.* [my italics]

Despite this dire warning, KERNEL32 continues to use a protected mode callback to access VxD services, specifically what are called Win32 services. Before Windows 95, VxDs only exported functions which could be used by other VxDs as a table of services. With Windows 95, VxDs can now export a table of services which can be accessed from ring-3 through a special protected mode callback. The table of Win32 services is constructed much like "regular" VxD services, by using several macros: **Begin_Win32_Services**, **End_Win32_Services**, and **Declare_Win32_Service**. Win32 services are dynamically registered with VMM using the VMM service **Register_Win32_Services**. Only a few VxDs export Win32 services at this time; the most notable are VMM and VWIN32 (IFSMgr does not).

To get the Win32 protected mode callback address, you need to use the Int 2Fh interface with the function **W386_Get_Win32_API**(168Dh), which is defined in *int2fapi.h* from the DDK. This function returns a PM callback in ES:DI. You can see the call to this function in the MultiMon trace shown in Figure 3-5. There is a catch-22 situation here. We need the callback address in a Win32 program but we can't retrieve it because software interrupts (Int 2Fh) are not allowed in a Win32 application! There are various work-arounds here; perhaps the easiest is to use an undocumented KERNEL32 function which has Ordinal 1. In the early Windows 95 beta, this function was exported as **VxDCall** and the name has stuck although the function is no longer exported by name in the retail release. KERNEL32 relies heavily on this interface to access Win32 services in VWIN32 and VMM. If you are curious about the details of how this Win32 callback works, see the section "The Win32 Callback."

Windows NT, in comparison, has a similar mechanism for user mode (ring-3) components to call into kernel mode (ring-0). Interrupt 2Eh, the system trap, is called with EAX holding a function number and EDX pointing to arguments on the stack. Since both user mode and kernel mode have the same "bitness," 16-bit and 32-bit stacks do not need to be distinguished.

The Win32 callback is an interface to IFSMgr but not a direct one, since IFSMgr does not provide Win32 services itself; rather, it is VWIN32 that provides the connection. Andrew Schulman, in *Unauthorized Windows 95*, describes the arguments required for **VxDCall**. Here is the passage in which he describes the Win32 service that provides Int 21h:

> VxDCall0 expects a VxD Win32 service number (such as 2A0010h), and any values for EAX and ECX on the stack. 2A0010h indicates VxD ID #002Ah, Win32 service #0010h. The PM callback in VMM decodes such Win32 service requests. VxD 2Ah is VWIN32, and the PM callback in VMM will call its Win32 service #10. VWIN32's Win32 service #10h issues INT 21h on behalf of Win32 applications by calling **Exec_PM_Int**, a VMM service new to Windows 95, with the parameter 21h.

This VWIN32 Win32 service is being called constantly but doesn't show up in our MultiMon trace because it was filtered out. Many Win32 file operations are converted into one or more calls to this service and many ultimately are handled by IFSMgr's protected mode Int 21h callback. There are other VWIN32 Win32 services which call IFSMgr services directly; we will examine these in the next chapter.

The real meat of the file system services is provided via the Win32 callback by way of VWIN32. Another Win32 interface to IFSMgr that we uncovered during our examination of the MultiMon trace is **DeviceIoControl**. IFSMgr exports this interface to MSNET32, the Network API Library for Microsoft Networks.

Accessing IFSMGR from Ring-0

Now we turn our attention to the topmost arrow in Figure 3-7, the arrow which represents the interfaces between ring-0 VxDs and IFSMgr. IFSMgr exports 117 services for use by other VxDs. Most of these are only needed by file system drivers, but others are more general purpose. For instance, using the **IFSMGR_Ring0_FileIO** services, VxDs may now perform DOS-like file operations.

IFSMgr provides services that allow other VxDs to install hooks into the file system. In some cases, a program needs to only monitor file activity. These services provide mechanisms for doing so.

IFSMgr also installs service hooks on a number of other VxDs at Init Complete time. These include:

VWIN32_ActiveTimeBiasSet (2a0015)
Schedule_Global_Event (1000e)
Resume_Exec(10085)
Suspend_VM(1002b)
Resume_VM(1002c)
No_Fail_Resume_VM(1002d)
Nuke_VM(1002e)
Close_VM(100ec)
Crash_Cur_VM(1002f)

So IFSMgr is even lurking around in VxD-land and doing a number on some standard VxD services.

The Win32 Callback

Many Win32 functions exported by KERNEL32 rely upon the Win32 callback for their implementation. Let's trace through the **GetLocalTime** function as an example. The first code section below is output captured from WinIce while tracing through this function. The trace skips over some of the initial parameter checks, etc., and picks up where the kernel is preparing to make an Int 21h function 2ah (Get Date) call. EDI points to a buffer where the return values (in AX, CX, and DX) will be stored. The function at BFF712B9 expects the DOS function number in AX and an optional parameter in ECX.

It pushes these registers and the Win32 service number for VWIN32's Int 21h provider and then calls yet another KERNEL32 service. This function, **ORD_0001** is exported as ordinal 1; it is also known as **VxDCall**. This function is a wrapper for the Win32 callback. It copies the first argument on the stack (the Win32 service number) to EAX and then pops the return address over the top stack argument, replacing the Win32 service number with another copy of the return address. It then performs an intersegment call using a far pointer (an FWORD in 32-bit land). It should come as no surprise that the address stored in CS:[BFFBC004] is none other than our Win32 callback address: 003b:000003da. The Int 30h interrupt gate then transfers us into ring-0.

```
0137:BFF767F8    MOV     EDI,[EBP+08]
0137:BFF767FB    MOV     AH,2A
0137:BFF767FD    CALL    BFF712B9
```

```
0137:BFF712B9    PUSH    ECX
0137:BFF712BA    PUSH    EAX
0137:BFF712BB    PUSH    002A0010
0137:BFF712C0    CALL    KERNEL32!ORD_0001

      KERNEL32!ORD_0001
      0137:BFF713D4    MOV     EAX,[ESP+4]
      0137:BFF713D8    POP     DWORD PTR [ESP]
      0137:BFF713DB    CALL    FWORD PTR CS:[BFFBC004]
            003B:000003DA    INT     30  ; #0028:C0236288   VMM(0D)+1288

0137:BFF712C5    RET     ---- this is where we return

0137:BFF76802    MOV     [EDI+02],DH
0137:BFF76805    MOV     [EDI+06],DL
0137:BFF76808    MOV     [EDI],CX
0137:BFF7680B    SUB     AH,AH
0137:BFF7680D    MOV     [EDI+04],AX
```

Before we look at the Win32 service handler, let's take a quick look at the Int 30h handler. This is the common entry point in VMM for all protected mode callbacks, not just for Win32 services. On entry into ring-0, the ring-3 register state is preserved in the client register structure. VMM checks whether the caller's ring-3 CS was selector 3bh on entry, i.e., VMM is expecting an Int 30h from the breakpoint segment to get us here. If that is true, then the caller's EIP is decremented by two to point to the beginning of the Int 30h instruction that caused the transfer. This value is then used to consult the breakpoint table to load the corresponding reference data to EDX before branching to the installed PM callback. Note that a number of other registers are also initialized before control is transferred: EBX is set to the current VM handle, EDI is set to the current thread handle, and ESP is set to the current thread's stack. Note also the check for an EIP value less than 200h; this signifies a default PM callback and requires a different handler which is responsible for reflection to V86 mode.

```
VMM(01)
+ 0b04    sub    esp,+04              ;no error code on stack
                                      ;for trap
+ 0b07    cld
+ 0b08    pushad                      ;complete the client
                                      ; register area
+ 0b09    mov    ebp,esp              ;set EBP to client
                                      ; register structure
+ 0b0b    mov    dword ptr [ebp+3c],ds  ;save segments to client
                                        ; registers
+ 0b0e    mov    dword ptr [ebp+38],es
+ 0b11    mov    dword ptr [ebp+40],fs
+ 0b14    mov    dword ptr [ebp+44],gs
+ 0b17    cmp    word ptr [esp+28],+3bh  ;client CS == 3bh?
+ 0b1d    jnz    short L_B5D
+ 0b1f    mov    ax,0030              ;set segment registers
+ 0b23    mov    ds,eax
```

```
    + 0b25        mov     ebx,dword ptr D1_F71C    ;current VM handle
    + 0b2b        mov     es,eax
    + 0b2d        mov     fs,eax
    + 0b2f        mov     gs,eax
    + 0b31        mov     eax,dword ptr [ebp+24]   ;client EIP
    + 0b34        sub     eax,+02                  ;backup to Int 30h
                                                   ; instruction
    + 0b37        mov     edi,dword ptr [ebx-20]   ;current thread handle
    + 0b3a        mov     dword ptr [ebp+24],eax   ;store adjusted EIP

        L_B3D:
    + 0b3d        xchg    dword ptr [edi+4c],esp
    + 0b40        sti
    + 0b41        push    offset C1_300            ;the handler will return
                                                   ; to C1_300
    + 0b46        cmp     ah,02                    ;callback offset < 200h?
    + 0b49        jc      L_1666                   ;branch to V86 reflection

    + 0b4f        mov     edx,dword ptr [eax*4+9390h]   ;retrieve refdata
    + 0b56        jmp     dword ptr [eax*4+938ch]       ;branch to ring-0
                                                        ; handler

        L_B5D:
    + 0b5d        mov     esi,0c0h
    + 0b62        jmp     L_2C0
    + 0b67        nop
```

We've finally arrived at the handler for Win32 services. A close study of this code reveals some interesting facts. The first thing it does is examine the caller's stack by testing SS from the client registers. SS is just a selector to which there corresponds a descriptor. The LAR assembly instruction returns a byte of attributes from the descriptor for a given selector. Only one bit is of interest here—the B-bit (big-bit). It tells us whether the stack segment is 32-bit (pushes and pops are 32 bits at a time) or whether it is 16-bit (pushes and pops are 16 bits at a time). If it is a 16-bit stack then VMM is careful to clear the upper 16 bits of ESI since it is an alias for SP and not ESP.

```
VMM(0D)
    + 1288        mov     ds,word ptr [ebp+34]     ;client SS
    + 128c        mov     esi,dword ptr [ebp+30]   ;client ESP
    + 128f        lar     eax,dword ptr [ebp+34]   ;load attribute byte of
                                                   ; SS descriptor
    + 1293        test    eax,400000h              ;test B-bit for 32-bit stack
                                                   ; (ESP)
    + 1298        jnz     short L_129D             ;branch if 32-bit
    + 129a        movzx   esi,si                   ;zero extend 16-bit stack
                                                   ; offset (SP)
```

Note that DS:ESI now points to the caller's stack, with the following contents:

```
BFF713E2 - return addr from CALL FWORD
00000137
BFF712C5 - return addr from CALL ORD_0001
```

```
00002A00 - Int 21h function number
00000000 - value of ECX pushed
BFF76802 - return address from BFF712B9
```

Continuing our trace, we see that VMM discards the Win32 callback and ORD_
0001 return addresses on the client stack by adding 12 to the stack pointer (ESI).
It sets the client CS:EIP to the return instruction in the procedure starting at
BFF712C5, as if returning from ORD_0001.

```
            L_129D:
  + 129d     mov     eax,dword ptr [esi+08]    ;get EIP to ORD_0001 return
  + 12a0     mov     edx,dword ptr [esi+04]    ;get CS  to ORD_0001 return
  + 12a3     mov     dword ptr [ebp+24],eax    ;store to client registers
  + 12a6     mov     word ptr [ebp+28],dx
  + 12aa     add     esi,+0c           ;remove return addresses from stack
```

Recall that EAX is loaded with the Win32 service number before entering the callback, so this argument is retrieved here and its device number is extracted. If the
device number is less than 40h, VMM consults a Win32 service table in an array
for faster lookup. If the device number is 40h or higher, the VxD list is searched
for a matching device ID. In either case, if the device ID is found and the device
has Win32 services registered for it, the service number is compared against the
total number of services offered. If this is within range, then a lookup in the
Win32 service table is made for the number of expected arguments (pushed on
the stack) and the address of the service routine.

```
  + 12ad     mov     eax,dword ptr [ebp+1c]    ;get client EAX
                                              ; (e.g. 002a0010)
  + 12b0     mov     edx,eax                   ;
  + 12b2     shr     edx,10                    ;extract device ID to EDX
  + 12b5     cmp     edx,+40                   ;device ID less than 40h?
  + 12b8     jnc     short L_12F4              ;branch if >= 40h
             ;
             ; Has this device registered Win32 services?
  + 12ba     mov     edx,dword ptr es:[edx*4+0c600h]
  + 12c2     or      edx,edx
  + 12c4     jz      short service_not_found


            lookup_Win32_service:
  + 12c6     movzx   eax,ax            ;extract Win32 service to EAX
  + 12c9     cmp     dword ptr es:[edx],eax    ;number of services >
                                              ; requested service# ?
  + 12cc     jbe     short service_not_found ;branch if service outside
                                              ; range

  + 12ce     inc     eax
  + 12cf     mov     ecx,dword ptr es:[edx+eax*8+04]    ;number of args
                                                       ; on stack
  + 12d4     mov     edx,dword ptr es:[edx+eax*8]       ;address of service
```

Now prepare the ring-0 stack before calling the service. A VWIN32 Int 21h service is passed two arguments on the stack, EAX and ECX, so 8 bytes are reserved on the ring-0 stack for these arguments.

Next, the current VM handle, then the address of the client register structure, and finally the address of the return procedure, are pushed onto the stack. The passed arguments are copied from the ring-3 stack to the reserved area on the ring-0 stack. This leaves ESI pointing at BFF76802 (the return address from BFF712B9) and it is stored as the new ESP in the client registers.

```
  + 12d8        pop    eax                      ;temporarily remove return
                                                ; proc addr
  + 12d9        shl    ecx,02                   ;allocate stack space for
                                                ; args*4 bytes
  + 12dc        sub    esp,ecx                  ;
  + 12de        mov    edi,esp                  ;
  + 12e0        push   ebx                      ;place current VM on stack
  + 12e1        push   ebp                      ;place client registers on
                                                ; stack
  + 12e2        push   eax                      ;put back return proc addr
  + 12e3        shr    ecx,02
  + 12e6        jz     short L_12EB
  + 12e8        cld
  + 12e9        repe   movsd                    ;copy ring3 stack args to
                                                ; ring0 stack


              L_12EB:
  + 12eb        mov    eax,ss                   ;restore DS
  + 12ed        mov    ds,eax
  + 12ef        mov    dword ptr [ebp+30],esi   ;save new stack ptr to
                                                ; client ESP
```

When control is transferred to the Win32 service, the ring-0 stack looks like this:

```
C0001300 - return address
EBP      - address of client register structure
EBX      - current VM handle
00002A00 - Int 21h function number
00000000 - value of ECX pushed

  + 12f2        jmp    edx                      ;branch to Win32 service


              L_12F4:  ; device ID is >= 40h
  + 12f4        mov    ecx,offset D1_C360       ;get base Device Descriptor
                                                ; Block

              next_DDB:
  + 12f9        mov    ecx,dword ptr es:[ecx]   ;last device?
  + 12fc        jecxz  short service_not_found  ;then exit loop
  + 12fe        cmp    word ptr es:[ecx+06],dx  ;matching device ID?
  + 1303        jnz    short next_DDB           ;no, then loop back
```

```
+ 1305      test   word ptr es:[ecx+0a],4000   ;device has Win32
                                               ; services?
+ 130c      jz     short service_not_found     ;no, then exit
+ 130e      mov    edx,dword ptr es:[ecx+38]   ;get Win32 service table
+ 1312      jmp    short lookup_Win32_service  ;

            service_not_found:
+ 1314      mov    dword ptr [ebp+1c],1h       ;set carry in client
                                               ; flags
+ 131b      mov    eax,ss                      ;restore DS
+ 131d      mov    ds,eax
+ 131f      mov    dword ptr [ebp+30],esi      ;store client ESP
+ 1322      retn                               ;return
```

This concludes our examination of the file system plumbing. In the next chapter we turn our attention to the file system APIs, especially the Win32 API.

4

File System API Mapping

In Chapter 3, *Pathways to the File System*, we saw how file system requests are channeled in diverse operating environments. The MS-DOS Int 21h interface forms the core API for the operating system modes: DOS/V86, Win16, and Win32. To a considerable extent, the Win32 file APIs are mapped to the extended MS-DOS API, although some additional assistance is needed from VWIN32 and VMM.

In this chapter, we will survey the Win32 and Win16 APIs and see how they map to the extended MS-DOS API. We'll also encounter the concept of KERNEL32 objects, a concept which will provide a framework for our examination of the Win32 APIs. Microsoft has us all believing that Win32 is the API of the future, so let's begin with a look at how the Win32 APIs are implemented, primarily those related to file I/O.

The Win32 API and KERNEL32 Objects

To begin our excursion, I've chosen **GetFileInformationByHandle** because it is short and yet illustrates several key aspects of KERNEL32's implementation.

A Sample Win32 API: GetFileInformationByHandle

The prototype for **GetFileInformationByHandle** and its C pseudocode are shown in Example 4-1. This function is designed to take a file handle as its input argument and fill-in and return a `BY_HANDLE_FILE_INFORMATION` structure as output. This structure contains fields for file create, modify, and access times as well as other information. The real meat of this function is in the assembly language lines preceding **Int21Dispatch**. Here we see registers getting loaded with BX set to the file handle, EDX pointing to the `BY_HANDLE_FILE_INFORMATION` structure, and AX set to the requested function 71A6h.

Int21Dispatch is a thin wrapper around a callback to VWIN32 Win32 service Int21. Here is the actual code:

```
Int21Dispatch proc near
    push    ecx
    push    eax
    push    2a0010h
    call    VxDCall
    retn
```

Function 71A6H is one of many new Int 21h services that have been added to Windows 95 to support long filenames and other extensions for MS-DOS and Win16 applications.*

There are still other calls to Int 21h hiding here. For instance, **x_GetExtendedError** is another thin wrapper around a Win32 callback. In this case the code is:

```
x_GetExtendedError    Proc Near
    push    ebx
    mov     eax,5900h
    call    Int21Dispatch
    movzx   eax,ax
    pop     ebx
    retn
```

The functions **x_MaybeChangePSP** and **x_RestorePSP** utilize interrupt 21h function 50h to set the current PSP.† These examples of Int 21h calls are typical of much of KERNEL32. You can see this for yourself by running MultiMon with the WIN32CB driver installed and the monitor for VWIN32 Int 21h enabled.

Example 4-1. Pseudo Source Code for GetFileInformationByHandle

```
BOOL GetFileInformationByHandle( HANDLE hFile,
       LPBY_HANDLE_FILE_INFORMATION lpFileInfo ) {
    DWORD wPSP;
    PK32FILEOBJ pK32FileObj;
    int retc;

    EnterMustComplete();
    x_MaybeChangePSP( hFile, &wPSP );
    pK32FileObj = retc = x_ConvertHandleToK32Object( hFile,
                          K32OBJ_INCREF|K32OBJ_FILE_TYPE, 0 );
    if ( pK32FileObj ) {
        _asm movzx ebx,word ptr pK32FileObj->hExtendedFileHandle
        _asm mov    edx,dword ptr lpFileInfo
        _asm mov    eax,71a6h
```

---

* You will find documentation for these functions in the *Programmer's Guide to Microsoft Windows 95, Part 5: Using Microsoft MS-DOS Extensions.* See *http://www.microsoft.com/msdn/sdk/platforms/doc/sdk/ win32/95guide/src/95func_28.htm.*

† A PSP (Program Segment Prefix) refers to the DOS data structure that describes a program's execution environment.

Example 4-1. Pseudo Source Code for GetFileInformationByHandle (continued)

```
                _asm stc
                retc = Int21Dispatch();
                if ( carry set ) {
                        if ( retc == 0x7100 ) retc = ERROR_NOT_SUPPORTED;
                        else  retc = x_GetExtendedError();
                        InternalSetLastError( retc );
                        retc = 0;
                        }
                else  retc = 1;
                }
        else if (x_ConvertHandleToK32Object(hFile,K32OBJ_ALL_TYPE,0)) {
                InternalSetLastError( ERROR_NOT_SUPPORTED );
                retc = 0;
                }
        x_RestorePSP( wPSP );
        LeaveMustComplete();
        return retc;
        }
```

There is a lot more going on in this function besides Win32 callbacks. Let's take a closer look. First, you'll notice some unfamiliar functions names: **EnterMustComplete**, **x_MaybeChangePSP**, **x_ConvertHandleToK32Object**, etc. These are names I've coined for some internal KERNEL32 functions.

The entire function is sandwiched with the **EnterMustComplete** and **LeaveMustComplete** calls. These place the body of the function in a must-complete section. This is a type of synchronization primitive that is supported by VMM. To quote the DDK Reference, a "must-complete section" is "block of code that must be executed in its entirety before any other thread or virtual machine can run."

Next, we see an inner sandwich of the functions **x_MaybeChangePSP** and **x_RestorePSP**. The first function looks at the Win32 handle and, depending on its value, may switch the thread to another PSP, storing the original PSP in the variable *wPSP*. On leaving **GetFileInformationByHandle**, **x_RestorePSP** restores the original PSP if it was changed.

Why would a thread want to change its PSP? In this case, it wants the PSP to match the owner of the handle. As we'll see later, the handle table is a per-process data structure and handles are indexes into this table. For instance, a handle of 5 in one process may reference a file, whereas in another process it may reference a pipe. However, KERNEL32 also recognizes global handles; these are handles which are associated with the KERNEL32 process and one of its PSPs. These global handles have a unique signature formed by the index value exclusive-ORed with 0x544a4d3f. To test if a handle is global, first AND it with 0xffff0000 and then compare with 0x544a0000.

So, **x_MaybeChangePSP** looks at the Win32 handle and checks whether it is a global handle. If it is, it switches the thread's PSP to a PSP which is associated with the KERNEL32 process. It does this using **Int21Dispatch**, function 50h (Set PSP), and BX set to the new PSP value. The current PSP is saved in *wPSP* so it can later be restored by a call to **x_RestorePSP**.

The last function that is also preparatory before making the **Int21Dispatch** is **x_ConvertHandleToK32Object**. Basically, this function converts any type of Win32 handle into a pointer to a KERNEL32 data structure that describes that object. In this case, we are asking it to take what we believe to be a file handle (*hFile*) and convert it into a KERNEL32 file data structure. Now, if the caller passes us, say, a console handle instead, the return value stored in *pK32FileObj* will be NULL causing the `else if (x_ConvertHandleToK32Object…)` clause to be executed. This time the call will look for any handle type (*K32OBJ_ALL_TYPE*). If this last call succeeds, the function fails and an ERROR_NOT_SUPPORTED will be returned by **GetLastError**.

If a valid file handle is supplied by the caller, then *pK32FileObj* will contain a pointer to a file object structure. The only piece of information we need from it is yet another file handle, one that IFSMgr will understand, an "extended file handle" in the field named *hExtendedFileHandle*. This is the handle that is ultimately passed to **Int21Dispatch** to acquire the `BY_HANDLE_FILE_INFORMATION` data structure.

Delving Into KERNEL32 Objects

Just as NT executive objects provide a unifying theme for Windows NT, KERNEL32 objects do the same for Windows 95. Quoting from Helen Custer (*Inside Windows NT*, Microsoft Press):

> In the NT executive, an object is a single, runtime instance of a statically defined object type. An object type comprises a system-defined data type, services that operate on instances of the data type, and a set of object attributes.

For example, a file is an instance of a file object type and an event is an instance of an event object type. As with Windows NT, instances of object types are created by services and are represented by object handles. Again using the same examples, a file is created by the service **CreateFile**, which returns a file handle; and an event is created by the service **CreateEvent**, which returns an event handle. Quoting again from Helen Custer, "An NT object handle is an index into a process-specific object table."

For each indexed entry in the object table there is a pointer to the object instance and a flags field specifying access rights and inheritance designations. Although there are a lot of similarities between NT executive objects and Windows 95

KERNEL32 objects, the KERNEL32 object is admittedly a very watered-down version of its NT counterpart; for instance, there is no support for security. Furthermore, in Windows NT, objects are created by a separate kernel mode component called the object manager.

Matt Pietrek has discussed KERNEL32 objects in Chapter 3 of *Windows 95 System Programming Secrets* (IDG Books). He has enumerated the 17 KERNEL32 object types and these are shown in Table 4-1. I have added the service names for creating and destroying each object type.

Table 4-1. The KERNEL32 Objects

Object	ID	Constructor	Destructor
K32OBJ_SEMAPHORE	1	CreateSemaphore	CloseHandle
K32OBJ_EVENT	2	CreateEvent	CloseHandle
K32OBJ_MUTEX	3	CreateMutex	CloseHandle
K32OBJ_CRITICAL_SECTION	4	InitializeCriticalSection	DeleteCriticalSection
K32OBJ_PROCESS	5	CreateProcess	CloseHandle
K32OBJ_THREAD	6	CreateThread	CloseHandle
K32OBJ_FILE	7	CreateFile	CloseHandle
K32OBJ_CHANGE	8	FindFirstChangeNotification	FindCloseChangeNotification
K32OBJ_CONSOLE	9	AllocConsole	FreeConsole
K32OBJ_SCREEN_BUFFER	10	AllocConsole	FreeConsole
K32OBJ_MEM_MAPPED_FILE	11	CreateFileMapping	CloseHandle
K32OBJ_SERIAL	12	CreateFile	CloseHandle
K32OBJ_DEVICE_IOCTL	13	CreateFile	CloseHandle
K32OBJ_PIPE	14	CreatePipe, CreateFile	CloseHandle
K32OBJ_MAILSLOT	15	CreateMailslot	CloseHandle
K32OBJ_TOOLHELP_SNAPSHOT	16	CreateToolhelp32Snapshot	CloseHandle
K32OBJ_SOCKET	17	socket	closesocket

For each of these object types, a block of data is allocated from the KERNEL32 heap to represent an object's instance. The KERNEL32 process object is also known as the process database, or PDB. Similarly, the KERNEL32 thread object is also known as the thread database, or TDB. Both of these data structures are described in detail in *Windows 95 System Programming Secrets*. Although each KERNEL32 object is represented by a different data structure, all KERNEL32 objects have the same header:

```
typedef struct { DWORD dwType;  DWORD dwRefCnt; } K32ObjectHeader;
```

The *dwType* field takes a value between 1 and 17 corresponding to its object type. The *dwRefCnt* field is used to maintain a usage count for the object. When a handle is closed and the *dwRefCnt* of its corresponding object has reached zero, the object is destroyed.

The KERNEL32 process object contains a member (at offset 0x44) which points to the table of object handles. The Win32 handles which are returned by **CreateFile**, **CreateMutex**, etc. are simply indices into this table. The function that we met in the last section, **x_ConvertHandleToK32Object**, is designed to retrieve an object from the object handle table given its Win32 handle. Thus given a handle of one of these 17 object types, we can get the address of its corresponding data structure, which was allocated from the KERNEL32 heap. Actually, there are two fields for each entry in the object handle table:

```
typedef struct { DWORD dwFlags;  PVOID pK32Object; } TableEntry;
```

The first DWORD in the object handle table contains the maximum number of entries in the table, so the handle table can be represented by this structure:

```
typedef struct {  DWORD dwMaxCnt; TableEntry entry[1]; }
ObjHandleTable;
```

Converting Win32 Handles to KERNEL32 Objects

Let's put together what we have just learned and see how **x_Convert-HandleToK32Object** works. First, from the listing that follows, we see that this function immediately calls another function, which I've named **x_RefHandleTo-K32Object**. One argument is added to this call, a pointer to the current process database (**ppCurrentProcess*).

```
K32ObjectHeader* x_ConvertHandleToK32Object( HANDLE hObject,
                                    DWORD fObjTypes, DWORD fAccess ) {
    return x_RefHandleToK32Object( *ppCurrentProcess,
                                    hObject, fObjTypes, fAccess );
}
```

Dropping down another level, we see in the listing below that **x_RefHandle-ToK32Object** sandwiches its body by acquiring a KERNEL32 mutex and releasing it on exit. We also see the reference count for the KERNEL32 object incremented on return from **x_Win32HandleToK32Object** if the *K32OBJ_INCREF* flag is set in *fObjTypes*.

```
K32ObjectHeader* x_RefHandleToK32Object(PPDB pProcess, HANDLE hObject,
                                    DWORD fObjTypes, DWORD fAccess ) {
    K32ObjectHeader* pK32Obj;
    DWORD fObjTypeFlags;

    _EnterSysLevel( pKrn32Mutex );
    fObjTypeFlags = fObjTypes;
```

```
        pK32Obj = x_Win32HandleToK32Object( pProcess, hObject,
                                            fObjTypes, fAccess );
        if ( pK32Obj && fObjTypeFlags & K32OBJ_INCREF )
            pK32Obj->dwRefCnt++;
        _LeaveSysLevel( pKrn32Mutex );
        return pK32Obj;
        }
```

Drilling down one more level brings us to **x_Win32HandleToK32Object**, shown in Example 4-2. This is where the interesting stuff happens. As we walk through it, keep in mind that this function is designed to take an object handle (*hObject*) from a given process (*pProcess*) and return its KERNEL32 object. The flags in *fObjTypes* and *fAccess* apply additional matching criteria.

Example 4-2. Source for the KERNEL32 Function x_Win32HandleToK32Object

```
K32ObjectHeader* x_Win32HandleToK32Object( PPDB pProcess,
            HANDLE hObject, DWORD fObjTypes, DWORD fAccess ) {

    DWORD handle = hObject;
    PPDB pPDB;
    K32ObjectHeader* pK32Obj;
    ObjHandleTable* pHdlTbl;

    if ( hObject & 0xffff0000 == 0x544a0000 ) { /* global handle? */
        pPDB = pK32Process;
        handle = hObject ^ 0x544a4d3f;
        }
    else pPDB = pProcess;

    switch( handle ) {
        case 0x7fffffff:        handle = pPDB->pEDB.hProcess;   break;
        case STD_ERROR_HANDLE:  handle = pPDB->pEDB.hStdErr;    break;
        case STD_OUTPUT_HANDLE: handle = pPDB->pEDB.hStdOut;    break;
        case STD_INPUT_HANDLE:  handle = pPDB->pEDB.hStdIn;     break;
        case 0xfffffffe:
            pK32Obj = *ppCurrentThread;
            if (1 << (pK32Obj->dwType-1)) & fObjTypes) return pK32Obj;
            else { InternalSetLastError( ERROR_INVALID_HANDLE );
                return NULL; }
            break;
        }

    pHdlTbl = pPDB->pHandleTable;
    if ( pHdlTbl->dwMaxCnt > handle ) {
        TableEntry* pEntry;
        pEntry = &pHdlTbl->entry[handle];
        pK32Obj = pEntry->pK32Object;
        if ( pK32Obj && pK32Obj != -1 ) {
            if ( fAccess ) {
                if (((pEntry->dwFlags & fAccess) & 0x130) != fAccess) {
                    InternalSetLastError( ERROR_ACCESS_DENIED );
                    return NULL;
                    }
```

Example 4-2. Source for the KERNEL32 Function x_Win32HandleToK32Object (continued)

```
                }

        if (1 << (pK32Obj->dwType-1)) & fObjTypes) return pK32Obj;
                }
        }
    InternalSetLastError( ERROR_INVALID_HANDLE );
    return NULL;
    }
```

This function can be split into roughly two halves. The first half massages the input handle to get it into a form that can be used to directly access the process's object handle table. The second half retrieves the entry in the object handle table and returns its *pK32Object* member.

First we see that the high-order word of the handle is tested for the signature 0x544a. Normally when an application creates KERNEL32 objects, the handles which are returned are nice small integer numbers, so we are talking handle values in the range 1 to say 1000. However, if you place a breakpoint at this location in the function, you will see handles are frequently passed which indeed have this 0x544a signature. The next two lines in the code help clarify what these handles signify. First, we switch to a different process (*pK32Process*), namely KERNEL32, and then the handle is exclusive-ORed with the value 0x544a4d3f. After this operation the handle value becomes a "nice small integer."

So what have we done? We have just created an index into KERNEL32's handle table and ultimately, when we return, we'll be returning a KERNEL32 object that actually belongs to the KERNEL32 process.

To summarize, the *hObject*s which are passed to **x_Win32HandleToK32Object** come in two flavors: global handles which have been exclusive-ORed with 0x544a4d3f, and private handles which are "small integer numbers." I've called these KERNEL32 handles "global" because an exported function is used to produce them, namely, **ConvertToGlobalHandle**.

In my statements above, I've simplified things a bit by separating handles into just two groups. There is actually a third group that might be called "standard handles;" these are handles every process has. For instance, the return value from **GetCurrentProcess** is always 0x7fffffff no matter which process you are calling from. Similarly, the return value from **GetCurrentThread** is always 0xfffffffe no matter which thread you call from. These magic values as well as the standard console handles are just constants that KERNEL32 translates into "real" object handles. In the switch statement, the first four magic values are translated into handles by looking up the values in the environment database (*pEDB*) of the process. The fifth value in the switch statement represents the handle of the current thread. Here, it is easier to just look up the KERNEL32 object for the current thread since it is stored in a global variable, rather than determine its index in the object handle table.

Before the KERNEL32 thread object is returned, we see that some test is performed. This test is in the form of the following expression:

```
(1 << (pK32Obj->dwType-1)) & fObjTypes
```

The first half of this expression simply takes a KERNEL32 object type number, decrements it by 1, and then left-shifts a single bit that number of times. In other words, it is converting the object type number to a bit position. For example, 0x00001 represents K32OBJ_SEMAPHORE, 0x00002 represents K32OBJ_EVENT, 0x00040 represents K32OBJ_FILE, and 0x10000 represents K32OBJ_SOCKET. *fObjTypes* is also a bit map of the types of KERNEL32 objects that the caller will accept a conversion into. We know that a thread object has a *dwType* of 6 so its bit map will be 0x00020. If the caller did not set this bit in *fObjTypes*, the function will fail and return NULL; otherwise it will return *pK32Obj* for the thread object.

Now, we are faced with the last half of the function. We have our Win32 handle massaged so it can index the object handle table, so we first find the object handle table *pHdlTbl* in the process database. Then the Win32 handle is compared with the range of the object handle table by verifying that it is less than the maximum handle value in the first DWORD of the table. If this test succeeds, the handle is used as an index into the array of table entries. The KERNEL32 object pointer in the entry is then tested to see that it is non-zero and not −1. If this holds true then the *fAccess* argument is tested for a non-zero value. If the caller has specified *fAccess* bits, then these are also tested. Finally, the requested object types *fObjTypes* are compared against the returned object type. If these match, then a pointer to the KERNEL32 object is returned.

Now that your curiosity about KERNEL32 objects has been whetted, let's fill in some more details about the following types: K32OBJ_FILE, K32OBJ_PIPE, K32OBJ_MAILSLOT, K32OBJ_CHANGE, K32OBJ_MEM_MAPPED_FILE, and K32OBJ_DEVICE_IOCTL.

The File Object

A file object represents a local or remote file that has been created or opened using the MS-DOS extension function 716ch. Note that this function takes 8.3 or long filenames as well as UNC filenames. A KERNEL32 file object is represented by a 28-byte data structure. The members of this structure are as follows:

00h DWORD dwType
    The constant value (0x7) that represents a KERNEL32 file object.

04h DWORD dwRefCnt
    The reference count for this object.

08h DWORD pK32ProcessObject

Pointer to the process database for the owning process.

0Ch DWORD pK32EventObject

Pointer to an event object which is created with each file object.

10h WORD hExtendedFileHandle

The file handle which is used by IFSMgr to reference this file. The undocumented Win32 API, **Win32HandleToDosFileHandle**, returns this value for a given Win32 file object handle.

12h WORD reserved

14h DWORD dwModeAndFlags

This member is 0 except for some special cases. If the file is opened with the *FILE_FLAG_DELETE_ON_CLOSE* flag, then this member is 0xffffffff. If the file handle is less than 0x200 (a DOS handle) then store the mode and flags word used to open or create the file.

18h DWORD pszFullPath

This member is 0 except for some special cases. If *dwModeAndFlags* is nonzero, the a heap allocation is made in which the full path of the file is stored; in that case, this member holds the pointer to that allocation.

There are numerous file object services supplied by the Win32 API. Some of these services are general purpose and work with many different types of KERNEL32 objects. **CreateFile** and **CloseHandle** are good examples of such general purpose services. Internally they have separate implementations for each object type. Table 4-2 enumerates the file object services and key **Int21Dispatch** calls used in their implementation. All of the Int 21h functions listed are documented.

Table 4-2. File Object Services

Win32 API	Key Int21Dispatch Calls	Other Win32 Callbacks
CloseHandle, _lclose	3eh	
CopyFile	7143h, 716ch, 42h, 3fh, 40h, 71a7h, 57xxh, 3eh	
CreateDirectory	7139h	
CreateDirectoryEx	7143h, 7139h	
CreateFile, _lcreat, _lopen	716ch	
DeleteFile	7141h	
DosDateTimeToFileTime	71a7h	
DuplicateHandle		_VWIN32DupHandle
FileTimeToDosDateTime	71a7h	
FindClose	71a1h	
FindFirstFile	714eh	

Table 4-2. File Object Services (continued)

Win32 API	Key Int21Dispatch Calls	Other Win32 Callbacks
FindNextFile	714fh	
FlushFileBuffers	6800h	
GetCurrentDirectory	19h, 7147h	
GetDiskFreeSpace	3600h	
GetDiskFreeSpaceEx (OSR2)	7303h (OSR2)	
GetDriveType	4408h, 4409h, 714eh, 71a1h	
GetFileAttributes	7143h	
GetFileInformationByHandle	71A6h	
GetFileSize	4200h, 4201h, 4202h	
GetFileTime	5700h, 5704h, 5706h	
GetFileType	4400h	
GetFullPathName	19h, 7147h	
GetLogicalDrives	4409h	
GetLogicalDriveStrings	4409h	
GetShortPathName	7160h, 4300h	
GetTempFileName	7143h, 2ch, 716ch, 3eh	
GetVolumeInformation	4409h, 440d/66h, 71a0h, 714eh, 71a1h	
LockFile	5c00h	
MoveFile	7156h (rename), 7143h, 716ch, 42h, 3fh, 40h, 71a7h, 57xxh, 3eh, 7141h (copy/delete)	
OpenFile	716ch, 4400h, 4401h	
ReadFile, _hread, _lread	3fh	
RemoveDirectory	713ah	
SearchPath		
SetCurrentDirectory	7143h, 713bh	
SetEndOfFile	42h, 40h	
SetFileAttributes	7143h	
SetFilePointer, _llseek	4200h, 4201h, 4202h	
SetFileTime	5707h, 5705h, 5701h	
SetVolumeLabel	Thunks[1] to KRNL386: 4409h, 2f00h, 1a00h, 4e00h, 1300h, 3ch, 3eh	
UnlockFile	5c01h	
WriteFile, _hwrite, _lwrite	40h	

[1] A *thunk* is a small section of code, similiar to a Remote Procedure Call (RPC) that handles the transitions between 16-bit and 32-bit code.

The File-Change Object

A file-change object is created by a call to **FindFirstChangeNotification**. It returns a Win32 handle which can be used as an argument to **WaitForSingleObject**, **Wait-ForMultipleObjects**, **WaitForSingleObjectEx**, or **WaitForMultipleObjectsEx** to wait for certain file-change notifications within a specified directory. A KERNEL32 file-change object is represented by a 20-byte data structure. The members of this structure are as follows:

00h DWORD dwType
> The constant value (0x8) that represents a KERNEL32 file-change object.

04h DWORD dwRefCnt
> The reference count for this object.

08h DWORD pK32ProcessObject
> Pointer to the process database for the owning process.

0Ch DWORD pK32EventObject
> Pointer to an event object which is created with each file-change object.

10h DWORD hFcnHandle
> IFSMgr's handle to the file-change context.

Table 4-3 enumerates the file-change object services and key **Int21Dispatch** calls used in their implementation. All of the Int 21h functions listed are *undocumented*.

Table 4-3. File-Change Object Services

Win32 API	Key Int21Dispatch Calls
FindFirstChangeNotification	71a3h
FindNextChangeNotification	71a4h
FindCloseChangeNotification	71a5h
WaitForSingleObject	
WaitForSingleObjectEx	
WaitForMultipleObjects	
WaitForMultipleObjectsEx	

The Pipe Object

A pipe object can represent an "anonymous pipe," which is created with the service **CreatePipe**, or the client-side of a "named-pipe," created with the service **CreateFile**. A KERNEL32 pipe object is represented by a 48-byte data structure. The members of this structure are as follows:

00h DWORD dwType
> The constant value (0xe) that represents a KERNEL32 pipe object.

04h DWORD dwRefCnt
The reference count for this object.

08h DWORD reserved

0Ch LPVOID pPipeBuffer
Item allocated from the KERNEL32 heap.

10h DWORD hExtendedFileHandle
This is the file handle which is used by IFSMgr to reference the pipe.

14h DWORD Counter1
Counter which controls when **SetEvent** is called on *pK32EventObject1*.

18h DWORD Counter2
Counter which controls when **SetEvent** is called on *pK32EventObject2*.

1Ch DWORD dwPipeBufferSize
Number of bytes allocated for pipe buffer.

20h DWORD unknown1
24h DWORD unknown2
The usage for these two doublewords is unknown

28h DWORD pK32EventObject1
2Ch DWORD pK32EventObject2
These are pointers to KERNEL32 Event Objects.

Table 4-4 enumerates the pipe object services and key **Int21Dispatch** calls used in their implementation. The Int 21h functions in the 5fxxh series are *undocumented.* (See Chapter 13 for more information.)

Table 4-4. Pipe Object Services

Win32 API	Key Int21Dispatch Calls
CallNamedPipe	5f37h
CreateFile	716ch
CreatePipe	
DuplicateHandle	
GetNamedPipeInfo	5f32h, 5f33h
PeekNamedPipe	5f35h
ReadFile	
ReadFileEx	
SetNamedPipeHandleState	5f34h, 5f3bh
TransactNamedPipe	5f36h
WriteFile	
WriteFileEx	

The Mailslot Object

Mailslots have server-side and client-side functions. On the server-side, a mailslot object is created by the service **CreateMailslot** and it is read from by **ReadFile** and **ReadFileEx**, and eventually closed by **CloseHandle**. The client-side uses **CreateFile** to create a mailslot object for writing only using **WriteFile** and **WriteFileEx**. A KERNEL32 mailslot object is represented by a 20-byte data structure. The members of this structure are as follows:

00h DWORD dwType

    The constant value (0xf) that represents a KERNEL32 mailslot object.

04h DWORD dwRefCnt

    The reference count for this object.

08H DWORD reserved

0CH DWORD pszMailslotName

    String tem allocated from the heap.

10H DWORD hExtendedFileHandle

    The file handle used by IFSMgr to reference the mailslot (a DOS handle is used).

Table 4-5 enumerates the mailslot object services and key **Int21Dispatch** calls used in their implementation. The Int 21h functions in the 5fxxh series are *undocumented*. (See Chapter 13 for more information).

Table 4-5. Mailslot Object Services

Win32 API	Key Int21Dispatch Calls	Other Win32 Callbacks
CreateFile		
CreateMailslot	5f4dh	
DuplicateHandle		_VWIN32DupHandle
GetMailslotInfo	5f4fh	
ReadFile	3f00h	
ReadFileEx		
SetMailslotInfo	5f3bh	
WriteFile	5f52h	
WriteFileEx		

The Memory-Mapped File Object

A memory-mapped file object is created by the service **CreateFileMapping**. A KERNEL32 memory-mapped file object is represented by a 48-byte data structure. The members of this structure are as follows:

00h DWORD dwType

The constant value (0xb) that represents a KERNEL32 memory-mapped file object.

04h DWORD dwRefCnt

The reference count for this object.

08h DWORD reserved

0Ch DWORD pMapName

An item allocated from the KERNEL32 heap to hold a copy of the map name if a map name is specified as a *CreateFileMapping* argument.

10h DWORD dwMapSize

Size of the mapping in bytes.

14h DWORD dwLinearBase

This is the linear address of the base of the mapping as returned by **PageReserve**.

18h DWORD dwPagerData

This value, shifted left by 12, is used as the starting value for the pager data argument to **PageCommit**.

1Ch DWORD dwModeAndFlags

If the KERNEL32 file object which is being mapped meets the following criteria:

— *hExtendedFileHandle* < 0x200,

— *pszFullPath* is non-zero,

— *dwModeAndFlags* is not 0xffffffff,

— and the **CreateFileMapping** was called with *PAGE_READONLY* protection,

then the *dwModeAndFlags* from the file object is copied here; otherwise it is assigned 0xffffffff.

20h DWORD pszFullPath

If the KERNEL32 file object which is being mapped meets the following criteria:

— *hExtendedFileHandle* < 0x200,

— *pszFullPath* is non-zero,

— *dwModeAndFlags* is not 0xffffffff,

— and the **CreateFileMapping** was called with *PAGE_READONLY* protection,

then a heap allocation is made and the file object's *pszFullPath* is copied to it, and the pointer is stored here; otherwise it is assigned 0.

24h DWORD pRing0Handle

> This is the ring0 file handle for the duplicated handle; this is a pointer to a `fhandle` structure.

28h DWORD dwFileSize

> This is the size in bytes of the mapped file.

2Ch BYTE bProtection

> One of the protection flags passed to **CreateFileMapping**: *PAGE_READONLY*, *PAGE_READWRITE*, or *PAGE_WRITECOPY*.

2Dh BYTE hPager

> This is the pager handle which is used by the **PageCommit** call. (See Chapter 10).

2Eh WORD wPSPSelector

> If the mapped file belongs to a Netware-managed drive, the PSP of the process is stored here; otherwise it is 0.

Table 4-6 enumerates the memory-mapped file object APIs and key Win32 services used in their implementation. (See Chapter 10, *Virtual Memory, the Paging File, and Pagers*, for more information.)

Table 4-6. Memory-Mapped File Object Services

Win32 API	Other Win32 Callbacks
CloseHandle	_VMMPageFree, _VWIN32Ring0CloseHandle
CreateFileMapping	_VWIN32DupHandle
FlushViewOfFile	
MapViewOfFile	_VMMPageReserve, _VMMPageCommit
MapViewOfFileEx	_VMMPageReserve, _VMMPageCommit
OpenFileMapping	
UnmapViewOfFile	

The Device Object

A KERNEL32 device object represents a statically or dynamically loaded virtual device which supports the device IOCTL interface. The **CreateFile** service can be used to obtain a handle to a device which meets these requirements. Note that this excludes virtual devices which do not support an IOCTL interface, such as Windows 3.x virtual drivers. A KERNEL32 device object is represented by a 28-byte data structure. The members of this structure are as follows:

00h DWORD dwType

> The constant value (0xd) that represents a KERNEL32 device object.

04h DWORD dwRefCnt

The reference count for this object.

08h DWORD reserved

This member always appears to be 0.

0Ch DWORD pDDB

Pointer to the ring-0 device descriptor block for the virtual device.

10h DWORD pszLoadPath

If the device object is created with the FILE_FLAG_DELETE_ON_CLOSE, this member contains a pointer to the pathname used to load the device, e.g., \\.\VTESTD. Later when the device is closed and its *dwRecCnt* reaches zero, **DeleteFile** will be performed on this path.

14h CHAR szDeviceName[8]

The name of the virtual device.

Unlike the file, file-change, pipe, and mailslot object services, which rely on IFSMgr for implementation support, the device object is dependent on VWIN32, specifically the Win32 service with ordinal 0x2a001f. This service takes 12 arguments and there appears to be three distinct ways of calling it. First, when a virtual device is loaded or opened by a call to **CreateFile**, the calling arguments take this form:

```
VxDCall(DWORD svc,   // has the Win32 service ordinal (0x2a001f)
        DDB pDDB,    // pointer to device descriptor block
        DWORD FuncAddr, // FuncAddr, is the address of a K32 procedure
        char* pszDevName,  // 8 character device name as it appears in
                           // the DDB
        BOOL bDoLoad,       // if TRUE load device, else search DDB list
        char* pszLoadPath, // pathname used to load the device
        DWORD unused0,      // has the value 0
        DWORD unused1,      // has the value 0
        DWORD InitialRing0ID,  // contains a ring-0 THCB
        DWORD unused2,      // has the value 0
        PPDB pProcess,      // pointer to the process database
        char* pszReturnName ); // pointer at which to store device name
```

This call is always made with *pDDB* equal to NULL. There are two variations based on the value of *bDoLoad*. If *bDoLoad* is FALSE, the Device Descriptor Block list is searched for a device with a name matching pszDeviceName. If *bDoLoad* is TRUE, the **VXDLDR_LoadDevice** service is used to attempt to load the device file *pszDeviceName*. It turns out that *bDoLoad* is TRUE if the device name has an extension, but FALSE if an extension is not specified. If the device is located or loaded successfully, the 8-character device name is copied to *pszReturnName* and a **DIOC_OPEN** (DIOC_GETVERSION) call is made to the device's control procedure. The arguments *FuncAddr* and *InitialRing0ID* appear to only be used for initialization of VWIN32 variables when the first call is made to Win32 service 0x2a001f.

When a virtual device is unloaded by a call to **DeleteFile**, the arguments to **VxDCall** take this form:

```
VxDCall(DWORD svc,      // has the Win32 service ordinal (0x2a001f)
        DDB pDDB,       // pointer to device descriptor block
        DWORD unused0,  // unused argument
        char* pszDevName,  // 8 character device name
        BOOL bDoLoad,      // if TRUE load device, else search DDB list
        char* pszLoadPath, // pathname used to load the device
        DWORD unused1,  // unused argument
        DWORD unused2,  // unused argument
        DWORD unused3,  // unused argument
        DWORD unused4,  // unused argument
        DWORD unused5,  // unused argument
        DWORD unused6); // unused argument
```

Furthermore, *pDDB* is NULL, *pszLoadPath* is −1, and *bDoLoad* is TRUE although the value is not tested.

Finally, when a virtual device is closed by a call to **CloseHandle** or an operation is requested via **DeviceIoControl**, the calling arguments take this form:

```
VxDCall( DWORD svc,    // has the Win32 service ordinal (0x2a001f)
         DDB pDDB,     // pointer to device descriptor block
         DWORD dwIoControlCode, // control code to process
         LPVOID lpvInBuffer,    // address of input buffer
         DWORD cbInBuffer,      // size, in bytes, of input buffer
         LPVOID lpvOutBuffer,   // address of output buffer
         DWORD cbOutBuffer,     // size, in bytes, of output buffer
         LPDWORD lpcbBytesReturned,   // # bytes transferred to
                                      //  lpvOutBuffer
         LPOVERLAPPED lpo, // address of OVERLAPPED structure,
                           //  if async command
         HANDLE hDevice,   // Win32 handle to device
         PPDB pProcess,    // pointer to process database
         char szDeviceName[] ); // pointer to 8 character device name
```

If the call is on behalf of **CloseHandle**, *dwIoControlCode* has the value DIOC_CLOSEHANDLE(−1); *lpvInBuffer*, *lpvOutBuffer*, *lpcbBytesRetuned*, and *lpo* are all NULL; and *cbInBuffer* and *cbOutBuffer* are both 0. If the call is on behalf of **DeviceIoControl**, *dwIoControlCode* takes a non-zero value which specifies the operation to perform. Depending on the control code and the manner in which the VxD processes it, input and output parameters may or may not be required.

IOCTL Services

Once an application retrieves a handle to a device object, it may use that handle to access IOCTL services using the **DeviceIoControl** API. It turns out that both

VWIN32 and IFSMgr offer public services of this kind, each with different sets of functionality.

VWIN32 provides a **DeviceIoControl** interface for a limited set of MS-DOS functions. It seems that these functions were added primarily for disk utility programs which require direct access to file system structures and need to request exclusive volume locks on the drives which are being manipulated. There are four *dwIoControlCode* values that are defined:

VWIN32_DIOC_DOS_INT13 *(4)*

This control code is used for BIOS level Int 13h. It allows access to the physical sectors of a disk drive *but only for the floppy disk drives in a system*. This behavior is documented by the MSDN KnowledgeBase Article Q137176: *PRB: DeviceIoControl Int 13h Does Not Support Hard Disks*. If you need BIOS Int 13h services for a fixed disk, this article shows how to thunk to a Win16 DLL that uses the DPMI Simulate Real Mode Interrupt function to issue Int 13h.

VWIN32_DIOC_DOS_INT25 *(3)*

This control code is used for issuing an absolute disk read on a specific volume. Int 25h reads chunks of disk storage which are referenced by logical sectors. To force a read from the physical disk, an exclusive volume lock needs to be acquired for the volume or the read may actually return cached data. This interrupt has been superseded by Int 21h Function 440dh Minor Code 61h, Read Track on Logical Drive.

VWIN32_DIOC_DOS_INT26 *(2)*

This control code is used for issuing an absolute disk write on a specific volume. Int 26h writes chunks of disk storage which are referenced by logical sectors. To write to the physical disk, an exclusive volume lock needs to be acquired for the volume; otherwise a write protect error will be returned. This interrupt has been superseded by Int 21h Function 440dh Minor Code 41h, Write Track on Logical Drive.

VWIN32_DIOC_DOS_IOCTL *(1)*

This control code is used for issuing Int 21h Functions in the range 4400h through 4411h. This range includes the "conventional" DOS IOCTL functions as well as the new volume locking functions.*

To issue the above **DeviceIoControl** calls, the *lpvInBuffer* and *lpvOutBuffer* reference **DIOC_REGISTERS** structures. These structures define the values of the 32-bit

---

* See *Programmer's Guide to Microsoft Windows 95*, Article 25, "Exclusive Volume Locking."

registers EAX, EBX, ECX, EDX, EDI, ESI, and flags. Note, however, that the segment registers are *not* specified.*

IFSMgr also provides a **DeviceIoControl** interface for use by Network Provider DLLs. The API which network programmers are familiar with consists of the "WNet" functions which are exported by the Multiple Provider Router (MPR) DLL. The Network Provider DLLs are never called by applications, only by the MPR. The most common Network Providers are Microsoft MSNet (*msnp32.dll*) and Novell Netware (*nwnp32.dll*). In the case of Microsoft Networks, these **DeviceIo-Control** calls are made by *msnet32.dll*, on behalf of the Network Provider, MSNP32. There are four *dwIoControlCode* values that are defined:

IFS_IOCTL_21 *(100)*

This control code is used for issuing Int 21h functions of the 5Fxxh series which are handled by IFSMgr's **dFunc5F** dispatch function (see Chapter 6, *Dispatching File System Requests*). Other Int 21h functions are passed to the IFSMgr_NetFunction hook chain (see Chapter 7, *Monitoring File Activity*). The *lpvInBuffer* and *lpvOutBuffer* arguments to **DeviceIoControl** reference **win32apireq** structures. These structures define the values of the 32-bit registers EAX, EBX, ECX, EDX, EDI, ESI, and EBP. There is also a field that will give the ID of the Network Provider and a field in which to store a return code. This structure is defined in *ifs.h* of the Windows 95 DDK.

IFS_IOCTL_2F *(101)*

This control code is used for issuing Int 2Fh functions. These are also passed to the **IFSMgr_NetFunction** hook chain. The same calling arguments are used as with control code *IFS_IOCTL_21*.

IFS_IOCTL_GET_RES *(102)*

This function takes a WORD size input buffer (*lpvInBuffer*) which holds an SFT or extended file handle that is owned by the calling process. The output is returned in a DWORD size output buffer (*lpvOutBuffer*) which holds the address of the file's **fhandle** structure after it has been exclusive-ORed with 0xa5a5a5a5 and rotated left by 13 bit positions.

IFS_IOCTL_GET_NETPRO_NAME_A *(103)*

This function takes a buffer containing an ASCIIZ UNC pathname (*lpvin-Buffer*) with the length of the pathname in *cbInBuffer*. It looks up the Net ID of the FSD which owns this UNC connection and returns it in the DWORD size output buffer (*lpvOutBuffer*). Net IDs are enumerated in the SDK header file *winnetwk.h*, e.g., the Net ID for Microsoft Networks is given the manifest constant *WNNC_NET_LANMAN* (0x00020000).

---

* For more details on using these functions, see *Programmer's Guide to Microsoft Windows 95*, Article 20, "Device I/O Control."

Implementation of VWIN32_ Int21Dispatch

Our survey of the Win32 API, as summarized in Tables 4-2 through 4-6, has shown that **Int21Dispatch** is the primary link that KERNEL32 has to IFSMgr. In Chapter 3, we traced a Win32 callback into VMM and looked at how a Win32 service was dispatched. For a review of that, see the section "The Win32 Callback" in Chapter 3. Now we are going to pick up where we left off there, and trace into the VWIN32's Win32 service 0x2a0010, which we'll refer to as **VWIN32_Int21Dispatch** hereafter. The assembly code for **VWIN32_Int21Dispatch** is shown in Examples 4-3 and 4-4.

Example 4-3. Source Code for VWIN32_Int21Dispatch, Part 1

```
VWIN32(4)
+ 0b2b    VMMcall Get_Cur_Thread_Handle
+ 0b31    or      dword ptr [edi].TCB_Flags,THFLAG_EXTENDED_HANDLES
+ 0b37    mov     ebx,dword ptr pCurrentThread    ;current K32 TDB
+ 0b3d    test    dword ptr [ebx].Flags,fOpenExeAsImmovableFile
+ 0b44    jz      short L_B4C
+ 0b46    or      dword ptr [edi].TCB_Flags,THFLAG_OPEN_AS_IMMOVABLE_FILE


          L_B4C:
+ 0b4c    mov     esi,dword ptr [edi].TCB_Flags
+ 0b4e    and     esi,THFLAG_CHARSET_MASK
+ 0b54    and     dword ptr [edi].TCB_Flags,NOT THFLAG_CHARSET_MASK
+ 0b5a    test    dword ptr [ebx].Flags,fOkToSetThreadOem
+ 0b61    jz      short L_B69
+ 0b63    or      dword ptr [edi].TCB_Flags,THFLAG_OEM


          L_B69:
+ 0b69    mov     eax,dword ptr [esp+0c] ;Int 21h function
+ 0b6d    mov     edx,dword ptr [esp+04] ;client register structure
+ 0b71    mov     dword ptr [edx].Client_EAX,eax
+ 0b74    mov     ecx,dword ptr [esp+10]       ;3rd VxDCall arg
+ 0b78    mov     dword ptr [edx].Client_ECX,ecx
+ 0b7b    push    dword ptr [edx].Client_FS ;preserve this


          ;Is the requested Int 21h function a read or write?
+ 0b7e    cmp     ah,3f
+ 0b81    jz      short r0_read_or_write
+ 0b83    cmp     ah,40
+ 0b86    jz      short r0_read_or_write


          nested_exec:
+ 0b88    mov     eax,21h
+ 0b8d    VMMcall Exec_PM_Int


          L_B93:
+ 0b93    pop     eax
+ 0b94    mov     edx,dword ptr [esp+04]
```

Example 4-3. Source Code for VWIN32_Int21Dispatch, Part 1 (continued)

```
+ 0b98    mov    word ptr [edx].Client_FS,ax    ;restore Client_FS
+ 0b9c    and    dword ptr [edi].TCB_Flags,NOT FILE_MASK
+ 0ba2    or     esi,esi
+ 0ba4    jz     short L_BA8
+ 0ba6    or     dword ptr [edi].TCB_Flags,esi ;restore charset flags

       ·L_BA8:
+ 0ba8    retn   0010
Note:
FILE_MASK  equ  (THFLAG_EXTENDED_HANDLES OR THFLAG_OPEN_AS_IMMOVABLE_FILE)
```

The raw disassembly has been cleaned up by adding equates from *VMM.INC* and using names that Matt Pietrek has assigned to members of the thread database structure (TDB). In the simplest case this function takes five steps. It modifies the current thread's flags, it initializes some client registers, it performs the Int 21h request, it restores some client registers, and it restores the current thread's flags before returning. Let's look at each of these steps.

Lines 0b2bh to 0b63h modify the current thread's flags. This starts with a call to **Get_Cur_Thread_Handle** which returns the handle, which is also the address, of the thread control block (*tcb_s* in *vmm.inc*). The first field of the thread control block contains the thread flags, *TCB_Flags*. The first flag to be modified is *THFLAG_Extended_Handles*; it is simply set. This informs IFSMgr that this thread uses extended file handles. The next flag which may be modified is *THFLAG_Open_As_Immovable_File*. Whether this flag is set depends upon the setting of the equivalent flag in the ring-3 thread database. Yes, even down in VWIN32, the current KERNEL32 thread object is being accessed! The DDK has this to say about this flag: "Used by VWIN32 to prevent defragmenter from moving an open file." Moving along to the last set of flags, *THFLAG_ANSI* and *THFLAG_OEM*, are both cleared, which implies use of the ANSI character set. Then the current KERNEL32 thread object is consulted to see if it is using the OEM character set; if so, the *THFLAG_OEM* bit is set.

Next, in lines 0b69h to 0b7bh, we see the calling arguments being accessed. Recall that on entry to **VWIN32_Int21Dispatch** the stack looks like this:

ESP   Return address

ESP+4   Address of client register structure

ESP+8   Current VM handle

ESP+C   2nd **VxDCall** argument (Int 21 function)

ESP+10   3rd **VxDCall** argument

We see that EAX is loaded with the requested Int 21h function number (the second **VxDCall** argument) and EDX is loaded with the address of the client register structure. Then we see EAX stored to *Client_EAX* and the third **VxDCall** argument stored to *Client_ECX*. Finally, the current value of *Client_FS* is pushed on the stack. These actions prepare the registers that will be used when Int 21h is invoked.

On lines 0b7eh to 0b86h, we see a check for AH values 3fh (read) and 40h (write). If either of these functions is being requested, a branch is made to the code shown in Example 4-4.

Example 4-4. Source Code for VWIN32_Int21Dispatch, Part 2

```
r0_read_or_write:
+ 0bab     push   esi
+ 0bac     push   ebx
+ 0bad     push   edx
+ 0bae     push   eax
+ 0baf     push   ecx
+ 0bb0     mov    ebx,dword ptr [edx].Client_EBX ;extended handle
+ 0bb3     mov    esi,dword ptr [edx].Client_EDX ; R/W buffer
+ 0bb6     VxDcall IFSMgr_Win32_Get_Ring0_Handle
+ 0bbc     pop    ecx
+ 0bbd     pop    eax
+ 0bbe     jc     short L_BF7
+ 0bc0     sub    ah,3f
+ 0bc3     movzx  eax,ah
+ 0bc6     add    eax,R0_READFILE_IN_CONTEXT  ;0d602h
+ 0bcb     VxDcall IFSMgr_Ring0_FileIO
+ 0bd1     pop    edx
+ 0bd2     push   edx
+ 0bd3     push   eax
+ 0bd4     mov    dword ptr [edx].Client_EAX,eax   ;save xfer count
+ 0bd7     sbb    eax,eax             ; carry set if error occurred
+ 0bd9     and    eax,+01
+ 0bdc     and    word ptr [edx].Client_Flags,0fffeh ;clr client carry
+ 0be1     or     word ptr [edx].Client_Flags,ax  ;set client carry on err
+ 0be5     test   eax,eax
+ 0be7     pop    eax
+ 0be8     jz     short L_BF6
+ 0bea     push   edi
+ 0beb     VMMcall Get_Cur_Thread_Handle
+ 0bf1     mov    word ptr [edi+34],ax   ;save error code
+ 0bf5     pop    edi

      L_BF6:
+ 0bf6     clc

      L_BF7:
+ 0bf7     pop    edx
+ 0bf8     pop    ebx
+ 0bf9     pop    esi
+ 0bfa     jc     short nested_exec ; try Int 21h
+ 0bfc     jmp    short L_B93
```

Finally, on lines 0b88h and 0b8dh, Int 21h is invoked by the service **Exec_PM_Int**. This service simulates the interrupt into the current virtual machine (the System VM). It first assures that the caller is in PM execution mode, and if not calls **Set_ PM_Execution_Mode**. Then it safeguards its stack from being paged out by locking it in place, using the service **Begin_Use_Locked_PM_Stack**. It uses the current client registers during the execution of the interrupt, except that a PM call-back is stored in CS:EIP. This breakpoint becomes the return address after the interrupt completes. The interrupt is then launched by the service **Exec_Int**, which in turn performs the **Simulate_Int** and **Resume_Exec** services. When the interrupt returns, control is regained at the breakpoint. Then the service **End_Nest_ Exec** is called, which restores CS:EIP and the original stack before returning from **Exec_PM_Int**.

Exec_PM_Int does pack quite a punch. It has a serious side effect too. The client registers and flags are modified to reflect the results of the software interrupt that was performed. Perhaps this is why the DDK warns us: "This service is intended to be used only by the Windows kernel; external virtual devices should not use it. External virtual devices should use the **Exec_Int** service instead."

On lines 0b93h to 0b98h, we see the original value of *Client_FS* being popped into EAX and then written back to the client register member *Client_FS*. So when **VxDCall** returns, the only client register which you can be sure of is FS! On lines 0b9ch to 0ba8h, **VWIN32_Int21Dispatch** undoes any changes it has made to thread control block flags and then returns.

Now let's look at the case where the requested function is a read or write. For these cases, VWIN32 tries to perform an optimization. Instead of sending the request to the protected mode Int 21h handler, it attempts to convert the extended file handle into a ring-0 file handle using the IFSMgr service **IFSMgr_ Win32_Get_Ring0_Handle**. This service takes an extended file handle in EBX and returns a ring0 handle, also in EBX. Extended file handles are numbers greater than 0x200, whereas ring-0 file handles are ring-0 addresses. If this conversion succeeds, then another IFSMgr service, **IFSMgr_Ring0_FileIO**, is used to perform the file read or write, thereby completely bypassing Int 21h.

IFSMgr_Ring0_FileIO supports a range of DOS-like file I/O services. For read and write, it takes the following arguments:

EAX	Service number
EBX	Ring-0 file handle
ECX	32-bit transfer count
EDX	File position at which to start operation
ESI	Linear address of read/write buffer

EBX and EDX are returned by **IFSMgr_Win32_Get_Ring0_Handle**, whereas ECX and ESI are set to the equivalent arguments for the Int 21h function 3fh or 40h calls. The service number used is either *RO_READFILE_IN_CONTEXT* (d602h) or *RO_WRITEFILE_IN_CONTEXT* (d603h). The "in context" modifier indicates that the operation takes place in the context of the current thread as opposed to a global context. On return, this service sets the carry flag if an error occurred and places an error code in AX. If the operation is successful, EAX will contain the number of bytes actually transferred.

Win16 File Services

This chapter would not be complete without some mention of Win16 file services. Table 4-7 summarizes Int 21h usage for some common Win16 APIs. A number of services have been updated to use the long filename form of the Int 21h calls. Remember that in the Win16 environment, software interrupts are allowed and are serviced by handlers installed in the protected mode IDT. Thus most of the Int 21h requests will arrive at the PM Int 21h handler installed by IFSMgr, as discussed in Chapter 3.

Table 4-7. Win16 File Services

Win16 API	PM Interrupt 21h	Thunk to Win32 API
_lcreat, _lopen	716ch, 6000h	
_hread, _lread	3fh	
_hwrite, _lwrite	40h	
_llseek	42h	
_lclose	3eh	
CreateDirectory	7139h	
DeleteFile	7141h	
FindClose		FindCloseA
FindFirstFile		FindFirstFileA
FindNextFile		FindNextFileA
FlushCachedFileHandle	3eh	
GetCurrentDirectory		GetCurrentDirectoryA
GetDiskFreeSpace	36h	
GetDriveType		
GetFileAttributes	7143h	
GetTempDrive	19h	
GetTempFileName	2ch, 5b00h, 3eh	
OpenFile	3dh	
OpenFileEx		?

Table 4-7. Win16 File Services (continued)

Win16 API	PM Interrupt 21h	Thunk to Win32 API
RemoveDirectory	713ah	
SetCurrentDirectory		SetCurrentDirectoryA
SetFileAttributes	7143h	

Table 4-7 shows an added twist for some of the new Win16 APIs. APIs such as **FindFirstFile**, **FindNextFile**, and **FindClose** thunk to the corresponding KERNEL32 routines. Thus, even though the function originates in a Win16 application, it will still generate **VWIN32_Int21Dispatch** calls.

5

*The "New" MS-DOS
File System*

Back in Chapter 3, *Pathways to the File System*, we saw that IFSMgr hooks several "legacy" interfaces. In this chapter we'll look at IFSMgr's handlers for these interrupts and see to what extent they are passed down the interrupt chain or handled within IFSMgr. Recall from Chapter 3 that there are five interrupts to be considered and they come in either PM or V86 modes, or both. Here again is the list of interrupts:

Int 21h	PM and V86
Int 25h	PM and V86
Int 26h	PM and V86
Int 2fh	V86
Int 17h	V86

Although the bulk of file I/O continues to be serviced through these interrupt interfaces, this need not be the case since ring-0 file services (**IFSMgr_Ring0_FileIO**) are also available and in a few instances are used directly for performance or design reasons.

Interrupt 21h Handlers

IFSMgr's protected mode and virtual-86 mode Int 21h handlers have many similarities. Disassemblies of these handlers are shown in Examples 5-1 and 5-2. Keep in mind that a protected mode handler consumes an interrupt by returning via **Simulate_Iret** and chains to the previous handler by a **Simulate_Far_Jmp**. In Example 5-1, the labels *SimIRet* and *NxtPM21* correspond to these two cases. On the other hand, a V86 interrupt handler consumes an interrupt by returning with *carry* clear and chains to the previous handler by returning with *carry* set. In Example 5-2, **NextV86Hook** and a return through line 1238h both set the *carry* flag, so the next V86 interrupt handler will be called. So to see which Int 21h functions are handled by IFSMgr and which are passed on, we need to examine how these handlers decide upon these alternatives.

Initially, both PM and V86 handlers look at the Int 21h function in the AH client register, to see if it lies below the constant *MAXDOSFUNC+1*. The functions between 0 and *MAXDOSFUNC* make up the MS-DOS API. For the retail release of Windows 95, *MAXDOSFUNC* is 71h, and for OSR2 it is 73h. Function numbers from *MAXDOSFUNC+1* to FFh correspond to APIs supported by various network providers, or vendor specific extensions; e.g., function EAh is used to detect if a Netware client is installed. Each of these groupings has a separate lookup table for it. The lookup table is indexed by the function number and the table entries are the addresses of preamble functions.

The first table of functions, called **Lower72_Preambles**, is filled in with default handlers by IFSMgr. The second table of functions, called **Upper8E_Preambles**, is not created by IFSMgr until a network provider or other client registers a preamble for a function in the range *MAXDOSFUNC+1* to FFh. When the table is initially created, it is filled with addresses of a preamble function which just sets *carry* and returns. A preamble function for either table can be registered using the IFSMgr service **IFSMgr_SetReqHook**, which is available during Device Init or Init Complete phases.

Example 5-1. Protected Mode Int 21h Handler at IFSMGR(1)+1140h

```
PM_Int21_Chain       Proc Near
1140         movzx   ecx,byte ptr [ebp].Client_AH
1144         cmp     cl,72
1147         jnc     short FuncGt71
1149         xor     edx,edx
114b         test    byte ptr HookerFlags,03      ; LOCALINT21 | UNUSEDFLAG
1152         jz      short TryPreamble0
1154         test    byte ptr HookerFlags,02      ; LOCALINT21
115b         jz      short TryPreamble1
115d         push    ebx
115e         add     ebx,dword ptr OfsVMCB
1164         test    byte ptr [ebx+08],10         ; LOCALINT21HOOKER
1168         pop     ebx
1169         jz      short TryPreamble0
116b         call    Is71_A3_A4_A5_A8
1170         jnc     short TryPreamble0
1172         jmp     short NxtPM21
        TryPreamble1:
1174         inc     edx
        TryPreamble0:
1175         mov     esi,0ffffffffh
117a         call    dword ptr Lower72_Preambles[ecx*4]
1181         jnc     short Dispatch_PM_Int21
1183         cmp     ecx,-01
```

Example 5-1. Protected Mode Int 21h Handler at IFSMGR(1)+1140h (continued)

```
1186          jz      short SimIRet
      NxtPM21:
1188          mov     ecx,dword ptr NextPM21Sel
118e          mov     edx,dword ptr NextPM21Ofs
1194          VMMjmp  Simulate_Far_Jmp
      FuncGt71:
119a          cmp     dword ptr Upper8E_Preambles,00
11a1          jz      short NxtPM21
11a3          mov     edx,dword ptr Upper8E_Preambles
11a9          mov     esi,0ffffffffh
11ae          call    dword ptr [edx+ecx*4-1c8h]
11b5          jc      short NxtPM21
11b7          mov     ecx,0d4h
      Dispatch_PM_Int21:
11bc          VxDcall IFSMgr_FillHeapSpare
11c2          mov     eax,dword ptr OfsVMCB
11c7          mov     edx,0ffffffffh
11cc          call    dword ptr [ebx+eax+0c]
11d0          jc      short NxtPM21
      SimIRet:
11d2          mov     ax,word ptr [ebp].Client_Flags
11d6          and     ax,+01
11da          VMMcall Simulate_Iret
11e0          and     word ptr [ebp].Client_Flags,-02
11e5          or      word ptr [ebp].Client_Flags,ax
11e9          retn
```

In Examples 5-1 and 5-2, you can see calls to the **Lower72_Preambles** at lines 117Ah and 122Ah. In each case, the Int 21h function number is multiplied by 4, the size of each doubleword address in the table, and added to the base of the table. You can also see calls to the **Upper8E_Preambles**, at lines 11AEh and 124Ah. In these cases, the offset is reduced by 1C8h (or 1D0h for OSR2), the offset to the base of the table ((*MAXDOSFUNC*+1) * 4).

In both Examples 5-1 and 5-2, we see that a number of tests are performed before a **Lower72_Preambles** function is called. The first test involves the *HookerFlags* variable, which uses two bits of one byte of storage. This variable is global in scope; that is, it is visible across all VMs. I've called bit 1 *LOCALINT21* and bit 0 *UNUSEDFLAG*. The *UNUSEDFLAG* bit is always zero. The *LOCALINT21* bit is set when V86 Int 21h is hooked in any VM. For instance, if I startup a DOS box and run a DOS application that hooks Int 21h, this flag will be set and will be seen from the System VM as well as other VMs. So we may interpret the four lines of code starting at 114bh in Example 5-1 and at 1200h in Example 5-2 as a three-way test. If both flags are clear, then call the preamble with EDX=0. If only the *UNUSEDFLAG* bit is set, call the preamble with EDX=1. And last, if only the *LOCALINT21* bit is set, continue performing additional tests.

Example 5-2. Virtual-86 Int 21h Handler at IFSMGR(1)+11eah

```
V86_Int21_Chain      Proc Near
11ea         VxDcall IFSMgr_FillHeapSpare
11f0         movzx ecx,byte ptr [ebp].Client_AH
11f4         mov    esi,0ffffffffh
11f9         cmp    cl,72
11fc         jnc    short _FuncGt71
11fe         xor    edx,edx
1200         test   byte ptr HookerFlags,03    ; LOCALINT21 | UNUSEDFLAG
1207         jz     short _TryPreamble0
1209         test   byte ptr HookerFlags,02    ; LOCALINT21
1210         jz     short _TryPreamble1
1212         push   ebx
1213         add    ebx,dword ptr OfsVMCB
1219         test   byte ptr [ebx+08],10       ; LOCALINT21HOOKER
121d         pop    ebx
121e         jz     short _TryPreamble0
1220         call   Is71_A3_A4_A5_A8
1225         jnc    short _TryPreamble0
1227         jmp    short NextV86Hook
      _TryPreamble1:
1229         inc    edx
      _TryPreamble0:
122a         call   dword ptr Lower72_Preambles[ecx*4]
1231         jnc    short Dispatch_V86
1233         cmp    ecx,-01
1236         jz     short _WasHandled
1238         stc
      _WasHandled:
1239         retn
      L_123A:
123a         retn
      _FuncGt71:
123b         cmp    dword ptr Upper8E_Preambles,00
1242         jz     short NextV86Hook
1244         mov    edx,dword ptr Upper8E_Preambles
124a         call   dword ptr [edx+ecx*4-1c8h]
1251         jc     short NextV86Hook
1253         mov    ecx,0d4h
      Dispatch_V86      Proc Near
1258         mov    eax,dword ptr lin_SDA_base
125d         movzx  edx,word ptr [eax+0e]
1261         movzx  eax,word ptr [eax+0c]
1265         shl    edx,04
1268         add    edx,eax
126a         add    edx,dword ptr [ebx+04]
126d         mov    eax,dword ptr OfsVMCB
1272         jmp    dword ptr [ebx+eax+0c]

      NextV86Hook:
1278         stc
1279         retn
```

Let's assume only *LOCALINT21* is set. We then drop into another bit test over the next five lines, starting at 115bh in Example 5-1, and at 1212h in Example 5-2. At this point, EBX is the current VM handle, which is also the base of the VM control block. During Device Init, IFSMgr calls **_Allocate_Device_CB_Area** to allocate a block of memory which is specific to IFSMgr and which is private to each VM. This block begins at offset *OfsVMCB* from the beginning of the VM control block; thus EBX + *OfsVMCB* is the address of the base of this **pervm** data structure (see Appendix C, *IFSMgr Data Structures*, for **pervm**'s typedef). The *pv_flags* member of this structure, a byte at offset 8, contains flag bits. Bit 4, which I've named *LOCALINT21HOOKER*, indicates whether there is a local Int 21h hooker in this VM. So this test is checking whether this VM is the VM which has installed the local hook. If not then the preamble is called with EDX=0.

Ok, now let's assume the *LOCALINT21* bit is set and we are in a VM which has a local Int 21h hook; then the function **Is71_A3_A4_A5_A8** is called. This is a simple function which returns with *carry* set if the requested function is *not* 71A3h, 71A4h, 71A5h, or 71A8h. So unless the Int 21h request is for one of these functions, the request will be passed to the next PM or V86 handler. It is interesting to note that functions 71A3h to 71A5h are undocumented but clearly are related to the implementation of Find Change Notification. Function 71A8h is used to generate a short name alias from a long filename.

In any event, if a preamble is called, the *carry* flag on return determines whether the function is ultimately dispatched. If the preamble returns with *carry* set, then the function is not handled and is passed on to the next handler. However, if the preamble returns with *carry* clear, then the function is dispatched to the file system at **Dispatch_PM_Int21** or **Dispatch_V86**. In either case, the address of the dispatch function is located in the VM's **pervm** data structure in the member *pv_dispfunc*. If the dispatch function fails, it also returns with *carry* set, and the function is passed on to the next handler in the chain.

The *LOCALINT21* bit of *HookerFlags* and the *LOCALINT21HOOKER* bit of the *pv_flags* member of the VM's **pervm** structure have a dramatic effect on the routing of Int 21h requests. When both bits are set for a VM, they essentially shut down the PM and V86 Int 21h handlers. This is a pretty drastic measure. Why would IFSMgr do this? Well, before we explore this mystery let's take a closer look at preamble functions.

Preamble Functions

Preamble functions are described in the DDK's *IFS Specification* under the section on the **IFSMgr_SetReqHook** service. This service takes two arguments, an unsigned int containing the interrupt number in the high word and the function number in the low word, and the address of the preamble function to install. At this time, this service only installs preambles for Int 21h. **IFSMgr_SetReqHook** returns the address of the previous preamble function, if successful, or 0 if the service fails. If a preamble function rejects an Int 21h request, it must chain to the previous preamble function.

A preamble function receives the following register-based arguments when it is invoked:

EBX

    The current VM handle

ECX

    The Int 21h function number

EBP

    A pointer to the client register structure

ESI

    The provider ID which is initialized to ANYPROID (–1)

The preamble function decides whether to accept or reject the Int 21h request. There is always a default preamble function installed for a given request number. The default preamble function will return with *carry* set if it wishes for the request to be rejected, and with *carry* clear if the request is to be accepted. An *installed* preamble function will return with *carry* clear if it accepts the request, but chains on to the next preamble if it rejects the request. So the net effect of calling a preamble function chain is to return with *carry* set to indicate rejection or clear to indicate acceptance. Note that this description is at odds with the IFS Specification, which *incorrectly* states that an installed preamble function should return with *carry* set if it accepts a request.

If an installed preamble function accepts a request, it needs to preserve the EBX and EBP registers. Optionally, it may set ESI to the specific provider ID of the file system driver that installed the preamble. If a specific provider ID is returned, then when the function is dispatched, it will only be seen by the file system driver for that provider ID. If ESI is left set as ANYPROID (any provider ID), then when the function is dispatched all file system drivers will be able to see the call.

If an installed preamble function rejects a request, it must preserve all registers and chain to the previous preamble.

Table 5-1 enumerates the default preamble functions which IFSMgr uses to initialize **Lower72_Preambles**. Functions 44h and 71h also have subtables indexed by the subfunction number in the AL register. These preamble functions are entered as 44xxh and 71xxh. The 71xxh series functions (except 71a0h–71aah) are remapped by the preamble into their non-long filename equivalent functions but with the LFN flag set (bit 30 of the ECX register). Functions 71a0h through

71aah are mapped to a different set of functions, but these also have the LFN flag set.

The functions which do not appear in Table 5-1 are not accepted by IFSMgr.

Table 5-1. Default Preamble Functions

Int 21h Function	Default Preamble
0Bh	IFSMGR(1)+127ch
0Dh,710dh	IFSMGR(3)+1e50h
0Eh	IFSMGR(3)+18f2h
1Ah	IFSMGR(3)+18c8h
1Bh, 1Fh	IFSMGR(3)+1a4eh
1Ch, 36h, 47h, 7147h	IFSMGR(3)+1a68h
25h	IFSMGR(3)+1b52h
29h	IFSMGR(3)+1bcfh
32h	IFSMGR(3)+1a62h
33h	IFSMGR(3)+1e89h
39h, 3Ah, 3Bh, 3Ch, 3Dh, 41h, 43h, 4Eh, 56h, 5Bh, 7139h, 713ah, 713bh, 7141h, 7143h, 714eh, 7156h	IFSMGR(3)+1c3fh
3Eh, 3Fh, 40h, 42h, 4400h, 4401h, 4402h, 4403h, 4406h, 4407h, 440ah, 4410h, 57h, 5Ch, 68h, 71a6h	IFSMGR(3)+000ch
44h	IFSMGR(3)+19b7h
4404h, 4405h, 4408h, 4409h, 440dh, 440eh, 440fh, 4411h	IFSMGR(3)+19d0h
45h, 46h	IFSMGR(3)+0000h
4Bh	IFSMGR(3)+182ch
4Dh	IFSMGR(3)+17fch
4Fh, 714fh	IFSMGR(3)+1aa5h
5Dh	IFSMGR(3)+1dc0h
5Eh	IFSMGR(3)+18b8h
5Fh	IFSMGR(3)+1840h
60h, 6Ch, 7160h, 716ch, 71a9h	IFSMGR(3)+1c38h
69h	IFSMGR(3)+1a3eh
71h	IFSMGR(3)+1f14h
71a0h, 71a1h, 71a2h, 71a3h, 71a4h, 71a5h, 71a7h, 71a8h, 71aah	IFSMGR(3)+1f8ch
7302h, 7303h, 7304h 7305h (OSR2 only)	IFSMGR(4)+1febh (OSR2)

The Preamble for Function 25h, Set Interrupt Vector

In Chapter 8 of *Unauthorized Windows 95*, entitled "The Case of the Gradually Disappearing DOS," Andrew Schulman performed some interesting experiments with Windows for Workgroups 3.11 and Windows 95. The experiments were performed with a simple DOS application, TEST21, which hooks Int 21h using DOS function 25h, set interrupt vector. TEST21 issues a sequence of Int 21h functions and tabulates a count of received Int 21h requests. It then compares the sent versus received counts for each function number.

When TEST21 is executed at the DOS prompt (outside of Windows), the sent and received counts are equal. However, if TEST21 is executed in a Windows for Workgroups 3.11 DOS box, the only Int 21h request which is received is the function 25h request; the other calls, functions 3D, 3F, 40, and 3E, are handled by IFSMgr without being reflected to DOS. When the same test is performed in a Windows 95 DOS box, all of the Int 21h requests *are* received by TEST21.

Schulman attributed the difference in behavior between Windows 95 and Windows for Workgroups 3.11 to the way that IFSMgr handles interrupt 21h function 25h for Windows 95. He found that changing the method used to hook Int 21h to a direct memory write to the interrupt vector table resulted in Windows 95 behaving the same as Windows for Workgroups, i.e., none of the Int 21h calls sent were received.

This interpretation is in line with Microsoft's documentation on Int 21h hookers. In a Microsoft white paper by Russ Arun, *Chicago File System Features—Tips & Issues* (April 22, 1994), the following explanation is given:

> On default all Int 21 interrupts, except file API Int 21s, are passed down to any hooker present in the system. The file API Int 21s are just passed to VM (local) hookers, but not to global (*autoexec.bat*) type hookers. This is done because there are new file APIs (new Int 21s) that support long filenames for delete, rename and so on that an older hooker won't understand anyway. Furthermore, not all file API calls are Int 21 calls. Specifically server calls and swapper calls to the file system are not Int 21 calls.

TEST21 falls into the category of a "local hooker" since it is executed in a DOS box (VM) after Windows is running. The reflection of file I/O Int 21h requests to a local hooker is a change from the Windows for Workgroups 3.11 behavior. Notice that the intent is not to actually service the interrupt requests in MS-DOS in virtual-86 mode; after all, that is what Windows 3.1 did. Instead, this change is intended to increase compatibility with local hookers as well as global hookers by allowing them to see Int 21h traffic.

By using the HOOKER21 TSR, which is on the companion diskette, you can confirm this behavior for yourself. HOOKER21 is a minimal TSR that calls set interrupt vector to establish a new Int 21h handler that does nothing except chain to the previous handler. If this TSR is placed in a *winstart.bat* file in the *windows* directory, it will be executed in the context of the System VM after IFSMgr has completed Device Init. Thus IFSMgr detects the re-vectoring of Int 21h and flags the System VM for Int 21h reflection.

To see this, perform a "before-and-after" test. Run MultiMon with the monitors "VWIN32 Int 21" and "V86 Int 21 (post-IFSMgr)" enabled. Generate some file activity by using the right mouse button to create a shortcut on the desktop. Most of the Int 21h requests which originate in VWIN32 do not make it as far as the V86 Int 21h handler. Now, perform the steps above after creating a *\windows\winstart.bat* file and having it load *hooker21.exe*. Then restart the system. Repeat the MultiMon test and generate some file activity. The MultiMon trace will now show a matching V86 Int 21h request for each VWIN32 Int 21h request (at least for the file I/O functions).

We can see why this is happening if we examine the code for the function 25h preamble in Example 5-3. First we see that this preamble is only interested in changes to the Int 21h vector and only if they originate in V86 mode. If the client making the request is executing in protected mode or if the vector being set is not for Int 21h, the preamble returns immediately. Next, the preamble determines whether the vector it is restoring is the original vector (whose linear address was stored in *LinV86I21Vec* during Device Init) or whether a new vector is being set. The vector argument in DS:DX is converted to a linear address for comparison with *LinV86I21Vec*, and execution continues at the label *ResVect* or *SetVect*, depending on the outcome.

The flags which track Int 21h reflection are found in three different locations. First, there is the *pv_flags* member of the VM's **pervm** structure. Next, there are *HookerFlags* and *HookedVMs* variables which reside in global IFSMgr memory. Finally, there are flags in the DOS device driver, *ifshlp.sys*. These flags are referenced as offsets from *lin_IFSHLP_data*, the linear address of a shared data area in *ifshlp.sys*.

The key flag is *LOCALINT21HOOKER* of *pv_flags* in the VM's **pervm** data structure. If it is getting cleared by the restoration of the Int 21h vector or if it is getting set because a new vector is installed, then all of the other flags also are updated. Setting the Int 21h vector multiple times in a VM has no affect on the flags after the first change.

Recall that when the *LOCALINT21* bit of *HookerFlags* and the *LOCALINT21HOOKER* bit of **pervm**'s *pv_flags* are both set, they essentially shut down the PM and V86 int 21h handlers for IFSMgr in that VM. We now understand the mechanism by which Int 21h is reflected into a VM but the connection with *ifshlp.sys* is still unclear. Let's look at the role it plays, shown in Example 5-3.

Example 5-3. Preamble for Function 25h at IFSMGR(3) + 1b52h

```
Preamble_25     Proc Near
1b52        test    dword ptr [ebx],VMSTAT_PM_EXEC
1b58        jnz     short Reject25
1b5a        cmp     byte ptr [ebp].Client_AL,21
1b5e        jnz     short Reject25
1b60        mov     edx,dword ptr OfsVMCB
1b66        add     edx,ebx
1b68        mov     edi,dword ptr lin_IFSHLP_data
1b6e        push    ecx
1b6f        movzx   ecx,word ptr [ebp].Client_DS
1b73        shl     ecx,04
1b76        movzx   eax,word ptr [ebp].Client_DX
1b7a        add     ecx,eax
1b7c        cmp     ecx,dword ptr LinV86I21Vec
1b82        pop     ecx
1b83        jnz     short SetVect
        ResVect:
1b85        test    byte ptr [edx+08],10      ; LOCALINT21HOOKER
1b89        jz      short Reject25
1b8b        and     byte ptr [edx+08],0ef     ; ~LOCALINT21HOOKER
1b8f        and     byte ptr [edi+12eh],0fe
1b96        dec     byte ptr HookedVMs
1b9c        jnz     short Reject25
1b9e        and     byte ptr HookerFlags,0fdh ; ~LOCALINT21
1ba5        and     byte ptr [edi+11],0f7
1ba9        jmp     short Reject25
        SetVect:
1bab        test    byte ptr [edx+08],10      ; LOCALINT21HOOKER
1baf        jnz     short Reject25
1bb1        or      byte ptr [edx+08],10      ; LOCALINT21HOOKER
1bb5        or      byte ptr [edi+12eh],01
1bbc        inc     byte ptr HookedVMs
1bc2        or      byte ptr HookerFlags,02   ; LOCALINT21
1bc9        or      byte ptr [edi+11],08
        Reject25:
1bcd        stc
1bce        retn
```

Bouncing Back from ifshlp.sys

In Chapter 3, in the section "Accessing IFSMgr," we summarized in Tables 3-2 and 3-3 all of the virtual devices which hooked Int 21h in either protected mode or virtual-86 mode. If none of these virtual devices accept the Int 21h request, it will get passed down the chain and arrive at the handler in the virtual-86 IVT (the "real-mode" interrupt vector table). This is represented by the last entry in the Int 21 column of Table 3-2. The address displayed there, 0c59:04a0, is the handler in *ifshlp.sys.*

If a VM has a local hooker installed, it will appear before *ifshlp.sys* in the IVT chain. There may also be other global hookers installed via *autoexec.bat* or *config.sys* that appear in the IVT chain before *ifshlp.sys* and any local hooker.

If a request gets routed all the way down to *ifshlp.sys*, what happens to it? Does it keep going and end up being serviced by MS-DOS? To answer these questions we'll need to look at the disassembly of the Int 21h handler in *ifshlp.sys*, shown in Example 5-4.

Example 5-4. Interrupt 21h Handler in ifshlp.sys

```
int_21h       proc      far
04A0          cmp       ah,72h
04A3          jae       next_in_chain
04A5          test      cs:flags,2
04AB          jz        try_preamble
04AD          test      cs:flags,0Ch
04B3          jz        try_preamble
04B5          test      cs:flags,4
04BB          jnz       haveOverride
04BD          test      cs:perVM_flags,1
04C3          jz        try_preamble
     haveOverride:
04C5          cmp       ah,0Bh
04C8          jb        try_preamble
04CA          push      ax
04CB          jmp       short bounce_back
     try_preamble:
04CD          push      ax
04CE          push      bx
04CF          mov       bl,ah
04D1          mov       bh,0
04D3          mov       al,cs:Lower72[bx]
04D8          mov       ah,0
04DA          pop       bx
04DB          add       ax,offset basePreamble
04DE          call      ax
04E0          jnc       bounce_back
04E2          pop       ax
     next_in_chain:
04E3          jmp       far ptr prevInt21
     bounce_back:
04E8          pop       ax
04E9          push      bx
04EA          mov       bl,ah
04EC          sub       bh,bh
04EE          jmp       cs:IFSMGR_V86CallBack
```

This handler routes requests in two possible directions. If line 4E3 is reached, the request is being sent down the interrupt chain to the next "real-mode" handler and may end up being serviced by MS-DOS. If line 4EE is reached, the *jmp* transfers control to a V86 callback which re-enters IFSMgr.

This 16-bit code bears some resemblance to the **PM_Int21_Chain** and **V86_Int21_ Chain** handlers shown in Examples 5-1 and 5-2. The *flags* variable resides in global memory and is modified by all VMs. Bit 1 signifies that IFSHLP has been initialized by a call from IFSMgr, bit 7 is equivalent to the *LOCALINT21* bit of *HookerFlags*, and bit 6 is equivalent to the *UNUSEDFLAG* bit of *HookerFlags*, as used in IFSMgr. The other variable tested here is *perVM_flags*. It lies in a region of IFSHLP which is instanced, i.e., which has a private copy mapped into each VM's address space.

The V86 callback to IFSMgr is called if, at least, the following conditions are met:

- Bit 1 is set in the *flags* variable, indicating IFSHLP has been initialized by IFSMgr;

- Bit 7 is set in the *flags* variable, indicating that some VM has a local Int 21h hooker;

- Bit 0 is set in the *perVM_flags* variable, indicating that the current VM has a local Int 21h hooker;

- The function number is 0Bh or greater but less than 72h.

The callback may also get called if a preamble returns with carry clear. Preambles may be called on the following Int 21h functions: 0Bh, 0Dh, 0Eh, 3Eh, 3Fh, 40h, 41h, 42h, 47h, 57h, 5Ch, 5Dh, 5Eh, 5Fh, 68h, and 71h.

One question still remains unanswered: who sets and clears these IFSHLP variables? We can find the answer back in Example 5-3 in the code for **Preamble_25**. IFSMgr stores away a linear address (in *lin_IFSHLP_data*) which points to offset 0024h in IFSHLP, the start of the shared data area. **Preamble_25** loads EDI with *lin_IFSHLP_data* and then uses EDI to reference bytes at offsets 11h and 12eh. If you add 24h to these offsets, you get the addresses of the *flags* and *perVM_flags* variables in IFSHLP.

Before we move on, let's recap. Several flags are maintained at a global scope and at a per-VM scope, to determine whether to reflect an Int 21h request downward towards MS-DOS land. IFSHLP is positioned along this downward path so that it can snatch up these requests and redirect them back to IFSMgr just before they drop into MS-DOS. For more details on how IFSMgr and IFSHLP exchange data, see the sidebar "The IFSHLP/IFSMgr Connection."

This excursion into IFSHLP and its role in Int 21h reflection has uncovered a "back door" into IFSMgr—that of the V86 callback. The ring-0 code for this callback is shown in Example 5-5. This routine's first order of business is to clean up the client stack. It does this by simulating a POP BX and then an IRET. Before BX is restored, the value of BX in the client registers is loaded into ECX to use as the function number. Except for the check for a special function value, BDh, which is

---

The IFSHLP/IFSMgr Connection

The connection between IFSHLP and IFSMgr is established during the Device Init stage. IFSMgr opens a handle to IFSHLP using the MS-DOS device name "IFSHLP". If successful, the handle is then used to acquire the entry point for subsequent calls. To do this, DOS function 4402h (receive control data from character device) is used. The caller passes in an 8-byte buffer, the first two words of which contain a version code: E970h followed by 3735h. If the call returns without error and 8 bytes are read, then the buffer should contain the following information: WORD 3735h, WORD EF70h, WORD entry_ofs, WORD entry_seg.

A call into IFSHLP takes the following form:

```
push word offset
push word segment
push word function number
call entry_seg:entry_ofs
add sp,6
```

The first two arguments (offset and segment) are not always used, although some values are pushed onto the stack. The function number is in the range 0 to 7. The functions have the following uses:

0   returns address of IFSHLP's shared data area in DX:AX

1   enables IFSHLP traps (int 17h,1bh,21h,2ah,2fh); IFSMgr's V86 callback passed to IFSHLP on the stack

2   disables IFSHLP traps (int 17h,1bh,21h,2ah,2fh);

3   unknown

4   unknown

5   unknown (unused by IFSMgr)

6   unknown (unused by IFSMgr)

7   unknown (unused by IFSMgr)

IFSMgr uses the return value from function 0 to initialize the following internal variables: *lin_IFSHLP_data, lin_IFSHLP_base, lin_SDA_base.*

---

vectored to the Int 17h handler, this code closely follows that of **V86_Int_Chain**. There is one small difference in the arguments to preamble functions: EDX has the value 2; when preambles are called from **PM_Int21_Chain** and **V86_Int_Chain**, EDX is either 0 or 1. If the preamble function rejects the request, or if IFSMgr fails the call, then the request is channeled back down the "real-mode" interrupt chain.

The address of the previous Int 21h handler is loaded from IFSHLP's shared data area. This address is passed to **Build_Int_Stack_Frame** to make it the new CS:EIP after the client registers *Client_CS* and *Client_EIP*, and *Client Flags* are pushed on the client stack. When the callback returns, execution resumes in the VM at this previous handler. Note that if the callback services the request, CS:EIP is set to the instruction following the Int 21h call since the request has been completed.

Example 5-5. V86 Callback Routine at IFSMGR(1) + 521

```
V86_CallBack_From_IFSHLP      Proc Near
521          VMMcall Simulate_Pop
527          VMMcall Simulate_Iret
52d          movzx ecx,word ptr [ebp].Client_BX
531          mov   word ptr [ebp].Client_BX,ax
535          cmp   cl,0bdh
538          jz    To_Int17_Chain
53e          cmp   cl,72
541          jnc   short AcceptBounceBack
543          mov   edx,2h
548          mov   esi,0ffffffffh
54d          mov   eax,21h
552          call  dword ptr Lower72_Preambles[ecx*4]
559          jc    short SendBackToDOS
     AcceptBounceBack:
55b          mov   eax,dword ptr lin_SDA_base
560          movzx edx,word ptr [eax+0e]
564          movzx eax,word ptr [eax+0c]
568          shl   edx,04
56b          add   edx,eax
56d          add   edx,dword ptr [ebx+04]
570          mov   esi,0ffffffffh
575          mov   eax,dword ptr OfsVMCB
57a          call  dword ptr [ebx+eax+0c]
57e          jc    short SendBackToDOS
580          retn
     SendBackToDOS:
581          mov   edx,dword ptr lin_IFSHLP_data
587          mov   cx,word ptr [edx+1ceh]
58e          movzx edx,word ptr [edx+1cch]
595          VMMcall Build_Int_Stack_Frame
59b          retn
```

Interrupt 2Fh Handler

IFSMgr's interrupt 2Fh handler is more straightforward than that for Int 21h. Of the many possible functions which could be intercepted, it is content with looking at only 05h (Critical Error Handler) and 11h (Network Redirector).

The handler for interrupt 2Fh function 05h, shown in Example 5-6, is quite simple. If AL is zero, the call is an installation check and AL is returned as 0FFh (installed). If AL is non-zero, the call is a request for an error string corresponding to the values in AL and BX. This request is converted into a function D2h and passed to the same dispatch routine utilized by the Int 21h handler, Dispatch_V86.

Example 5-6. V86 Interrupt 2Fh Function 05h Handler at IFSMGR(3)+1130

```
Int2f_05xx_Handler     Proc Near
1130        mov    edx,dword ptr [ebp].Client_EAX
1133        test   dl,dl
1135        jnz    short L_113C
1137        mov    byte ptr [ebp].Client_AL,0ff
113b        retn
    L_113C:
113c        mov    ecx,0d2h
1141        push   edx
1142        call   Dispatch_V86
1147        pop    edx
1148        test   byte ptr [ebp].Client_Flags,01
114c        jnz    short L_114F
114e        retn
    L_114F:
114f        mov    dword ptr [ebp].Client_EAX,edx
1152        stc
1153        retn
```

The handler for the Network Redirector functions (11xxh) is more complicated. The disassembly for this routine is shown in Example 5-7. For each minor function number (in client AL), a table in IFSHLP is consulted to see if it is supported. The linear address for the table is at *lin_IFSHLP_data* + 2eh. This table lies in the instanced portion of the IFSHLP data area, so the address in the current VM's address space is found by adding [EBX].**CB_High_Linear**, where EBX is the current VM handle. This table is indexed by the minor function number. If the high order bit of the byte at the indexed location is set, then a function in the array, **Table_2f11**, is called. Otherwise, the previously installed V86 Int 2Fh handler will get control.

Example 5-7. V86 Interrupt 2Fh Function 11h Handler at IFSMGR(3)+1104

```
Int2f_11xx_Handler     Proc Near
1104   movzx  ecx,byte ptr [ebp].Client_AL
1108   mov    edx,dword ptr lin_IFSHLP_data
110e   add    edx,dword ptr [ebx].CB_High_Linear
1111   test   byte ptr [ecx+edx+2e],80
1116   jz     prev_V86_Int2f
111c   cmp    cl,80
111f   cmc
1120   sbb    edx,edx
1122   and    edx,0fffffec8h
1128   jmp    dword ptr Table_2f11[edx+ecx*4]
```

The code which determines the index into **Table_2f11** is a little tricky. If the minor function number is less than 80h, then the comparison at line 111c will set the *carry* flag. The instruction at line 111f then complements the *carry* flag, thereby clearing it, so that the subtract with borrow at line 1120 makes EDX zero. The net effect is that **Table_2f11** is indexed by (function*4). However, if the minor function number is 80h or greater, then the comparison at line 111c will clear the *carry* flag. Complementing the *carry* flag then sets it so that the subtract with borrow leaves EDX equal to ffffffffh. The subsequent AND with fffffec8 sets EDX to that value. This is equivalent to c8h–(80h*4). The net effect is that minor functions 80h or greater index a section of Table_2f11 starting at offset c8h.

Table 5-2 summarizes the functions for which handlers are installed by IFSMgr. Most of the functions are mapped to a different function number and then sent to **Dispatch_V86**.

Table 5-2. Network Redirector Functions, Int 2Fh, 11xxH

Minor Function	Handler	Action
00h	IFSMGR(3)+12a9h	
01h, 02h, 03h, 04h, 05h, 0Dh, 0Eh, 0Fh, 10h, 11h, 12h, 13h, 14h, 15h, 16h, 17h, 18h, 19h, 1Bh, 2Eh	IFSMGR(3)+1411h	Dispatch as (minor function + 76h)
06h, 08h, 09h	IFSMGR(3)+12d6h	Dispatch as (minor function + 76h)
0Ch	IFSMGR(3)+1500h	Dispatch as function 82h
1Ah, 1Ch	IFSMGR(3)+147eh	
1Dh	IFSMGR(3)+14b9h	Dispatch as function 93h
21h	IFSMGR(3)+1315h	Dispatch as function 97h
23h	IFSMGR(3)+1154h	
25h	IFSMGR(3)+1288h	
31h	IFSMGR(3)+132eh	Dispatch as function b8h
80h, 81h, 82h, 84h, 86h, 8Bh, 8Ch, 8Dh, 8Eh, 8Fh, 90h, 91h	IFSMGR(3)+14b1h	Dispatch as (minor function + 26h)

Note that in MS-DOS the Network Redirector functions are called by DOS. The functions which are enumerated here are not called internally. For more information on the Network Redirector, see Chapter 8 of *Undocumented DOS* by Andrew Schulman et al.

Interrupt 25h and 26h Handlers

Protected mode as well as virtual-86 mode interrrupt 25h and 26h handlers are implemented by IFSMgr. The two handlers are very similar, so only the protected mode code is shown here in Example 5-8. On entry, AL contains the drive number on which the read or write is to be performed. If the drive number is validated, the request is sent to the dispatch point as function DDh for Int 25h or function DEh for Int 26h. After the request is dispatched and returns, the client flags are pushed onto the client stack. This is done to simulate the "quirky" behavior of these software interrupts.

Example 5-8. Protected Mode Int 25h / 26h Handler at IFSMGR(3)+162f

```
PM_Int25_26_Chain      Proc Near
162f          mov    eax,edx
1631          movzx  edx,byte ptr [ebp].Client_AL
1635          call   ValidateDrive
163a          jc     short next_pm_int
163c          mov    ecx,0ddh
1641          cmp    eax,+25
1644          jz     short dispatch_int
1646          mov    ecx,0deh
        dispatch_int:
164b          VMMcall Simulate_Iret
1651          mov    eax,dword ptr OfsVMCB
1656          mov    edx,0ffffffffh
165b          call   dword ptr [ebx+eax+0c]
165f          mov    eax,dword ptr [ebp].Client_EFlags
1662          VMMcall Simulate_Push
1668          retn

        next_pm_int:
1669          mov    ecx,dword ptr NextPM25Sel
166f          mov    edx,dword ptr NextPM25Ofs
1675          cmp    eax,+25
1678          jz     short L_1686
167a          mov    ecx,dword ptr NextPM26Sel
1680          mov    edx,dword ptr NextPM26Ofs
        L_1686:
1686          VMMjmp Simulate_Far_Jmp
```

Interrupt 17h Handler

The virtual-86 mode Int 17h handler for BIOS printer services would take several pages if we were to display it all. However, it is relevant to discuss one aspect of it. This is that even printer services are channeled to the **Dispatch_V86** routine. The function number which they are dispatched under is CCh.

IFSMGR's Common Dispatch Routine

Our survey of IFSMgr's interrupt handlers has revealed a surprising fact. If an interrupt request is accepted, in most cases it is directed to a single dispatch routine, a routine whose address is stored in IFSMgr's **pervm** data structure. Placing the address in a per-VM data location would seem to lend itself to customization, depending on the kind of application executing in the VM. There is no evidence that this is the case since the same dispatch address is used in the System VM as well as DOS boxes.

Storing the dispatch address in such a convenient location makes it easy to write a simple hook for monitoring traffic through the dispatch point. The IFSDSPAT monitor driver does just that. It hooks the dispatch point in all VMs and displays each dispatched function and some associated registers. This driver works in conjunction with MultiMon, so its output is displayed in MultiMon's application window along with the output from other monitors that are also enabled.

The output in Example 5-9 was generated in response to clicking the right mouse button on the desktop and selecting "New Folder." These are just the first few lines; the complete trace spans several pages. The lines of output that we see here are from three different monitors:

- **w21**, VWIN32's Int 21h dispatcher (WIN32CB)

- **p21**, protect-mode Int 21h hook before IFSMgr (I21HELP1)

- **dsp**, hook at IFSMgr's dispatch point (IFSDSPAT)

Example 5-9. MultiMon Output for Creating a Folder

```
Explorer p21  Seek(42)   (0) handle=024c offs=2b400
Explorer  dsp Func=      42 EDX=ffffffff ESI=ffffffff
Explorer p21  Read(3f)  handle=024c cnt=1000 buf=7b:f000
Explorer  dsp Func=      3f EDX=ffffffff ESI=ffffffff
Explorer w21  LFN(71)Get File Attr(43)
Explorer p21  LFN(71)Get File Attr(43)
Explorer  dsp Func=40000043 EDX=ffffffff ESI=ffffffff
Explorer p21  Seek(42)   (0) handle=024c offs=32400
Explorer  dsp Func=      42 EDX=ffffffff ESI=ffffffff
Explorer p21  Read(3f)  handle=024c cnt=1000 buf=7b:f000
Explorer  dsp Func=      3f EDX=ffffffff ESI=ffffffff
Explorer p21  Seek(42)   (0) handle=024c offs=30400
Explorer  dsp Func=      42 EDX=ffffffff ESI=ffffffff
Explorer p21  Read(3f)  handle=024c cnt=1000 buf=7b:f000
Explorer  dsp Func=      3f EDX=ffffffff ESI=ffffffff
Explorer w21  LFN(71)MkDir(39) C:\WINDOWS\Desktop\New Folder
Explorer p21  LFN(71)MkDir(39) C:\WINDOWS\Desktop\New Folder
Explorer  dsp Func=40000039 EDX=ffffffff ESI=ffffffff
Explorer w21  LFN(71)(a4)
Explorer p21  LFN(71)(a4)
Explorer  dsp Func=400000e1 EDX=ffffffff ESI=ffffffff
```

For each Int 21h function, two or three lines are displayed. If the interrupt request originated in VWIN32, then the trace begins with the Win32 callback shown as a **w21** line. VWIN32's interrupt dispatcher then generates a protected-mode nested execution of the interrupt which produces the **p21** line. If the interrupt request is handled by IFSMgr, then it gets sent to the dispatch point and we get a dsp line.

The Func value shown on each **dsp** line is the function number. We see that this is usually the same as the Int 21h function number. The get file attributes function, 7143h, is mapped to function 43h with the long filename flag set in the high order byte giving us 40000043h. We also see this apply to the make directory function, 7139h. Something different is happening with the last function call in the trace. Here, 71A4h becomes 400000e1h when it is dispatched. In this case, there is no standard implementation of function A4h so it is mapped to an available number above 71h, which happens to be E1h. In fact we have been seeing this kind of mapping in the handlers for interrupts 2Fh, 25h, 26h, and 17h.

Here is a more formal description of the calling convention for the dispatch point:

ECX

> The dispatched function number in the low byte, the high byte consists of several flag bits

EBX

> The current VM handle

EAX

> The offset to IFSMgr's **pervm** data structure for the VM

EBP

> Pointer to the client register structure

ESI

> The provider ID (usually –1 for ANYPROID)

EDX

> ? (may be function specific)

EDI

> ? (may be function specific)

The file API which IFSMgr exports to other VxDs, **IFSMgr_Ring0_FileIO**, is also a thin veneer around a call to the dispatch point. Unfortunately, the dispatch routine is called directly and not through the entry in IFSMgr's area of the VM control block. So our hook doesn't show these calls.

Implementing a Dispatch Hook

We've spent a lot of time looking at disassembled code in this chapter, so for a break let's look at how the IFSDSPAT virtual device is implemented. There are two interesting problems that need to be resolved to get this monitor to work.

The first involves determining the offset of IFSMgr's VM control block area, and the other is how to track the dispatch function for each VM separately.

To get IFSMgr's VMCB offset, I used a direct approach: just load before IFSMgr, hook the **_Allocate_Device_CB_Area** service, and watch for IFSMgr's call. The code for this is shown in Example 5-10. This function has a special header in order to support **Unhook_Device_Service**; HOOK_PREAMBLE is the macro which achieves this. At the center of the code is the indirect call to *pPrevAllocDevCB*, a variable which holds the previous service address when the **Hook_Device_Service** returns. The key to knowing which VxD has made the call is to look at the return address on the stack. This address is passed to **_GetVxDName** to let it do the grunge work of figuring out which device that address belongs to. For instance, if IFSMgr is making the call, the string returned might be "IFSMGR(2)+c01234567". The intrinsic function **memcmp()** then compares the first 6 characters returned against "IFSMGR". If we get a match, then we've got what we're after and store the returned offset in the global variable *OfsIfsVMCB*. Since our hook has served its purpose, we unhook it before returning—that way it won't get called again.

Example 5-10. Service Hook for _Allocate_Device_CB_Area

```
HOOKPROC MyAllocDevCB( void ) {
        PVOID pReturnAddr;
        char szBuf[80];
        DWORD dwOfs;
        HOOK_PREAMBLE(pPrevAllocDevCB)

        _asm push ebp
        _asm mov ebp,esp
        _asm sub esp,__LOCAL_SIZE
        _asm pushad

        _asm mov eax,[ebp+4]
        _asm mov pReturnAddr,eax

        _asm push [ebp+0ch]
        _asm push [ebp+08h]
        _asm call dword ptr pPrevAllocDevCB
        _asm add esp,8
        _asm mov dwOfs,eax

        if ( _GetVxDName( pReturnAddr, szBuf ) &&
                !memcmp( szBuf, szMatchStr, 6 ) ) {
            OfsIfsVMCB = dwOfs;
            Unhook_Device_Service( ___Allocate_Device_CB_Area,
                                    MyAllocDevCB );
        }

        _asm popad
        _asm mov eax,dwOfs
        _asm mov esp,ebp
```

Example 5-10. Service Hook for _Allocate_Device_CB_Area (continued)

```
_asm pop ebp
_asm ret
}
```

The second problem I needed to address was how to keep track of each VM's dispatch function address so that if MultiMon shuts down, the original dispatch function can be restored on a per-VM basis. Currently, all VMs use the same dispatch function but IFSMgr's design allows multiple dispatch addresses, so let's support that.

The solution to this is fairly simple. IFSDSPAT also uses **_Allocate_Device_CB_Area** to allocate a private doubleword in each VM. This is accomplished by these lines in the Device Init message handler:

```
_asm push 0 // flags
_asm push 4 // sizeof DWORD
VxDCall( _Allocate_Device_CB_Area );
_asm add esp,8
_asm mov OfsMyVMCB,eax
```

This doubleword of storage lies at the address VMHandle+*OfsMyVMCB* for each VM. The original dispatch address for a VM is stored in this location before it is replaced with the dispatch hook function.

6

Dispatching File System Requests

This chapter is going to look at what is our first taste of the real IFS. So far, we have been hovering about looking at the various ways we arrive at the IFSMgr and its services, but now we have arrived. The dispatch point is the ultimate IFS service. It is the entry point to the file system or systems, the gateway to local and remote file systems as well as character-based I/O to printers; I/O to mailslots and named-pipes also passes through here. At this point, we start utilizing data structures and file system drivers that are uniquely those of IFSMgr. We are no longer propping up legacy APIs. However, IFSMgr borrows a lot from DOS and builds upon it, so we can't claim a clean break with the past.

This dispatch point is just another API of sorts. It is not one that has been documented in the IFS Specification, although key data structures that are part of it have been partially documented. Unlike the many interrupt-based APIs we have been looking at, this new API is based upon a packet or block of data describing a desired operation. This packet is constructed from a set of input parameters, one of which is a function number. This function number lies in the range 0 to *MAXIFSFUNC*, where *MAXIFSFUNC* is E7h for the retail release of Windows 95 and EAh for OSR2. The values 0 through *MAXDOSFUNC* (see Chapter 5, *The "New" MS-DOS File System*) overlap with the corresponding DOS function numbers, although there are large gaps in the coverage, especially for those functions which are not file-related. Other legacy APIs are also mapped in this function range; for instance, Int 25 and Int 26h are mapped to functions DDh and DEh, and Int 17h is mapped to function CCh.

This API is not just a convergence of legacy interrupts into a single linear range of function numbers; it is more fundamental than that. By moving the function description into a packet structure, a function request can be more completely described. It can carry a complete description of the register state and pointers to important system data structures upon which the command depends. Packets can also be scheduled to execute as an event providing a mechanism for asynchronous operations.

Since the packet is such a key part of this new API, we'll start by examining how these packets are constructed. The dispatch point is where this process begins.

The Dispatch Point

In the last chapter, we saw that I/O requests from the file system are funneled through the dispatch point. The dispatch point is not entered as a service or even as a fixed location, but rather via an indirect call or jump through the *pv_dispfunc* member of the **pervm** structure for the current VM. This allowed us to write a simple hook to monitor calls through the dispatch point.

Although the dispatch point is primarily the common entry point for ring-3 file system requests, there are two ring-0 IFSMgr services which also use it. First, the service **IFSMgr_Ring0_FileIO** enters the dispatch point directly using a near call. On the other hand, **IFSMgr_ServerDOSCall** enters the dispatch point using an indirect jump through *pv_dispfunc*.

The dispatch point routine needs to do several things. It builds an `ifsreq` packet and passes it to a function handler. After the function handler returns, it performs some optional cleanup and other completion handling chores.

Think for a minute about who will be calling this routine. Just about every component in the system will be executing this code—applications, system services, and ring-0 clients—on different threads and in different process contexts. Is this interface going to be synchronous or asynchronous? Will it be re-entrant? If so, how might these objectives be achieved?

The standard way to support re-entrancy is by eliminating static variables. You can't quite get rid of all static variables, but at least you can reduce the number that need to be worried about. Well, the designers of the file system did just this. The dispatch point handler builds the `ifsreq` packet on the stack through a series of pushes and copies to the stack frame. Note that the `ifsreq` packet is the unit which IFSMgr works with. The IFS documentation only describes the `ioreq` structure which is a structure nested within the `ifsreq`. The `ifsreq` structure is 260 bytes in length whereas the `ioreq` structure is only 116 bytes long. (Note that these sizes are applicable to IFSMgr version 0x22.)

Figure 6-1 portrays the `ifsreq` packet, showing its members and the groupings which are initialized by the dispatch point handler. For details on each of the members, see Appendix C, *IFSMgr Data Structures*. There are four groupings of members that are distinguished in Figure 6-1. At the bottom of the `ifsreq` packet, storage is set aside for saving the client register structure. On top of the client register structure is a group of members which are undocumented. These start with the member *ifs_pdb* and ends with member *ifs_VMHandle*. These are all initialized in the dispatch point handler. Then there is a section which is initialized to zero, followed by the topmost members of the structure. The topmost members are documented in the IFS Specification. Of these, members *ir_length* through *ir_data* are initialized by the dispatch point handler.

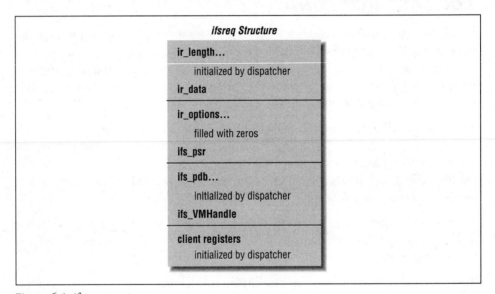

Figure 6-1. ifsreq structure

It would be interesting to walk through the dispatcher code, but it would take us four or five pages just to display it in pseudocode form. Instead, Table 6-1 distills this routine into a chart of *ifsreq* members and how each member gets its value from the execution of the dispatcher code. Although the main purpose of the dispatcher is to get the *ifsreq* packet into a good known state before passing it on, it also performs other chores such as passing CTRL-C down to IFSHLP if CTRL-C checking is turned on and the VM is not the system VM. It also performs a series of post-dispatch cleanup steps which, under some circumstances may include suspending a VM, adjusting a thread's execution priority, or even terminating a Win32 application, to name a few.

Table 6-1. ifsreq Initialization

Member	Initial Value	Notes
ir_length	*[EBP].Client_ECX*	From EBP on entry; only 16 bits of ECX used if 16-bit PM client
ir_flags	*[EBP].Client_AL*	From EBP on entry
ir_user	from byte at IFSMGR(1) + 64c8h	
ir_sfn	00FFh	

ir_pid	IFSMgr_Ring0_FileIO:
	    FFFFFFFFh
	IFSMgr_ServerDOSCall/LFN:
	    (*DPL32_UID* << 16) + *DPL32_PID*	

ir_ppath	FFFFFBBBh	
ir_aux1	EDX	From EDX on entry

ir_data	IFSMgr_Ring0_FileIO:
	    [EBP].Client_ESI
	IFSMgr_ServerDOSCall/LFN:
	    DPL32_EDX
	Other:
	    [EBP].Client_DS, [EBP].Client_DX	

ir_options	0	
ir_error	0	
ir_rh	0	
ir_fh	0	
ir_pos	0	
ir_aux2	0	
ir_aux3	0	
ir_pev	0	
ir_fsd[16]	{0}	
ifs_pfh	0	
ifs_psft	0	
ifs_psr	0	

ifs_pdb	IFSMgr_Ring0_FileIO:
	    FFFFFFFFh
	IFSMgr_ServerDOSCall/LFN:
	    FFFFFBDBh
	IFSMgr_ServerDOSCall:
	    (current PSP) << 4
	Other:
	    (current PSP) << 4	

ifs_func	CL, between 00h and *MAXISFUNC*	From CL on entry
ifs_drv	*ir_vmbc->curdrv* + 1	From VM's control block
ifs_hflag	?	?

Table 6-1. ifsreq Initialization (continued)

Member	Initial Value	Notes

ifs_proid	IFSMgr_Ring0_FileIO:
	  ESI
	IFSMgr_ServerDOSCall:
	  FFFFFFFFh
	Other:
	  ESI
		From ESI on entry

ifs_nflags	80h - **IFSMgr_ServerDOSCall** 40h - LFN 20h - Uses Extended Handles 10h - **IFSMgr_Ring0_FileIO** 08h - 8.3 Match Semantics 04h - Caller is Win32 app 02h - BCS/Unicode 01h - ANSI/OEM character set	From ECX on entry
ifs_pbuffer	FFFFFBBBh	
ifs_VMHandle	EBX(current VM handle)	From EBX on entry
ifs_PV	EBX(current VM) + EAX(offset to IFS control block)	From EBX and EAX on entry
ifs_crs	Copy of VM's client registers; for **IFSMgr_Ring0_FileIO** calls EBP points to a shortened register structure of only 48 bytes; for **IFSMgr_ServerDOS-Call** calls, EBP also points to a shortened register structure	From EBP on entry

Once `ifsreq` is initialized, it is passed as an argument in a call to a function handler. The function handlers are arranged in a table which is indexed by the function number. The function number is stored in *ifs_func*. As the `ifsreq` packet moves through the routines called by the handler, the members of `ifsreq` are interpreted and changed in ways which are unique to each command. On return, the changes to `ifsreq` will reflect the results of the function.

Table 6-2 shows the contents of an `ifsreq` before and after a file create operation: creating a shortcut on the Windows 95 desktop. The Int 21h function that is behind the ultimate dispatch call is 716ch.

Table 6-2. ifsreq for a File Create Operation

Entry	Value	Return	Value
ir_length (*ir_attr*)	FILE_ATTRIBUTE_ARCHIVE (20h)	*ir_length* (*ir_attr*)	FILE_ATTRIBUTE_ARCHIVE (20h)
ir_flags	ACCESS_READWRITE | SHARE_DENYNONE | OPEN_FLAGS_NOINHERIT (c2h)	*ir_flags*	ACCESS_READWRITE | SHARE_DENYNONE | OPEN_FLAGS_NOINHERIT (c2h)

Table 6-2. ifsreq for a File Create Operation (continued)

Entry	Value	Return	Value
ir_user	01h	*ir_user*	01h
ir_sfn	00ffh	*ir_sfn*	0248h
ir_pid	000121e3h	*ir_pid*	000121e3h
ir_ppath	FFFFFBBBh	*ir_ppath*	C0087af4h (`ParsedPath`)
ir_aux1	FFFFFFFFh	*ir_hfunc*	c1084f38h
ir_data	c3400012h	*ir_data*	0066f450h (`Client_ESI`)
ir_options	0	*ir_options*	ACTION_CREATED (0002h)
ir_error	0	*ir_error*	0
ir_rh	0	*ir_rh*	c1058db8h (sr_rh)
ir_fh	0	*ir_fh*	c10869b8h (fh_fh)
ir_pos	0	*ir_size*	0
ir_aux2	0	*ir_dostime*	205ca94dh
ir_aux3	0	*ir_upath*	c0087f04h
ir_pev	0	*ir_pev*	0
ir_fsd[16]	{0}	*ir_fsd[16]*	filled by FSD
ifs_pfh	0	*ifs_pfd*	c1084f38h (`fhandle`)
ifs_psft	0	*ifs_psft*	0
ifs_psr	0	*ifs_psr*	c1039b28h (`shres`)
ifs_pdb	00021e20h	*ifs_pdb*	00021e20h
ifs_proid	FFFFFFFFh	*ifs_proid*	FFFFFFFFh
ifs_func	6Ch	*ifs_func*	6Ch
ifs_drv	03h	*ifs_drv*	03h
ifs_hflag	00h	*ifs_hflag*	00h
ifs_nflags	60h	*ifs_nflags*	60h
ifs_pbuffer	FFFFFBBBh	*ifs_pbuffer*	c0087af4h (`ParsedPath`)
ifs_VMHandle	c35200e8h	*ifs_VMHandle*	c35200e8h
ifs_PV	c35202ach	*ifs_PV*	c35202ach

In the Return column, several of the `ioreq` members have different names than
the operation started with in the Entry column. These represent overlays of
different members of a union. For example, *ir_aux1* is a union of type **aux_t**.
The `ioreq` structure declaration in *ifs.h* declares this member as:

```
aux_t      ir_aux1;    /* secondary user data buffer (CurDTA) */
```

The *ifs.h* header file also contains this declaration of the union *aux_t*:

```
typedef union {
    ubuffer_t      aux_buf;
    unsigned long  aux_ul;
```

```
    dos_time      aux_dt;
    vfunc_t       aux_vf;
    hfunc_t       aux_hf;
    void          *aux_ptr;
    string_t      aux_str;
    path_t        aux_pp;
    unsigned int  aux_ui;
} aux_t;
```

Any of these members can be combined with *ir_aux1*. So if this field happened to represent an unsigned long volume handle, then it would be referred to as *ir_aux1.aux_ul*, or if it represents a table of handle-based functions, it would be referred to as i*r_aux1.aux_hf. ifs.h* has gone further and defined macros for some common union references:

```
    #define ir_volh    ir_aux1.aux_ul  /* VRP address for Mount */
    #define ir_hfunc   ir_aux1.aux_hf  /* file handle function vector */
```

The *ir_hfunc* member is one of the more interesting return values on a file create. It points to a table of functions in the FSD that support read, write, and other handle-based operations. The results column also contains three different forms of handles. The member *ir_sfn* contains the System File Number for the newly created file. This is the number that backs up a Win32 file object (see Chapter 4, *File System API Mapping*). The field *ifs_pfh* is a pointer to a **fhandle** structure which also happens to be used as a ring-0 file handle. And lastly, *ir_fh* is a file handle that is private to the FSD.

It is interesting to follow what has happened to the file name that was passed to the function. Originally, it was a pointer in the client registers, specifically, **Client_ESI**, and it pointed to the long filename *C:\WINDOWS\Desktop\New Shortcut.lnk*.

On return, four different fields contain some representation of the original file name: *ir_ppath, ir_data, ir_upath*, and *ifs_pbuffer*. Now, *ir_data* just holds the original pointer to the filename but the other three pointers are different. The member *ir_upath* is declared as type **string_t**, which is unsigned short *, i.e., a Unicode string. This string is also "unparsed"—it is a straight conversion of the input path to Unicode. The members *ir_ppath* and *ifs_pbuffer*, on the other hand, are of type **ParsedPath**. A path which is represented by a **ParsedPath** structure is called a *canonicalized* path. Here is the declaration for the **ParsedPath** type:

```
    struct ParsedPath {
        unsigned short  pp_totalLength;
        unsigned short  pp_prefixLength;
        struct PathElement pp_elements[1];
    };
```

The member *pp_totalLength* gives the total length of the pathname including the size of the **ParsedPath** structure (4 bytes). The member *pp_prefixLength* gives

the offset of the last path element in the pathname relative to the start of the
ParsedPath structure. These members are followed by zero or more **PathElement** structures. A **PathElement** structure has this declaration:

```
struct PathElement {
    unsigned short  pe_length;
    unsigned short  pe_unichars[1];
};
```

The member *pe_length* gives the length in bytes of *pe_unichars*, including its null
termination. The member *pe_unichars* contains the zero or more Unicode characters that make up the path element string. The **PathElements** in a pathname are
delimited by the path separator character ("\" or "/") but the separator character is
removed from the extracted Unicode string.

An example will make this much more clear. Here is the **ParsedPath** representation for our "New Shortcut":

```
0046h    0024h
0010h    "WINDOWS"
0010h    "DESKTOP"
0022h    "NEW SHORTCUT.LNK"
```

In this example, the total length of the path, 46h, is equal to the sum of the
lengths of the **PathElements** (10h+10h+22h) plus the length of the **ParsedPath**
structure (4). We also see that *pp_prefixLength*, which has a value of 24h, gives us
the offset to the filename portion of the path. Note that all elements are converted
to uppercase and the strings are in Unicode. These canonicalized paths are
always relative to the root of the volume, and a volume designator is not part of
the path description. For instance, a root path can be represented by a **Parsed-
Path** structure containing a *pp_totalLength* of 4 and a *pp_prefixLength* of 4.

There is a lot more information that we could extract from Table 6-2, but it will
make more sense once we have better grounding in the IFSMgr's internal data
structures.

Dispatch Functions

The dispatch function table contains functions for handling each command type,
as shown in Tables 6-3 through 6-5. For instance, the command 6Ch can come in
several forms. If it is function 6Ch using a short filename, then the LFN command
flag will be cleared. However, if it was called using function 716Ch, then the LFN
bit will be set. Or, it may have been invoked in response to an **IFSMgr_Ring0_
FileIO** service and the command **LFN** and **IFSMgr_Ring0_FileIO** flags will be set.
Yet another variation in command flags would be seen if the call was made via
IFSMgr_ServerDosCall. Although several different calling methods could be used,
the same dispatch function will service all of these requests for function 6Ch.

Tables 6-3, 6-4, and 6-5 enumerate the functions in the dispatch function table. Each known function has been given a descriptive name in these tables. These are simply names that I have created for convenience; you will not find them documented anywhere. If a function number is not represented in the tables but lies in the range 0 through *MAXIFSUNC*, the default handler shown in Example 6-1 is called. This routine does nothing but return with a error code of 1. However, if a kernel debugger is loaded, a breakpoint will occur at the int 3 instruction. The contents of the ECX, EAX, EDX, and EBX will indicate which command was attempted and where it originated. In reality, this function should not get called; the preamble routines should weed out any unsupported functions.

Table 6-3. Dispatch Functions 00-69h

Name	Function Number(s)
dResetDrive	0Dh
dDriveData	1Bh, 1Ch, 36h
dOpenCreate	3Ch, 3Dh, 5Bh, 6Ch
dGetDefDPB	1Fh
dGetDPB	32h
dMkRmDir	39h, 3Ah
dChDir	3Bh
dClose	3Eh
dReadWrite	3Fh, 40h
dDelete	41h
dSeek	42h
dAttribs	43h
dIoctl	44h
dDup	45h
dForceDup	46h
dGetCurDir	47h
dFindFile	4Eh, 4Fh
dRename	56h
dFileDateTime	57h
dLock	5Ch
dFunc5E	5Eh
dFunc5F	5Fh
dGetFullName	60h
dCommit	68h
dDiskSerial	69h

Table 6-3 consists entirely of Int 21h functions with the table function number corresponding to the Int 21h function. In Table 6-4, many of the functions are handlers for the Int 2fh function 11xxh interface. Where this is the case, the function number is indicated in parentheses. Similarly, in Table 6-5, where the originating interrupt is known, it is indicated in parentheses along with a function number. Table 6-5 contains dispatch functions for many of the Win32 MS-DOS extensions and several **IFSMgr_Ring0_FileIO** functions (those beginning with "dR0").

Table 6-4. Dispatch Functions 77h-CFh

Name	Function Number(s)
dFunc77	77h(2f/1101h), 78h(2f/1102h), 79h(2f/1103h), 7Ah(2f/1104h)
dChDir	7Bh(2f/1105h)
dFunc7C	7Ch(2f/1106h)
dFunc7E	7Eh(2f/1108h), 7Fh(2f/1109h)
dFunc82	82h(2f/110Ch)
dFunc83	83h(2f/110Dh), 84h(2f/110Eh)
dFunc85	85h(2f/110Fh), 86h(2f/1110h)
dFunc87	87h(2f/1111h), 88h(2f/1112h)
dFunc89	89h(2f/1113h), 8Ah(2f/1114h)
dFunc8B	
dFunc8F	8Fh(2f/1119h), 90h(2fh/111Ah), 91h(2f/111Bh), 92h(2f/111Ch)
dProcExit	93h(2f/111Dh)
dFunc5F	94h(2fh/111eh)
dFunc5E	95h(2f/111fh)
dSeek	97h(2f/1121h)
dNetFunc	A6(2f/1180h), A7(2f/1181h), A8(2f/1182h), AAh(1184h), B1(2f/118Bh), B2(2f/118Ch), B3(2f/118Dh), B4(2f/118Eh)
dFuncB8	B8h(2f/1131h)
dFuncBE	BEh, BFh, C0h, C1h, C2h, C3h, C4h, C5h, C6h
dFuncC9	C9h
dFuncCC	CCh
dFuncCD	CDh
dFuncCF	CFh

Table 6-5. Dispatch Functions D0h-EAh

Name	Function Number(s)
dFuncCF	D0h
dFuncD1	D1h

Table 6-5. Dispatch Functions D0h-EAh (continued)

Name	Function Number(s)
dCritErr	D2h (2f/05)
dFuncD3	D3h
dFuncA6	D4h
dR0_OpenCreate	D5h
dR0_ReadWrite	D6h
dR0_Close	D7h
dR0_FileSize	D8h
dGetVolInfo	DBh (21/71A0h)
dFindClose	DCh (21/71A1h)
dAbsReadWrite	DDh (25h), DEh (26h)
dFuncDF	DFh
dFcnFirst	E0h (21/71A3h)
dFcnNext	E1h (21/71A4h)
dFcnClose	E2h (21/71A5h)
dGetByHandleInfo	E3h (21/71A6h)
dConvertTime	E4h (21/71A7h)
dGenShortName	E5h (21/71A8h)
dOpenCreate	E6h (21/71A9h)
dSubst	E7h (21/71Aah)
dSetDPB (OSR2)	E8h (21/7304h)
dSetDPBAllocInfo (OSR2)	E9h (21/7305h)
dFuncEA (OSR2)	Eah

Example 6-1. Default Dispatch Function

```
mov     ecx,dword ptr [edi].ifs_func
mov     eax,dword ptr [edi].ifs_crs.Client_EAX
movzx   edx,word ptr [edi].ifs_crs.Client_CS
mov     ebx,dword ptr [edi].ifs_crs.Client_EIP
int     3
mov     word ptr [edi].ir_error,0001
retn
```

To get a feel for how a dispatcher function is implemented, we'll take a look at
the pseudocode for **dGetVolInfo**, one of the shorter functions (see Example 6-2).
The *Programmer's Guide to Microsoft Windows 95* describes the input and output
parameters for this function in the section "Interrupt 21h Function 71A0h Get
Volume Information." There is essentially one input, the root path of the volume
for which information is requested. This string takes the form "C:\". Upon arrival
at **dGetVolInfo**, the pointer to the rootname, which was originally in DS:DX or

Example 6-2. Pseudocode for dGetVolInfo

```
void dGetVolInfo( ifsreq* pifs ) {
  int retc;

  retc = _PathToShRes( pifs, 0 );
  if ( !retc ) {
    if ( pifs->ifs_drv == 2 &&    // drive B
         (DriveAttribs[1] & 0x08) &&  // single drive system
         !(DriveAttribs[1] & 0x80) &&
         pifs->ifs_VMHandle == hvmSystem ) {
      pifs->ifs_ir.ir_error = ERROR_INVALID_DRIVE;
      return;
      }

    pifs->ifs_ir.ir_options = 2; // Level 2 Request

    if ( pifs->ifs_nflags & 0x04 ) // Win32 call
       pifs->ifs_ir.ir_data = pifs->ifs_crs.Client_EDI;
    else // convert Client_ES : Client_DI to linear address
       pifs->ifs_ir.ir_data = MapFlat_Seg_Ofs( 0x3800 );

    pifs->ifs_ir.ir_length = pifs->ifs_crs.Client_CX;//size of name buffer
    pifs->ifs_ir.ir_pos = 0;

    if ( ! Call_FSD( pifs->ifs_psr->sr_func->vfn_func[VFN_QUERY],
                     IFSFN_QUERY, pifs, FALSE ) ) {

      pifs->ifs_crs.Client_BX = pifs->ifs_ir.ir_options; // FS flags
      pifs->ifs_crs.Client_AX = pifs->ifs_ir.ir_pos; // cache block size

      if ( HookerFlags & 0x01 ) { //OVERRIDE flag (see Ch.5)
        pifs->ifs_crs.Client_CX = 0x000c; // Max fn len
        pifs->ifs_crs.Client_BX = 0x8000; // File system flags
        pifs->ifs_crs.Client_DX = 0x0050; // Max path len
        }
      else { // use values returned by FSD for volume
        pifs->ifs_crs.Client_CX = pifs->ifs_ir.ir_length; // Max fn len
        pifs->ifs_crs.Client_DX = (pifs->ifs_ir.ir_length >> 16);
        }
      }
    return;
    }

  if ( retc == 0xffffffc0 ) {
    if ( IsPhysicalDrive( pifs->ifs_drv ) ) {
      pifs->ifs_crs.Client_CX = 0x000c; // Max fn len
      pifs->ifs_crs.Client_BX = 0x8000; // FS flags
      pifs->ifs_crs.Client_DX = 0x0050; // Max path len
      pifs->ifs_ir.ir_error = 0;
      }
    else pifs->ifs_ir.ir_error = ERROR_INVALID_DRIVE;
    }
}
```

EDX, is now stored in the `ifsreq` member *ir_data*. Other members of `ifsreq` are filled in as outlined in Table 6-1.

The dispatcher function wants to pass the request to a file system driver, specifically the driver's **FS_QueryResourceInfo** routine which is designed to return its "Volume Information." To do this, it has to find which FSD handles the requested volume. The call to **_PathToShRes** (my name) achieves this by processing the `ifsreq` packet. It relies upon the service **IFSMgr_ParsePath** to convert the path in member *ir_data* into a `ParsedPath` with a pointer to it left in *ir_ppath* (and *ifs_pbuffer*) on return. This service also fills in *ir_uFName* (*ir_aux2*), *ir_upath* (*ir_aux3*), and, most importantly, *ifs_psr*. This last member is important because a `ParsedPath` only contains the path components and not the drive letter. The *ifs_psr* member is a pointer to an IFSMgr *shell resource*; it describes the volume to which the `ParsedPath` refers. When **IFSMgr_ParsePath** returns, **_PathToShRes** does some additional processing and also fills in the *ir_rh* member. This is a resource handle for the volume; a handle which the FSD returned when the volume was initially mounted.

Once the `ifsreq` packet is primed with this information, we know how to call the FSD. Before doing so, there are few more parameters which need to be set up: *ir_options* is set to 2 for a level 2 request, *ir_data* is now pointed at the buffer which will hold the file system name on return, *ir_length* contains the length of this buffer, and *ir_pos* is set to 0. The `ifsreq` structure is now ready for a **FS_QueryResourceInfo** call (for a description of the calling parameters see the DDK's *IFS Specification*).

This brings us to the **Call_FSD** function. The first argument to this function is key—it is the address of the FSD function to be called. How does it know which FSD and which function? By using *ifs_psr*. This pointer to the shell resource gives us access to a function "exported" by the FSD. The shell resource's member *sr_func* is a pointer to a `volfunc` structure, which is an array of all of the volume-based entry points in the FSD. This structure is defined in *ifs.h* along with manifest constants for each function. In our case, we need *VFN_QUERY*, which corresponds to **FS_QueryResourceInfo**. The *pir* argument to **Call_FSD** will be passed as an argument on the call to the FSD function.

The FSD's **FS_QueryResourceInfo** function will retrieve various bits of volume information and store them in the designated locations of the `ifsreq` structure. So on return, we see *ir_options*, *ir_pos*, and *ir_length* being accessed to transfer the results back to registers. At this level, we are supporting an Int 21h function, so the return values are placed into the BX, CX, and DX registers. This is where having the saved copy of the client register structure included in the `ifsreq` structure is very convenient. It is this image of the client registers which will be restored before the Int 21h request ultimately returns. By changing this image we are assured that the caller will see the returned values.

From this example we have seen that volume-based FSD functions are found in a shell resource structure for a given local or remote drive. There are also handle-based FSD functions which are found in the **fhandle** structure corresponding to the file's SFN. So, just as the **ifsreq** member *ifs_psr* is required for volume-based FSD function calls, *ifs_pfh* is required for handle-based FSD function calls. Detailed descriptions of **fhandle** structures and shell resource are given in Appendix C. In the next two sections we will examine these key file system structures in more detail.

Shell Resources and the FSD's Volume-Based Function Table

IFSMgr maintains several data structures that relate to the mounted volumes in the system, whether these are local or remote volumes. At the base of the chain of structures is the system volume table, **SysVolTable[]**, which is an array of pointers to **volinfo** structures (see Appendix C for **volinfo**'s typedef). **SysVolTable** can hold up to 32 entries and is indexed by a zero-based drive number. The **volinfo** structure contains several members, the most important of which is the very first entry, a pointer to the volume's shell resource structure, **shres** (see Figure 6-2). **SysVolTable** and **volinfo** structures are kept pretty well hidden, since they are not exposed through any services and they are not cross referenced by other data structures. The shell resource, however, is included as an undocumented member of the **ifsreq** packet. For most dispatch table functions, the shell resource is resolved and inserted into the **ifsreq** structure prior to dispatching the function.

Descriptions of the members of the shell resource are given in Appendix C. For our purposes now, we are interested in the *sr_func->vfn_func* and *sr_rh* entries. When a file system driver registers with IFSMgr during the Device Init stage, the address of the **FS_MountVolume** function provided by the FSD is supplied. When the first access is made to this volume, the **FS_MountVolume** function is called to mount the volume. This establishes its table of volume-based functions and the FSD returns a unique handle, *sr_rh*, which is then passed to the FSD on future calls. This handle is not interpreted by IFSMgr, so the FSD is free to use the address of a data structure or any other unique value to identify a volume.

The contents of the FSD's volume-based function table is shown in Table 6-6. At the head of the table, version and revision are given first, followed by the table size, and then the actual function entries (this structure is defined in *ifs.h*). The

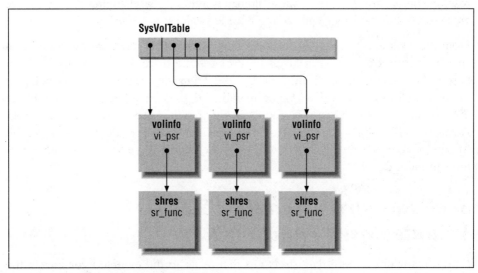

Figure 6-2. Volume-related data structures

corresponding **FS_** function name for each table entry is also shown. These are
the functions which are described in the *IFS Specification*.

Table 6-6. Volume-Based Function Table

Table Entry	Value
vfn_version	IFS version (030Ah)
vfn_revision	IFS interface revision (10h)
vfn_size	15
vfn_func[VFN_DELETE]	FS_DeleteFile
vfn_func[VFN_DIR]	FS_Dir
vfn_func[VFN_FILEATTRIB]	FS_FileAttributes
vfn_func[VFN_FLUSH]	FS_FlushVolume
vfn_func[VFN_GETDISKINFO]	FS_GetDiskInfo
vfn_func[VFN_OPEN]	FS_OpenFile
vfn_func[VFN_RENAME]	FS_RenameFile
vfn_func[VFN_SEARCH]	FS_SearchFile
vfn_func[VFN_QUERY]	FS_QueryResourceInfo
vfn_func[VFN_DISCONNECT]	FS_DisconnectResource
vfn_func[VFN_UNCPIPEREQ]	FS_NamedPipeUNCRequest
vfn_func[VFN_IOCTL16DRIVE]	FS_Ioctl16Drive
vfn_func[VFN_GETDISKPARMS]	FS_GetDiskParms
vfn_func[VFN_FINDOPEN]	FS_FindFirstFile
vfn_func[VFN_DASDIO]	FS_DirectDiskIO

IFSMgr calls an internal function during Device Init to construct the `SysVolTable`, its `volinfo` members, and the shell resource structures. These initial structures are based upon **IRS_drv_get** calls to **IOS_Requestor_Service** over the range of drives ending with the DOS last drive. The DOS current directory structures (CDS) are copied into the `volinfo` structure for each drive.

fhandle Structures and the FSD's Handle-Based Function Table

IFSMgr maintains several data structures for tracking open files, shown in Figure 6-3. SFNs, or system file numbers, are used to reference each file. SFNs are split into two groups: those numbering 0 through FFh, which refer to DOS file handles backed by a VM specific SFT entry, and extended file handles, which are numbered 200h and above and which are allocated at a global scope—global in the sense that a single table is shared by all VMs.

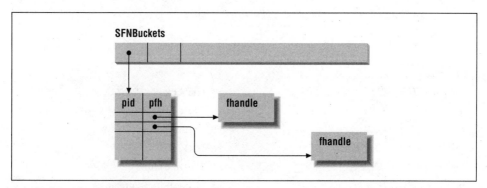

Figure 6-3. File-related data structures

Several data structures are used to represent a system file number. Initially a single `SFNBucket` is allocated; it is a pointer that references a block of storage able to hold 256 files. As more handles are required, additional `SFNBuckets` are allocated by IFSMgr. The maximum number of `SFNBuckets` that can be accomodated is 254, so the file system has a capacity for 65024 files.

Each block of memory referenced by a `SFNBucket` contains 256 8-byte structures. The first member of the structure is the owner's process ID (*pid*, in Figure 6-3) and the second member is a pointer to a `fhandle` structure (*pfh*, in Figure 6-3). A ring-0 file handle, such as that used by the **IFSMgr_Ring0_FileIO** service, is the address of a `fhandle` structure. The service **IFSMgr_Win32_Get_Ring0_Handle** is used to convert an extended file handle to a ring-0 handle, i.e., given an SFN it returns the address of its `fhandle` structure.

Descriptions of the members of the `fhandle` structure are given in Appendix C. The first four members of fhandle are provided by the FSD. When a file is opened on a volume, the volume's FSD returns three pointers: a pointer to a read function, **fh_hf.hf_read**; a pointer to a write function, **fh_hf.hf_write**; and a pointer to the table of other handle-based functions, **fh_hf.hf_misc**. The FSD also returns a unique handle, *fh_fh*, which is then passed to the FSD on future calls for this file. As with its shell resource counterpart, *fh_fh* is not interpreted by IFSMgr; it is simply treated as a "magic cookie."

The contents of the FSD's handle-based function table is shown in Table 6-7. At the head of the table, version and revision are given first, followed by the table size and then the actual function entries (this structure is defined in *ifs.h*). The corresponding **FS_** function name for each table entry is also shown. Note that the functions **FS_ReadFile** and **FS_WriteFile** correspond to the members *hf_read* and *hf_write* and are not included in the table pointed to by **fh_hf.hf_misc**.

Table 6-7. Handle-Based Function Table

Table Entry	Value
hm_version	IFS version (030Ah)
hm_revision	IFS interface revision (10h)
hm_size	8
hm_func[HM_SEEK]	FS_FileSeek
hm_func[HM_CLOSE]	FS_CloseFile
hm_func[HM_COMMIT]	FS_CommitFile
hm_func[HM_FILELOCKS]	FS_LockFile
hm_func[HM_FILETIMES]	FS_FileDateTime
hm_func[HM_PIPEREQUEST]	FS_NamedPipeRequest
hm_func[HM_HANDLEINFO]	FS_NetHandleInfo
hm_func[HM_ENUMHANDLE]	FS_EnumerateHandle

The FSD function **FS_FindFirstFile** is similar to a file open (**FS_OpenFile**). It returns addresses of *hf_read*, *hf_write*, and *hf_misc* members but their contents are different. In this case, *hf_read* contains the address of a **FS_FindNextFile** function, and *hf_write* is not defined, so it is set to an error function. Most of the entries in the table *hf_misc* are filled with the address of an error function, the two exceptions being *HM_CLOSE*, which contains the address of an **FS_FindClose** function, and *HM_ENUMHANDLE*, which contains a pointer to a **FS_Enumerate-Handle** function.

Calling into a File System Driver

Now that we know about these FSD function tables, we can re-examine the use of **Call_FSD** in **dGetVolInfo**. Here is the call into **Call_FSD** as it appears in assembly language:

```
push   00
push   esi
push   +27
mov    eax,dword ptr [esi+7c]
mov    eax,dword ptr [eax+0c]
push   dword ptr [eax+24]
call   Call_FSD
add    esp,+10
```

ESI is a pointer to an **ifsreq** packet, *pifs*, and [ESI+7c] references its member *ifs_psr*, the shell resource. EAX is assigned the address of the **shres** structure, so [EAX+0c] references its member, *sr_func*, the **volfunc** structure. Finally, the function at offset 24h in the structure is pushed on the stack as an argument. This corresponds to *sr_func->vfn_func[VFN_QUERY]*. In C the function call would look like this:

```
Call_FSD( pifs->ifs_psr->sr_func->vfn_func[VFN_QUERY],
        IFSFN_QUERY, pifs, FALSE );
```

The constant *IFSFN_QUERY* is part of an enumeration of FSD functions that IFSMgr uses. These are defined in *ifs.h*.

The volume-based call was straightforward. Now let's take a look at a handle-based call from the dispatch handler: **dByHandleInfo**. Here is the call into **Call_FSD** as it appears in assembly language:

```
push   00
push   esi
push   +11
mov    eax,dword ptr [esi+74]
mov    eax,dword ptr [eax+08]
push   dword ptr [eax+20]
call   Call_FSD
add    esp,+10
```

ESI is a pointer to an **ioreq** packet, *pifs*, and [ESI+74] references its member *ifs_pfh*, the **fhandle** structure. EAX is assigned the address of the **fhandle** structure, so [EAX+08] references its member, *fh_hf->hf_misc*, the handle-based function table. Finally, the function at offset 20h in *hf_misc* is pushed on the stack as an argument. This corresponds to *fh_hf->hf_misc.hm_func[HM_ENUMHANDLE]*. In C the function call would look like this:

```
Call_FSD( pifs->ifs_pfh->fh_hf->hf_misc.hm_func[HM_ENUMHANDLE],
        IFSFN_ENUMHANDLE, pifs, FALSE );
```

From these two examples, we see that the first argument to **Call_FSD** is the address of either a volume-based or handle-based FSD function. The other arguments include a constant which identifies the FSD function, a pointer to the `ifsreq` packet, and a Boolean. To gain some further insight into this function, take a look at its pseudocode in Example 6-3.

Call_FSD is just a wrapper around the call to the FSD function which is passed as the first argument. **Call_FSD** decides whether or not to call a file system API hook rather than making a direct call to the FSD. The Boolean argument *bHookLock* plays a role in making this decision. If *bHookLock* is FALSE, which is the most common situation, the file system API hook will *not* be called if the volume referenced by the `ifsreq` packet has a lock on it.

Example 6-3. Pseudocode for Call_FSD

```
#define ALLRES   (IFSFH_RES_UNC|IFSFH_RES_NETWORK|
                  IFSFH_RES_LOCAL|IFSFH_RES_CFSD)

int Call_FSD( pIFSFunc FSDFnAdr,int Func,ifsreq* pifs,BOOL bHookLock ){
  fhandle* pfh = pifs->ifs_pfh;
  shres* psr = pifs->ifs_psr;
  DWORD flags, drive, retc;
  BOOL bCallHook = bHookLock;

  if ( bHookLock ) // decide if hook will be called
    if ( !psr->sr_LockType ) bCallHook = FALSE;
  else if ( !psr->sr_LockType )
    bCallHook = TRUE;

  // If a file system API hook has been installed ...
  if ( pFSHook != NULL && bCallHook ) {
    if ( Func==IFSFN_CLOSE || Func==IFSFN_READ ) {
      if ( pfh->fh_type & 0x0c ) {
        if ( Func==IFSFN_CLOSE ) Func=IFSFN_FINDCLOSE;
        else Func=IFSFN_FINDNEXT;
        if ( pfh->fh_type & 0x08 ) {
          if ( Func==IFSFN_CLOSE ) Func=IFSFN_FCNCLOSE;
          else Func=IFSFN_FCNNEXT;
          }
        }
      }
    flags = psr->sr_flags;
    if ( flags & IFSFH_RES_NETWORK ) {
      if ( Func <= IFSFN_ENUMHANDLE ) drive =0xffffffff;
      else drive = pifs->ifs_drv;
      }
    else drive = psr->sr_uword + 1;

    if ( Func == IFSFN_CONNECT && D1_6844 )
      drive = pifs->ifs_drv + 1;

    _asm  inc cntHookCalls
```

Example 6-3. Pseudocode for Call_FSD (continued)

```
    retc = (*pFSHook)( FSDFnAdr, Func, drive,
            flags & ALLRES,
            pifs->ifs_nflags & (BCS_WANSI|BCS_OEM),
            pifs );
    _asm   dec cntHookCalls

    _asm   cmp claimHookerList,0
    _asm   jz  not_claimed
    _asm   cmp cntHookCalls,0
    _asm   jnz not_claimed
    _asm   mov claimHookerList,0
    IFSMgr_WakeUp( &claimHookerList );
   not_claimed:
    return retc;
    }


    // No hook call - call direct to FSD
    return (*FSDFnAdr)(pifs);
    }
```

If it is decided that the file system hook will be called, then some additional work is needed to prepare the arguments to the hook function. Here is a prototype for this function:

```
    int FileSystemApiHookFunction( pIFSFunc FSDFnAddr, int FunctionNum,
                                   int Drive, int ResourceFlags,
                                   int CodePage, pioreq pir );
```

The first argument is simply the address of the FSD function to be called. The second argument is the function number being called. This is the same as the second argument to **Call_FSD** and would be *IFSFN_QUERY* or *IFSFN_ENUM-HANDLE* in the examples shown above. There are some special cases, however. If the second argument to **Call_FSD** is either *IFSFN_CLOSE* or *IFSFN_READ*, these may need to be translated. For *IFSFN_CLOSE*, *IFSFN_FINDCLOSE* or *IFSFN_FCNCLOSE* may be substituted if the `fhandle` indicates it refers to a find or file change handle. Similarly, *IFSFN_READ* may be replaced with *IFSFN_FINDNEXT* or *IFSFN_FCNNEXT*, if appropriate.

The drive argument for a local drive is derived from the *sr_uword* member of the shell resource. This is a zero-based drive number so one is added to it. If the drive is remote, the drive is set to –1 for functions less than *IFSFN_ENUMHANDLE*; otherwise the drive number in the `ifsreq` packet is used. The *ResourceFlags* argument is the value of the *sr_flags* member of the shell resource ANDed with the mask ALLRES. The *CodePage* is determined by the corresponding bits in the `ifsreq` member *ifs_nflags*.

Before each call into the file system hook, the global variable *cntHookCalls* is incremented; when the file system hook returns, this count is decremented. If this variable is zero, there are no calls executing or blocked which were initiated from the file system hook chain. A related global variable, *claimHookerList*, is a syncronization primitive used to control access to the list of installed file system hooks. When either **IFSMgr_InstallFileSystemApiHook** or **IFSMgr_RemoveFileSystemApiHook** attempt to modify the hook list, the critical section around the hook list needs to be claimed. If *cntHookCalls* is non-zero, then these services block until all pending hook calls complete. Threads are blocked waiting for this critical section when *claimHookerList* is non-zero. The blocked threads are awakened by the call **IFSMgr_WakeUp**(&*claimHookerList*), once *cntHookCalls* drops to zero.

FSDs as Providers

The idea of a "provider" stems from the WOSA (Windows Open System Architecture) concept of a SP and SPI, a service provider and service provider interface. IFSMgr and its file system drivers are part of the WOSA-SPI layer, and thus are considered service providers. During the Device Init stage of system initialization, each FSD registers with IFSMgr using one of the registration services and thereby establishes its provider ID. There are four types of providers that an FSD can supply and these have distinct registration functions: **IFSMgr_RegisterMount** for local drives, **IFSMgr_RegisterNet** for remote drives, **IFSMgr_RegisterCFSD** for character devices, and **IFSMgr_RegisterMailSlot** for mailslots. Each of these registration functions returns a provider ID on success.

IFSMgr_RegisterMount allows up to ten providers to register with it. A FSD supplies its type when it registers, either NORMAL_FSD or DEFAULT_FSD. Only one FSD is allowed to register with type DEFAULT_FSD; this FSD is used to mount a drive if all other FSDs refuse to mount it. The provider IDs which **IFSMgr_RegisterMount** returns are in the range 0 through 9, with 0 reserved for a DEFAULT_FSD. On each call to **IFSMgr_RegisterMount**, the supplied FSD function address is added to a table (`MountVolTable[]`). Later, when a local disk volume is mounted, this table will be consulted to find a potential **FS_MountVolume** function.

IFSMgr_RegisterNet allows up to eight providers to register with it. A FSD supplies its Net ID when it registers. The provider IDs which **IFSMgr_RegisterNet** returns are in the range 0Ah through 11h. On each call to **IFSMgr_RegisterNet**, the supplied FSD function address is added to a table (`ConnectNetTable[]`) and the supplied Net ID is also added to another parallel table (`NetIDs[]`). Later, when a connection is attempted, the `ConnectNetTable` table will be consulted to find a potential **FS_ConnectNetResource** function.

Enumerating Shell Resources and fhandles

To make it easy to examine the system shell resources and **fhandles**, a couple of windows utilities are included on the companion diskette. *sr.exe* displays shell resource structures for all drives reported by a call to the Win32 API **GetLogicalDrives**. Figure 6-4 displays some sample output.

Drive	Sr Address	sr_sig	sr_idx	sr_next	sr_func	sr_inUse	sr_uword	sr_HndCnt	sr_flags	sr_Proid
A	c105d094	Sr	04	c0fd4d4c	c002ae44 (VDEF(01) + 000001D4)	00000002	0000	0000	10	00000000
C	c1021e74	Sr	00	00000000	c001fde8 (VFAT(01) + 00000F54)	00000086	0002	0084	10	00000002
D	c0fd4d4c	Sr	02	c1038950	c001fde8 (VFAT(01) + 00000F54)	0000001a	0003	0018	10	00000002
E	c1038950	Sr	01	c1021e74	c001fde8 (VFAT(01) + 00000F54)	0000000c	0004	000a	10	00000002
F	c1074718	Sr	05	c105d094	c001fde8 (VFAT(01) + 00000F54)	00000002	0005	0000	10	00000002
G	c10cd6e4	Sr	03	c1074718	c0fd7554 (CDFS(01) + 00000944)	00000004	0006	0002	10	00000001
K	c107f1d4	Sr	06	00000000	c00379d0 (VREDIR(01) + 00004818)	00000004	0000	0002	09	0000000a

Figure 6-4. SR sample output

Each column in Figure 6-4 corresponds to a member of the **shres** structure (see Appendix C for details) with the exception of the Drive and Sr Address columns which contain the drive letter and the address of each line's **shres** structure, respectively. The shell resource structures are arranged in a singly linked list; the links are shown in the *sr_next* column. The lists for local drives and remote drives are kept separately. The *sr_func* column contains the address of this drive's volume-based function table. The address is decomposed into the FSD's name, segment, and address, The system that this output was produced on has a floppy drive A which has not had a floppy inserted since system startup. Until it sees some media inserted, the default FSD is used: VDEF. The other local drives all use VFAT except for a CD-ROM which is using the CDFS driver. A connection to *SERVER**SERVER_C* is mapped to drive K and it is represented by the MSNet redirector VREDIR. Note that each of these FSDs has a unique provider ID given in the *sr_Proid* column.

If you run ScanDisk on a volume and at the same time capture output from *sr.exe*, you will see results like those in Figure 6-5. You may refresh the SR display while the ScanDisk operation proceeds, by selecting **Refresh** from the **Operations** menu. In this case, ScanDisk is being executed on drive D. The *sr_LockType* column shows the type of volume lock currently active, with 0 corresponding to none, 1 to a level 0, 2 to a level 1, 3 to a level 2, etc. It is interesting that the *sr_func* column now indicates that IFSMgr owns the volume function table for this drive; the original function table address is stored in *sr_LockSavFunc*. This reflects the fact that IFSMgr takes over the function tables for drives that are volume locked.

Shell Resources

Operations About

Drive	sr_serial	sr_func	sr_uword	sr_flags	sr_LockPid	sr_LockSavFunc	sr_LockType	sr_LockFlags
A	00	c002ae44 (VDEF(01) + 000001D4)	0000	10	00000000	00000000	00	0000
C	00	c001fde8 (VFAT(01) + 00000F54)	0002	10	00000000	00000000	00	0002
D	25	c001e6ec (IFSMGR(01) + 00006AD8)	0003	10	000121a3	c001fde8	03	0022
E	00	c001fde8 (VFAT(01) + 00000F54)	0004	10	00000000	00000000	00	0002
F	00	c001fde8 (VFAT(01) + 00000F54)	0005	10	00000000	00000000	00	0002
G	00	c0fd7554 (CDFS(01) + 00000944)	0006	10	00000000	00000000	00	0000
K	0f	c00379d0 (VREDIR(01) + 00004818)	0000	09	00000000	00000000	00	0000

Figure 6-5. SR output with volume lock

To retrieve the shell resource, *sr.exe* relies upon a dynamically-loaded VxD, *volsr.vxd*. This virtual driver supports a **DeviceIoControl** interface. A shell resource structure is requested from VOLSR by supplying it with a drive number and a buffer in which to copy the structure. VOLSR retrieves the `shres` by installing a file system hook and the calling **IFSMgr_Ring0_FileIO** to get the drive's the root directory attributes. When the **FS_FileAttributes** call is detected at the hook, the `shres` structure passed in via *ifs_psr* member of the `ifsreq` structure is copied. When the **IFSMgr_Ring0_FileIO** call completes, the file system hook is removed and the results are returned to SR.

Another windows utility, *fh.exe*, displays `fhandle` structures for currently open files on a specified volume. Each column in Figure 6-6 corresponds to a member of the `fhandle` structure (see Appendix C for details) with the exception of the *sfn*, Pathname, and *pfh* columns which contain the system file number, the associated pathname, and the address of each line's `fhandle` structure, respectively. You may select a different drive or refresh the FH display by selecting the corresponding option from the **Operations** menu.

Open Files (fhandles) on Drive C

Operations About

sfn	Pathname	pfh	fh_devflags	fh_type	fh_ref_count	fh_mode	fh_prev	fh_next	fh_sfn	fh_mmsfn	fh_pid
021c	\WINDOWS\SYSTEM\USER32.DLL	c1061bcc	0042	42	0001	00a0	c1061ce4	c105fc78	021c	0000	0001166d
021a	\WINDOWS\SYSTEM\USER.EXE	c105fc78	0042	02	0001	0080	c1061bcc	c105fb60	021a	0000	0001181d
0218	\WINDOWS\FONTS\VGAOEM.FON	c105fb60	0042	02	0001	0080	c105fc78	c105fa48	0218	0000	0001181d
0217	\WINDOWS\FONTS\VGAFIX.FON	c105fa48	0042	02	0001	0080	c105fb60	c105f930	0217	0000	0001181d
0216	\WINDOWS\FONTS\VGASYS.FON	c105f930	0042	02	0001	0080	c105fa48	c105f614	0216	0000	0001181d
0215	\WINDOWS\SYSTEM\ADVAPI32.DLL	c105f614	0042	42	0001	00a0	c105f930	c105f4fc	0215	0000	0001166d
0214	\WINDOWS\SYSTEM\GDI32.DLL	c105f4fc	0042	42	0001	00a0	c105f614	c105f3d4	0214	0000	0001166d
0213	\WINDOWS\SYSTEM\GDI.EXE	c105f3d4	0042	02	0001	0080	c105f4fc	c105f2bc	0213	0000	0001181d
0212	\WINDOWS\SYSTEM\COMM.DRV	c105f2bc	0042	02	0001	0080	c105f3d4	c105f1a4	0212	0000	0001181d
0211	\WINDOWS\SYSTEM\MMSOUND.DRV	c105f1a4	0042	02	0001	0080	c105f2bc	c105f08c	0211	0000	0001181d
0210	\WINDOWS\SYSTEM\DIBENG.DLL	c105f08c	0042	02	0001	0080	c105f1a4	c105ef74	0210	0000	0001181d
020f	\WINDOWS\SYSTEM\DMSSTL3D.DRV	c105ef74	0042	02	0001	0080	c105f08c	c105ee5c	020f	0000	0001181d
020d	\WINDOWS\SYSTEM\MOUSE.DRV	c105ee5c	0042	02	0001	0080	c105ef74	c0fd04dc	020d	0000	0001181d
020c	\WINDOWS\SYSTEM\KEYBOARD.DRV	c0fd04dc	0042	02	0001	0080	c105ee5c	c0fde538	020c	0000	0001181d
020b	\WINDOWS\SYSTEM\SYSTEM.DRV	c0fde538	0042	02	0001	0080	c0fd04dc	c0fd00c0	020b	0000	0001181d
0208	\WINDOWS\SYSTEM\UNICODE.NLS	c0fd00c0	0042	22	0001	00a0	c0fde538	c1039c10	0208	0209	0001181d
0206	\WINDOWS\SYSTEM\LOCALE.NLS	c1039c10	0042	22	0001	00a0	c0fd00c0	c1039ac4	0206	0207	0001181d
0204	\WINDOWS\SYSTEM\CP_437.NLS	c1039ac4	0042	22	0001	00a0	c1039c10	c1039188	0204	0205	0001181d
0202	\WINDOWS\SYSTEM\CP_1252.NLS	c1039188	0042	22	0001	00a0	c1039ac4	c0fd57d4	0202	0203	0001181d
0201	\WINDOWS\SYSTEM\KERNEL32.DLL	c0fd57d4	0042	42	0001	00a0	c1039188	00000000	0201	0000	0001181d

Figure 6-6. Sample FH Output

The first few entries of the list of files open on a system drive (drive C) are shown in Figure 6-6. The numbers in the *sfn* column appear to have gaps in the sequence. In some cases this is because the file was opened as a memory-mapped file. A memory-mapped has two handles refer to it, the initial `fhandle` used to open it (*fh_sfn*) and a duplicate handle used for the memory-mapping (*fh_mmsfn*).

To retrieve a list of open files on a volume, *fh.exe* relies upon a dynamically loaded VxD, *filefh.vxd*. This virtual driver supports a **DeviceIoControl** interface. A list of open files is requested of FILEFH by supplying it with volume number and a buffer in which to copy the `fhandle` structures and associated file names. FILEFH creates the list by first installing a file system hook and then requesting a level 1 volume lock on the specified volume. One of the activities associated with acquiring a level 1 lock is to build a list of open files on the volume. To do this, the volume locking function (interrupt 21h, function 440dh, subfunction 084ah) calls **FS_EnumerateHandle** repeatedly to get the names of all the open handles associated with the volume. As each **FS_EnumerateHandle** call comes in, the *ifs_pfh* and *ir_sfn* members of the `ifsreq` structure are copied. After the **FS_EnumerateHandle** call completes, the filename is also copied. When the volume lock function completes, the volume is immediately unlocked and the file system hook is removed. One advantage of using a volume lock to get the file list is that it creates a snapshot at one instant in time.

7

In this chapter:
• *The File System API Hook*
• *The NetFunction Hook*
• *Hooking a Path*

Monitoring File Activity

IFSMgr provides at least three methods for hooking file system notifications. The most general technique is to install a file system API hook. This method allows an application to see much of the `ifsreq` packet traffic that passes through to file system drivers. This method can also change the way a request is handled, and so can serve to override the behavior of a FSD. Another source of notifications can be tapped by installing a hook (using **Hook_Device_Service**) on the service **IFSMgr_NetFunction**. IFSMgr makes various internal broadcasts through this function, such as when a drive appears in a system or when a drive goes away. This service is also called when a "hooked" Int 21h function is called. Here, the term "hooked" means that a preamble has been installed for an Int 21h function which is greater than 71h. Some Int 2fh functions also generate events here. Yet another source of notifications can be received by way of **IFSMgr_ParsePath** (or **IFSMgr_ FSDParsePath**) to allow a FSD installed path checking routine to get a first crack at parsing a path. This path checking routine is installed with the service **IFSMgr_ SetPathHook**.

The File System API Hook

One of the most popular IFS features is the file system hook. This hook provides functionality similar to an Int 21h hook under DOS and Windows 3.x. Unlike its DOS/Windows 3.x counterpart, there are a variety of APIs (besides Int 21h) that ultimately pass through a file system hook. The hook gets called whenever the dispatch handler for a particular function calls into a file system driver via **Call_ FSD**. Unlike the Int 21h hook, the file system hook will only see file-related calls so it is not appropriate for every need.

A file system API hook is installed using the IFSMgr service **IFSMgr_InstallFileSystemApiHook**. Once it is installed, it is not permanent, it can be removed using the companion service **IFSMgr_RemoveFileSystemApiHook**. This makes it easy for a dynamic VxD to install and remove a file system hook as an adjunct to a Win32 application. However, we will find it useful to install a file system hook during Device Init so we can track events during system startup.

Under what conditions is the file system hook called? Generally, any file system request, either local or remote, will pass through the installed hook function. The hook will also see activity on any character FSDs, such as LPTn and PRN of *spooler.vxd* and PIPESTDX of *vcond.vxd*. **IFSMgr_Ring0FileIO** and **IFSMgr_Server-DOSCall** services are also routed through the file system hook.

Having said that, you should be aware of some exceptions. IFSMgr does not always use **Call_FSD** as the gateway into file system drivers. For instance, there are circumstances where **FS_MountVolume** is called directly using the addresses in `MountVolTable[]`. Similarly, **FS_ConnectNetResource** sometimes is called directly through `ConnectNetTable[]`.

Even if **Call_FSD** is used, recall that one argument to that function controls whether a file hook will be called when a volume lock is taken. So, if a volume lock is in place you won't see the FSD calls on that volume. Another peculiarity occurs with the functions that support file change notifications. The **FindFirstFile-ChangeNotification** call does not go through the file system hook although the **FindNextChangeNotification** and **FindCloseChangeNotification** functions do. Although, some "change" notification functions do go through the file system hook, they do not get serviced by a file system driver; rather they are routed back into IFSMgr.

A file system hook has this interface:

```
int FileSystemApiHookFunction( pIFSFunc FSDFnAddr,
                               int FunctionNum, int Drive,
                               int ResourceFlags, int CodePage,
                               pioreq pir )
```

We saw this function called in the routine **Call_FSD** in the previous chapter.

The first argument, *FSDFnAddr*, is simply the address of the function to call in the FSD. It corresponds to one of the addresses in the volume-based or handle-based tables (see Table 6-6 and Table 6-7). Most commonly this address resides in another VxD, although there are cases where this address will reside in IFSMgr (the change notification functions and the mailslot functions).

The value of the *FunctionNum* argument tells us which FSD function is being called. There is a mapping between the set of *FunctionNum* values and the entries in the FSD's volume-based and handle-based function tables. Table 7-1, later in the chapter, shows this relationship. There are two exceptions to this rule: *IFSFN_FCNNEXT* and *IFSFN_FCNCLOSE* do not have FSD functions corresponding to them. This is because the support for file change notifications is done entirely within IFSMgr without the participation of FSDs. Still, these functions are sent down the file system hook before being processed by IFSMgr, and IFSMgr has an internal handle-based function table which is referenced by the `fhandle` structure which **FindFirstChangeNotification** creates. **FindFirstChangeNotification** is not sent down to the file system hook, so there is no *FunctionNum* corresponding to it.

The third argument, *Drive*, is the 1-based volume number to which the function refers. If the volume resource is a UNC name, this argument has the value −1. There are situations where *Drive* can have the value 0. This may happen when the target resource is a character FSD. In general, you can think of *Drive* as corresponding to *ir_rh*, the resource handle, and *ifs_psr*, the address of the shell resource structure.

The fourth argument, *ResourceFlags*, is a collection of four bits extracted from the shell resource that indicate whether the resource is a character FSD, whether it is local, whether it is remote, and whether it is represented by a UNC name.

The *CodePage* argument indicates which of the ANSI or OEM code page character sets should be used with the function. The corresponding manifest constants are *BCS_WANSI* and *BCS_OEM*.

The last argument, *pir*, is a pointer to the `ioreq` or `ifsreq` structure. This is the only argument passed to the FSD. The other arguments here are provided as a convenience to the file hook.

So what can a file system hook do when it gets called? Here is what Microsoft says, in *DOS/Win32 Installable File System Specification*, p. 70:

> The hooker gets control before the FSD is called to perform the function and it can do anything it wants. Hookers can do one of four things when they get called on a hooked call:
>
> — Ignore the call and chain on to the previous hooker in the hook chain.
>
> — Process the call and return directly to the IFS manager.
>
> — Change the call or make multiple calls to the FSD directly, and then return to the IFS manager.
>
> — It can call down the chain and do some processing on the way back.
>
> Basically, the hooker has complete control over how it wants to process the call.

From this description it would appear that anything is possible in a hook function. The documentation does not elaborate on how to go about making "multiple calls to the FSD directly." It does hint that:

> The preferred method for hookers to perform other functions while on a hooked call is to use the ring-0 APIs. It is usually quite safe to issue a ring-0 API call while on a file system API hook; the IFS manager is re-entrant.

These statements bear a closer examination. Re-entrancy comes into play in at least four possible ways:

- A thread executing a dispatch routine is blocked waiting for results. While it is blocked other threads may continue to execute within the dispatch routines.

- A thread may deliberately re-enter the dispatch point by calling a ring-0 API such as **IFSMgr_Ring0_FileIO** or **IFSMgr_ServerDOSCall** from a file system API hook.

- While executing a dispatch function, a page fault occurs as part of normal system paging activity; the file system may be re-entered to read-in or write-out pages.

- If a thread is executing in a dispatch routine and a thread switch occurs which causes the newly scheduled thread to also execute a dispatch routine.

By "ring-0 API call" one would have to consider that both **IFSMgr_Ring0_FileIO** and **IFSMgr_ServerDOSCall** are fair game. An equally attractive alternative is to perform a direct call into the FSD without performing re-entrant calls to the dispatch point. This requires that we use our knowledge of undocumented fields in the `ifsreq` structure, namely *ifs_psr* and *ifs_pfh*, to access the volume-based and handle-based function tables. It is clear that this is what is implied in the statement "make multiple calls to the FSD directly." We'll work through a few examples to give you a feel for these different approaches.

FSHook

FSHook is a file system API hook that reports all FSD calls to MultiMon for display. Its predecessor, FILEMON, was the basis for an article on monitoring file system activity in Windows 95 that appeared in what was then called *Windows/ DOS Developer's Journal* ("Monitoring Windows 95 File System Activity in Ring 0," July 1995; now *Windows Developer's Journal*). The file monitor presented here is much improved. It is configurable through MultiMon's filter settings; it spools its output to a file for later display and the spooler file is accessed using ring-0 APIs. These changes eliminate the buffer overrun problems that FILEMON had. FSHook output can be combined with other monitor output to gain a multidimensional picture of system activity.

FSHook displays one line of output for each FSD call. Each FSD call is identified by a function number (see Table 7-1 for a list of possible values). Output from FSHook tends to be rather lengthy if all functions are included, so usually it helps to filter out Read, Write, and Seek functions. Figure 7-1 contains a trace fragment that was collected during the system's response to a right mouse-button click on the icon for drive A, when the drive did not contain a floppy diskette. The first column, which contains "Explorer," is the process which was executing when the call was made. *fsh* is an identifier for file system hook entries in the trace. The next column contains the name of the operation; here we see **FS_MountVolume** for **IFSFN_CONNECT**, **FS_Ioctl16Drive** for **IFSFN_IOCTL16DRIVE**, and **FS_FileAttribs** for **IFSFN_FILEATTRIB**. The dispatch function (**ifs_func**) associated with an operation is shown in parentheses. The Flags1 column shows the settings for **ifs_nflags** and the *ResourceFlags* passed in to the file hook function. For the **FS_MountVolume** entries, *ifs_func* and *ifs_nflags* are both 0, indicating that these FSD calls did not directly originate from a dispatch call; rather, they were "spun off" to bring the volume online. For the **FS_FileAttributes** entries we see the dispatch function 43h, which corresponds to the Int 21h function number for getting or setting file attributes. The *ifs_nflags* indicate two conditions accompany this function. It is a long filename call (**L**) and it uses extended handles (**X**), i.e., this was Int 21h function 7143h. The first five characters in the Flags1 column are a sequence of 5 letters, **eclnu**. An **e** indicates the call reported an error, a **c** indicates the call is to a character FSD, an **l** indicates the call is to a local FSD, an **n** indicates the call is to a network FSD, and a **u** indicates that the remote volume is referenced by an UNC name. From this we see that all of the **FS_MountVolume** function calls for drive A have failed. The Device column gives the name of the FSD which was called. Here we see an attempt to mount drive A through VFAT, but that fails. The next available local FSD is VDEF, the default FSD. A mount is attempted through its **FS_MountVolume**, and it also fails. If there were additional local FSDs in the system, they would be called before VDEF. Finally, we see the call to **FS_FileAttributes** getting passed to VDEF and it fails. The **Gt** signifies get attributes and "A:" is the path for which the attributes are requested.

Table 7-1. FSD Function Numbers

FunctionNum	FSD Function	IFS Specification API
IFSFN_READ (0)	hf_read	FS_ReadFile
IFSFN_WRITE (1)	hf_write	FS_WriteFile
IFSFN_FINDNEXT (2)	hf_read	FS_FindNextFile
IFSFN_FCNNEXT (3)	hf_read	- - - - - -
IFSFN_SEEK (10)	hm_func[HM_SEEK]	FS_FileSeek
IFSFN_CLOSE (11)	hm_func[HM_CLOSE]	FS_Close
IFSFN_COMMIT (12)	hm_func[HM_COMMIT]	FS_CommitFile
IFSFN_FILELOCKS (13)	hm_func[HM_FILELOCKS]	FS_LockFile
IFSFN_FILETIMES (14)	hm_func[HM_FILETIMES]	FS_FileDateTime
IFSFN_PIPEREQUEST (15)	hm_func[HM_PIPEREQUEST]	FS_NamedPipeRequest
IFSFN_HANDLEINFO (16)	hm_func[HM_HANDLEINFO]	FS_NetHandleInfo
IFSFN_ENUMHANDLE (17)	hm_func[HM_ENUMHANDLE]	FS_EnumerateHandle
IFSFN_FINDCLOSE (18)	hm_func[HM_CLOSE]	FS_FindClose

Table 7-1. FSD Function Numbers (continued)

FunctionNum	FSD Function	IFS Specification API
IFSFN_FCNCLOSE (19)	hm_func[HM_CLOSE]	- - - - -
IFSFN_CONNECT (30)	MountVolTable[], NetConnectTable[], ...	**FS_MountVolume, FS_ConnectNetResource**
IFSFN_DELETE (31)	vfn_func[VFN_DELETE]	**FS_DeleteFile**
IFSFN_DIR (32)	vfn_func[VFN_DIR]	**FS_Dir**
IFSFN_FILEATTRIB (33)	vfn_func[VFN_FILEATTRIB]	**FS_FileAttributes**
IFSFN_FLUSH (34)	vfn_func[VFN_FLUSH]	**FS_FlushVolume**
IFSFN_GETDISKINFO (35)	vfn_func[VFN_GETDISKINFO]	**FS_GetDiskInfo**
IFSFN_OPEN (36)	vfn_func[VFN_OPEN]	**FS_OpenFile**
IFSFN_RENAME (37)	vfn_func[VFN_RENAME]	**FS_RenameFile**
IFSFN_SEARCH (38)	vfn_func[VFN_SEARCH]	**FS_SearchFile**
IFSFN_QUERY (39)	vfn_func[VFN_QUERY]	**FS_QueryResourceInfo**
IFSFN_DISCONNECT (40)	vfn_func[VFN_DISCONNECT]	**FS_DisconnectResource**
IFSFN_UNCPIPEREQ (41)	vfn_func[VFN_UNCPIPEREQ]	**FS_NamedPipeUNCRequest**
IFSFN_IOCTL16DRIVE (42)	vfn_func[VFN_IOCTL16DRIVE]	**FS_Ioctl16Drive**
IFSFN_GETDISKPARMS (43)	vfn_func[VFN_GETDISKPARMS]	**FS_GetDiskParms**
IFSFN_FINDOPEN (44)	vfn_func[VFN_FINDOPEN]	**FS_FindFirstFile**
IFSFN_DASDIO (45)	vfn_func[VFN_DASDIO]	**FS_DirectDiskIO**

Module	Type	Function	Flags1	Device	Args	Flags2
Explorer	fsh	FS_MountVolume (00)	E_clnu_slxrmwoa	VDEF	drive: A	m
Explorer	fsh	FS_Ioctl16Drive (440d)	e_cLnu_slxrmwoA	VDEF	drive: A	
Explorer	fsh	FS_FileAttributes (43)	e_cLnu_sLXrmwoa	VFAT	C:\WIN...	Gt
Explorer	fsh	FS_MountVolume (00)	E_clnu_slxrmwoa	VDEF	drive: A	m
Explorer	fsh	FS_Ioctl16Drive (4408)	e_cLnu_slXrmwoa	VDEF	drive: A	
Explorer	fsh	FS_MountVolume (00)	E_clnu_slxrmwoa	VFAT	drive: A	m
Explorer	fsh	FS_MountVolume (00)	E_clnu_slxrmwoa	VDEF	drive: A	m
Explorer	fsh	FS_FileAttributes (43)	E_cLnu_sLXrmwoa	VDEF	A:	Gt
Explorer	fsh	FS_MountVolume (00)	E_clnu_slxrmwoa	VFAT	drive: A	m
Explorer	fsh	FS_MountVolume (00)	E_clnu_slxrmwoa	VDEF	drive: A	m
Explorer	fsh	FS_FileAttributes (43)	E_cLnu_sLXrmwoa	VDEF	A:	Gt
Explorer	fsh	FS_FileAttributes (43)	e_cLnu_sLXrmwoa	VFAT	C:\WIN...	Gt

Figure 7-1. MultiMon/FSHook sample output.

Figure 7-2 shows another sample fragment. Here we see a sequence of **FS_Read-File** calls on a local volume supported by the VFAT FSD. For **FS_ReadFile** and **FS_WriteFile** functions, the FSD name is followed by system file number, some function arguments, and another set of flags in the Flags2 column. The possible characters in the Flags2 column are msn, where an m indicates a memory-mapped file access, an s indicates a swap file access, and an n indicates that caching should *not* be used on the call. What is significant about the calls in this sample is that they are reads from the paging file and they all have a system file number of 200h, the base value for the range of extended file handles. Also notice the value of the dispatch function (d6h) and the R flag under Flags1. These indicate that the read originated as an **IFSMgr_Ring0_FileIO** call.

Module	Type	Function	Flags1	Device	Handle	Args	Flags2
Explorer	fsh	FS_ReadFile (d6)	e_cLnu_sLxRmwoa	VFAT	200	cnt=1000H ofs=388000H ptr=c135f000H	-sn
Explorer	fsh	FS_ReadFile (d6)	e_cLnu_sLxRmwoa	VFAT	200	cnt=1000H ofs=373000H ptr=c135f000H	-sn
Explorer	fsh	FS_ReadFile (d6)	e_cLnu_sLxRmwoa	VFAT	200	cnt=1000H ofs=372000H ptr=c135f000H	-sn

Figure 7-2. A second MultiMon/FSHook sample fragment

For a complete reference to the meanings of the various fields in FSHook output, see Appendix B, *MultiMon: Monitor Reference.*

To ease implementation of FSHook (and other samples), all of the IFSMgr services have been wrapped as C-callable routines and made available through *ifswraps.clb.* (For more information see Appendix D, *IFS Development Aids.*)

The simplest scenario for installing a file system hook would start with a call to **IFSMgr_InstallFileSystemApiHook** during Device Init phase. This function takes the address of the hook function to be installed and returns the address of the previous hook function you chain onto. Example 7-1 shows the simplest possible hook function, where **ppPrevHook** is a pointer to the previous hook function. It simply calls the previous hook function and returns.

Example 7-1. Simplest File System Hook

```
int __cdecl FileHook( pIFSFunc pfn, int fn, int drv,
                      int res, int cp, pioreq pir ) {
    return (*(*ppPrevHook))(pfn, fn, drv, res, cp, pir);
    }
```

In response to System VM Terminate, your driver would remove this hook by calling **IFSMgr_RemoveFileSystemApiHook** and passing it the address of your file hook routine.

The **FileHook** function used by FSHook examines the function number to determine the type of function call and fills in an event structure describing the function call. When the call into the previous hook function returns, the error status and sometimes other values are retrieved and added to the event structure before it is sent to MultiMon. FSHook uses a passive hook; it doesn't attempt to modify the call or to make additional calls into the FSD. To see how one might make additional calls into the FSD, let's look at some examples.

FSHQuery

FSHQuery demonstrates how to "piggyback" an additional call to a FSD whenever a **FS_DeleteFile** is attempted. The piggybacked call is a **FS_QueryResourceInfo**, the equivalent of a **GetVolumeInformation** Win32 call for local drives or a **WNet-GetConnection** for a remote drive. The code for FSHQuery's file system hook function is shown in Example 7-2. This is a stand-alone driver that is installed by making an entry in the *system.ini* file. To see its output you need to execute it with a kernel debugger (WinIce or WDEB386).

Example 7-2. FSHQuery: File System Hook

```
int __cdecl FileHook( pIFSFunc pfn, int fn, int drv,
                      int res, int cp, pioreq pir ) {

  // Look for a volume-based FS_DeleteFile call,
  if ( fn == IFSFN_DELETE ) {
    ifsreq* pifs;
    pIFSFunc pQueryFunc;

    // Call-down into the FSD using a modified copy
    //         of the ifsreq passed in.
    pifs = IFSMgr_GetHeap( sizeof( ifsreq ) );
    if ( pifs != NULL) {
      memcpy( pifs, pir, sizeof( ifsreq ) );
      // Get Level 0 Information if we are dealing
      //       with a Network Resource
      if ( res & IFSFH_RES_NETWORK ) {
        _QWORD qw;
        ParsedPath* pUniResource;
        char* pszName;
        pszName = IFSMgr_GetHeap( MAX_PATH );
        if ( pszName != NULL ) {
          pUniResource = IFSMgr_GetHeap( 1024 );
          pifs->ir_options = 0; // Level 0
          pifs->ir_ppath = (DWORD)pUniResource;
          pQueryFunc = pifs->ifs_psr->sr_func->vfn_func[VFN_QUERY]
          (*(*ppPrevHook))( pQueryFunc, IFSFN_QUERY, drv, res,
                            cp, (pioreq)pifs );
          memset( pszName, 0, MAX_PATH );
          qw = UniToBCSPath( pszName, pUniResource->pp_elements,
                             MAX_PATH, cp );
          if ( qw.ddLower )
            Debug_Printf( "Query level 0, drive = %d resource name = %s\n",
                          drv, pszName );
          IFSMgr_RetHeap( pUniResource );
        }
```

Example 7-2. FSHQuery: File System Hook (continued)

```
        IFSMgr_RetHeap( pszName );
      }
    }

    // Get Level 2 Information if we are dealing
    //         with a Local Resource
    else {
      char szFileSystemName[32];
      pifs->ifs_ir.ir_options = 2; // Level 2
      pifs->ifs_ir.ir_length = sizeof(szFileSystemName);
      pifs->ifs_ir.ir_data = (DWORD)szFileSystemName;
      pQueryFunc = pifs->ifs_psr->sr_func->vfn_func[VFN_QUERY];
      (*(*ppPrevHook))( pQueryFunc, IFSFN_QUERY, drv, res,
                        cp, (pioreq)pifs );
      Debug_Printf( "Query level 2, drive = %d file system = %s\n",
                    drv, szFileSystemName );
      Debug_Printf( "             maxpath = %d, maxcomp = %d\n",
                    pifs->ifs_ir.ir_length >> 16,
                    pifs->ifs_ir.ir_length & 0xffff );
      Debug_Printf( "             flags = %04x, cache block size = %d\n",
                    pifs->ifs_ir.ir_options, pifs->ifs_ir.ir_pos );
    }
    IFSMgr_RetHeap( pirx );
  }
}

return (*(*ppPrevHook))( pfn, fn, drv, res, cp, pir );
}
```

The general approach is to clone the **ifsreq** packet that is used by the **FS_Delete-File** call. This gives us a painless way to get the *ir_pid*, *ir_user*, *ir_rh*, *ifs_psr*, *ifs_VMHandle*, and *ifs_PV* fields. Some of the remaining fields will require initialization for the **FS_QueryResourceInfo** call. Specifically, it is necessary to set the *ir_options* member to the "query level," level 2 for local resources and level 0 for remote resources. If it is a level 2 query, we need to provide a buffer to hold the returned file system name string, in *ir_data*, with the length of the buffer given by *ir_length*. On the other hand, for a level 0 query, we just provide a pointer, in *ir_ppath*, to a buffer for the returned **ParsedPath** structure which represents the name of the remote resource.

Several of the fields require buffers—one to contain the cloned **ifsreq**, one to contain a **ParsedPath** structure, etc. You'll notice that **_HeapAllocate** is not used here, but instead IFSMgr's heap routines: **IFSMgr_GetHeap** and **IFSMgr_RetHeap**. IFSMgr creates its heap in pages of locked system memory. There is a main heap and a "spare heap"; the latter is allocated prior to entering the dispatch point by a call to **IFSMgr_FillHeapSpare**. The advantage of using the **IFSMgr_GetHeap** routine is that for requests less than a page in size, it will not trigger paging activity. This is a requirement for file hooks and FSDs that are accessing the swap file or a memory-mapped file. IFSMgr's heap routines avoid paging by returning pieces of its pre-allocated locked heap. (See the section entitled "Heap Management" in Chapter 12, *A Survey of IFSMgr Services*.)

In Example 7-2, the actual call into the FSD occurs at the following lines:

```
pQueryFunc = pifs->ifs_psr->sr_func->vfn_func[VFN_QUERY];
(*(*ppPrevHook))( pQueryFunc, IFSFN_QUERY, drv, res, cp, (pioreq)pifs
);
```

The variable *pifs* is a pointer to the `ifsreq` structure, which is described in Appendix C, *IFSMgr Data Structures*. Its *ir_psr* member is a pointer to the shell resource structure for the volume which is being queried. The declaration of the shell resource structure is also given in Appendix C. Its *sr_func* member is a pointer to the volume-based function table (see Table 6-6). The *vfn_func[VFN_QUERY]* member gives us the FSD's address for the **FS_QueryResourceInfo** function. The address of this function is then passed to the previous hooker function, thereby giving downstream file hooks an opportunity to see the request. When this call returns, the results are stored in the `ifsreq` structure. The member p*ifs->ifs_ir.ir_error* is zero if the call succeeded and a non-zero error code otherwise.

Note that the *res* argument to the **FileHook** function distinguishes a remote from a local resource call by the bits *IFSFH_RES_NETWORK* and *IFSFH_RES_LOCAL*. If the resource flags indicate a remote resource, then a level 0 query is performed; otherwise a level 2 query is performed. On a level 0 query, a `ParsedPath` structure is returned, which represents the name of the remote resource. To convert this into a printable form, the IFSMgr service, **UniToBCSPath**, is used to convert it into a byte-wide string in the selected character set (ANSI/OEM).

FSHEnum

FSHEnum demonstrates how to piggyback an additional call to a FSD whenever a **FS_CloseFile** is attempted. The piggybacked call is a **FS_EnumerateHandle**, subfunction *ENUMH_GETFILENAME*. There is no Win32 or Int 21h call that directly maps to this function. The closest ones are **GetFileInformationByHandle** which maps to **FS_EnumerateHandle**, subfunction *ENUMH_GETFILEINFO*, and Int 21h Function 440dh Subfunction 086dh, Enumerate Open Files. The code for FSHEnum's file system hook function is shown in Example 7-3. This is a stand-alone driver that is installed by making an entry in the *system.ini* file. To see its output you need to execute it with a kernel debugger (WinIce or WDEB386).

Here again we clone the `ifsreq` packet that, in this case, is used by the **FS_Close-File** call. This gives us a painless way to get the *ir_pid*, *ir_user*, *ir_rh*, *ir_sfn*, *ir_fh*, *ifs_psr*, *ifs_pfh*, *ifs_VMHandle*, and *ifs_PV* fields. Some of the remaining fields will require initialization for the **FS_EnumerateHandle** call. Specifically, it is necessary to set the *ir_flags* member to *ENUMH_GETFILENAME* to request the filename for the given resource handle (*ir_rh*) and FSD file handle (*ir_fh*). We also need to provide a pointer, in *ir_ppath*, to a buffer for the returned `ParsedPath` structure which represents the name of the file.

Example 7-3. FSHEnum: File System Hook

```
int __cdecl FileHook( pIFSFunc pfn, int fn, int drv,
                      int res, int cp, pioreq pir ) {

  // Look for a handle-based FS_CloseFile call,
  //    but skip any character FSDs
  if ( fn == IFSFN_CLOSE && !(res & IFSFH_RES_CFSD) ) {
    // Call-down into the FSD using a modified copy
    //       of the ifsreq passed in.
    _QWORD qw;
    ifsreq ifs;
    pIFSFunch pEnumHandle;
    ParsedPath* pUniPPath;
    char* pszName;
    pszName = IFSMgr_GetHeap( MAX_PATH );
    if ( pzName != NULL) {
      pUniPPath = IFSMgr_GetHeap( 1024 );
      if ( pUniPPath != NULL ) {
        memcpy( &ifs, pir, sizeof( ifsreq ) );
        ifs.ifs_ir.ir_flags = ENUMH_GETFILENAME;
        ifs.ifs_ir.ir_ppath = (DWORD)pUniPPath;
        pEnumHandle = ifs.ifs_pfh->fh_hf.hf_misc->hm_func[HM_ENUMHANDLE];
        (*(*ppPrevHook))( pEnumHandle, IFSFN_ENUMHANDLE, drv, res,
                          cp, (pioreq)&ifs );
        memset( pszName, 0, MAX_PATH );
        qw = UniToBCSPath( pszName, pUniPPath->pp_elements, MAX_PATH, cp );
        if ( qw.ddLower ) {
          Debug_Printf( "Closing file %s\n", pszName );
          }
        IFSMgr_RetHeap( (void*)pUniPPath );
        }
      IFSMgr_RetHeap( pszName );
      }
    }

  return (*(*ppPrevHook))( pfn, fn, drv, res, cp, pir );
  }
```

It is important to note that the filename is not stored by IFSMgr. It is the job of the FSD to store this information for files which are opened on its drives. IFSMgr only holds onto the FSD file handle and `fhandle` information. When an open occurs the FSD receives a name in a standard canonicalized form (a `ParsedPath`). Whether the drive accepts a particular name depends on its underlying filesystem. So it makes sense that, given a SFN (System File Number), it would be necessary to retrieve its name from its FSD.

In Example 7-3, the actual call into the FSD occurs at the following line:

```
pEnumHandle = ifs.ifs_pfh->fh_hf.hf_misc->hm_func[HM_ENUMHANDLE];
(*(*ppPrevHook))( pEnumHandle , IFSFN_ENUMHANDLE, drv, res, cp,
                 (pioreq)&ifs );
```

The variable *ifs* is an **ifsreq** structure as described in Appendix C. Its *ifs_pfh* member is a pointer to the **fhandle** for the file which is being enumerated. The declaration of the **fhandle** structure is also given in Appendix C. Its *fh_hf.hf_misc* member is a pointer to the handle-based function table (see Table 6-7). The *hm_func[HM_ENUMHANDLE]* member gives us the FSD's address for the **FS_EnumerateHandle** function. The address of this function is then passed to the previous hooker function, thereby giving downstream file hooks an opportunity to see the request. When this call returns, the filename is stored in the buffer pointed to by *ir_ppath*. This is a **ParsedPath** structure, which represents the canonicalized filename. To convert this into a printable form, the IFSMgr service, **UniToBCSPath**, is used to convert it into a byte-wide string in the selected character set (ANSI/OEM) of the current code page.

When I was testing this code with Build 950 of Windows 95, I found an interesting bug in VCOND, the virtual console device for Win32 console applications. VCOND registers a character FSD with IFSMgr called PIPESTDX. This is used when redirecting output from a console application, such as running NMAKE from an editor and collecting its output to a file. **FS_CloseFile** is called on a handle of this character FSD. The bug appears when attempting to call **FS_EnumerateHandle** for this handle—it will always crash the system. The problem occurs because VCOND's handle-based function table does not contain a valid function address for *HM_ENUMHANDLE* (it is always 00000001h). It should implement an error handler if it doesn't support the function.

To work around this problem, you'll see the following code:

```
if ( fn == IFSFN_CLOSE && !(res & IFSFH_RES_CFSD) )
```

This ignores **FS_CloseFile** for character FSDs.

FSHAttr

For a final file system hook example, we'll use **IFSMgr_Ring0_FileIO** to create a re-entrant call into the dispatch point. We aren't able to take the FSHQuery or FSHEnum examples and redo them using this ring-0 API because they each use FSD APIs that are not exposed through the ring-0 interface. So in some cases, the "direct call to FSD" approach is the only one viable.

FSHAttr demonstrates how to piggyback a ring-0 call to Get File Attributes whenever a **FS_DeletcFile** is attempted. The piggybacked call is a **IFSMgr_Ring0_FileIO**, subfunction *RO_FILEATTRIBUTES*. This is equivalent to a Int 21h function 7143h call. The code for FSHAttr's file system hook function is shown in Example 7-4. This is a stand-alone driver that is installed by making an entry in the *system.ini* file. To see its effect, you need to look at the trace output from FSHook after performing some file deletes.

Example 7-4. FSHAttr: File System Hook

```
int __cdecl FileHook( pIFSFunc pfn, int fn, int drv,
                      int res, int cp, pioreq pir ) {
  // Look for a volume-based FS_DeleteFile call,
  if ( fn == IFSFN_DELETE && (res & IFSFH_RES_LOCAL) ) {
    short attr;

    // Get file attributes for pathname
    _QWORD qw;
    char *pszName, *p;

    p = pszName = IFSMgr_GetHeap( MAX_PATH );
    if ( pszName != NULL ) {
      memset( pszName, 0, MAX_PATH );
      *p++ = '@' + drv;
      *p++ = ':';
      qw = UniToBCSPath( p, pir->ir_ppath->pp_elements, MAX_PATH, cp );
      if ( qw.ddLower ) {
        EREGS r;
        int retc;
        r.r_eax = R0_FILEATTRIBUTES | GET_ATTRIBUTES;
        r.r_esi = (DWORD)pszName;
        retc = IFSMgr_Ring0_FileIO(&r);
        attr = (retc==0) ? r.r_ecx : 0;
        Debug_Printf( "FSHATTR: %s attribs: %04x\n", pszName, attr );
        }
      IFSMgr_RetHeap( pszName );
      }
    }
  return (*(*ppPrevHook))( pfn, fn, drv, res, cp, pir );
  }
```

In this example, **FS_DeleteFile** is called with a complete pathname. We can convert it from a `ParsedPath` structure to a byte-string for passage to the ring-0 API. The **IFSMgr_Ring0_FileIO** service wrapper provided by *ifswraps.clb* uses the **EREGS** structure to pass values of register-based arguments. The **FileAttributes** function requires that the following registers be loaded prior to invoking the service:

```
AH = 43h, AL = 00h,
ESI = linear address of pathname.
```

On return, if *carry* is clear, then the attributes are in the CX register; if *carry* is set, AX holds the error code.

There is an error in the IFS Specification regarding the arguments to this function. It shows the calling parameters as AH=*RO_FILEATTRIBUTES*. This has the effect of setting AH to 0 because *RO_FILEATTRIBUTES* is defined as 0x4300 in *ifs.h*. Instead, you should set AX=*RO_FILEATTRIBUTES* and then adjust AL to 0 for a get and 1 for a set.

Figure 7-3 shows the FSHook trace when deleting *c:\windows\desktop\test.txt* from Explorer. The **FS_FileAttributes** entry preceding the **FS_DeleteFile** shows that the re-entrant ring-0 API call goes through the file system hook.

Module	Type	Function	Flags1	Device	Args	Flags2
Explorer	fsh	FS_FileAttributes [43]	e_cLnu_sLXRmwoa	VFAT		Gt
					C:\WINDOWS\DESKTOP\TEST.TXT	
Explorer	fsh	FS_DeleteFile [41]	e_cLnu_sLXrmwoa	VFAT		
					C:\WINDOWS\DESKTOP\TEST.TXT	

Figure 7-3. MultiMon/FSHook output on delete

The NetFunction Hook

Another function which IFSMgr uses for notifications is **IFSMgr_NetFunction**. Unlike the file system hook, this service is used mostly by network redirectors and other network components. This is not a service which is called but a service which is intended to be hooked, using VMM's service **Hook_Device_Service**. On the occurrence of various events, IFSMgr calls this service as a broadcast to all hookers.

An **IFSMgr_NetFunction** hook will receive four arguments on each call. These are a pointer to an `ifsreq` structure appropriate for the call, a pointer to the client registers structure, a provider identifier, and a flag indicating whether the call originated from a Win32 API (see Example 7-5). All of the arguments actually reference the contents of the `ifsreq` structure, i.e., *pRegs* is &(*pir->ifs_crs*), *proId* is *pir->ifs_proid*, and *flags* is given by the expression (*pir->ifs_nflags* & 0x04). A **NetFunction** handler will need to examine the *Client_AX* value in the client registers structure to determine the type of call. The calls can be grouped into three different categories: IFSMgr broadcasts, dispatch handlers, and **DeviceIoControl** handlers.

Example 7-5. Prototype for IFSMgr_NetFunction

```
int IFSMgr_NetFunction( pioreq pir, PCRS pRegs, int proId, int flags );
```

Table 7-2 shows the function values for IFSMgr broadcasts. The first five entries in the table correspond to events generated by IFSMgr. The function type is given by the value of *Client_AX* in the client register structure. Functions 1 and 2 occur when a drive (local or remote) appears or disappears from the system. When these events are broadcast, the `ifsreq` structure contains the resource handle for the drive (*ir_rh*), the 1-based drive letter (*ir_flags*), and the provider ID for the FSD which handles the drive (*ir_aux1.aux_ul*). Functions 3, 4 and 5 report events for network printers. For these functions, *proId* contains the provider ID of the printer handler, and `ifsreq` holds the resource handle (*ir_rh*) for the printer, a buffer to contain a returned job ID (*ir_data*), or an index (0-8 for LPT1 through LPT9) to the printer (*ir_flags*). For each of these calls, the return value is stored to the *ir_error* member of the `ifsreq` structure.

Table 7-2. NetFunction Broadcasts

Function Type	ifsreq	Provider ID	Event Description
NF_DRIVEUSE(1)	ir_rh, ir_flags, ir_aux1	ANYPROID	new drive appears in system
NF_DRIVEUNUSE(2)	ir_rh, ir_flags, ir_aux1	ANYPROID	drive goes away
NF_GETPRINTJOBID(3)	ir_rh, ir_data	ID of printer handler	IFSMgr needs a print job ID from FSD
NF_PRINTERUSE(4)	ir_rh, ir_flags	ID of printer handler	Network printer is attached
· NF_PRINTERUNUSE(5)	ir_rh, ir_flags	ID of printer handler	Network printer is disconnected
NF_PROCEXIT(111Dh)	ir_pid	ANYPROID	process exits

The last entry in Table 7-2 corresponds to an Int 2Fh function call and should be lumped together with the dispatch handlers. *DOS/Win32 Installable File System Specification*, p. 91, has this to say about **NetFunction**s:

> This service is provided to export certain functions most of which are specific to the network FSDs. These functions can come from a variety of sources: Int 21h and int 2fh functions that the IFS hooks but does not support, Int 21h functions that the IFS does not support that are hooked via **IFSMgr_SetReqHook**…

Several of the dispatch functions listed in Table 6-3 call into **IFSMgr_NetFunction**. These include **dProcExit**, **dFunc5F**, and **dNetFunc**. **dProcExit** corresponds to the Int 2fh call 111dh. Some other Int 2fh functions are sent to **dNetFunc**: 1180h, 1181h (*NF_NetSetUserName*), 1182h, 1184h, 118bh, 118ch, 118dh, and 118eh. **dFunc5F** handles several Int 21h functions in the range 5f00h through 5f53h. Many of the functions in this range and all those greater than 5f54h are routed to **IFSMgr_NetFunction**. For some of these functions, IFSMgr does provide an implementation (e.g., **dProcExit**) and the call to **IFSMgr_NetFunction** is only another form of broadcast. However, in most cases IFSMgr only goes as far as wiring the functions up to the dispatcher so that a FSD can use a **NetFunction** hook to provide an implementation.

Actually, IFSMgr takes this interface a step further by allowing some Int 21h functions to be attached to the **dNetFunc** dispatch function. This is done by installing a preamble for the function using **IFSMgr_SetReqHook**. We looked at preamble functions back in Chapter 6, *Dispatching File System Requests*. There we concentrated on the preambles which IFSMgr installs by default for Int 21h functions in the range 00 through *MAXDOSFUNC*. Here, we are interested in the Int 21h functions from *MAXDOSFUNC+1* to FFh.

The preamble function decides whether it wishes to accept the Int 21h function call. It "accepts" by returning with the *carry* flag cleared. For functions greater than *MAXDOSFUNC*, an accepted request will be dispatched as command 0x00d4 (see Figure 6-1 and Example 6-1), which has **dNetFunc** as its handler. The preamble function only decides whether it wants to accept the call; it is the **IFSMgr_NetFunction** hook which will actually look for the function call by examining the *Client_AX* register value. Unlike the broadcasts from IFSMgr, which provide information, these calls to **IFSMgr_NetFunction** are requests for a service. This implies that if a FSD completes the request it should *not* pass the request down the chain. Rather, it should return with the same value that it stuffed into *ir_error*.

One additional source of calls into **IFSMgr_NetFunction** come from IFSMgr's **DeviceIoControl** interface. In Chapter 4, several IOCTL Services were described. Two of these, **IFS_IOCTL_21** and **IFS_IOCTL_2F**, use the contents of the win32apireq structure to fill the client register portion of an ifsreq packet. The remainder of the packet is initialized and then, for functions of the 5fxxh series, are sent to **dFunc5f**. Others are routed to the chain of **IFSMgr_NetFunction** hooks.

NetFunc

NetFunc is a **IFSMgr_NetFunction** hook that reports all calls to MultiMon for display. NetFunc shows one line of output for each NetFunction call. Figure 7-4 shows a sample trace fragment that was collected while running a simple program from DEBUG in a DOS box. The first column, which contains "VM2", indicates the process was executing in a second VM (DOS box) when the call was made. *nfn* is an identifier for NetFunction entries in the trace. The next column contains the function number. 8000h corresponds to an Int 21h function that NetFunc has installed. Function 111dh is recorded when DEBUG is terminated. The Args field shows the values of the EDX and ESI registers. The four bytes that comprise EDX, from most significant to least significant, are: *ifs_nflags*, *ifs_hflag*, *ifs_drv*, and *ifs_func* from the ifsreq structure; ESI contains the value of the provider ID passed to the hook function. In Figure 7-4, we see interrupt 21h function 80h map to the dispatcher function D4h and we see interrupt 2fh function 111dh map to dispatcher function 93h.

Module	Type	Function	Args
VM2	nfh	Func=00008000	EDX=010003d4 ESI=ffffffff
VM2	nfh	Func=0000111d	EDX=01000393 ESI=ffffffff
VM2	nfh	Func=0000111d	EDX=01000393 ESI=ffffffff

Figure 7-4. NetFunc sample output

The hook function installed by NetFunc is shown in Example 7-6. This function does not use a stack frame so that the HOOK_PREAMBLE macro can insert extra information to allow the hook to be removed. This also requires that the calling arguments be moved into local variables so they can be referenced by C statements. There are two main sections here. In the clause beginning if (bEnabled)..., the routine is checking if MultiMon has enabled monitoring of **IFSMgr_NetFunction** calls. If so, it prepares a notification structure and sends it. The next interesting clause begins if (pRegs->Client_AX == 0x8000).... This checks if the function we are being called on is one that we have installed a handler for. If it is, we just print out a message and return. Otherwise, we restore the original stack frame and jump to the next hook function.

Example 7-6. IFSMgr_NetFunction Hook

```
HOOKPROC MyNetFunction( pioreq pir, PCRS pRegs, int proId, int flags ) {
  PEBLOCK pBlk;
  ifsreq _pifs;
  struct Client_Word_Reg_Struc* _pRegs;
  int _provider;
  HOOK_PREAMBLE(pPrevNetFunc)
  _asm push ebp
  _asm mov ebp,esp
  _asm sub esp,__LOCAL_SIZE

  _asm mov eax, [ebp+0ch]
  _asm mov _pRegs, eax
  _asm mov eax, [ebp+10h]
  _asm mov _provider, eax
  _asm mov eax, [ebp+8]
  _asm mov _pifs, eax

  if ( bEnabled ) {                                 // monitor enabled?
    if ( Get_Cur_Thread_Handle() != pFmon2TCB ) {    // not MultiMon thread?
      if ( Directed_Sys_Control1( pFilemon2, REQUEST_EVENT_BLK, &pBlk ) ) {
        FillDispBlk( pBlk, _pRegs->Client_AX, _provider,
                     _pifs->ifs_func, IFS_NETFUNC );
        Directed_Sys_Control1( pFilemon2, EVENT_NOTIFY, pBlk );
        }
      else if ( pBlk != NULL ) {
        pBlk->type = OVR_ERROR;
        Directed_Sys_Control1( pFilemon2, EVENT_NOTIFY, pBlk );
        }
      }
```

Example 7-6. IFSMgr_NetFunction Hook (continued)

```
    }

  // This is for handling our "bogus" Int 21h Function 8000h
  if ( _pRegs->Client_AX == 0x8000 ) {
    Debug_Printf( "Int 21h Function 8000h called\n" );
    _asm mov esp,ebp
    _asm pop ebp
    _asm ret
    }

  _asm mov esp,ebp
  _asm pop ebp
  // Chain to the next Net Function Hooker
  _asm jmp dword ptr pPrevNetFunc
  }
```

To show how **IFSMgr_NetFunction** and **IFSMgr_SetReqHook** work together, I select an Int 21h function, which is unused by MS-DOS, say 80h. To get our Int 21h Function 8000h to create **IFSMgr_NetFunction** calls, we install a preamble for it as shown in Example 7-7. This code fragment is executed as part of Device Init. The address of the previous preamble function is saved in *pPrevPreamble* so that if we decide to reject the request, we can chain on to the previous preamble function.

Example 7-7. Installation of Preamble During Device Init

```
  pPrevPreamble = IFSMgr_SetReqHook( 0x00210080, MyPreamble );
```

The actual preamble function, **MyPreamble**, is shown in Example 7-8. This function simply clears the *carry* flag and returns. Some logic may be required to decide whether to accept or reject the request.

Example 7-8. Preamble Function for Int 21h Function 80h

```
void __declspec( naked ) MyPreamble( void ) {

  #ifdef NOT_HOOKED
  // ... If we don't handle it, call the next preamble
  _asm jmp dword ptr pPrevPreamble
  #else
  // ... Do whatever checks are required
  _asm clc    // Clear carry if we accept the function call
  _asm ret
  #endif
  }
```

To test our preamble and NetFunction hook we need to generate an Int 21h Function 80h call in either V86 or protected mode. The simplest way to do this is to open a DOS box and run DEBUG. At the – prompt, type the following four-line program:

```
-a100
mov ax,8000
int 21
mov ax,4c00
int 21
-g
```

Then let it execute. To see the message "Int 21h Function 8000h called," a kernel debugger will have to be running (WinIce or WDEB386). This little program also creates the MultiMon trace shown in Figure 7-4 when the IFSMgr NetFunction filter is enabled.

Hooking a Path

The last hook function that we'll take a look at, **IFSMgr_SetPathHook**, is closely tied to **IFSMgr_ParsePath** (and **IFSMgr_FSDParsePath**). Recall that **IFSMgr_Parse-Path** is called for the volume-based FSD functions that receive a path string (in `ifsreq` member *ir_data*). In other words, in preparation for calling **FS_OpenFile**, **FS_FileAttributes**, etc., a call into **IFSMgr_ParsePath** is needed to set up the `ifsreq` packet. By parsing the path string, this service fills in the *ifs_psr* member of the `ifsreq` packet, as well as the **ParsedPath** structure required for *ir_ppath*.

IFSMgr_SetPathHook has the following function prototype:

```
void* IFSMgr_SetPathHook( void* PathCheckFunc ).
```

This service installs a *path check* routine and returns a previous path check routine. The service is available at Device Init or Init Complete time. The path check routine is called by **IFSMgr_ParsePath** if the input path does not contain leading \, /, or **d:** characters. What does a path check routine do? Here is what Microsoft has to say in *DOS/Win32 Installable File System Specification*, p. 90:

> This service has been provided for FSDs to check for special path prefixes and process them separately. The FSD can register a routine with the IFS manager that is called every time a path is parsed. If this is a prefix the FSD wants to process, it can claim it and the IFS manager will then call the FSD directly on the path-based operation.

If the path check routine does not "claim" the path, then it needs to jump to the previous path check routine with all registers preserved. The last path check routine in the chain is supplied by IFSMgr; it just sets the *carry* flag and returns. This tells the parser to use default handling.

The inputs to and outputs from the path check function are summarized in Table 7-3. As you can see it is entirely register-based, so it needs to be written in inline assembly code. We also see from the input arguments that by the time the path check function is called, the *ir_data* member of `ifsreq` has been translated into a Unicode string (ESI); however, the `PathElements` (EDI) have not been created yet.

Table 7-3. Path Check Function Arguments and Returns

Input	Output	Description
ESI		Pointer to Unicode pathname
EDI		Destination buffer to hold `PathElements`
	EAX	Length (*pe_length*) of last `PathElement` consumed and stored to buffer at EDI
	EBX	Pointer to Unicode string of the last `PathElement` consumed by the FSD
	EDX	Provider ID of FSD that claimed the path
	ESI	Pointer to Unicode pathname, next char to parse
	EDI	Pointer to buffer holding zero or more consumed `PathElements`
	Carry Flag	Return Clear—request is hooked; else jump to previous path check routine

The path check routine can look for a specific signature at the beginning of the string pointed to by ESI. This string can be a prefix which is stripped off from the remainder, or it may convert the prefix into some other string or character and store it to a `PathElement` structure in the buffer pointed to by EDI. The prefix string may also just be copied to a `PathElement`. There is considerable flexibility here: from one extreme, the string may be completely parsed into `PathElements` before returning; to the other extreme, the entire path might be passed back and no parsing is done, only the provider ID is set. If any of the string is passed back to **IFSMgr_ParsePath** to complete parsing, then that portion must follow the convention that elements are delimited by / or \ characters.

In any case, when **IFSMgr_ParsePath** returns, *ir_ppath* will contain a `ParsedPath` structure comprised of the `PathElements`, some or perhaps all of which were extracted by the path check routine. This canonicalized path is really private to the FSD that has "claimed" it. The path becomes claimed because **IFSMgr_Parse-Path** modifies the contents of the `ifsreq` structure to earmark it for a specific FSD. It does this by clearing *ifs_psr*, to indicate that there is no associated shell resource and by setting *ifs_proid* to the FSD's provider ID. The net effect is that instead of calling a volume-based function based on default parsing behavior, the volume-based functions that correspond to the specified provider ID are used .

8

In this chapter:
- *FSD to IFSMgr Linkage*
- *FSDs Come in Three Flavors*
- *FSD Mechanics*
- *FSD Linkage*
- *MONOCFSD: A Character File System Driver*
- *FSINFILE: A Remote File System Driver*

Anatomy of a File System Driver

Over the course of this book we have progressively stripped away the layers of the Windows 95 file system. We have seen that the programming APIs converge upon a dispatch point that has the characteristics of an extended Int 21h interface. Many of the dispatch functions require support from an underlying file system driver. In the last chapter we used MultiMon, with the FSHook driver, to monitor the calls into the underlying FSDs. In this chapter we will shift our focus to the file system drivers.

FSD to IFSMgr Linkage

A file system driver is a virtual device driver containing entry points which are only accessed by IFSMgr (or a file system API hook). There are three stages by which a FSD exposes these entry points. In the initial registration step, an FSD passes the address of a **FS_MountVolume** or **FS_ConnectNetResource** entry point. The next stage occurs when a file system resource is first used. IFSMgr determines which FSD maps to the resource and then performs the "mount" or "connect" operation by calling the entry point which was supplied during the registration step. As a result of the mount or connect, IFSMgr is returned the FSD's table of volume-based entry points. Amongst the entry points in this table, some provide an "open" type operation. For instance, **FS_OpenFile** opens a file and **FS_FindFirst-File** opens a find context. When an open is performed, the FSD exposes its last layer of entry points. In response to these calls, IFSMgr receives a handle and a table of handle-based entry points. Table 8-1 illustrates these relationships for a local FSD; the same relationships apply to remote and character FSDs.

Table 8-1. FSD/IFSMgr Linkage

	File System Driver		IFSMgr
Registration	Pass address of FS_MountVolume	→	IFSMgr_RegisterMount
Volume Mounting	FS_MountVolume	←	Mount call
	returns `volfunc[]`	→	
File Open	FS_OpenFile	←	Open call
	returns `hdlfunc[]`	→	

FSDs Come in Three Flavors

Although all FSDs exhibit the linkage characteristics described above, three types of FSDs are distinguished by IFSMgr: character, local, and remote.

Character FSDs

The term *character* originated in the UNIX world to distinguish block and character devices. Block devices are characterized by data transfers of blocks of data of a fixed size (usually the sector size), whereas character devices transfer data byte-at-a-time in a serial fashion. This is also the meaning attached to character as it applies to FSDs.

Character FSDs register with IFSMgr by calling the service **IFSMgr_RegisterCFSD**. The registering FSD passes the address of the **FS_MountVolume** entry point and a pointer to an array of pointers to one or more device names. When a listed device is first accessed, **FS_MountVolume** is called for its name. Each name registered is separately mounted. Each successful mount creates a shell resource for the specified device name.

Some examples of character FSDs include *vcond.vxd* and *spooler.vxd*. VCOND, the virtual console driver, exposes a number of Win32 VxD services which are used by KERNEL32 to provide support for Win32 console applications. Tucked away inside this driver is a character FSD, which registers under the name PIPESTDX. This device is opened by *redirect.mod*, which in turn is loaded by KERNEL32, to enable redirection for certain kinds of console applications. SPOOLER, the other example given, is a character FSD registered for the system printer devices: LPT1 through LPT9 and PRN.

Character FSDs are good candidates for modeling devices which transfer data a byte at a time and which do not already have an existing driver class. It is the lack of dependency on the I/O subsystem or network protocol stack that makes this type of FSD most flexible.

Local FSDs

A local FSD provides support for local storage devices, such as floppy disk drives, fixed disk drives, and CD-ROM drives.

Local FSDs register with IFSMgr by calling the service **IFSMgr_RegisterMount**. The registering FSD passes the address of its **FS_MountVolume** entry point. Local storage devices are partitioned into volumes, and when a volume is first accessed, **FS_MountVolume** is called on each local FSD until one recognizes the media and claims it. This establishes a shell resource for the local device and the volume-based function table which provides linkage to IFSMgr.

The system registers one default local FSD through **IFSMgr_RegisterMount**. When IFSMgr searches for a local FSD to claim a volume, the search may fail. The default local FSD is there to claim those volumes that other local FSDs do not recognize. Some common situations where this would occur include an unformatted volume or a floppy drive without media inserted.

Some examples of local FSDs include *vfat.vxd, cdfs.vxd* and *vdef.vxd*. VFAT is the protected mode FAT file system driver that provides access to most floppy and fixed media. CDFS is the protected mode ISO-9660 file system driver that provides access to CD-ROM media. VDEF is the default local FSD (the source for *vdef.vxd* is given in the DDK).

Each storage device present in the system requires one or more hardware drivers that fall under the umbrella of the I/O subsystem. These drivers hide the differences in bus types and controller chip sets, and present a logically consistent view of the various devices, to the file system drivers. Thus, local FSDs rely upon the I/O subsystem services for their implementation. Local FSDs also conceal knowledge of the disk layout for a specific file system. A local FSD just accepts properly constructed filenames and returns handles through which logical operations may be performed.

Remote FSDs

A remote FSD connects to a resource which is shared by a server. There are two scenarios. In a peer-to-peer network, each system may be a client and a server and the protocol stacks of the client and server match, layer for layer. In a non–peer-to-peer network, a client PC system connects to a server host; there is no peer server.

The remote FSD, which resides in a client machine, connects to the server through some network medium and protocol. IFS requests on the client machine are redirected by the remote FSD to the server. The shared resource can be a character or block storage device.

Remote FSDs register with IFSMgr by calling the service **IFSMgr_RegisterNet**. The registering FSD passes the address of its **FS_ConnectNetResource** entry point. Dynamic connections to remote resources are made using the service **IFSMgr_SetupConnection** and broken by IFSMgr's internal function **IoreqDerefConnection**. These services call **FS_ConnectNetResource** and **FS_DisconnectResource**, respectively. A connection is attempted when a UNC path is resolved to a remote server and share. If the connection is mapped to a volume, then the connection persists until the volume is explicitly unmapped. Each connection to a unique remote server and share is represented by a shell resource.

To support the Windows 95 peer-to-peer networking, Microsoft Networks and Microsoft Netware Networks clients and servers are included in the package. The Microsoft Networks client is the remote FSD, *vredir.vxd*, and its matching server is *vserver.vxd*. These components work with NetBEUI, TCP/IP, and IPX/SPX protocols through the NetBIOS interface. When an IFS request is redirected by VREDIR, it is in the form of the Server Message Block (SMB) protocol. VSERVER interprets the SMB protocol and, if appropriate, generates an IFS request on the server machine using the **IFSMgr_ServerDOSCall** service. The results of the request are then returned via the SMB protocol.

In a similar fashion, the Netware Networks client is the remote FSD, *nwredir.vxd*, and its matching server is *nwserver.vxd*. These components work with the IPX/SPX protocols. When an IFS request is redirected by NWREDIR, it is in the form of the Netware Core Protocol (NCP). NWSERVER interprets the NCP protocol and, if appropriate, generates an IFS request on the server machine using the **IFSMgr_ServerDOSCall**. The results of the request are then returned via NCP.

FSD Mechanics

There are certain characteristics of an FSD that you must understand to use them properly: the contents of the Device Description Block; whether it is static or dynamic; how it can be segmented; and how it is affected by multiple threads.

Device Descriptor Block

As with other VxDs, an FSD requires a Device Descriptor Block. Generally, there is no need to export services or APIs, since linkage with IFSMgr is established dynamically. This implies that the DDB's protected-mode and virtual-86 API entries, as well as its service table, will be empty. This rule holds at least for local FSDs, but the other types of FSDs do not fit this mold. Remote FSDs export services that are needed by other network components and in the case of VCOND, a character FSD, it has every possible interface: V86 and PM APIs, Win32 services, and standard VxD services.

Initialization order for a static FSD is important. The header file *vmm.h* defines the manifest constant *FSD_INIT_ORDER* (0xa0010100) as the base value for FSDs. This assures that they load after IFSMgr. This is the *Init_Order* assigned to VFAT, CDFS, and VDEF. But again there are exceptions to the rule. In the case of remote FSDs, the *Init_Order* may also require that other network components be loaded before the FSD. For example, VREDIR has an *Init_Order* of 0xa0021000, which assures that it loads after IFSMgr and also after *vnetsup.vxd*. VCOND breaks even this rule by having an *Init_Order* of *UNDEFINED_ORDER* (0x80000000) that is less than IFSMgr. It gets away with this because VCOND does not register its character device with IFSMgr until a V86 API is called in response to running a console application. This is long after IFSMgr has completed its initialization.

All VxDs have a control procedure and FSDs are no different.

Static or Dynamic?

The *DOS/Win32 Installable File System Specifcation* is emphatic about FSDs being static drivers. On page 3, it states:

> The FSDs will be loaded and initialized when the system starts up. Once they are loaded they will remain loaded until the system hardware is shutdown or rebooted.

This makes sense because a file system has to be in place for the operating system to start up. However, there may be circumstances where an FSD might load dynamically; this is especially true of character FSDs.

If you intend to unload the FSD as well, one precaution needs to be observed. This arises because registering an FSD with IFSMgr creates a permanent linkage to the mount entry point and, in the case of character FSDs, a list of device names. Removing these from memory by performing an unload may eventually lead to a page fault. One work-around is to make the segment containing the mount entry point and device names a static segment.

OEM Service Release 2 appears to expand the options available to FSDs. Although the services are undocumented at this time, two new services are provided for registering and deregistering FSDs with IFSMgr. (See Chapter 12, *A Survey of IFSMgr Services.*)

Segmentation

This section may seem to be an anachronism; after all, weren't segments supposed to go away with 32-bit code? Segmentation as used here might be more accurately thought of as groupings of code or data with similar attributes. For instance, some code gets discarded after Device Init, other code is locked in memory and never swapped to disk, while pageable code may be paged-out when demands upon system memory require it. Although these code and data areas are distinct "objects" with different memory attributes, they are part of the continuum of the 4-gigabyte address space and thus don't require selector changes when switching from one to another.

The segmentation of a VxD is rooted in its linear executeable (LE) file format. Each grouping of code or data is assigned to a distinct object in the file. The attributes of each object determine what the loader does with it. An object will be created for each unique (non-empty) segment in the assembly language source. Traditionally, a macro from *vmm.inc* is used to specify the segment directives in a VxD.

Using C to write VxDs is more typical today and this change requires using a different sort of macro to specify segmentation. These new macros are found in *vmm.h*. The more common ones are reproduced in Example 8-1.

Example 8-1. Segmentation Pragmas

```
#define VxD_LOCKED_CODE_SEG      code_seg("_LTEXT", "LCODE")
#define VxD_LOCKED_DATA_SEG      data_seg("_LDATA", "LCODE")
#define VxD_INIT_CODE_SEG        code_seg("_ITEXT", "ICODE")
#define VxD_INIT_DATA_SEG        data_seg("_IDATA", "ICODE")
#define VxD_PAGEABLE_CODE_SEG    code_seg("_PTEXT", "PCODE")
#define VxD_PAGEABLE_DATA_SEG    data_seg("_PDATA", "PDATA")
#define VxD_STATIC_CODE_SEG      code_seg("_STEXT", "SCODE")
#define VxD_STATIC_DATA_SEG      data_seg("_SDATA", "SCODE")
```

The keywords **code_seg** and **data_seg** are pragma directives specific to the Microsoft compiler. The first argument in parentheses is the Portable Executable section name and the second argument is a class name. At the compile stage, a COFF object module is created with each segment name mapped to the named section. At the link stage, instead of creating a portable executeable (PE) format EXE file, the linker generates a VxD with the OBJ's sections mapped to linear executeable objects.

Example 8-2 shows a C code fragment using pragmas to set the code and data segments. The assembly language output from the compiler for this fragment is given in Example 8-3. To assure that *pageable_item* is assigned to the proper segment (*_PDATA*), it is necessary to initialize it; otherwise the variable will be assigned to the *_DATA* segment, the default segment for uninitialized data.

Segmentation also affects which library routines are statically linked to a VxD. The libraries VXDWRAPS and IFSWRAPS create six versions of each routine, one specific to each of the main segment types. The name of a library routine is prefixed by the name of the segment it resides in. By default, the header file *vxdwraps.h* sets the macro **CURSEG()** to return LCODE, so locked segment versions are used. For instance, if you are calling **IFSMgr_InstallFileSystemApi-Hook** only from Device Init, but you link in the "locked" segment version, that routine will remain part of your memory image after initialization, although you have no intention of calling it again. To call a library routine in a specific segment, redefine `CURSEG()` to the required segment; for example, `CURSEG` is defined as PCODE in Example 8-2.

Example 8-2. Pageable C Code and Data

```
/////////////////////////////
#pragma VxD_PAGEABLE_CODE_SEG
#pragma VxD_PAGEABLE_DATA_SEG
#pragma warning (disable:4005)
#define CURSEG() PCODE
#pragma warning (default:4005)
/////////////////////////////
int pageable_item = 0;
void pageable_func() {}
```

Example 8-3. Assembly Language for C Sample

```
_PDATA                        SEGMENT
_pageable_item DD 00H
_PDATA                        ENDS


PUBLIC                        _pageable_func
_PTEXT                        SEGMENT
_pageable_func PROC NEAR

; 494  : void pageable_func() {}

  00000                   55      push ebp
  00001                   8b ec   mov  ebp, esp
  00003                   53      push ebx
  00004                   56      push esi
  00005                   57      push edi
$L5493:
  00006                   5f      pop  edi
  00007                   5e      pop  esi
  00008                   5b      pop  ebx
  00009                   c9      leave
  0000a                   c3      ret  0
_pageable_func ENDP
_PTEXT                        ENDS
```

The segment prefixes are as follows:

> LCODE for VXD_LOCKED_CODE_SEG
> ICODE for VxD_INIT_CODE_SEG
> PCODE for VXD_PAGEABLE_CODE_SEG
> SCODE for VXD_STATIC_CODE_SEG

DCODE for VXD_DEBUG_ONLY_CODE_SEG
CCODE for VXD_PNP_CODE_SEG

An FSD may have a need for all of the segment types in Example 8-1. Only general recommendations can be given here. Here are some general rules of thumb for placement of FSD code and data into segments:

- If the code or data will be hit during swap file or memory-mapped file handling, then this code and data must be locked. This will apply to most of the code and data in a local FSD which supports a swap file. We see this with VFAT, where the bulk of the code lies in VXD_LOCKED_CODE_SEG and VXD_LOCKED_DATA_SEG.

- A character FSD may place the bulk of its implementation in pageable segments.

- Any initialization code and data, such as routines specific to System Critical Init, Device Init, and Init Complete phases, should be placed in VXD_INIT_CODE_SEG and VXD_INIT_DATA_SEG segments. Usually, an FSD will check the IFSMgr version number and register with IFSMgr at this time. This code is discarded after Init Complete phase.

- As with other VxDs, the control procedure and device descriptor block must reside in locked code and data segments.

- If the FSD is dynamically loaded and unloaded, place its mount entry point and device names (if a character FSD) in static code and data segments.

Multi-Threading Considerations

As noted in Chapter 7, *Monitoring File Activity*, the path through the file system is multi-threaded. This will have an impact on the design of an FSD. Any global data accessed by more than one thread in an FSD must be protected by synchronization primitives. A variety of synchronization services are supplied by VMM to fill this need.*

In the sample FSDs described at the end of this chapter, I use a simple technique based on blocking identifiers. To gain access to a critical section containing a shared resource, the following page-locked code acts as a guard:

```
DWORD claim_resource = -1;
...
    _asm    pushfd    /* save interrupt flag */
  get_resource:
    _asm    cli
```

---

* For a good discussion of synchronization services, see Walter Oney's account in *Systems Programming for Windows 95* (Microsoft Press), Chapter 9.

```
    _asm    inc     claim_resource
    _asm    jz      got_resource
    _BlockOnID( (DWORD)&claim_resource, 0 );
    _asm    jmp     short get_resource
got_resource:
    _asm    popfd       /* restore interrupt flag */
```

The variable *claim_resource* is initialized to −1. If another thread is currently using the resource, then on entry *claim_resource* will be greater than or equal to 0, and the increment instruction will not set the zero flag. This will cause the thread to execute the VMM service **_BlockOnID**, which will block the thread on the specified blocking ID (the address of the variable claim_resource). Interrupts are disabled to assure that **_SignalID** is not called before the thread blocks.

If the resource was not already in use when entering the above code, then *claim_resource* will be set to 0 and the thread will continue execution at the label got_resource. The thread then does whatever it needs to do within the critical section, and then on leaving it executes this code:

```
    _asm    dec     claim_resource
    _asm    jl      released_resource
    _asm    mov     claim_resource,-1
    _SignalID( (DWORD)&claim_resource );
released_resource:
```

If only a single thread has attempted to claim the critical section, then on leaving, the variable *claim_resource* will be 0, and decrementing it will restore it to −1 and execution will continue at the label released_resource. However, if one or more threads have been blocked attempting to get at the resource, then *claim_count* will be greater than or equal to zero after the decrement operation. In this case, *claim_resource* is reset to −1, all threads which are currently blocked on the specified blocking ID are signaled by the call to the service **_SignalID**, and then the critical section is left. Since all threads blocked on the &*claim_resource* ID will be awakened, the first one to retry the get_resource test above will be able to access the critical section.

FSD Linkage

Although much of IFSMgr's internals are undocumented, perhaps an area where documentation is most sorely missed is in how IFSMgr and FSDs establish their linkage. A better understanding of this linkage can help when analyzing certain kinds of bugs, like "Why doesn't IFSMgr call my FSD?" or "Why isn't my FSD mounted?"

The process of making a device visible to IFS is called *mounting* if the device is local, or *connecting* if the device is remote. The reverse processes, *dismounting* or *disconnecting*, remove a device from the system. At the FSD level, mounting is handled by **FS_MountVolume**, connecting is handled by **FS_ConnectNetResource**, and dismounting and disconnecting are handled by **FS_DisconnectResource**.

First, we'll review how FSDs register with IFSMgr. Then we'll examine the processes of mounting and dismounting, as well as connecting and disconnecting, in detail. In the descriptions which follow, only the commonly traversed pathways through the file system are examined during the mounting and dismounting of local drives and character devices. Many "corner cases" are left unexplored so as not to distract you with additional details that do not clarify the overall picture.

FSD Registration

The **FS_MountVolume** and **FS_ConnectNetResource** functions are installed by each FSD through one of the registration calls to IFSMgr. Recall that there are three different types of registration: **IFSMgr_RegisterMount**, **IFSMgr_RegisterNet**, and **IFSMgr_RegisterCFSD**, corresponding to local FSDs, remote FSDs, and character FSDs. The provider IDs returned by **IFSMgr_RegisterMount** and **IFSMgr_ RegisterNet** form a continuous range 0 through 9 for local FSDs and 10 through 17 for remote FSDs. IFSMgr creates a function pointer table, `MountVolTable[]`, of 18 entries, where **FS_MountVolume** and **FS_ConnectNetResource** addresses are stored. (When searching for a remote FSD, sometimes the elements 10 through 17 are treated as a separate table, `ConnectNetTable[]`.) Given a provider ID, a mount operation is performed by a call, such as

```
(*MountVolTable[provider ID])(pifs)
```

or, if a file system hook is to see the call, by

```
Call_FSD(MountVolTable[provider ID], IFSFN_CONNECT, pifs, FALSE)
```

Character devices store their mount function pointers in a table separate from local and remote FSDs. The elements in this table are structures with two members:

```
typedef struct { int (*mntfunc)(); PathElement* pDevName[]; }
       CHARDEV, *PCHARDEV;
```

The first member, *mntfunc*, holds the address of the mount function, and the second member, *pDevName*, is a pointer to an array of pointers to device names stored as `PathElements`. Up to 8 character FSDs can be registered with IFSMgr and these are stored in an array I've named `MountCharTable[]`. Once a matching device name is located in `MountCharTable[]`, its accompanying mount function can be called like this:

```
Call_FSD(MountCharTable[i].mntfunc, IFSFN_CONNECT, pifs, FALSE)
```

Mounting a Local Drive

A local drive will be mounted the first time it is accessed and on the first access after its media has changed. Any file system request that references a volume may initiate a mount operation if that volume is not already mounted. In practice, the system drive will be accessed first and mounted first, but only after IFSMgr has completed its Device Init phase. It is during the Device Init phase that IFSMgr initializes its internal data structures to reflect known drives in the system as determined by examining the DOS CDS array and querying IOS for drive information. For each such drive detected, a zero-filled `volinfo` structure is allocated and its address stored in `SysVolTable[]`. Recall from Figure 6-2 that for each local volume (*volnum* 0-31), `SysVolTable[volnum]` contains the address of a `volinfo` structure. The first member of the `volinfo` structure, *vi_psr*, is a pointer to the volume's shell resource structure (see Appendix C, *IFSMgr Data Structures*, for details on the `volinfo` structure).

The first access to a local drive typically occurs through IFSMgr's Int 21h dispatch routines. These routines indirectly rely upon a pair of IFSMgr's internal functions to check if a mount is needed (**_NeedMount**) and to actually perform the mount (**_Gen_FSMount_IFSReq**). The prototype for **_NeedMount** has this form:

```
BOOL _NeedMount( ifsreq* pifs, int Drive, BOOL bChgReset )
```

If the function returns TRUE, the specified zero-based *Drive* needs to be mounted. The variable *pifs* holds a pointer to the ifsreq structure for the current file system request, and the variable *bChgReset* indicates whether the IOS function for media change reset is to be called.

One indicator that a drive needs to be mounted is given by `SysVolTable[]`. If the indexed entry is NULL, or if the `volinfo` member which points to the shell resource (*SysVolTable[drive]->vi_psr*) is NULL, the drive needs to be mounted. After a successful mount, `volinfo` and shell resource structures are allocated and initialized.

To do the mounting operation, _Gen_FSMount_IFSReq is called. It has the prototype:

```
int _Gen_FSMount_IFSReq( int Drive, int arg2 )
```

This function and subfunctions which it calls ultimately call **FS_MountVolume** on the FSD which supports the drive. The steps which are taken can be summarized as follows:

- Allocate an `ifsreq` structure and initialize its contents
- If `SysVolTable[Drive]` is NULL, allocate a `volinfo` structure and insert it in `SysVolTable[Drive]`

- Allocate a shell resource structure

- Fill in the **ifsreq** structure with parameters specific to a **FS_MountVolume** call:

  — *ir_volh* = address of IOS's VRP structure for *Drive*

  — *ir_rh* = address of first DOS DPB

  — *ir_fh* = address of shell resource

  — *ir_mntdrv* = *Drive*

  — *ir_flags* = the type of mount operation (*IR_FSD_MOUNT*)

  — *ifs_drv* = *Drive* + 1

  — *ifs_psr* = address of shell resource

- look up the provider ID in the array **Vol_to_ProId[]** indexed by *Drive*

  — if the value is 0xff, start with provider ID of the last registered local FSD

  — if the value is 0, start with the provider ID of last registered local FSD

  — for any other value, use it as an initial provider ID

- **Step A**: attempt to mount *Drive* using **FS_MountVolume** function by calling:

  ```
  Call_FSD( MountVolTable[provider ID], IFSFN_CONNECT, pifs, FALSE );
  ```

  If mount succeeds, add address of shell resource to **SrTable[]**:

  1. Fill in the shell resource structure,

  2. Insert address of shell resource in the **volinfo** structure,

  3. Send an **IFSMgr_NetFunction** broadcast of type *NF_DRIVEUSE*,

  4. **Call_FSD**(*pifs->pfs_psr->sr_func.vf[VFN_DIR]*, *IFSFN_DIR*, *pifs*, *FALSE*) to check that the directory in the drive's CDS (current directory structure) exists,

  5. Update IOS's VRP structure for *Drive*,

  and save the succeeding provider ID in **Vol_to_ProId[*Drive*]**; go to **step** B

- If mount fails, and provider ID > 0, decrement provider ID, and repeat from **step A**;

- If mount fails, and provider ID is 0, go to **step B**;

- **Step B**: if provider ID > 0, notify IOS of the mount using **IRS_MountNotify**

- Free the **ifsreq** structure

- Return the *ir_error* value

A drive created as a **subst** alias of an existing logical drive and subdirectory is a special case. In this case, a **volinfo** structure is created which references the parent drive's shell resource. Three members of a `volinfo` structure are used to track the **subst** drive: *vi_drv* contains the volume number for the referenced drive, *vi_subst_path* is the null-terminated Unicode string of the complete path to which the **subst** drive refers, and *vi_leng* contains the length of the Unicode string in bytes. While the creation of such a drive generates **IFSMgr_NetFunction** (*NF_DRIVEUSE*) notifications, there is no underlying call to the parent FSD's **FS_MountVolume** entry point. Figure 8-1 shows the relationships between the various data structures used to track standard and **subst** local drives.

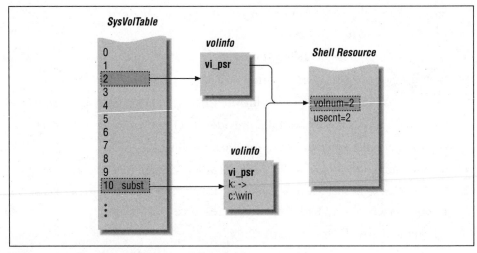

Figure 8-1. subst drive K mapping to C:\WIN

Mounting a Character Device

As with local drives, a character device will be mounted the first time it is accessed. Any file system request that references a registered device name will initiate a mount operation if that device name is not already mounted. The first access to a character device typically occurs through IFSMgr's Int 21h dispatch routines. These routines rely upon IFSMgr's internal function, **_PathToShRes**, to convert a pathname into a shell resource. This function distinguishes device names, local file pathnames, and UNC names by inspecting an undocumented return code from **IFSMgr_ParsePath** (see Chapter 12). The parser always checks the last `PathElement` to see if it is a registered device name or a DOS device name.

The function prototype for **_PathToShRes** has this form:

```
int _PathToShRes( ifsreq* pifs, int wildcards )
```

where *pifs* is a pointer to the `ifsreq` structure for the current file system request and *wildcards* indicates how wildcards are to be treated; a value of 0 for no wildcards, a value of 1 to accept long filename wildcards, and a value of 2 to accept "8.3" wildcard names. Calling _PathToShRes with *pifs->ifs_psr* set to NULL and with *pifs->ir_data* containing a pathname which is a device name will initiate mounting of the character device. Here, in summary, are the steps taken:

- Using the last `PathElement` parsed in the input pathname, search through `MountCharTable[]` for a matching registered device name; if a match is found, return two indexes, one to `MountCharTable[]` and one to `MountCharTable[i].pDevNames[]`

- Insert this device into the `CharSrTable[]` array; each entry consists of two DWORDS: the first is the pair of indexes returned in the previous step and the second will hold the address of the corresponding shell resource; `CharSrTable[]` can hold up to 64 device names

- Allocate and initialize an `ifsreq` structure

- Allocate storage for a shell resource

- Fill in the `ifsreq` structure with parameters specific to a **FS_MountVolume** call:

  — *ir_volh* = address of IOS's VRP structure for the character device; if one is returned by **IOS_Requestor_Service**, *IRS_GET_VRP*; otherwise NULL

  — *ir_fh* = address of shell resource

  — *ir_flags* = the type of mount operation (*IR_FSD_MOUNT*)

  — *ifs_psr* = address of shell resource

  — *ifs_proid* = provider ID of character device (index to `MountCharTable[]`)

  — *ir_aux2* = index into `MountCharTable[provider ID].pDevName[]`

- Call the **FS_MountVolume** entry point for the device using:

  Call_FSD(*MountCharTable[i].mntfunc, IFSFN_CONNECT, pifs*, FALSE)

- If the mount succeeds, insert the address of the shell resource into `CharSrTable[]`

- Initialize the contents of the shell resource

Figure 8-2 illustrates the relationships between the data structures used to track character devices.

Dismounting a Local Drive

Mounts of local drives are intended to be static, with the exception of drives which support removable media. For example, CD-ROM FSDs are provided with the services **IFSMgr_CDROM_Attach** and **IFSMgr_CDROM_Detach**, to asynchronously mount and dismount a CD-ROM drive. Fixed media drives will only

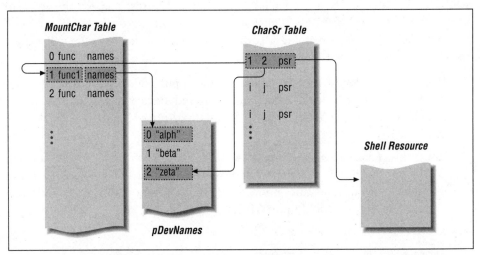

Figure 8-2. Using a CharSrTable to get device name ("zeta") and mount function (func1)

dismount at system shutdown. To be more exact, when IFSMgr receives the System Exit control message, it will procede to dismount local drives, in reverse order, from the last mounted to the first.

IFSMgr uses an internal function to perform the dismount (_Dismount_Local_ Drives). The prototype for **_Dismount_Local_Drives** has this form:

```
void _Dismount_Local_Drives( ifsreq* pifs )
```

The variable *pifs* holds an **ifsreq** structure which has been allocated and initialized for the function call.

_Dismount_Local_Drives and the functions it calls attempt to reduce the reference counts on the various data structures that track the local drives. This involves closing any open files, reclaiming heap allocations, and ultimately calling **FS_ DisconnectResource** on each volume.

IFSMgr maintains a single table, **SrTable**, containing addresses of shell resource structures for local drives and remote connections. Two separate one-way linked lists thread their way through the table. The heads for these lists are *Head_Local_ Srs*, for the shell resources which refer to local drives, and *Head_Net_Srs*, for shell resources which refer to network resources. To dismount all local drives, IFSMgr starts at *Head_Local_Srs* and walks the list to remove each shell resource. The steps which are taken to dismount each shell resource can be summarized as follows:

1. Walk list of local shell resources (a nested walk) for those having a matching VRP address close open files on the volume.

2. Walk list of local shell resources (a nested walk) for those having a matching VRP address and a non-zero *sr_inUse*. Remove any remaining references such as **subst** drives.

3. Do a final **IoreqDerefConnection** which reduces the *sr_inUse* to zero and forces a **FS_DisconnectResource** call on the volume; this call also frees the shell resource structure if it succeeds, followed by removal of the resource from the `SrTable` with adjustment of *Head_Local_Srs*.

Finally, for each drive which has been removed, perform these steps:

1. Generate an **IFSMgr_NetFunction** broadcast of type *NF_DRIVEUNUSE*.

2. Free the `volinfo` structure storage.

3. For **subst** drives, also copy the complete pathname to the DOS CDS structure.

Dismounting a Character Device

As with local drives, mounts of character devices are usually static, with IFSMgr automatically dismounting the devices when the system exits and IFSMgr receives the System Exit control message. However, IFSMgr also provides the service **IFSMgr_FSDUnmountCFSD** for dynamically dismounting a character FSD.

IFSMgr uses an internal function to perform the dismount (**_Dismount_Char_Devices**). The prototype for **_Dismount_Char_Devices** has this form:

```
void _Dismount_Char_Devices( ifsreq* pifs )
```

The variable *pifs* holds a pointer to an `ifsreq` structure which has been allocated and initialized for the function call. **_Dismount_Char_Devices** and the functions it calls attempt to reduce the reference counts on the various data structures that track the character device. This involves closing any open handles, reclaiming heap allocations, and ultimately calling **FS_DisconnectResource** on each device.

IFSMgr maintains a separate table, `CharSrTable`, containing addresses of shell resources for character devices and printers. A one-way linked list threads through the table. The head for the list is *Head_Char_Srs*, and starts with the most recently mounted character device. To dismount all character devices, IFSMgr starts at *Head_Char_Srs* and walks the list, removing the resources associated with each device. The steps which are taken at each shell resource in the list can be summarized as follows:

- If the resource has a non-zero *sr_inUse* and a valid pointer to a chain of fhandles, the corresponding handles are closed, thereby reducing the *sr_inUse*.

- *Sr_inUse* is decremented.

- The internal function, **IoreqDerefConnection**, is called for the shell resource; if the *sr_inUse* decrements to zero, **FS_DisconnectResource** is called for the character device, the heap allocation for the resource is freed, and it is removed from **CharSrTable** with adjustment to *Head_Char_Srs*.

FSD Connecting

Some examples of connections are mapping a local drive letter to a remote server and share name, and accessing a remote file by a UNC pathname.

Drive-based connections

When mapping a local drive to a remote drive and directory, the standard connection dialog is displayed in response to the **WNetConnectionDialog1** API. The information gathered by this dialog is used by the Multiple Provider Router (MPR) to route the request to an appropriate Network Provider and call that provider's **NPAddConnection** SPI.

The Network Provider then passes the request to the remote FSD, using the **DeviceIoControl, IFS_IOCTL_21**, interface. As an example, for Microsoft Networks, Int 21h function 5F47h (NetUseAdd, a Lan Manager DOS extension), is called. This function receives the following register arguments: BX is the level number, either 1 or 2; CX is the size of the **use_info** structure; and ES:DI is a pointer to the **use_info** structure. The **use_info** structure which is passed to NetUseAdd is either a **use_info_1** or a **use_info_2** structure, depending on the level of the call. As part of its argument checking, IFSMgr verifies the size (CX) of the **use_info** structure to be either 26 bytes for **use_info_1** or 52 bytes for **use_info_2**. This function is actually handled by IFSMgr's dispatch function **dNetFunc**. A similar Int 21h function, **Make Net Connection**, 5F03h, serves the same purpose but uses different arguments.

The handlers for Int 21h functions 5F03h and 5F47h massage the input parameters and call a common internal IFSMgr function which I've named **_UseAdd**. This function can also be accessed at ring-0 through the service **IFSMgr_UseAdd**. This internal function, **_UseAdd**, is a frontend to a call to **IFSMgr_SetupConnection**. The function prototype for **_UseAdd** takes this form:

```
_UseAdd( ifsreq* pifs, void* pinfo, int connstatus, int bStatic )
```

The calling arguments consist of *pifs*, a pointer to the **ifsreq** structure; *pinfo*, a structure containing information about the mapping; *connstatus*, an integer having the value 0 if the resource is setup connected and 1 if the resource is setup disconnected; *bStatic*, a Boolean which is 0 if the connection is to be established at system startup (static), and 1 if the connection is established by the user.

The `use_info_1` structure has the following declaration:

```
typedef struct use_info_1 {
  char  ui2_local[9];   // ASCIIZ local drive letter ("F:") or device
                        //  name
  char  ui2_pad_1;      // unused
  char* ui2_remote;     // pointer to ASCIIZ remote UNC pathname
  char* ui2_password;   // pointer to ASCIIZ password (NULL if none)
  WORD  ui2_status;     //
  WORD  ui2_asg_type;   // type of resource connected to
                        //  (USE_DISKDEV,etc.)
  WORD  ui2_refcount;   //
  WORD  ui2_usecount;   //
  }
  use_info_1, * puse_info_1;
```

The declaration for the `use_info_2` structure is given in *ifsmgrex.h* on the companion disk. The only members which _UseAdd cares about are *ui2_local*, *ui2_remote*, *ui2_password*, and *ui2_asg_type*, whether *pinfo* points to a `use_info_1` or `use_info_2` structure. (Note that the `use_info_2` structure given in the DDK file *ifsmgr.inc* is not correct.)

_UseAdd performs several preliminaries prior to calling **IFSMgr_SetupConnection**:

- Validates the local drive (from *ui2_local*) to use in a mapping, and verifies it is not a drive in use and does not exceed the "last drive" limit; the local drive number (1-based) is placed into *pifs->ifs_drv*.

- If a printer port is specified in place of a drive letter, e.g., LPT1, a drive number is assigned in the range 21h to 29h for LPT1 to LPT9 and is placed into *pifs->ifs_drv* (it isn't clear how generic character devices are redirected).

- Validates the server name and share name (from *ui2_remote*) via a call to **IFSMgr_ParsePath**; this path must be a UNC path or a path which has been parsed by a custom parser installed via **IFSMgr_SetPathHook**; the resultant `ParsedPath` is stored to *pifs->ir_ppath*, e.g., *SERVER**SHARE*.

- Allocates a volinfo structure which is stored to SysVolTable[pifs->ifs_drv-1].

_UseAdd then calls **IFSMgr_SetupConnection** with these arguments:

```
IFSMgr_SetupConnection( pifs, RESOPT_DEV_ATTACH, RESTYPE_DISK )
```

The contents of the `ifsreq` structure are modified to reflect the arguments passed to _UseAdd. This form of connection is referred to as a "drive-based" connection in the IFS specification.

Now what does **IFSMgr_SetupConnection** do internally? Without getting into all of the details and handling of error and exceptional conditions, here are the basic steps it takes:

1. Allocate a block in which to store a shell resource structure.

2. If an explicit *ifs_proid* is stored in `ifsreq`, then call the **FS_ConnectNetRe-source** function indexed in the `MountVolTable[]`; this call is direct to the table function.

3. If *ifs_proid* is ANYPROID (any provider), then look up the server name in the name cache and if found, convert the returned NetID to a provider ID; then call the **FS_ConnectNetResource** function indexed in `MountVolTable[]`; this call is made via **Call_FSD**, so it will be seen by a file system hook.

4. If *ifs_proid* is ANYPROID and the server name is not in the name cache, then attempt to call **FS_ConnectNetResource** for each registered net provider in the table `ConnectNetTable[]`, until one succeeds or the list is exhausted; these calls are made via **Call_FSD**, so they will be seen by a file system hook.

5. If **FS_ConnectNetResource** succeeds, then add the server name to the name cache; adjust the *ir_ppath* member of the `ifsreq` structure to advance past the first two `PathElements` for server and share names; insert the address of the shell resource into the `SrTable` and, finally, fill in the shell resource structure; the *sr_flags* member of the shell resource has only the *IFSFH_RES_NETWORK* attribute.

6. If **FS_ConnectNetResource** fails, then **IFSMgr_SetupFailedConnection** is called to give an FSD that hooks this function a chance to emulate network services when the net provider is not available; the default implementation of this service by IFSMgr simply returns the error *ERROR_BAD_NET_PATH* (35h); finally, the block of memory allocated for the shell resource is freed.

If **IFSMgr_SetupConnection** returns to **_UseAdd** without error, the `volinfo` structure is filled in with the address of the shell resource. An **IFSMgr_NetFunction** broadcast is generated of type NF_DRIVEUSE, indicating that a new drive has appeared in the system. The DOS CDS structure for the drive is also updated for each VM. Finally, a callback is scheduled (using **SHELL_CallAtAppyTime**) to a function which broadcasts a plug-and-play event using the function call:

```
IFSMgr_PNPEvent( DBT_DEVICEARRIVAL, drvnum, PNPT_VOLUME | DBTF_NET )
```

_UseAdd also clears the *ifs_psr* member of the `ifsreq` structure. This step assures that the connection's reference count is not immediately decremented by a call to **IoreqDerefConnection**.

UNC-based connections

The path that we have just traced is the system response to the deliberate mapping of a drive. **IFSMgr_SetupConnection** is also called when a UNC pathname is processed by IFSMgr's Int 21h dispatch routines. Many of the dispatch routines, including **dRing0_OpenCreate, dOpenCreate, dMkRmDir, dChDir, dGet-CurDir, dAttribs, dGetVolInfo, dDelete, dGetFullName, dFindFile, dRename,**

dSubst, and **dIoctl**, use IFSMgr's internal function **_PathToShRes** to convert a path-name, UNC or otherwise, into a shell resource. These "connections on demand" are made by a call to **IFSMgr_SetupConnection**, which takes this form:

```
IFSMgr_SetupConnection( pifs, RESOPT_UNC_REQUEST, RESTYPE_WILD )
```

This call establishes what the IFS specification refers to as a *UNC-based* connection. It follows the same basic steps as described above for *drive-based* connections. The *sr_flags* member of the shell resource for a UNC-based connection has both *IFSFH_RES_NETWORK* and *IFSFH_RES_UNC* attributes set.

One of the main differences between a UNC-based and a drive-based connection is in the way the connection's reference count is maintained. For a UNC-based connection the reference count is decremented by a call to **IoreqDerefConnection** as soon as the dispatch function completes. This happens because the *ifs_psr* member of **ifsreq** is not cleared before returning to the dispatcher. This would seem to suggest that UNC-based connections only last for the length of a file system request if the reference count drops to zero. This is not the case and we'll see why when we look at how UNC-based disconnection occurs.

FSD Disconnecting

Some examples of disconnection are removing a drive letter mapping to a remote server and share name and automatic disconnection after a period where a connection is not used.

Drive-based disconnection

Disconnecting a mapping of a local drive to a remote drive and directory is accomplished by the **WNetCancelConnection2** API. The parameters passed to this function are used to create a call to **NPCancelConnection** corresponding to the Network Provider for the specified server. The Network Provider then passes the cancel request to the remote FSD, again using the **DeviceIoControl**, IFS_IOCTL_ 21, interface. As an example, for Microsoft Networks, Int 21h function 5F48h (**NetUseDel**, a Lan Manager DOS extension) is called. This function receives the local drive name or the remote device UNC name which is to have the mapping canceled. This function is actually handled by IFSMgr's dispatch function **dNet-Func**. A similar Int 21h function, **Delete Net Connection**, 5F04h, serves the same purpose but uses different arguments.

The handlers for Int 21h functions 5F04h and 5F48h massage the input parameters and call a common internal IFSMgr function which I've named **_UseDel**. This function can also be accessed at ring-0 through the service **IFSMgr_UseDel**. This internal function, **_UseDel**, is a frontend to a call to another internal function, **IoreqDerefConnection**.

The function prototype for **_UseDel** takes this form:

```
_UseDel( ifsreq* pifs, int drvnum, int ForceLevel );
```

The calling arguments include *pifs*, a pointer to the `ifsreq` structure; *drvnum*, the one-based local drive which is to be unmapped; and *ForceLevel*, the force level to use for the disconnection. There are four force levels which are interpreted differently depending on the resource connected to. In the case of a drive-based disconnection, force levels 0 and 1 will fail if there are any open files on the mapped drive or if it is the current drive, whereas force level 2 closes open files and then disconnects the drive, but will fail if it is the current drive, and force level 3 closes open files and disconnects the drive even if it is the current drive.

_UseDel performs the following steps when called with a mapped-drive argument:

1. Reconcile drive number, provider ID, and shell resource.

2. Look up `volinfo` structure in `SysVolTable[]`; if connection is static, fails the disconnect unless *ForceLevel* is greater than or equal to 4.

3. Verify that drive's DOS CDS attributes word at offset 43h has the value 0xC000.

4. If the *ForceLevel* is less than 3, check if the mapped drive is the current drive in any VM; if so, then fail the disconnect.

5. If the *ForceLevel* is less than 2 and there are open files on the mapped drive, fail the disconnect; if the *ForceLevel* is 2 or greater and there are open files on the mapped drive, close the files one by one.

6. Remove `volinfo` from `SysVolTable[]`.

7. Decrement the reference count in the shell resource, *vi_psr*.

8. Broadcast **IFSMgr_NetFunction** *NF_DRIVEUNUSE*, to notify that the drive has gone away.

9. Clear the drive's DOS CDS entries for each VM.

10. Free the memory block used by `volinfo`.

11. Schedule callback to broadcast a Plug and Play event:

```
IFSMgr_PNPEvent( DBT_DEVICEREMOVECOMPLETE, drvnum,
                 PNPT_VOLUME|DBTF_NET )
```

12. **IoreqDerefConnection** decrements the shell resource's reference count; since it drops to zero and this resource does not have the *IFSFH_RES_UNC* attribute, call **FS_DisconnectResource** on this resource, remove it from `SrTable`, and free the shell resource's memory block.

UNC-Based Disconnection

UNC-based connections persist as long as the connection's reference count does not drop to zero. Some actions on a connection keep the connection open until the actions are explicitly undone, e.g., opening a file will increment the reference count until a close on that file decrements the reference count.

Other file system requests will only keep the reference count incremented for the duration of the operation. For example, checking the file attributes on an explicit UNC pathname will create a UNC-based connection via a call to **_PathToShRes**. After the request has been completed, the dispatcher will check for a non-zero *ifs_psr* member of the `ifsreq` structure. If it is non-zero, **IoreqDerefConnection** will be called to decrement its reference count. If the reference count drops to zero, then the *sr_flags* for the shell resource are checked for the *IFSFH_RES_UNC* attribute. If this attribute is set, the connection is not immediately disconnected, as would be the case with a drive-based connection. Instead, the shell resource's reference count is left as zero to *mark* the connection for removal.

In order for one of these marked UNC-based connections to get removed it needs to "age" a few minutes. To handle the aging of these connections and their eventual removal, IFSMgr schedules a recurring event every 120 seconds. The event handler walks the list of current connections and looks for two special connection states. The first state is a UNC-based connection which has a reference count of zero. When a connection with this state is found it is advanced to the next state. The state change is indicated by modifying the shell resource's *sr_flags* from *IFSFH_RES_NETWORK | IFSFH_RES_UNC* to *IFSFH_RES_NETWORK | IFSFH_RES_UNC | 0x02*.

If the connection to this particular server and share gets used before it is removed, the state gets reset on a call to **IoreqDerefConnection**. However, if the connection remains idle for 120 seconds until the next event, the event handler changes the sr_flags once more from *IFSFH_RES_NETWORK | IFSFH_RES_UNC | 0x02* to *IFSFH_RES_NETWORK | 0x02*.

The connection's reference count is *incremented* to 1 and then **IoreqDeref-Connnection** is called. This disconnects the resource, removes it from the shell resource list, and frees the resource's memory block.

MONOCFSD: A Character File System Driver

In this section, we'll look at a sample file system driver, MONOCFSD, which is a character FSD that drives a monochrome monitor. The complete source for

MONOCFSD is on the companion diskette. This makes a good example for introducing the structure of an FSD since we don't have to worry about IOS or network protocol details. In the next section, we'll look at an example of a remote FSD, FSINFILE.

Features

Basically, MONOCFSD is an FSD for a standard 80x25 monochrome display adapter. It associates a single device name, MONO, with the character device. Multiple file handles can be opened on MONO. It accepts independent writes on these separate open handles. Any programming language that supports file open, file write, and file close can use MONO as an output device. Multiple processes can write to MONO simultaneously. MONO is equally accessible from Win32, Win16, and DOS/V86 operating environments.

Output to the MONO device is buffered in the driver. A primitive keyboard interface allows scrolling of the display using line up, line down, and clear screen operations, using keys on the numeric keypad.

MONOCFSD fails initialization if a monochrome display adapter is not detected.

Design

The design centers on using a file model to interact with the monochrome display device. A client uses the MONO device much like one would use stdout, except that an explicit open is required. Thus for a client to use MONO, an open is performed, which returns a handle if successful. Output is sent to the device by performing writes to the handle. A separate line buffer is managed for each handle. A line will be displayed when either a carriage return and line feed are received or the 80 character buffer fills. Thus, all screen output is in complete lines. This allows multiple processes to interleave lines of output. The combined output of all clients is stored in a 200-line buffer. Normally, only the most recent 25 lines are displayed. A line-up operation will scroll back through the buffer by one line; a line-down operation will scroll forward through the buffer by one line. A keyboard interface to the scroll operations is achieved by assigning each to a hotkey.

MONOCFSD supports up to 10 clients; this is an arbitrary limit. MONOCFSD loads as a static VxD.

Implementation

During Device Init phase, MONOCFSD registers with IFSMgr using **IFSMgr_RegisterCFSD**, passing it the address of a mount function and the single device name,

MONO. The list of device names is passed as an array of pointers to `PathElements`, with the end of array marked by a NULL pointer. The device name is given by the `PathElement` { 10, 'M', 'O', 'N', 'O' }. The first element is the total length of the array which is 5 * **sizeof**(WORD) since the characters are in Unicode.

The mount function for MONOCFSD will get called the first time the "MONO" device is accessed. The source for the mount function is shown in Example 8-4.

Example 8-4. MONOCFSD's FS_MountVolume Function

```
int FS_MountCharDevice( pioreq pir ) {
  MonoPrint( "FS_MountVolume\n" );
  ifs_resource_hdl = pir->ir_fh;                  // save shell resource
  pir->ir_vfunc = &vf;              // return our volume function table
  pir->ir_rh = (void*)'MONO';                     // MONO's resource handle
  memset( OpenHandles, 0, 10*sizeof(void*) );   // init file handles
  return ( pir->ir_error = 0 );
  }
```

The mount function exchanges parameters with IFSMgr using the `ioreq` structure. As input, MONOCFSD receives the resource handle that IFSMgr is using to track this device (what we have referred to as a shell resource). MONOCFSD does not interpret this handle but does store it away, in *ifs_resource_hdl*, for possible future use in calls to certain IFSMgr services. MONOCFSD returns to IFSMgr a pointer to the structure containing all of the volume-based entry points. This address is placed in the `ioreq` member *ir_vfunc*. This structure is shown in Example 8-5. The other value returned to IFSMgr is a resource handle known only to the FSD. This handle is placed in the `ioreq` member *ir_rh*. It can be the address of an internal data structure or other guaranteed unique value. IFSMgr does not interpret this value, it simply passes it in on calls into MONOCFSD corresponding to this particular mount. The FSD can use this value to validate calls and also to distinguish mounts under different device names. As an example, the screen might be split into scrolling and non-scrolling regions, and these could be given separate device names. The non-scrolling screen might be treated as a fixed-size file, using a file seek to position the output cursor. For our needs it is sufficient to use the unique integer value 'MONO'.

Example 8-5. MONOCFSD's Volume-Based Function Table

```
struct volfunc vf = {
     IFS_VERSION, IFS_REVISION, NUM_VOLFUNC,
    { FailFsdCall,   /* VFN_DELETE */
     FailFsdCall,    /* VFN_DIR */
     FailFsdCall,    /* VFN_FILEATTRIB */
     FailFsdCall,    /* VFN_FLUSH */
     FailFsdCall,    /* VFN_GETDISKINFO */
     FS_OpenFile,    /* VFN_OPEN */
     FailFsdCall,    /* VFN_RENAME */
```

Example 8-5. MONOCFSD's Volume-Based Function Table (continued)

```
    FailFsdCall,   /* VFN_SEARCH */
    FailFsdCall,   /* VFN_QUERY */
    FS_Disconnect, /* VFN_DISCONNECT */
    FailFsdCall,   /* VFN_UNCPIPEREQUEST */
    FS_Ioctl,      /* VFN_IOCTL16DRIVE */
    FailFsdCall,   /* VFN_GETDISKPARMS */
    FailFsdCall,   /* VFN_FINDOPEN */
    FailFsdCall,   /* VFN_DASDIO */
  } };
```

The volume-based function table in Example 8-5, which supplies the linkage to IFSMgr, provides a function for every entry in the array. For most of the functions, the routine **FailFsdCall** is used. This function sets the *ir_error* member of the `ioreq` structure to *ERROR_INVALID_FUNCTION* and returns that value. This informs IFSMgr that the function is not implemented. The functions which are implemented include **FS_OpenFile**, **FS_Ioctl**, and **FS_Disconnect**. Of these, **FS_Disconnect** has the simplest implementation; it just sets *ir_error* to *ERROR_SUCCESS* and returns that value. This allows MONO to be dismounted without returning an error.

The **FS_Ioctl** function, shown in Example 8-6, is required to support the Int 21h function 4400h, Get Device Data. For all other **Ioctl** functions, an *ERROR_INVALID_FUNCTION* error code is returned. The *ir_flags* member of the `ioreq` structure contains the **Ioctl** subfunction number, and only subfunction 0 is checked for. Depending on the value of the *ir_options* member, a pointer to the client registers structure is retrieved from either *ir_data* or *ir_cregptr* (*ir_aux2*). Within the client registers, bit 7 of DX is set to 1 to indicate that the handle in BX refers to a device.

Example 8-6. MONOCFSD's FS_Ioctl Function

```
int FS_Ioctl( pioreq pir ) {
  PCRS pClientRegs;
  if ( pir->ir_flags == 0 ) { // "Get Device Data 0x4400"
    if (pir->ir_options == IOCTL_PKT_LINEAR_ADDRESS ) {
      pClientRegs = (PCRS)pir->ir_data;
      }
    else {
      pClientRegs = (PCRS)pir->ir_cregptr;
      }
    pClientRegs->Client_EDX = 0x00000080;  // is a device
    return ( pir->ir_error = 0 );
    }
  pir->ir_error = ERROR_INVALID_FUNCTION;
  return ( pir->ir_error );
  }
```

Example 8-7 shows the implementation of the **FS_OpenFile** function. First, a sanity check is performed on *ir_rh*, which should have the value 'MONO' that we returned when the device was mounted. Rather than just return a pointer to a handle-based function table, the *ir_hfunc* member contains a pointer to the location where the handle-based function pointers should be written. This location is initialized with three addresses: the address of the **FS_ReadFile** function, the address of the **FS_WriteFile** function, and the address of the "miscellaneous" handle-based function table (see Example 8-8). Since we don't support a read operation, the address of **FailFsdCall** is used for **FS_ReadFile**. **FS_OpenFile** then adds an entry to the **OpenHandles** array; the entry is the address of an 80-character line buffer structure. This address is also returned in *ir_fh* as a unique value representing this handle; IFSMgr will pass this value to other handle-based functions. Note that access to the global array **OpenHandles** is protected with a claim and release of the critical section. Finally *ir_options* is set to the value *ACTION_OPENED* and *ir_error* to *ERROR_SUCCESS* to indicate that the open succeeded.

Example 8-7. MONOCFSD's FS_OpenFile Function

```
int FS_OpenFile( pioreq pir ) {
    struct hndlfunc* phf;
    LINE* pl;
    int i;

    if ( pir->ir_rh == (void*)'MONO' ) {
        phf = pir->ir_hfunc; // get location where IFSMgr expects pointers
        phf->hf_read  = FailFsdCall;  // no FS_ReadFile support
        phf->hf_write = FS_WriteFile; //  .. only write supported
        phf->hf_misc  = &hm; //  .. table of other handle-based functions
        ClaimHandleArray(); // Critical section around OpenHandles[]
        for (i=0; i<MAXHDL; i++)
            if ( !OpenHandles[i] ) break;
        if ( i == MAXHDL ) {
            ReleaseHandleArray();
            return ( pir->ir_error = 4 ); // ERROR_TOO_MANY_OPEN_FILES
            }
        pl = IFSMgr_GetHeap( sizeof( LINE ) ); // zero initialized
        if ( pl == 0 ) {
            ReleaseHandleArray();
            return ( pir->ir_error = 1 );
            }
        OpenHandles[i] = pl;
        ReleaseHandleArray(); // End critical section
        // we use the line buffer as our open instance
        pir->ir_fh = (void*)pl;
        pir->ir_options = ACTION_OPENED;
        return ( pir->ir_error = 0 );
        }
    else {
        return ( pir->ir_error = 1 );
        }
    }
```

Only two handle-based functions are supported for the MONO device: **FS_Write-File** and **FS_CloseFile**. The remainder of the functions in the handle-based function table (see Example 8-8) call into **FailFsdCall**, to indicate that they are not implemented.

Example 8-8. MONOCFSD's Miscellaneous Handle-Based Function Table

```
struct hndlmisc hm = {
    IFS_VERSION, IFS_REVISION, NUM_HNDLMISC,
    { FailFsdCall,      // HM_SEEK
      FS_CloseFile,     // HM_CLOSE
      FailFsdCall,      // HM_COMMIT
      FailFsdCall,      // HM_FILELOCKS
      FailFsdCall,      // HM_FILETIMES
      FailFsdCall,      // HM_PIPEREQUEST
      FailFsdCall,      // HM_HANDLEINFO
      FailFsdCall       // HM_ENUMHANDLE
    } };
```

Example 8-9 shows the implementation of the **FS_CloseFile** function. Again, a sanity check is performed on *ir_rh*, which should have the value 'MONO' that we returned when the device was mounted. The handle to MONO which is being closed is passed in *ir_fh*. It is just the address of one of the line buffer structures which are stored in the **OpenHandles** array. To validate the handle, **OpenHandles** is searched for a matching entry. If a match is found, then the current index of the buffer is checked to see if anything needs to be flushed to the screen. Finally, the allocation for the line buffer is freed and *ir_error* is set to *ERROR_SUCCESS*.

Example 8-9. MONOCFSD's FS_CloseFile Function

```
int FS_CloseFile( pioreq pir ) {
    void* hMono;
    LINE* pl;
    int i;

    if ( pir->ir_rh == (void*)'MONO' ) {
        hMono = pir->ir_fh;
        // First validate the handle
        ClaimHandleArray();       // Critical section around OpenHandles[]
        for (i=0; i<MAXHDL; i++)
            if ( OpenHandles[i] == hMono ) break;
        if ( i == MAXHDL ) {
            ReleaseHandleArray();
            return ( pir->ir_error = 6 );   // ERROR_INVALID_HANDLE
            }
        ReleaseHandleArray();     // End critical section
        pl = hMono;               // handle is our line buffer
        if ( pl->idx > 0 ) {      // flush any pending characters
            pl->pLine[pl->idx+1] = '\0';
```

Example 8-9. MONOCFSD's FS_CloseFile Function (continued)

```
            MonoPrint( pl->pLine );
            }
        IFSMgr_RetHeap( OpenHandles[i] );   // free the line buffer
        ClaimHandleArray();          // Critical section around OpenHandles[]
        OpenHandles[i] = 0;
        ReleaseHandleArray();        // End critical section
        return ( pir->ir_error = 0 );
        }
    else {
        return ( pir->ir_error = 1 );
        }
    }
```

The last function that we'll take a look at is **FS_WriteFile**, shown in Example 8-10. On each write, *ir_length* contains the number of characters written, *ir_data* contains a pointer to the buffer containing the characters to be written, and *ir_fh* contains the particular MONO handle to which to write the data. The handle in *ir_fh* is validated by checking that it is contained in the **OpenHandles** array. If the handle is found to be valid, then the handle is cast to a pointer to a line buffer structure. The characters in the buffer at *ir_data* are transferred into the line buffer starting at the current line buffer index. If a carriage return/line feed pair is encountered or if the line buffer fills (80 characters), the accumulated line is written to the monochrome monitor, using the **MonoPrint** function. The index into the line buffer is then reset to the beginning and the process continues until *ir_length* is exhausted. Multiple writes to a handle may be made before the assembled line is actually written to the monitor.

Example 8-10. MONOCFSD's FS_WriteFile Function

```
int FS_WriteFile( pioreq pir ) {
    char* pChar;
    char lastChar = 0;
    int cnt, i;
    LINE* pl;
    void* hMono;

    pChar = pir->ir_data;    // characters to be written to MONO
    cnt   = pir->ir_length;  // count of characters
    pl = hMono = pir->ir_fh; // line buffer for this handle
    // Validate the handle
    ClaimHandleArray();       // Critical section around OpenHandles[]
    for (i=0; i<MAXHDL; i++)
        if ( OpenHandles[i] == hMono ) break;
    if ( i == MAXHDL ) {
        ReleaseHandleArray();
        return ( pir->ir_error = 6 ); // ERROR_INVALID_HANDLE
        }
    ReleaseHandleArray();    // End critical section
    i = pl->idx;             // current index to line buffer
```

Example 8-10. MONOCFSD's FS_WriteFile Function (continued)

```
while( cnt > 0 ) {
    if ( i < 80 ) pl->pLine[i] = *pChar;
    if ( lastChar == 0x0d && *pChar == 0x0a ) {
        pl->pLine[i+1] = '\0';
        MonoPrint( pl->pLine );
        // Reset line buffer variables and continue
        lastChar = '\0';
        pChar++;
        i = 0;
        cnt--;
        continue;
        }
    lastChar = *pChar;
    pChar++;
    if ( i < 80 ) i++;
    cnt--;
    }
pl->idx = i;            // save the current line buffer index
return ( pir->ir_error = 0 );
}
```

Using MONOCFSD

To illustrate how one might use MONOCFSD, we'll show typical usage from a C program. First, the device must be opened using statements like the following:

```
FILE* fMono;
fMono = fopen( "mono", "r+" );
```

Then, at points where output is to be displayed, any of the standard C stream I/O functions could be used with the **fMono** stream. For example, the following lines output a single line of text:

```
fprintf( fmono, "In function %s, SomeVariable=%lx\n",
                "SomeFunc", SomeVar );
fflush( fmono );
```

Since stream I/O is buffered by default, **fflush** forces the text to be written immediately. Another way to accomplish this is to use the functions **setbuf** or **setvbuf** to disable buffering for the stream. Finally, the program would release the MONO handle with a call to **fclose**. MONO might also be used from a DOS box as a target for redirection, as in the command **dir > mono**.

FSINFILE: A Remote File System Driver

In this section, we'll look at the sample file system driver, FSINFILE, which is a remote FSD that contains a file-system-in-a-file. The complete source for FSINFILE is on the companion diskette. This example is more complicated than MONOCFSD, and implements many more FSD functions.

Features

FSINFILE creates a file called *fsif.bin* in the *windows* directory. The creation of and reads and writes to this file are done using the **IFSMgr_Ring0FileIO** service. Internally, *fsif.bin* contains the structure of a simple file system. It is divided into three sections: allocation bitmap, root directory entries, and user space. The unit of user space is a 512 byte sector. For each sector in user space, there corresponds a single bit in the allocation bitmap. If a bit is set, the sector is allocated; otherwise it is free. Directory entries hold the 8.3 names of files which are stored in user space, as well as a creation date and time, size, attributes, and a map of allocated sectors. This is not a "production" file system, but it does provide a great test-bed for experimenting with FSD functions and exploring interactions with IFSMgr. A production remote file system would also supply a Network Provider DLL to support drive enumeration and other WNet functions.

Implementation Notes

The source code for FSINFILE is amply documented, so refer to the companion disk for complete information. Here, I will just single out one aspect of its implementation that is a little unusual. The file system registers through **IFSMgr_RegisterNet** as a network FSD. I use a "bogus" Net ID, i.e., a value which lies outside the range of currently assigned networks. This registration returns a provider ID which is used with subsequent IFSMgr services.

If you think about it, a remote FSD just maps local file operations to operations in another domain. This applies equally well to our situation except instead of our file system residing on another machine across the network, it resides on our machine and it is embedded in a local file.

The main reason for using this approach is that it is the simplest way to create a drive. IFSMgr provides facilities which make connections to network drives easy to setup and tear down. This facility is supported through the services **IFSMgr_UserAdd** and **IFSMgr_InitUseAdd**. I use the latter because it allows us to create the drive implicitly at system startup by assigning it the next available drive in the range of available drives as shown in Figure 8-3 (the upper limit is set by the **LastDrive** command if it is issued in *config.sys,* otherwise the default is either 26, or if you have the Netware client installed, 32). **IFSMgr_InitUseAdd** uses the supplied provider ID and `use_info_2` structure to create a properly formed IFS request to the service **IFSMgr_SetupConnection**. The latter prepares the **FS_ConnectNetResource** call into the FSD which matches the provider ID. This initial call is used to

Figure 8-3. Drive H (\\.\fsinfile), a FSINFILE remote driver

mount our file system, by either creating or opening the file *fsif.bin* and initializing the file system's internal state.

9

VFAT: The Virtual FAT File System Driver

The FAT file system was invented in 1977 as a method for storing data on floppy disks for Microsoft Stand-Alone Disk BASIC. It achieved wider usage in 1981 as the floppy disk storage mechanism used by MS-DOS Version 1 shipped with the first IBM PC. At that time, the OS code ran in 8 KB of memory and 5.25" floppy disk media only had a single level directory. With the introduction in 1982 of the IBM PC-XT with a 10 MB fixed disk, MS-DOS underwent a major revision. In MS-DOS Version 2, we saw the introduction of a hierarchical directory structure, support for fixed disks as well as floppy disks, and a UNIX-like handle-based file structure. Filenames were a maximum of 8 characters long with a 3 character extension and a pathname could be up to 64 characters long. Since then, the various releases of MS-DOS have extended support for larger and larger hard disks, but much of the underlying file structure has remained unchanged.

VFAT was introduced with Windows for Workgroups Version 3.11. Up until that time, the manipulation of file system structures in Windows 3.x was done by MS-DOS code executing in virtual-86 mode. Although the actual FAT file structures on the disk still mirrored those of MS-DOS 5 and 6.x, VFAT and IFSMgr provided file system services that executed in ring-0 protected mode.

The latest version of VFAT which accompanied the rollout of Windows 95 goes further by making some changes to the FAT file structures on the disk in order to support long filenames. Even more recent changes to VFAT, in OEM Service Release 2 (October 1996), increased the size of entries in the file allocation from

16 bits to 32 bits, thereby increasing the maximum allowable drive size to 2047 gigabytes.

The role of VFAT is to control reads from and writes to the disk in accordance with the FAT file structure. It understands how to convert a pathname into the chain of disk clusters and then return the contents of those sectors. Or, it can reverse direction and create long filename directory entries from a pathname and allocate clusters of storage and save a file's image within them. Before we dig into some aspects of VFAT's implementation, let's review the FAT file structure. In large measure, the DOS 6.x structure remains the same in Windows 95.

DOS 6.x FAT, Boot Record, and Directory Entries

A storage device has natural divisions based upon its design. There are multiple read/write heads which sweep over platters coated with ferromagnetic material. The read/write heads trace out concentric rings called *tracks*, and the tracks are divided by gaps into sectors. This sector is the unit by which hard disk storage is read and written and it usually contains 512 bytes of data.

With multiple megabyte and gigabyte storage commonplace, keeping track of in-use and available space at the granularity of a sector would require rather large data structures. By increasing the granularity to a grouping of sectors, smaller data structures can be used.

The term *cluster* is used to refer to the fundamental unit by which disk storage is allocated. The size of a cluster is measured in sectors. A cluster may contain 1, 2, 4, 8, ... sectors; it is always an integral power of 2. The sectors which comprise a cluster are consecutively numbered logical sectors.

The *file allocation table* (FAT) is used to track the usage of a volume's clusters. The table is organized as an array of either 12-bit or 16-bit cluster numbers. Cluster numbers start at 2, since the first two entries in the table are reserved. For 12-bit cluster numbers the maximum value is FEFh, whereas for 16-bit cluster numbers the maximum is FFEFh. A cluster number of 0 indicates that the cluster is available for allocation. The values FF7h or FFF7h are used to flag a cluster which contains a bad sector.

Directory entries specify a starting cluster number for a file or directory. This number is used as an index into the FAT. If the value is in the range for a valid cluster number, then that cluster is allocated to the file or directory and serves as an index to the next cluster. The total allocation is determined by following this chain of cluster numbers until the last cluster indicator is reached. The last cluster indicator is FF8-FFFh for 12-bit FATs, and FFF8-FFFFh for 16-bit FATs.

A volume will usually contain space for two FATs which are mirror images of each other. The extra FAT is used to detect disk corruption and allows recovery from some minor FAT problems.

Following the two FATs, space is set aside for the root directory entries. This is a part of the disk structure that has undergone some change with the Windows 95 version of VFAT. We will take a closer look at directory entries below. The space following the root directory entries is available for user data, and the first sector here marks the beginning of cluster number 2.

The *boot record* is always present as the first sector whether the volume is bootable or not. In addition to containing the OS boot code, it begins with a BOOTSECTOR structure which describes the layout of the disk volume. This includes such parameters as the size of a sector, the size of a cluster, the number of sectors used up by the FAT, the number of entries in the root directory, and the total number of sectors in the volume.

The information in the boot record is sufficient to delineate the starting positions of all of the important volume structures. The diskette accompanying this book contains the utility DUMPDISK, which displays the contents of the boot record, portions of the FATs, and the root directory entries for a fixed or floppy diskette. It is a Win32 console application (see source on the diskette) that illustrates use of the **DeviceIoControl** interface to VWIN32 to do direct disk reads. Some sample output from DISKDUMP is shown in Example 9-1. In this particular example, a fixed disk of 455 MB, sectors 0 through 467 are set aside for the boot record, the FATs, and the root directory entries. The first sector available for allocation to files and subdirectories is at 468.

Example 9-1. DUMPDISK Sample Output

```
Sector 0 - BOOTSECTOR structure ...
   OEM Name:                     MSWIN4.0
   Bytes/Sector:                 0200
   Sectors/Cluster:              10
   Reserved Sectors:             0001
   Number FATs:                  02
   Number Root Directory Entries: 0200
   Total number Sectors:         000d8db5
   Media Descriptor:             F8
   Number of Sectors/FAT:        00d9
   Sectors/Track:                003b
   Heads:                        0010
   Hidden Sectors:               0000003b
   BIOS Drive Number:            80
   Boot Signature:               29
   Volume ID:                    1f285e7a
   Volume Label:
   File System Type:             FAT16
```

Example 9-1. DUMPDISK Sample Output (continued)

```
Sector 1 - First File Allocation Table ...
 fff8 ffff ffff 0004 0005 0006 0007 ffff
 0009 000a 000b 000c ffff 000e 000f ffff
 ...
Sector 218 - Second File Allocation Table ...
 fff8 ffff ffff 0004 0005 0006 0007 ffff
 0009 000a 000b 000c ffff 000e 000f ffff
 ...
Sector 435 - Root Directory Entries ...
```

Name		Attrib	Creation Date/Time	Last Access	Start Cluster	Size	Chksum
IO	DOS	---shr	08-10-94 13:16:02	xx-xx-xx	0003	40854	
MSDOS	DOS	---shr	05-31-94 06:22:00	xx-xx-xx	0008	38138	
COMMAND	DOS	-----r	08-10-94 15:54:46	xx-xx-xx	04cf	54710	
COMMAND	COM	a-----	07-11-95 09:50:00	03-29-96	22a8	92870	
WETSUIT		a-v---	09-08-95 10:51:42	xx-xx-xx	0000	0	
DOS		-d----	09-08-95 11:51:52	xx-xx-xx	0002	0	
EXTMSDOS	SYS	---shr	12-12-94 14:18:40	xx-xx-xx	000d	22368	
WINA20	386	a-----	05-31-94 06:22:00	12-11-95	01cf	9349	
BOOTLOG	TXT	a---h-	12-21-95 16:50:34	12-21-95	0391	21894	
DBLSPACE	BIN	---shr	07-11-95 09:50:00	xx-xx-xx	228e	71287	
AUTOEXEC	BAT	a-----	05-02-96 09:14:18	05-20-96	c022	317	
SCSI		-d----	09-08-95 12:09:42	xx-xx-xx	031f	0	
CONFIG	DOS	a-----	09-08-95 12:17:34	xx-xx-xx	0397	270	
AUTOEXEC	DOS	a-----	09-08-95 12:17:34	xx-xx-xx	0396	148	
MSDOS	---	----h-	09-08-95 12:32:22	xx-xx-xx	0755	22	
SETUPLOG	TXT	a---h-	09-08-95 13:10:16	09-08-95	0756	46604	
SUHDLOG	DAT	----hr	09-08-95 13:01:48	xx-xx-xx	231b	5166	
WINDOWS		-d----	09-08-95 12:46:52	xx-xx-xx	079e	0	
DETLOG	TXT	a--sh-	01-20-96 19:44:40	01-20-96	21be	67944	
NETLOG	TXT	a-----	09-08-95 12:51:36	04-07-96	0798	1364	
CONFIG	SYS	a-----	03-24-96 21:35:00	05-20-96	9398	235	
MSDOS	SYS	a--shr	03-24-96 21:39:28	03-24-96	7dbd	1641	
BOOTLOG	PRV	a---h-	12-21-95 16:39:40	12-21-95	001d	21420	
A Program Files		--vshr					20
PROGRA~1		-d---r	09-08-95 12:52:40	xx-xx-xx	0ac8	0	
SYSTEM	1ST	---shr	09-08-95 13:01:36	xx-xx-xx	224d	312424	
DRVSPACE	BIN	---shr	07-11-95 09:50:00	xx-xx-xx	2298	71287	
DETLOG	OLD	---sh-	01-18-96 22:52:00	01-18-96	3e90	67946	
IO	SYS	---shr	07-11-95 09:50:00	xx-xx-xx	22fc	223148	

```
...
 Sector 468 - First available cluster.
```

Note that the Chksum column is blank except for the longname entry "Program Files." The checksum is only used on longname entries; however, the checksum is calculated on its associated alias entry (which follows on the next line).

Windows 95 Directory Entries

Starting with Windows 95, there are now three distinct types of directory entries written to the disk. The *shortname* entry is the same as the existing directory entry used by MS-DOS 5 and 6.x. This directory entry can represent 8.3 filenames, directory names, and the volume label. The other two types of directory entries consist of a sequence of one or more *longname* entries followed by a single *alias* entry (see Example 9-2). The alias entry is a shortname entry with an additional member for the last access date.

The longname directory entry is needed to represent case-preserved names or long filenames. As you can see in Example 9-2, most of the space in the 32-byte entry is consumed by 13 Unicode characters. The attribute byte is at the same offset as it occurs in shortname and alias entries, but because it contains a set of "impossible" settings, it is not recognized by DOS disk utilities. Thus legacy programs will only recognize and display the shortname and alias directory entries.

Example 9-2. Directory Entry Structures

```
typedef struct _DIRENTRY {
    char    deName[8];           // base name
    char    deExtension[3];      // extension
    BYTE    deAttributes;        // file or directory attributes
    BYTE    deReserved[6];
    WORD    deLastAccessDate;    // *New Win95* - last access date
    WORD    deEAhandle;          //
    WORD    deCreateTime;        // creation or last modification time
    WORD    deCreateDate;        // creation or last modification date
    WORD    deStartCluster;      // starting cluster of the file or directory
    DWORD   deFileSize;          // size of the file in bytes
    }
    DIRENTRY, *PDIRENTRY;

typedef struct _LONGDIRENTRY {
    char    leSequence;          // sequence byte:1,2,3,.. last entry is
                                 //   ORed with 40h
    wchar_t leName[5];           // Unicode characters of name
    BYTE    leAttributes;        // Attributes: 0fh
    BYTE    leType;              // Long Entry Type: 0
    BYTE    leChksum;            // Checksum for matching short name alias
    wchar_t leName2[6];          // More Unicode characters of name
    WORD    leZero;              // reserved
    wchar_t leName3[2];          // More Unicode characters of name
    }
    LONGDIRENTRY, *PLONGDIRENTRY;
```

Since each longname entry can hold 13 characters, if a filename is longer than that, additional longname entries are needed to store the additional characters.

The first byte in a longname entry serves as an integral sequence number starting at 1. The sequence number of the last longname entry is ORed with 40h. A typical sequence of longname entries is shown in Example 9-3.

Example 9-3. Directory Entries for a Long Filename

```
Name            Attrib    Creation         Last      Start     Size    Chksum
                          Date/Time        Access    Cluster
--------------- ------ ---------------- --------- -------- ------- -----
C ilename       --vshr                                               1e
2 ee_direntry_f --vshr                                               1e
1 This_is_a_thr --vshr                                               1e
   THIS_I~1     a----- 05-20-96 16:57:08 05-20-96   247c       8
```

This sample sequence of entries (shown in Example 9-3) consists of three long-name entries followed by a single alias entry. The filename which is spread over the three longname entries is *This_is_a_three_direntry_filename*. The sequence numbers are 1, 2, and C (43h). Adjacent to the first longname entry is the alias entry which contains an 8.3 format name, *THIS_I~1*, which is a capitalized and compressed version of the long filename. The alias entry is crucial for recording the actual attributes, creation date/time, starting cluster, and file size. The checksum value which is stored in the longname entry is computed on the alias name. This provides a means for reconciling a longname entry with an alias entry.

Changes in Disk Layout with FAT32

A number of changes have been made to disk data structures in order to accommodate the new 32-bit FAT. These changes are serious enough that they will break FAT16 disk utilities. For example, when I first tried DUMPDISK on a FAT32 drive, it failed miserably. After adding new code to detect and support FAT32 drives, it displays these disk data structures too. Example 9-4 shows sample output from DUMPDISK for a 1.79 gigabyte FAT32 partition:

Example 9-4. Sample FAT32 Output from DUMPDISK

```
Sector 0 - FAT32 BOOTSECTOR structure ...
  OEM Name:                        MSWIN4.1
  Bytes/Sector:                    0200
  Sectors/Cluster:                 08
  Reserved Sectors:                0020
  Number FATs:                     02
  Number Root Directory Entries:   0000
  Media Descriptor:                F8
  Number of Sectors/FAT:           0000
  Sectors/Track:                   003f
  Heads:                           0080
  Hidden Sectors:                  0000003f
  Big Total number Sectors:        00397641
  *Big Sectors per FAT:            00000e5a
```

Example 9-4. Sample FAT32 Output from DUMPDISK (continued)

```
*Extended flags:            0000
*File System Version:       0000
*Root Dir Start Cluster:    00000002
*File System Info Sector:   0001
*Backup Boot Sector:        0006
*Reserved[0]:               0000
*Reserved[1]:               0000
*Reserved[2]:               0000
*Reserved[3]:               0000
*Reserved[4]:               0000
*Reserved[5]:               0000
BIOS Drive Number:          80
Boot Signature:             29
Volume ID:                  361810f7
Volume Label:               NO NAME
File System Type:           FAT32

Sector 1   - FAT32 FS Info Sector...
Signature:                  61417272
Free Clusters:              0005c017
Next Free Cluster:          00031b1a

Sector 32 - First File Allocation Table ...
 0 ffffff8 fffffff fffffff 0000000 0000000 0000000 0000000 0000000
 8 0000000 0000000 0000000 0000000 0000000 0000000 0000000 0000000
16 0000000 0000000 0000000 0000000 0000000 0000000 0000000 0000000
24 0000000 0000000 0000000 0000000 0000000 0000000 0000000 0000000
32 0000000 0000000 0000000 0000000 0000000 0000000 0000000 0000000
40 0000000 0000000 0000000 0000000 0000000 0000000 0000000 0000000
48 0000000 0000000 0000000 0000000 0000000 0000000 0000000 0000000
56 0000000 0000000 0000000 0000000 0000000 0000000 0000000 0000000
...

Sector 3706 - Second File Allocation Table ...
 0 ffffff8 fffffff fffffff 0000000 0000000 0000000 0000000 0000000
 8 0000000 0000000 0000000 0000000 0000000 0000000 0000000 0000000
16 0000000 0000000 0000000 0000000 0000000 0000000 0000000 0000000
24 0000000 0000000 0000000 0000000 0000000 0000000 0000000 0000000
32 0000000 0000000 0000000 0000000 0000000 0000000 0000000 0000000
40 0000000 0000000 0000000 0000000 0000000 0000000 0000000 0000000
48 0000000 0000000 0000000 0000000 0000000 0000000 0000000 0000000
56 0000000 0000000 0000000 0000000 0000000 0000000 0000000 0000000
...

Sector 7380 - First available cluster.

Sector 7380 - Root Directory Entries ...
```

Name	Attrib	Creation Date/Time	Last Access	Start Cluster	Size	Chksum
SUHDLOG DAT	----hr	04-15-97 11:26:04	04-16-97	6bc0	7802	
SUHDLOG BAK	----hr	04-15-97 10:35:24	04-15-97	c88b	7802	

Example 9-4. Sample FAT32 Output from DUMPDISK (continued)

```
  BOOTLOG  TXT  a---h- 04-16-97 17:16:16 04-16-97     3780       53596
  IO       SYS  ---shr 04-08-97 14:23:00 04-15-97     6b84      219158
  RECYCLED      -d-sh- 03-01-97 19:51:00 03-01-97     84ab           0
  AUTOEXEC DOS  a----- 03-01-97 18:04:14 04-15-97     00bf        1111
  CONFIG   DOS  a----- 09-29-96 18:04:22 03-02-97     0061         312
  WINICE        -d---- 03-03-97 11:32:38 03-03-97     2b86           0
  SCANDISK LOG  a----- 04-16-97 17:10:50 04-16-97     3781         448
  CONFIG   BAK  a----- 04-15-97 10:35:24 04-15-97     c88a         167
  CONFIG   SYS  a----- 04-16-97 17:51:32 04-18-97     3874         167
  DETLOG   TXT  a--sh- 04-16-97 21:39:52 04-16-97     599c       69781
  HIMEM    SYS  a----- 09-29-96 17:32:28 03-02-97     009a       33191
  MSDOS    SYS  a--shr 04-16-97 18:03:40 04-16-97     38a2        1702
  SIW95         -d---- 03-10-97 16:35:42 03-10-97     a92e           0
  ASPI2DOS SYS  a----- 09-27-94 03:10:00 04-15-97     00af       28728
  ASPICD   SYS  a----- 09-27-94 03:10:00 03-01-97     00b7       29244
A My Documents  --vshr                                                   d7
  MYDOCU~1      -d---- 03-16-97 18:10:00 03-16-97     142b           0
  DBLSPACE BIN  ---shr 04-08-97 14:23:00 04-15-97     5c89       65271
  ...
```

The first thing you'll notice is that the boot sector has expanded. Actually, the SDK does not define a BOOTSECTOR structure as was the case with MSDOS. Instead you have to piece together a "BOOTSECTOR32" structure like this:

```
typedef struct _BOOTSECT32 {
    BYTE    bsJump[3];           // jmp instruction
    char    bsOemName[8];        // OEM name and version

    // This portion is the FAT32 BPB
    A_BF_BPB  bpb;

    BYTE    bsDriveNumber;       // 80h if first hard drive
    BYTE    bsReserved;
    BYTE    bsBootSignature;     // 29h if extended boot-signature record
    DWORD   bsVolumeID;          // volume ID number
    char    bsVolumeLabel[11];   // volume label
    char    bsFileSysType[8];    // file-system type (FAT12 or FAT16)
    }
    BOOTSECTOR32, *PBOOTSECTOR32;
```

The structure named A_BF_BPB is a new expanded BPB (BIOS Parameter Block) for FAT32. It is documented in the SDK and it is this portion of the BOOTSECTOR32 structure where the change has occurred. If you look back at the DUMPDISK output, a range of entries in the BOOTSECTOR area are marked with asterisks. These members are either new to the FAT32 BPB or are "widened" members, i.e. they have expanded from 16 to 32 bits. The Reserved Sectors entry tells us the number of sectors before the start of the first FAT; in this case it is 20h or 32 sectors. On this particular drive, only 6 of these sectors are put to use. Four of these sectors are used for the boot sector, two for a primary copy and two for a backup copy. Two sectors are now needed for the boot sector because the BPB has expanded in size causing the boot code to spill over to another sector.

The other two sectors are for a primary and a backup copy of a FS INFO sector. The SDK describes the structure in this way:

> ...there is a sector in the reserved area on FAT32 drives that contains values for the count of free clusters and the cluster number of the most recently allocated cluster. These values are members of the BIGFATBOOTFSINFO (FAT32) structure which is contained within this sector. These additional fields allow the system to initialize the values without having to read the entire file allocation table.

This sector is sandwiched between the two boot sectors on this particular drive.

Another peculiarity about FAT32 partitions is that the BPB indicates they have 0 root directory entries. Instead of specifying a fixed number of entries, a FAT32 root directory is treated like a file. It has a minimum size consisting of a single starting cluster but can be expanded by adding more clusters to its chain. Note that for the example FAT32 DUMPDISK output above, the first available cluster on the drive is also the first cluster of the root directory.

As its name implies, FAT32 File Allocation Tables contain 32-bit cluster numbers. The SDK notes that "...the high 4 bits of the 32-bit values in the FAT32 file allocation table are reserved and are not part of the cluster number. Applications that directly read a FAT32 file allocation table must mask off these bits and preserve them when writing new values." The first cluster which can be allocated is number 2. A look at the FAT tables reveals a 0xffffffff at this location; this signifies the end of a cluster chain.

The sample code for DUMPDISK illustrates some techniques for determining whether a system supports FAT32 and whether a particular drive is a FAT32 drive. It also includes typedefs for some of the FAT32 data structures.

IOS and the Layered Driver Model

So far in this book, I have avoided discussing the layered nature of the file system in any detail. This is because IFSMgr has closer affiliations with application APIs than it does with the underlying hardware. Also, the layered driver model only applies to local file system drivers; it is not a common structure for all classes of devices as is the case with the Windows Driver Model (see Chapter 14, *Looking Ahead*).

The layered model is comprised of 32 distinct layers of drivers. The layering represents both the ordering of initialization (from the bottom up), and the servicing of requests (from the top down). At the very top of the hierarchy is IFSMgr and immediately beneath it are the file system drivers. The other 30 layers are occupied by drivers that handle physical aspects of disk I/O and are referred to in the DDK as the Layered Block Device Drivers. The layered driver model in Windows 95 is implemented in a VxD called the I/O Supervisor (IOS).

The subject of the IOS could easily fill another book.* Here, we will be content with addressing only two aspects of IOS: the types of drivers which make up the layered model and the role which IOS serves.

Some of the common types of block device drivers which Windows 95 uses fall into these categories, arranged from highest to lowest:

Volume trackers

> The volume tracking driver, or VTD, makes sure that the target drive for an incoming request matches the media that is actually in the drive. The VTD is only needed for drives which have removable media, e.g., floppy drives and CD-ROMs.

Type-specific drivers

> All devices of a certain class have a common type specific driver, or TSD. The TSD is responsible for casting the logical view of a device, as it is viewed from an FSD, into its physical view. This might involve translating a logical block address into the physical head, cylinder, and sector. TSDs also know about drive partitions and are able to match up a volume identifier with a sub-section of a fixed disk as defined in its master boot record.

Vendor-supplied drivers

> Several slots in the hierarchy are set aside for vendor supplied drivers, or VSDs. This is a provision for adding vendor specific functionality for a device by inserting an auxiliary driver in the path of I/O requests.

SCSI manager and miniport drivers

> The SCSI device architecture is inherited from Windows NT. The SCSI Manager is a device independent layer that abstracts the behavior of SCSI controller cards. A miniport driver is the lower layer which supports the SCSI manager for a specific type of SCSI adapter.

Port drivers

> For non-SCSI controller cards a port driver is required. The port driver controls the hardware. It does such things as write to I/O ports, program DMA transfers, and service hardware interrupts, in order to take control of a disk drive or other device which is attached. Port drivers are also inherited from Windows NT.

---

* For more extensive coverage, see the DDK, and Walter Oney's book, *Systems Programming for Windows 95*, Chapter 15, "Block Device Drivers." For a higher-level account, see Chapter 7, "The Filesystem," in *Inside Windows 95*, by Adrian King.

Real-mode mappers

In cases where no protected-mode driver exists for a piece of hardware, calls to a real-mode driver are passed from protected mode to real mode using this type of driver.

Here are a couple of examples. A standard floppy disk drive is represented by drivers from three layers. It has a volume tracking driver for detecting a media change; a disk-type specific driver, and a port driver for an NEC floppy controller card. An IDE fixed disk also has three layer drivers. It has a disk-type specfic driver, a miscellaneous port driver (layer 19), and a port driver for an IDE controller card.

Three basic services which IOS supplies to clients are **IOS_Register**, **IOS_SendCommand**, and **IOS_Requestor_Service**. **IOS_Register** is the means by which IOS becomes aware of a driver. It receives a DRP (Driver Registration Packet) structure which specifies what level the driver will occupy in the hierarchy. An FSD will use the **IOS_SendCommand** interface to make requests of a device. An I/O packet, or IOP, is passed through this interface and IOS routes it through the driver layers using the calldown chain. The **IOS_Requestor_Service** interface supplies a number of utility functions for clients.

As drivers initialize during startup, each driver for a device specifies the level at which it wishes to be called in the layered hierarchy. In response, IOS builds a chain of target functions, the *calldown chain*, in the correct order. Later, when an I/O request is routed to a device, the order of the functions in the calldown chain determines the order in which the layered drivers will be called. When a driver receives an I/O packet, it decides what to do with it; it may decide to pass it down the chain, or possibly complete the request and not pass it down.

VFAT Initialization and Registration

VFAT, as a local FSD, needs to support linkage with IFSMgr and it does this with volume-based (see Table 6-6) and handle-based (see Table 6-7) function tables. As with other FSDs, VFAT establishes the first entry point, **FS_MountVolume**, by registering with IFSMgr using the **IFSMgr_RegisterMount** service during the Device Init phase.

In order for VFAT to access the local disk, it relies upon IOS. To gain access to IOS services, VFAT registers with IOS during the Device Init phase. To register, VFAT calls the service **IOS_Register** with a DRP (Driver Registration Packet) structure as an argument. The contents of the DRP are shown in Example 9-5 along with the values that VFAT uses in its **IOS_Register** call.

Example 9-5. DRP Passed to IOS_Register

```
typedef struct DRP {
    CHAR    DRP_eyecatch_str[8];   // "XXXXXXXX"
    ULONG   DRP_LGN;               // DRP_TSD
    PVOID   DRP_aer;               // Async_Event_Rtn
    PVOID   DRP_ilb;               // Address of ILB structure
    CHAR    DRP_ascii_name[16];    // "Flatfat FileSysD"
    BYTE    DRP_revision;          // 0
    ULONG   DRP_feature_code;      // 0
    USHORT  DRP_if_requirements;   // 0
    UCHAR   DRP_bus_type;          // 0
    USHORT  DRP_reg_result;        // 0
    ULONG   DRP_reference_data;    // 0
    UCHAR   DRP_reserved1[2];      // reserved; must be zero
    ULONG   DRP_reserved2[1];      // reserved; must be zero
} DRP, *PDRP;
```

The *DRP_LGN* member specifies the driver's load group and initialization layer. Each bit of *DRP_LGN* corresponds to one of 32 initialization layers. The lower the bit, the higher the layer and the later it will be initialized. At the top of the hierarchy is IFS manager, followed by FSDs, etc. The *DRP_LGN* value also informs IOS of the driver's registration type. Noncompliant registration is used for FSD's and IFS drivers; this means the driver will not receive AEP (asynchronous event packet) notifications at its asynchronous event routine. Since VFAT supplies an asynchronous event routine (**Aysnc_Event_Rtn**), it uses a load group of *DRP_TSD*, giving it the same initialization order as a type specific driver.

The *DRP_ilb* member supplies the address of an ILB (IOS linkage block) structure, which IOS will fill in before returning. The members of this structure are shown in Example 9-6. This structure contains several IOS entry points for requesting services.

Example 9-6. ILB Returned by IOS_Register

```
typedef struct ILB {
    PFNISP ILB_service_rtn;        // addr of service routine
    PVOID  ILB_dprintf_rtn;        // addr of dprintf routine
    PVOID  ILB_Wait_10th_Sec;      // addr of wait routine
    PVOID  ILB_internal_request;   // addr of request routine
    PVOID  ILB_io_criteria_rtn;    // addr of IOR criteria routine
    PVOID  ILB_int_io_criteria_rtn; // addr of IOP criteria routine
    ULONG  ILB_dvt;                // addr of driver's DVT
    ULONG  ILB_ios_mem_virt;       // addr of IOS memory pool
    ULONG  ILB_enqueue_iop;        // addr of enqueue routine
    ULONG  ILB_dequeue_iop;        // addr of dequeue routine
    ULONG  ILB_reserved_1;         // reserved; must be zero
    ULONG  ILB_reserved_2;         // reserved; must be zero
    USHORT ILB_flags;              // flags
    CHAR   ILB_driver_numb;        // number of calls to AEP_INITIALIZE
    CHAR   ILB_reserved_3;         // reserved; must be zero
} ILB, *PILB;
```

The DRP structure resides in a VxD_INIT_DATA_SEG segment and thus is discarded after initialization completes; however, the ILB is placed in a VxD_LOCKED_DATA_SEG segment since it will be used for accessing IOS services.

Mounting a VFAT Volume

Example 9-7 shows the top level C pseudocode for the **FS_MountVolume** function. Of the six different mount types, only the IR_FSD_MOUNT case is shown; this case corresponds to the standard, mount drive operation. This is truly pseudocode because VFAT is not implemented using the C language. For instance, internally the EBP register is used as a pointer to the `ioreq` structure, whereas in a C implementation EBP would point to the base of the stack frame.

Example 9-7. VFAT's FS_MountVolume Function

```
int FS_MountVolume( pioreq pir ) {
   register PIOREQ ebp_pir = pir;
   register short retc;

   ebp_pir->ws.ior_error = 0;
   ebp_pir->ws.b35 = 0;
   ebp_pir->ws.hi_options = 0;
   ebp_pir->ws.w38 = 0;

   switch( ebp_pir->ir_flags ) {
      case IR_FSD_MOUNT:
         _Claim_Level2();
         _asm bts dword ptr D1_9E66,00

         retc = _MountVol();
         ebp_pir->ir_vfunc = VolFunc;

         _Release_Level2();
         _asm btr dword ptr D1_9E66,00

         if ( !retc ) ebp_pir->ir_tuna = D1_A3AC & 1;
         break;

      /*** other cases not shown here ***/

      default:
         retc = ERROR_INVALID_FUNCTION;
         break;
   }
   return ( ebp_pir->ir_error = retc );
}
```

On entry to **FS_MountVolume**, the `ioreq` structure contains four members which are of special significance to this function call: *ir_volb* (*ir_aux1*) contains a pointer to a VRP (Volume Request Parameters), *ir_rh* contains the linear address of the DOS DPB (Disk Parameter Block) chain, *ir_mntdrv* (*ir_aux2*) contains the drive number of the volume to be mounted, and *ir_fb* contains the address of IFSMgr's as yet unfilled shell resource structure. On return, *ir_rb* will contain VFAT's resource handle for the volume and *ir_vfunc*, will contain the address of the table of volume-based entry points.

The first four lines in **FS_MountVolume** (see Example 9-7) initialize members of the structure WS. Recall that the *ir_fsd* member of **ioreq** is a 64-byte "provider work space" for use by FSDs. VFAT puts this entire area to use.

Most of the logic for mounting the volume is implemented in the routine **_MountVol**. It reads the first logical sector of the volume, which should be a DOS boot sector. Using the BOOTSECTOR structure (see the *Microsoft MS-DOS Programmer's Reference*, Version 5 or newer, for a description of this structure) at the beginning of this sector, VFAT creates a Resource Block structure for the volume and adds it to a doubly-linked list of such structures. The C volume gets special treatment; if it is being mounted, the DOS DPB structure is compared field-by-field with corresponding members of the Resource Block structure. If there is a mismatch, an error message is displayed via VMM's **Fatal_Error_Handler** service.

Using IOS to Read the Boot Sector

Reading a sector using IOS services takes several steps; it's not as straightforward as using the BIOS Int 13h interface. The first step is to ask IOS to allocate an IOP (I/O Request Packet). An IOS service request is made by pushing the address of an ISP (IOS Services Packet) on the stack and calling the address of the IOS service routine in the **ILB_service_rtn** member of the ILB.

The form and content of the ISP varies from service to service. Example 9-8 shows how the ISP is structured for an ISP_CREATE_IOP service.

Example 9-8. ISP Structure for Create IOP Service

```
typedef struct ISP_IOP_create {
  USHORT ISP_func;          // ISP_CREATE_IOP
  USHORT ISP_result;        // filled in on return
  USHORT ISP_IOP_size;      // size of IOP to allocate (in bytes)
  ULONG ISP_delta_to_ior;   // offset to IOR within IOP
  ULONG ISP_IOP_ptr;        // on return: address of IOP
  UCHAR ISP_I_c_flags;      // various allocation flags
  UCHAR ISP_pad2[1];        // pad to DWORD boundary
  } ISP_IOP_alloc;
```

The first two members of this structure are common to all ISP structures, and the remaining members are unique to the **Create IOP** call. The following members are initialized prior to making the call: *ISP_func* is set to *ISP_CREATE_IOP*, *ISP_IOP_size* is set to *pVRP->VRP_max_req_size*, *ISP_delta_to_ior* is set to *pVRP->VRP_* *delta_to_ior*, and *ISP_I_c_flags* is set to 0. If the service succeeds then on return, *ISP_IOP_ptr* contains the address of the allocated IOP. Nested within an IOP is an IOR (I/O Request Descriptor); in fact, the address of the IOR is given by the expression *ISP_IOP_ptr + ISP_delta_to_ior*. It is the IOR that is needed for the next step.

If you have followed along this far, you'll be relieved to know that we're almost ready to actually read something from the disk, but first we have to fill in the IOR structure. The members of the IOR structure are detailed in Example 9-9.

Example 9-9. Contents of IOR Structure for Boot Sector Read

```
typedef struct _IOR {
    ULONG     IOR_next;
    USHORT    IOR_func;               // IOR_READ: function to perform
    USHORT    IOR_status;             // returned status
    ULONG     IOR_flags;              // IORF_VERSION_002|IORF_HIGH_PRIORITY|
                                      //   IORF_BYPASS_VOLTRK
    CMDCPLT   IOR_callback;           // completion callback routine
    ULONG     IOR_start_addr[2];      // vol relative starting addr
    ULONG     IOR_xfer_count;         // sector count of 1
    ULONG     IOR_buffer_ptr;         // 2048 byte buffer
    ULONG     IOR_private_client;
    ULONG     IOR_private_IOS;
    ULONG     IOR_private_port;
    union     urequestor_usage _ureq; // 5 dwords, "working area"
    ULONG     IOR_req_req_handle;
    ULONG     IOR_req_vol_handle;     // address of volume's VRP
    ULONG     IOR_sgd_lin_phys;
    UCHAR     IOR_num_sgds;
    UCHAR     IOR_vol_designtr;       // zero-based volume number
    USHORT    IOR_ios_private_1;
    ULONG     IOR_reserved_2[2];
} IOR, *PIOR;
```

I'll confine our discussion to just the elements of IOR that are initialized for the boot sector read; for more details on the IOR structure see the Windows 95 DDK documentation for layered block drivers.

The bits which are *not* set in the *IOR_flags* member are more revealing than those which are. *IORF_CHAR_COMMAND* flag clear implies **IOR_xfer_count** refers to sectors rather than bytes. *IORF_SYNC_COMMAND* flag clear implies that the command is asynchronous and **IOR_callback** is called on completion. *IORF_LOGICAL_START_SECTOR* flag clear implies that **IOR_start_addr** is a physical address which is in the range *pVRP->VRP_partition_offset* to *pVRP->VRP_partition_offset* + total sectors in the volume.

The address of the IOR is placed in the ESI register and EDI is set to the address of the DCB (Device Control Block) for the physical device which holds the volume. Then the **IOS_SendCommand** service is invoked to perform the read. This call sets the wheels in motion by passing the request down through the layers of the IOS subsystem. Before the disk access is completed, **IOS_SendCommand** will return, since VFAT made an asynchronous request.

Upon return from **IOS_SendCommand**, VFAT suspends the current thread until **IOR_callback** is called. To coordinate the suspension and resumption of the thread, the first two doubleword elements of IOR's _ureq_ member are used; the first doubleword is used as a simple flag and the address of the second double-word serves as a blocking identifier.

Example 9-10 shows the code used to suspend the thread. Interrupts are disabled to assure that the test and call to block are treated as an "atomic" operation. The doublewords at EBX+2Ch and EBX+30h are elements in the _ureq_ member of IOR. Bit 0 of the first element is set by the callback handler once the requested service completes. So on the first execution of this loop, the bit test will return with the carry flag clear, and the function **Cli_Block_Thread** will be called. This function takes the address of a blocking identifier; it increments the contents of that address and then calls **IFSMgr_Block**. **IFSMgr_Block**, in turn, is a wrapper for the VMM service **_BlockOnID**, which is passed the same blocking identifier and the flags *BLOCK_ENABLE_INTS* and *BLOCK_SVC_INTS*. These flags force interrupts to be re-enabled.

Example 9-10. Suspending Thread

```
call  Send_IOS_Cmd            ; request boot sector read
   pop   ebx                  ; restore EBX, ptr to IOR
 wait_for_IOR_callback:
   cli
   bt    dword ptr [ebx+2c],00  ; has callback occurred?
   jc    short continue
   lea   eax,[ebx+30]         ; addr of _ureq dword as blocking ID
   call  Cli_Block_Thread     ; wrapper to IFSMgr_Block
   ;
   ; thread resumes when signaled by IOR_callback handler
   jmp   short wait_for_IOR_callback
 continue:
   sti
```

The function **Cli_Block_Thread** will not return until the blocking identifier is signaled. This, of course, is done in the callback handler and the code fragment which achieves this is shown in Example 9-11. The **Wakeup_Thread** function is a wrapper to **IFSMgr_Wakeup** which in turn, is a call to **_SignalID** with the given blocking ID.

Example 9-11. Resuming Thread

```
or    dword ptr [ebx+2c],+01
lea   eax,[ebx+30]
jmp   Wakeup_Thread                  ; wrapper to IFSMgr_Wakeup
```

When control does return from **Cli_Block_Thread**, the bit test will set the *carry* flag, and execution will resume at the label *continue*. The *IOR_status* member will then reveal whether the request was successful. If an error is reported by IOS, **_MountVol** calls the IOS service **IOSMapIORSToI21**, to convert the error code into an equivalent Int 21h error code before returning.

Creating a VFAT Resource Block Structure

Once VFAT has successfully read in the boot sector, it will proceed to examine the contents of the BOOTSECTOR structure at the beginning of the buffer. Several criteria that must be met before VFAT accepts a non-removable volume for mounting:

- The sector size must be one of 200h, 400h, 800h, or 1000h bytes
- The number of sectors per cluster must be 2 or greater
- The number of FATs must be either 1 or 2
- The number of system sectors must be less than the total number of sectors on the drive

Once a volume is found to be acceptable, a Resource Block (Example 9-12) is constructed using the contents of the BOOTSECTOR structure. VFAT maintains a linked list of mounted volumes. The list can be traversed from the front by starting with a head pointer or from the backend by starting with the tail pointer. A Resource Block for a new volume is added at the head of the linked list. Before a new volume is added, the list is searched for a matching volume. A match is based on the following Resource Block members: *VolumeID*, *VolumeLabel*, and the range of members from *sector_size* to w32. If a match is found, the mount is failed with the error code *ERROR_IFSVOL_EXISTS* (0x11C).

Example 9-12. Resource Block Structure

```
typedef struct _resource_block {
0    struct _resource_block* pnext;
4    struct _resource_block* pprev;
8    DWORD total_sectors;        // total sectors in the volume
C    DWORD d0C;                  // number system sectors that are partial 4K
10   DWORD d10;                  // value of ebp_pir->ir_pos
14   VRP* pVRP;
18   WORD second_fat;           // sector offset to 2nd FAT
1C   BYTE d1C;                   // init'ed to 1
1D   BYTE volnum;                // zero-based volume number
1E   BYTE mapvol;                // mapped volume number
1F   BYTE b1F;
20   WORD sector_size;          // sector size in bytes
22   WORD sector_byte_mask;     // sector_size - 1
```

Example 9-12. Resource Block Structure (continued)

```
24   BYTE cluster_mask;           // (sectors per cluster) - 1
25   BYTE cluster_shift;          // sectors per cluster, as power of 2
26   WORD reserved_sectors;       // sectors used by boot record, etc.,
                                  //    before first FAT
28   WORD root_entries;           // number of entries in root directory
2A   WORD first_sector;           // sector number of first sector
                                  //    in the first cluster
2C   WORD max_cluster;            // maximum number of clusters in volume
2E   WORD FAT_size;               // size of FAT in sectors
30   WORD dir_sector;             // first sector containing the
                                  //    root directory
32   WORD w32;                    // init'ed to 2
34   WORD w34;                    // init'ed to 0xffff
36   BYTE FAT_count;              // number of FATs
37   BYTE cluster_byte_shift;     // cluster size in bytes, power of 2
38   WORD cluster_byte_mask;      // size of cluster in bytes, less one
3A   BYTE sector_byte_shift;      // sector size in bytes, power of 2
3B   BYTE sectors_in_page;        // number of sectors in 4K
3C   BYTE sectors_in_page_mask;   // sectors_in_page - 1
3D   BYTE b3D;
3E   WORD w3E;
40   WORD flags;
42   char VolumeLabel[11];
4D   BYTE b4D;
4E   BYTE media;                  // F8h for fixed disk
4F   BYTE b4F;
50   DWORD VolumeID;
54   DWORD d54;
58   DWORD d58;
5C   DWORD d5C;
60   DWORD d60;
64   DWORD d64;
68   DWORD d68;
6C   DWORD buffer_idle_timeout;
70   DWORD buffer_age_timeout;
74   DWORD latest_system_time;
78   DWORD volume_idle_timeout;
7C   DWORD d7C;
80   DWORD d80;
84   DWORD d84;
88   DWORD d88;
8C   DWORD d8C;
90   DWORD d90;
94   DWORD d94;
98   DWORD d98;
9C   DWORD pNameCache;
A0   DWORD dA0;
A4   DWORD dA4;
} RESOURCE_BLK, *PRESOURCE_BLK;
```

Opening a VFAT File—Top Level

Examples 9-13 and 9-14 show the top level C pseudocode for the **FS_OpenFile** function. There are many parameters in the `ioreq` structure which affect this function, these are detailed in the IFS Specification. The *ir_options* parameter determines the function to perform; it essentially boils down to opening an existing file or creating a new file. If creating a file, *ir_attr* supplies the desired attributes for the new file. The *ir_flags* parameter specifies the desired access and share mode for the returned handle. The *ir_rh* member contains the resource handle for the volume on which file is opened or created. It is the address of the VFAT Resource Block structure which was returned when the volume was mounted. If the call succeeds, *ir_fh* will return the FSD file handle; this is the address of a VFAT File Instance Block structure.

To get a feel for how this function works, let's trace through the open of an existing file. To make it interesting, let's select a long filename, say *d:\windows\ desktop\old_forum_messages.txt.*

Execution begins at lines 10 through 16, in Example 9-13, where several members of the FSD's working area structure, WS, are initialized. The first test occurs at line 18 where *ir_options* is examined to separate two distinct types of operations. In our case, *ir_options* has the value *ACTION_OPENEXISTING*, so the first half of the if clause is true and the function **_Claim_Level1** is called. Under certain conditions this function will block the current thread; thus this function serves to mark the beginning of a VFAT critical section. When **_Claim_Level1** returns, initialization of the FSD's working area structure continues, with values for *new_file_attrib, access_ share_mode,* and *standard_options* retrieved from **ioreq** members *ir_attr, ir_flags,* and *ir_options,* respectively. At line 36, the *standard_options* are tested for validity and, if they are found to be invalid, an error return is made.

At line 41, the function **_AllocInstanceBlock** allocates 44 bytes for a VFAT File Instance Block. The address of this block is stored to the *ir_fh* member of the **ioreq** structure, and thus is used to represent the FSD's file handle. At line 42, the pointer to the caller's **hndlfunc** structure is retrieved from *ir_hfunc* in the **ioreq** structure. At lines 43, 44, and 45, members of the caller's **hndlfunc** structure are initialized with the addresses of VFAT handle-based function pointers.

With these preliminaries out of the way, *standard_options* is used once again at line 48, to decide which action to take. If the open options are *ACTION_OPENEX- ISTING* (0x01) or *ACTION_OPENALWAYS* (0x11), then the function **_OpenExisting** will be called at line 49. If the open options are any of *ACTION_CREATENEW* (0x10), *ACTION_CREATEALWAYS* (0x12), or *ACTION_REPLACEEXISTING* (0x02), then the function **_CreateNew_ReplaceExisting** at line 63 is called, assuming that the drive is not write protected (this is checked at line 57).

Example 9-13. FS_OpenFile Function, Part 1

```
1  int FS_OpenFile( pioreq pir ) {
2    register pioreq ebp_pir = pir;
3    register BYTE opt;
4    register struct hndlfunc* phf;
5    int action, errcode=0;
6    DWORD entry_ir_fh;
7    struct instance_block* poi;
8    struct open_block* pob;
9
10   ebp_pir->ws.special_options = (ebp_pir->ir_options &
11     (OPEN_FLAGS_NO_CACHE|RO_SWAPPER_CALL|RO_MM_READ_WRITE)) >> 8;
12   ebp_pir->ws.w38 = 0x2000;
13   ebp_pir->ws.ior_error = 0;
14   ebp_pir->ws.b35 = 0;
15   ebp_pir->ws.d6C = ebp_pir->ws.vcache_handle = 0;
16   entry_ir_fh = ebp_pir->ir_fh;
17
18   if (!ebp_pir->ir_options & (ACTION_CREATENEW|ACTION_REPLACEEXISTING))
19     _Claim_Level1();
20   else {    _Claim_Level2();
21     ebp_pir->ws.w38 |= 0x0800;
22     if ( !C_3EF4() ) C_3FFD();
23     }
24   ebp_pir->ws.ir_fh = 0;
25   ebp_pir->ws.new_file_attrib = (BYTE)ebp_pir->ir_attr;
26   ebp_pir->ws.b45 = 0x16;
27   ebp_pir->ws.b46 = 0;
28
29   if ((ebp_pir->ir_flags & 0x7f) == 0x7f) {
30     ebp_pir->ir_flags = ACCESS_READWRITE;
31     ebp_pir->ws.access_share_mode = 0x0082;
32     }
33   else   ebp_pir->ws.access_share_mode = ebp_pir->ir_flags & 0x7f;
34
35   opt = ebp_pir->ws.standard_options = (BYTE)ebp_pir->ir_options;
36   if ( opt==0 || (opt&0xf)>2 || opt & 0xe0 ) {
37     errcode = 1;
38     goto error_exit;
39     }
40
41   ebp_pir->ir_fh = __AllocInstanceBlock();
42   if (carry_flag) goto error_exit;
43   phf = ebp_pir->ir_hfunc;
44   phf->hf_read = FS_ReadFile;
45   phf->hf_write = FS_WriteFile;
46   phf->hf_misc = HdlFunc;
47
48   (ebp_pir->ir_fh)->open_mode = ebp_pir->ws.access_share_mode;
49   if ( ebp_pir->ws.standard_options & ACTION_OPENEXISTING ) {
50     action = _OpenExisting();
51     if (carry_flag)
52         if ( (action != 2) ||
```

Example 9-13. FS_OpenFile Function, Part 1 (continued)

```
53                 (! ebp_pir->ws.standard_options & ACTION_CREATENEW))
54         goto error_exit;
55      else goto store_results;
56      }
57   if ((ebp_pir->ir_rh)->pVRP->VRP_event_flags & VRP_ef_write_protected){
58      errcode = 0x13;
59      goto error_exit;
60      }
61   if (ebp_pir->ws.new_file_attrib & 0x08 )
62      ebp_pir->ws.b45 = 0x08;
63   action = _CreateNew_ReplaceExisting();
64   if (carry_flag) goto error_exit;
```

Since we are tracing the open of an existing file, the function **_OpenExisting** will be called. If the function succeeds, the *carry* flag will be clear on return and the *action* variable will be assigned the return value *ACTION_OPENED*, and execution will continue at line 1 (with the label **store_results**) in Example 9-14. If the *carry* flag is set on return, the open failed and execution continues at line 26 (with the label **error_exit**) in Example 9-14.

Example 9-14. FS_OpenFile Function, Part 2

```
1   store_results:
2    poi = (struct instance_block*)ebp_pir->ir_fh;
3    if ( ebp_pir->ir_options & OPEN_FLAGS_COMMIT )
4       poi->w0E |= 0x0083;
5    pob = poi->pob;
6    if ( ebp_pir->ws.special_options & R0_SWAPPER_CALL ) {
7       D1_9E38 = ebp_pir->ir_fh;
8       _Init_PageFile();
9       (ebp_pir->ir_rh)->w40 |= 0x4000;
10       if (ebp_pir->ir_rh->pVRP->VRP_demand_flags &
11           VRP_dmd_lock_unlock_media)
12          _Lock_Removable_Media();
13       }
14    if ( (!ebp_pir->ir_options & OPEN_FLAGS_ALIAS_HINT) &&
15          ebp_pir->ir_pos != 0 ) {
16       pob->record_lock_list = ebp_pir->ir_pos;
17       IFSMgr_ReassignLockFileInst( ebp_pir->ir_pos,
18          entry_ir_fh, ebp_pir->ir_fh );
19       }
20    ebp_pir->ir_size    = pob->file_size;
21    ebp_pir->ir_dostime = pob->create_date_time;
22    ebp_pir->ir_attr    = pob->fattrib;
23    pob->d14--;
24    if ( pob->d14 < 0 ) C_540D();
25    ebp_pir->ir_options = action;
26   error_exit:
27    if ( ebp_pir->ws.w38 & 0x2000 ) {
28       DWORD tmp, tmp2;
29       tmp = ebp_pir->ws.d6C;
```

Example 9-14. FS_OpenFile Function, Part 2 (continued)

```
30      ebp_pir->ws.d6C = 0;
31      if (tmp) { tmp2 = D1_A260;
32          D1_A260 = tmp;
33          if (tmp2) _HeapFree(tmp2,0);
34          }
35      }
36   ebp_pir->ir_error = errcode;
37   if (! ebp_pir->ws.special_options &
38      (OPEN_FLAGS_NO_CACHE|R0_SWAPPER_CALL)) {
39      if (ebp_pir->ws.w38 & 0x0004){
40          BYTE old_ior_err = ebp_pir->ws.ior_error;
41          ebp_pir->ws.ior_error = 0;
42          new_err = C_979C();
43          ebp_pir->ws.ior_error =
44              carry_set ? new_err:old_ior_err;
45          ebp_pir->ir_error = new_err;
46          }
47      }
48   if ( Level2_ClaimCnt ) {
49          if ( (ebp_pir->ws.special_options &
50                  (R0_SWAPPER_CALL|R0_MM_READ_WRITE)) &&
51              (Level1_ClaimCnt & 0xffffff) ) _Release_Level1();
52          else {
53          _Release_Level2();
54          goto finish;
55          }
56      }
57   else _Release_Level1();
58  finish:
59   if (ebp_pir->ws.ior_error)    ebp_pir->ir_error = IOSMapIORSToI21();
60   if ( ebp_pir->ws.b35 ) {
61      (ebp_pir->ir_rh)->d1A &= (~(1 << ebp_pir->ws.b35));
62      if ( D1_9DAC ) Wakeup_Thread( &D1_9DAC );
63      }
64 }    // end of FS_OpenFile
```

After a successful open of an existing file, return values are extracted from the VFAT File Instance Block and File Open Block structures. These values are stored to the *ir_size*, *ir_dostime*, and *ir_attr* members of the `ioreq` structure. The value of the *action* variable, returned by **_OpenExisting**, is stored to *ir_options*.

The common cleanup code starts at line 27 where the first `if` clause checks if an allocation needs to be freed or just placed on the free list. Then at line 36, the current error code value (0 if no error) is stored to the *ir_error* member of the `ioreq` structure. At line 37, a check is made to see if the file open was for a ring-0 swapper file or memory-mapped file; if so special action is taken here.

Finally, at line 48, the *Level2_ClaimCnt* variable is checked to see if a **Claim_Level2** call has occurred in the interim. If not, the **Release_Level1** function is called to "unclaim" the critical section.

This top level view of **FS_OpenFile** reveals some interesting aspects of VFAT's implementation, but we need to descend to lower levels to see how the file is located on the disk and to learn more about the File Instance and Open Block structures.

Opening a VFAT File—Lower Level

Let's continue to "zoom-in" on **FS_OpenFile**, by examining one of its core functions: **_OpenExisting**. The pseudocode for this function is shown in Example 9-15.

Example 9-15. Pseudocode for Function _OpenExisting

```
int _OpenExisting() {
1    register DWORD eax_reg, ebx_reg, edx_reg, esi_reg;
2    BYTE mode, share_mode;
3    PDIRENTRY pdir;
4    PINST_BLK poi;
5
6    eax_reg = 0xc000;
7    edx_reg = ebp_pir->ir_attr;
8    _Init_PathAttribs();
9
10   mode = ebp_pir->ws.access_share_mode & 0x77;
11   share_mode = mode & 0x70;
12   if ( ( share_mode > SHARE_DENYNONE ) ||
13       ( share_mode ^ mode > 4 ) ) return_carry( 0x0c ); // invalid access
14
15   eax_reg = ebp_pir->ir_ppath;
16   if ( eax_reg == NULL ) {
17       esi_reg = ebp_pir->ir_uFName; // SFTOpenInfo
18       _SFT_Open();
19       if ( carry_flag ) return_carry( 0x02 ); // file not found
20       }
21   else {
22       _FindPath();
23       if ( carry_flag ) {
24           if ( zero_flag ) return_carry( 0x02 ); // file not found
25           return_carry( 0x03 ); // path not found
26           }
27       if ( zero_flag ) return_carry( 0x05 ); // access denied
28       }
29   pdir = ebx_reg; // EBX points to directory entry
30   poi = ebp_pir->ir_fh;
31   if ( pdir->deAttributes & ATTR_READONLY ) {
32       if ( ebp_pir->ws.access_share_mode & 0x0080 ) {
33           poi->open_mode = SHARE_DENYNONE; //0x40;
34           ebp_pir->ws.access_share_mode = 0x00c0;
35           }
36       if ( poi->open_mode & 0x03 != ACCESS_READONLY ) // 0
37           if ( poi->open_mode & 0x03 != ACCESS_EXECUTE ) // 3
38               if ( ebp_pir->ir_options & OPEN_FLAGS_REOPEN == 0 ) // 0x800
39                   return_carry( 0x05 ); // access denied
```

Example 9-15. Pseudocode for Function _OpenExisting (continued)

```
40      }
41    if ( ebp_pir->ws.vcache_handle )
42        VCache_Hold( ebp_pir->ws.vcache_handle );
43    _Add_Open_Instance();
44    cf = carry_flag;
45    if ( ebp_pir->ws.vcache_handle )
46        VCache_Unhold( ebp_pir->ws.vcache_handle );
47    if ( cf ) return;
48    if ( ebp_pir->ir_options & OPEN_FLAGS_NO_COMPRESS ) {
49        poi = ebp_pir->ir_fh;
50        poi->pob->b25 |= 0x10;
51      }
52    if ( pdir->deStartCluster == 0 ) return 1;
53    if ( ebp_pir->ws.special_options &
54        (OPEN_FLAGS_NO_CACHE|R0_SWAPPER_CALL) ) return 1;
55    eax_reg = 0; // amount to read
56    edx_reg = 0; // starting read position
57    _ReadAhead();
58    return 1;
59  }
```

This function starts out by extracting the path-parsing flags which were passed into **FS_OpenFile** in the upper word of the *ir_attr* member of the **ioreq** structure. This is accomplished by the call to **_Init_PathAttribs** on line 8. The path-parsing flags as well as other path-related attributes are combined into e*bp_pir->ws.path_attribs*, a word-sized member of the **ioreq**'s working area, WS structure.

Next, on lines 10 through 13, the validity of the access and sharing modes is verified. If invalid values are detected here, the error code *ERROR_INVALID_ACCESS* (0x0c) is returned to the caller and the *carry* flag is set. These operations are combined in the macro **return_carry()**.

At line 15, the EAX register is initialized with the address of *ir_ppath*, the pointer to the **ParsedPath** structure for the canonicalized input filename. A special case is checked at line 16, where this address is NULL, signifying an open using an **SFTOpenInfo** structure. In this situation, the address of this structure is contained in the *ir_uFName* member of the **ioreq** structure. This is passed via the ESI register to the function **_SFT_Open**, where the file is opened not by pathname, but by logical cluster number, directory entry index, and an 8.3 FCB-style name. The IFS specification states that, "This special kind of open is issued by the IFS manager when it is taking over a file handle left open by a TSR before booting into Windows." We are more interested in the other half of the **if** clause which starts at line 22.

The **_FindPath** function, which is called at line 22, attempts to walk the disk through each of the path elements in the *ir_ppath* member of the **ioreq** structure. It follows a sequence like this: For each path component, starting from the root, locate the directory entry for the path component (using the function _Find-DirEntry). A "located" path component has a pointer to a cache buffer containing the corresponding directory entry. The starting cluster of the directory entry is then used to retrieve the next directory level, where an attempt is made to locate the next path component. This process is repeated for all the components in the path and ultimately, if a filename is specified, it is searched for in the last located directory.

_FindPath also makes use of the Path Cache and the Name Cache. Before starting to walk the disk for a pathname, it consults the Path Cache to see if it holds an entry for the path portion of a filename. If it finds an entry, the starting cluster for the specified directory is returned, thereby saving one or more directory entry traversals. Similarly, the Name Cache is consulted to see if it has an entry for the filename portion of the pathname. If it does, the starting cluster and directory entry index for the file are used to vector more directly to the file's contents.

Eventually, when _FindPath returns, the EBX register contains a pointer to the directory entry structure for the file, if the search was successful. An error return is indicated by setting either the *carry* flag, the zero flag, or both, and returning an error code. On a successful return, the attribute byte in the directory entry is checked for read-only attributes (see line 31). If this is true, then some special actions are taken in lines 32 through 40.

The next significant event occurs at line 43. Here, the call to _Add_Open_Instance uses the information in the file's directory entry to fill in VFAT's file structures. The first of these structures is a File Instance Block; the address of this block becomes VFAT's file handle which is returned in the *ir_fb* member of `ioreq`. The second structure is an Open File Block, which is added to VFAT's table of open files. Only one Open File Block is created for each unique file, whereas a separate File Instance Block a created for each file open or create. Note that **Vcache_Hold** and **Vcache_Unhold** calls are used to make sure that the cache block for the directory entry is not discarded while it is in use during the _Add_Open_Instance call.

Finally, before returning from _OpenExisting, some of the file is loaded into the cache. This is accomplished by the call to _ReadAhead at line 57.

Locating a Directory Entry

In the previous section, the _FindPath function was described. It takes a sequence of path components in a `ParsedPath` structure and attempts to walk the corresponding directories on the disk. The VFAT function _FindDirEntry meets this need. Let's see how it is used to traverse the path:

```
d:\windows\desktop\old_forum_messages.txt
```

In this example _FindDirEntry uses three arguments: ECX, an option argument; EBX, the starting sector of the directory of interest; and EAX, a pointer to the current *pp_elements* path component to be found. There are also variables shared via the *ir_fsd* area of the `ioreq` structure: starting cluster, sectors per cluster, and starting sector. These are also initialized prior to calling _FindDirEntry.

On entry, _FindDirEntry clears and initializes its workspace buffer, null terminates the path element it receives, and then makes an initial read from the specified start sector. The read may actually be avoided if the sector is found in the cache. Following this initialization, the search loop begins. Here are the various steps taken:

Next entry:

- If the first byte of the directory entry is 0, then the end of the used portion of the directory has been reached. Go to *Match failed.*

- Examine the attribute byte of the directory entry in the cache buffer; if it is a 0fh attribute, go to *Long entry.* Otherwise, go to *Short entry.*

Short entry:

- Copy the 8.3 BCS (byte character set) filename and extension from the directory entry to the workspace buffer.

- Create a Unicode FCB style name using IFS manager's **BCSToUni** service to convert the BCS filename and extension.

- Use the IFS manager service **FcbToShort** to convert the Unicode FCB style name to a Unicode 8.3 name with a dot separating primary and extension components.

- If a longname buffer exists which has been created from long directory entries preceding the alias directory entry, go to *Alias entry.*

- Now use the IFS manager service, **IFSMgr_MetaMatch**, to compare the input Unicode path component with the Unicode 8.3 name created from the directory entry. For this example, the *UFLG_NT* flag is passed to this service to select NT matching semantics.

  If a match is found go to *Match attributes*; otherwise, continue at the label *Increment entry.*

Long entry:

- If this directory entry has the last-in-sequence indicator (it is encountered first), the number of directory entries in this sequence is determined from the first byte of the entry and stored as a counter. The checksum byte for the shortname alias is also saved.

- For all long directory entries, append the Unicode characters in the fields of the directory entry to a longname buffer and decrement the entry count. If the directory entry does not have the last-in-sequence indicator, compare its checksum against that which was initially saved. Go to *Increment entry*.

Alias entry:

- A checksum is calculated on the 11-character name in the alias directory entry and it compared against the value found in the preceding long directory entries.

- If the path component is a filename, and the path portion was added to the Path Cache, then the filename portion is added to the Name Cache.

- Now use the IFS manager service **IFSMgr_MetaMatch** to compare the input Unicode path component with the long filename created from the one or more long directory entries. For this example, the *UFLG_NT* flag is passed to this service to select NT matching semantics. If this match succeeds, perform an uppercase comparison with the alias name up until the first "~" character is encountered. If this also succeeds, go to *Match attributes*.

- If the previous compare fails, use **IFSMgr_MetaMatch** to compare the input Unicode path component with the Unicode 8.3 name created from the alias directory entry. For this example, the *UFLG_NT* flag is passed to this service to select NT matching semantics. If this match succeeds, go to *Match attributes*, otherwise go to *Increment entry*.

Match attributes:

- If the directory attributes match the input criteria, then go to *Match return*; otherwise go to *Increment entry*.

Increment entry:

- The directory index is incremented and the cache buffer pointer is advanced to the next directory entry. If the cache pointer exceeds the cache block range, then the cache block for the next sector will have to be filled.

- If the end of the directory is reached go to *Match failed*; otherwise go to *Next entry*.

Match return:

- Replace the null termination of the path component with the original value.

- Set EAX to 0.

- The EBX register points to the short or alias directory entry for the match.

Match failed:

- Replace the null termination of the path component with the original value.

- Set *carry* flag to indicate failure.

VFAT's File Structures

In our earlier examination of the function **_OpenExisting**, we came across the routine **_Add_Open_Instance**. This is where File Open Blocks and File Instance Blocks are initialized. The declarations for these data structures are shown in Examples 9-16 and 9-17. VFAT's table of open files is rooted in a header block containing four pointers (see Example 9-16). The first two pointers appear to be reserved, but the third pointer addresses the head of the open file list and the fourth pointer addresses the tail of the open file list. Each entry in this linked list is an **OPEN_BLK** shown in Example 9-17. The links are followed forward with the pnext member until it reaches the address of the header block. Links can also be followed backwards with the *pprev* member.

Example 9-16. Header Block for Open Files

```
OpenFileTable

0           unused ?
4           unused ?
8           POPEN_BLK   first_open_block
C           POPEN_BLK   last_open_block
```

When a file is opened, an **OPEN_BLK** structure is created for it and the first **INST_BLK** structure is created to reference it. As new file handles are requested on the open file, additional **INST_BLK** structures are created to reference the single **OPEN_BLK** structure. Initially, the *pfirst_inst* and *plast_inst* members of the **OPEN_BLK** point to the single **INST_BLK** structure. As new instances of the file are opened, each new **INST_BLK** is added to the head of the list at *pfirst_inst*. The **INST_BLK** structure contains *pnext* and *pprev* members for traversing forwards and backwards through the list of instances. The last *pnext* pointer and the first *pprev* pointer point to the referenced **OPEN_BLK** structure. There is also a *pob* member which points to the common **OPEN_BLK** structure.

Example 9-17. File Open Block (92 bytes)

```
typedef struct _open_block {
0    struct _instance_block* pfirst_inst;
4    struct _instance_block* plast_inst;
8    struct _open_block* pnext;
C    struct _open_block* pprev;
10   DWORD record_lock_list;
14   DWORD d14;
18   DWORD d18;
1C   DWORD d1C;
20   DWORD d20;
24   BYTE fattrib;               // attribute byte[1]
25   BYTE b25;
26   WORD start_clus;            // starting cluster number[1]
```

Example 9-17. File Open Block (92 bytes) (continued)

```
28  DWORD rh;                    // volume's resource handle from ioreq
2C  DWORD create_date_time;      // creation date & time1
30  DWORD file_size;             // file size1
34  WORD access_date;            // last access date1
36  DWORD d36;
3A  BYTE b3A;
3B  BYTE b3B;
3C  DWORD d3C;
40  DWORD d40;
44  BYTE dir_entry;              // directory entry index
45  char fcb_name[11];           // FCB format 8.3 name1
50  DWORD sector_pos;            // sector offset to beginning of file
54  DWORD cluster_table;         // table of clusters in file
58  WORD table_size;             // size of cluster table
5A  WORD w5A;
} OPEN_BLK, *POPEN_BLK;
```

1 Value retrieved from directory entry.

Example 9-18. File Instance Block (44 bytes)

```
typedef struct _instance_block {
0    struct _instance_block* pnext;
4    struct _instance_block* pprev;
8    struct _open_block* pob;
C    WORD open_mode;             // ir_flags & 0x7f
E    WORD w0E;                   // init'ed to 0x004c
10   DWORD user;                 // ir_user
14   DWORD pid;                  // ir_pid
18   DWORD d18;
1C   DWORD d1C;
20   DWORD d20;                  // init'ed to 1
24   DWORD d24;
28   DWORD d28;
} INST_BLK, *PINST_BLK;
```

Recall that the **_AllocInstanceBlock** function call, in **FS_OpenFile**, returns an address which is assigned to *ir_fb*. This allocation is an **INST_BLK** structure in which a unique file is referenced via a pointer to an **OPEN_BLK** structure. In the subsequent call to **_Add_Open_Instance**, VFAT checks if other open instances of this file already exist. This check is done by traversing the table of open files and looking for a match on three keys: directory entry index, sector position, and resource handle. If no match is found, an **OPEN_BLK** structure is allocated and its contents initialized from the directory entry. On the hand, if a match is found, then the new open will be granted only if the desired access and sharing mode are permitted by IFSMgr.

To determine if the open should succeed VFAT calls the service **IFSMgr_CheckAccessConflict**. One of the arguments to this service is the address of an enumeration function. This function is called by IFSMgr for each open instance of the file. On each call to the enumeration function, VFAT returns information about an instance of the open file. The enumeration function returns 1 for enumeration to continue and 0 for enumeration to stop. When the enumeration is complete, **IFSMgr_CheckAccessConflict** returns 0 if the desired access and sharing mode can be granted, or an error code if not.

10

Virtual Memory, the Paging File, and Pagers

Virtual memory and paging have been the topics of numerous texts. If you would like some background in these areas, I recommend *Operating System Concepts*, by Abraham Silberschatz and Peter Galvin (Addison-Wesley, March 1994), especially Chapter 8 on memory management and Chapter 9 on virtual memory. Paging in Windows 95 is, of course, dependent on hardware support in the x86 family of microprocessors. Many books have described the details of page directories, page tables, and page faults of the Intel microprocessors—*Programming the 80386* by John Crawford and Patrick Gelsinger is one that I refer to frequently. This background is really essential to understanding this chapter, although I'll throw in a brief refresher for some of the thornier topics.

Paging is not new to Windows 95. Earlier versions of Windows utilized the paging capability of the 386 and 486. Andrew Schulman's article, "Exploring Demand-Paged Virtual Memory in Windows Enhanced Mode," in *Microsoft System Journal*, December 1992, examines paging in Windows 3.1. More recently, Matt Pietrek, in Chapter 5 of his book, *Windows 95 System Programming Secrets*, looks at memory paging as a prelude to his in-depth discussion of Win32 memory management.

The Windows 95 Paging File

One of the new features touted in Windows 95 is the use of a dynamic paging file. To quote from the *Microsoft Windows 95 Resource Kit*, p. 562, "It can shrink or grow based on the operations performed on the system and based on available disk space."

This is in contrast to the Windows 3.x paging file which, for best performance, had to be a fixed file contiguously allocated. The file *386part.par* was created in the root directory with system attributes and accessed via either the Windows block device driver or Int 13h. In the *windows* directory another file was created called *spart.par*, which gave the size and location of *386part.par*.

Windows 3.x also had the option to use a temporary swap file which it created while Windows was running and deleted automatically on exit. It also could grow or shrink as necessary. This was a DOS file with normal attributes, called *win386.swp*. Since access was via Int 21h in virtual-86 mode, performance suffered compared to the fixed file option. Although the temporary swap file was not a popular option with Windows 3.x users, it is the only option available in Windows 95.

Paging or Swapping?

A leisurely scan of the *Microsoft Windows 95 Resource Kit* reveals several references to the Windows 95 *swap file*. For instance, in Chapter 17 on Performance Tuning, there is a section on "Optimizing the Swap File," and in Chapter 31 on Windows 95 Architecture there is a section on "Windows 95 Swap File." The file that is being referred to is stored under the filename *win386.swp*. The term *swapping* has traditionally referred to the process of moving entire processes to and from the disk (see *Operating System Concepts*, pp. 303-304). This is *not* the mechanism used by Windows 95. The technically correct term is *paging*. The distinction is that a *pager* moves page-sized chunks (4096 bytes) of code or data to main memory from the disk but only when that page is needed. On the other hand, a *swapper* brings in the code and data for the entire process, while moving a process to disk to make room. You will see the terms *swapping* and *paging* used interchangeably in Windows 95 documentation.

Exploring with MultiMon

To start our excursion into Windows 95 paging, I'm going to perform a simple experiment using MultiMon. Here are the steps I used to set up MultiMon to collect the results shown in Figure 10-1:

1. Launch MultiMon.

2. Select only the FSHook and BOOTMGR monitors in the **Add/Remove Drivers** dialog that you get from the **Options** Menu, **Add/Remove Drivers...** command. FSHook will allow us to capture file system events and, when used in conjunction with BOOTMGR, we can capture events during system startup.

3. Bring up the **Filter Options** dialog by clicking the **Filters** button on the toolbar. Select "IFSMgr Filehook" and then check the boxes for the following

> APIs: **FS_GetDiskInfo** and **Ring0SwapperIO**. Then press the dialog button labeled **Save As Default**.

4. Restart the system. (It isn't necessary to shut down.)

5. Launch MultiMon. You should be greeted with a message box that states "BOOTMGR has captured a log file. Do you wish to display it now?" Press the **Yes** button. You should now be viewing an output screen similar to that shown in Figure 10-1.

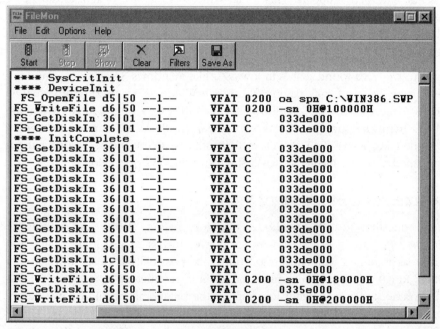

Figure 10-1. Paging file activity reported by MultiMon

In Figure 10-1, groups of lines are separated by tags that BOOTMGR inserts to flag the stages of system initialization: "****** DeviceInit**", "****** InitComplete**", etc. The third line in the listing shows an **FS_OpenFile** command being sent to VFAT for the file named *c:\win386.swp*. The field d5|50 indicates the dispatched command and accompanying flags. Referring back to Chapter 6, *Dispatching File System Requests*, we know that the command **d5** corresponds to a ring-0 open or create, the function I named **dR0_OpenCreate** (see Table 6-5). The flags byte 50 signifies the LFN and **IFSMgr_Ring0_FileIO** bits. These pieces of information point to a IFSMgr_Ring0_FileIO call and in this case the subfunction R0_OPENCREATEFILE.

We can read more into this call from the flags which accompany the open. The characters "oa" signify *ACTION_OPENALWAYS*, meaning open an existing file but if it doesn't exist, create it. The special options "spn" are "s" for *RO_SWAPPER_ CALL*, "p" for *OPEN_FLAGS_NO_COMPRESS*, and "n" for *OPEN_FLAGS_NO_ CACHE*. Another thing to note is that the value 200h (*ir_sfn*) is the first value in the range of extended file handles.

Scanning down the listing, you will also note a few **FS_WriteFile** calls on this extended file handle using "-sn" attributes: *RO_SWAPPER_CALL* and *RO_NO_ CACHE*. It's interesting that the length of the writes is 0 but the position of the write is not, e.g., 0H@100000H. This initial write sets the size of *win386.swp* to 1 megabyte. If we were to extend our logging and launch some applications, we would see **FS_WriteFile** and **FS_ReadFile** calls on the handle 200h with lengths which are a multiple of 1000h, the size of a page.

To sum up, we have found that Windows 95, like Windows 3.x, uses a temporary file called *win386.swp* for its paging file. While Windows 3.x used only virtual-86 DOS calls to access this file, Windows 95 uses IFSMgr's ring-0 APIs (when the underlying hardware supports it). As we have seen, these APIs are a thin veneer to the underlying FSD, VFAT. VFAT in turn utilizes IOS services. These changes have breathed new life into what was a sluggish Windows 3.x option.

Who Accesses win386.swp?

A natural question to ask is who is opening, reading from, and writing to *win386.swp*? Perhaps the easiest way to answer this is to use a debugger and place a breakpoint at a well-chosen location. One possibility is to set a breakpoint at **IFSMgr_Ring0_FileIO** and examine the calling parameters in each case. This would be rather tedious. A better location for the breakpoint would be just before we chain into the next file system hook (or call into the FSD) in FSHook. This is after FSHook has decided to report the event but before it passes the request down to the FSD.

FSHook has a registry option for just such a need. This is not a feature that most users will want to experiment with, so it is left as a registry entry that is set manually using REGEDIT. In Figure 10-2, the registry values under the **MultiMon_ fshook** key are shown. The value name "Int3On" will not be defined unless you have experimented with this feature already. To add this value, select the menu **Edit**, submenu **New**, followed by **DWORD Value**. Type in **Int3On** for the value name. The DWORD associated with this is a Boolean, 1 for "on" and 0 for "off."

A breakpoint is inserted as an assembly language Int 3 instruction. In order for your kernel debugger to respond to these breakpoints you may have to issue a command. For instance, with WinIce the command **I3Here On** must be executed. Once you have made the necessary adjustments, repeat the experiment we performed in the last section. Now, when the first **FS_OpenFile** call is encountered you will break into your debugger.

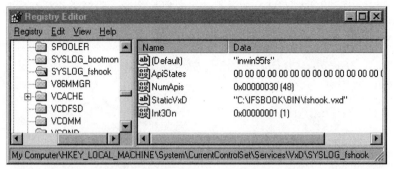

Figure 10-2. Setting FSHOOK's Int3On option using RegEdit

When the breakpoint occurs, execution stops on the instruction following the Int
3. The actual code, in both C and indented assembly, is shown in Example 10-1.
Here you see the call to the previous file system hook function, which looks a
little strange because of the double indirection involved, (*(*ppPrevHook)). Using
the debugger to step forward we can watch as each of the arguments are pushed
onto the stack in preparation for calling down into the FSD. Right now, I'm interested in seeing who is making this call, so I won't step into the FSD code, but
rather step over it. By continuing to step through code we work our way up
through the series of nested functions which initiated the call into **FS_OpenFile**.

Example 10-1. FSHook Code in Vicinity of Breakpoint

```
if ( bIssueInt3 ) _asm int 3
   CMP     DWORD PTR [_bIssueInt3],00
   JZ      C00B59AD
   INT     3
retc = (*(*ppPrevHook))( pfn, fn, drv, res, cp, pir );
   MOV     EAX,[EBP+1C]   ;pir=C33E5C84 (ptr to ioreq)
   PUSH    EAX
   MOV     EAX,[EBP+18]   ;cp=00000000 (ANSI codepage)
   PUSH    EAX
   MOV     EAX,[EBP+14]   ;res=00000010 (local drive)
   PUSH    EAX
   MOV     EAX,[EBP+10]   ;drv=00000003 (C drive)
   PUSH    EAX
   MOV     EAX,[EBP+0C]   ;fn=00000024 (IFSFN_OPEN)
   PUSH    EAX
   MOV     EAX,[EBP+08]   ;pfn=C008FEE4 (FS_OpenFile)
   PUSH    EAX
   MOV     EAX,[_ppPrevHook];=C33F709C
   CALL    [EAX];=C0086D20
   ADD     ESP,18
```

The nested hierarchy of functions is shown in Example 10-2. It shouldn't come as
too big of a surprise that *pageswap.vxd* and *dynapage.vxd* are the virtual drivers
from which the paging file calls originated. Although the VxD file has the name

DYNAPAGE, internally, in its Device Descriptor Block, this driver goes by the name PAGEFILE. PAGEFILE and PAGESWAP are not new to Windows 95. They are revamped versions of their Windows 3.x counterparts.

Example 10-2. Tracing the Initial Open of the Paging File

```
                  FS_OpenFile       VFAT
              FileHook             FSHOOK
            Call_FSD               IFSMGR(1)+194a
          C1_3A14                  IFSMGR(1)+3a90
        dRing0_OpenCreate          IFSMGR(1)+3939
      Dispatcher1                  IFSMGR(1)+07c4
    IFSMgr_Ring0_FileIO            IFSMGR(1)+38a3
  PageFile_Init_File               PAGEFILE(2)+01f3
 PageSwap_Init_File                PAGESWAP(2)+000e
VMM(5)+622D                        VMM(5)+622d
```

The Roles of PAGESWAP and PAGEFILE (DYNAPAGE)

The DDK documentation is not particularly illuminating about the relative roles of two virtual drivers, PAGESWAP and PAGEFILE. PAGESWAP exports the services listed in the first column of Table 10-1. The PAGEFILE services shown in the second column are called by the PAGESWAP services in the first column. As you can see, there is almost a one-to-one correspondence. Contrary to the documentation, PAGESWAP is little more than a thin layer over the PAGEFILE services.

Table 10-1. Correspondence Between PAGESWAP and PAGEFILE Services

PAGESWAP Services	PAGEFILE Services Used by PAGESWAP
PageSwap_Init_File	PageFile_Get_Version, PageFile_Init_File
PageSwap_Get_Version	
PageSwap_Test_IO_Valid	PageFile_Test_IO_Valid
PageSwap_Grow_File	PageFile_Grow_File
PageSwap_Read_Or_Write	PageFile_Read_Or_Write

Fortunately, we are given the entire source code for the PAGEFILE (DYNAPAGE) driver; it can be found in the Windows 95 DDK directory ..*base**samples*\ *dynapage*. Using this source as a guide, we can place the **IFSMgr_Ring0_FileIO** call, which we traced above, into the context of **PageFile_Init_File**. Here is a thumbnail sketch of what this function does:

- Gathers the values of the following *system.ini* profile strings:

  — **Paging**. If this Boolean value is off, then paging is disabled and **PageFile_Init_File** returns with EBX equal to 0, to indicate an error.

  — **MinPagingFileSize**. This optional setting determines the minimum size of the paging file in Kbytes. The default is 0.

— **MinUserDiskSpace**. This optional setting determines the amount of space (in Kbytes) to reserve as free on the disk containing the paging file. The default is 512 Kbytes.

— **MaxPagingFileSize**. This optional setting determines what the upper limit is for growing the paging file. This value is also given in Kbytes. The default is 2 gigabytes.

— **PagingFile**. This optional entry determines the path and filename for the paging file. The path must include a drive letter, i.e., it overrides *PagingDrive*. The default is *win386.swp*.

— **PagingDrive**. This optional entry specifies the volume where the paging file will be created. If this option is specified, the paging file is created in the root directory of the specified volume; otherwise the Windows drive and directory are used unless *PagingFile* is specified.

- Uses **IOS_Requestor_Service**, subfunction IRS_IS_DRVCOMPRESSED, to see if the drive containing the paging file is using a real-mode compression driver; if so, moves the paging file to the host drive.

- Checks **IFSMgr_Ring0GetDriveInfo** to see if the paging drive is being handled by IFS and whether it is using protect-mode or real-mode drivers. Some IFS drives use real-mode drivers, i.e., real-mode mapper. If the drive doesn't pass this test, it has to use DOS for paging.

- If the system has a protect-mode IFS driver, double checks the drive using **IOS_Requestor_Service**, sub function IRS_GET_DRVINFO. This will tell us if it has any DOS-like characteristics, e.g., the driver uses pageable code. If the drive has any of these "undesireable" characteristics, it too uses DOS for paging.

At this point there are two possibilities: paging is provided through the virtual-86 DOS Int 21h interface, or paging is provided through IFSMgr's ring-0 APIs. We'll only show the ring-0 case for the remainder.

- Uses **IFSMgr_Ring0_FileIO** subfunction R0_OPENCREATEFILE to create the paging file with normal attributes. Perform the create using the special flags: *R0_SWAPPER_CALL*, *R0_NO_CACHE*, and *OPEN_FLAGS_NO_COMPRESS*.

- Uses **IFSMgr_Ring0_FileIO** subfunction R0_WRITEFILE to set the initial length of the paging file to the value specified by *MinPagingFileSize*. If this fails then tries again using a different value. If the system has less than 9 megabytes of RAM under control of the memory manager (as reported by **_GetDemandPageInfo**), then sets the file size to 9216 Kbytes (amount of physical RAM in Kbytes). Otherwise retries with a size of 0.

- On success, returns the maximum paging file size in EAX (in pages) and the current paging file size in EBX (in pages).

The call trace shown in Figure 10-1 also reveals several calls to **FS_GetDiskInfo**. Those which are marked by command and flag bytes of 36|01 are the result of Int 21h function 36h requests. Note that only the ANSI code page flag is set, so these calls are not invoked using **IFSMgr_Ring0_FileIO**. Instead, they originate as **Exec_VxD_Int** calls in **PageFile_Get_Size_Info**. This latter function reports the minimum, maximum, and current size of the paging file. The amount of free space on the disk containing the paging file enters into the calculations of these parameters. **PageFile_Get_Size_Info**, in turn, is called by two VMM services: **_GetDemandPageInfo** and **_PageGetAllocInfo**.

The last four lines shown in Figure 10-1 are two pairs of **FS_GetDiskInfo** and **FS_WriteFile** calls. Both of these calls are made via **IFSMgr_Ring0_FileIO**. Each pair of calls corresponds to a single call to **PageFile_Grow_File** requesting that the paging file grow by 80h pages (512 Kbytes). Growing and shrinking the paging file is an ongoing process. Any service that commits "swappable pages" (e.g., **_Page-Commit**) adds that number of pages to a running total. The requests are not acted on until the total outstanding exceeds the current paging file size by at least 80h pages. Similarly, decommitting swappable pages reduces the size of the paging file by a like amount, but the paging file is not shrunk until its new size would be at least 80h pages less than its current size. While the growth of the paging file occurs directly in response to committing new swappable pages, shrinking the paging file goes on as a background process from a callback installed by the VMM service **Call_When_Idle**. Pages which are allocated as fixed or which are subsequently locked do not require space in the paging file, since they will never be candidates for page-outs. Also, some pages use a different backing file, such as those for memory-mapped files, and are not counted as swappable.

The key PAGEFILE service for moving pages to and from the paging file is **PageFile_Read_Or_Write**. This service takes a single argument, a pointer to a PageSwapBufferDesc structure (see Example 10-3). PAGEFILE converts the parameters in this structure into an **IFSMgr_Ring0_FileIO** call for either R0_READ-FILE or R0_WRITEFILE, depending on the value of *PS_BD_Cmd*.

Example 10-3. Structure Passed into PageFile_Read_Or_Write

```
typedef struct {
DWORD PS_BD_Next;              // ignored
BYTE  PS_BD_Cmd;               // PF_Read_Data(0) or PF_Write_Data(1)
BYTE  PS_BD_Priority;          // ignored
BYTE  PS_BD_Status;            // return: PFS_Failure or PFS_Success
BYTE  PS_BD_nPages;            // number of pages to read or write
DWORD PS_BD_Buffer_Ptr;        // linear address to transfer to or from
DWORD PS_BD_File_Page;         // page offset within paging file
} PageSwapBufferDesc;
```

The transfer count is equal to *PS_BD_nPages* * 4096 bytes. The file position at which the operation begins is determined by *PS_BD_File_Page* * 4096. The paging file remains open, so the handle returned by the **OpenCreateFile** call in **PageFile_Init_File** is still valid and used by PAGEFILE here. Note that although we can't explicitly specify the *RO_NO_CACHE*, *RO_SWAPPER_CALL*, and *OPEN_FLAGS_NO_COMPRESS* options as we did on the **OpenCreateFile** call, these attributes are stored with the `fhandle` structure. Before the call is passed down to the FSD, IFSMgr propagates these attributes to the *ir_options* member of the `ifsreq` structure, so they will be seen by **FS_WriteFile** and **FS_ReadFile**.

To see how **PageFile_Read_Or_Write** is put to use, we need to get acquainted with VMM's pagers.

Pagers

Pagers are a new addition to the VMM in Windows 95. A pager is simply code called by the VMM to move pages in and out of memory. A pager does not have to reside in a virtual device, and in fact several pager routines are located in KERNEL32.

Pagers are used for loading and initializing both swappable and fixed pages. Pagers are involved during the entire lifetime of a page, from the time it is committed until it is freed. Not all pages fall under the control of a pager though; the exceptions include hooked pages, instanced pages, and pages committed using the service **_PageCommitPhys**.

A pager exposes one or more action functions through a Pager Descriptor (PD) structure (see Example 10-4). Each pager action function (e.g., *pd_virginin*) has the following prototype:

```
ULONG _cdecl FUNPAGE( PULONG ppagerdata,
                      PVOID ppage, ULONG  faultpage );
```

If a function pointer member of the PD structure is zero, the pager will not be notified when the corresponding action is taken. It is customary that a pager will not implement all action functions.

Example 10-4. Pager Descriptor Structure

```
struct pd_s {
PFUNPAGE pd_virginin;
PFUNPAGE pd_taintedin;
PFUNPAGE pd_cleanout;
PFUNPAGE pd_dirtyout;
PFUNPAGE pd_virginfree;
PFUNPAGE pd_taintedfree;
PFUNPAGE pd_dirty;
ULONG pd_type; .
};
```

A virtual device may register a pager with VMM using the **_PagerRegister** service. This service takes a pointer to a PD structure as its only argument. It returns a handle, actually a 1-based index, that represents the pager. This handle can be passed to other services, such as **_PagerQuery**, to retrieve the pager's PD structure, or **_PagerDeregister**, to remove the pager from VMM.

All system pages which are under control of a pager have such a handle associated with them. The association is made at the time pages are committed through **_PageCommit**. Here are the parameters passed in to **_PageCommit**:

```
ULONG _PageCommit( ULONG page, ULONG pages,
                   ULONG hpd,  ULONG pagerdata, ULONG flags );
```

- *page* is the linear page number, i.e., the linear address returned by **_PageReserve** divided by 4096

- *pages* specifies the number of pages to commit but can be no larger than the number of pages initially reserved by the call to **_PageReserve**

- *hpd* is the handle of the pager whose action functions will be called for these pages. VMM supplies four internal pagers with handles 1 to 4, which are:

    PD_ZEROINIT(1) for swappable zero-initialized pages

    PD_NOINIT(2) for swappable uninitialized pages

    PD_FIXEDZERO(3) for fixed zero-initialized pages

    PD_FIXED(4) for fixed uninitialized pages

- *pagerdata* is a 32-bit value associated with this page or pages; if used in conjunction with the *PC_INCR* flag, then *pagerdata* is incremented by one for each page in the range

- *flags* specifies various options such as whether the pages are permanently locked, are accessible by ring-3 applications, etc.

A typical Windows 95 configuration will have 12 different pagers. Of these, VMM contributes its four internal pagers. But where do the other eight come from? We'll see shortly that VWIN32 and KERNEL32 are responsible.

The System Pagers

On the book's companion diskette, there is a utility called PAGERS which dumps out all of the registered pagers in a system. Figures 10-3 and 10-4 show its output for a standard system configuration. Imagine Figure 10-4 as a continuation of Figure 10-3 to the right. Corresponding lines in the two figures can be found by matching up the pager handle (hPD) in the first column.

For each pager action function there is a corresponding column, VirginIn, TaintedIn, etc. The addresses displayed in these columns are given as *Device(obj)* +

hPD	Description	VirginIn	TaintedIn	CleanOut
1	Swappable Zero-Init	VMM(E)+370	VMM(1)+5843	0
2	Swappable Un-Init	0	VMM(1)+5843	0
3	Fixed Zero-Init	VMM(E)+370	0	0
4	Fixed Un-Init	0	0	0
5	Win32 Sys DLL Data	VWIN32(1)+268	VMM(1)+5843	0
6	Win32 Sys DLL Code	VWIN32(1)+268	VWIN32(1)+268	0
7	Win32 Zero-Init Sys DLL Data	VMM(E)+370	VWIN32(1)+268	0
8	Win32 EXE/DLL Data	bff7b4b6	VMM(1)+5843	0
9	Win32 EXE/DLL Code	bff7b4b6	0	0
10	Win32 Safe Mapped File	bff7eefa	bff975d7	0
11	Win32 Unsafe Mapped File	bff7eefa	bff975d7	0
12	Win32 Copy-On-Write Mappe...	bff7eefa	VMM(1)+5843	0
13	Test Pager	_VirginIn	_TaintedIn	_CleanOut

Figure 10-3. First half of pagers output

hPD	DirtyOut	VirginFree	TaintedFree	Dirty	Type
1	VMM(1)+5670	0	VMM(1)+5868	VMM(1)+58B6	SWAPPER
2	VMM(1)+5670	0	VMM(1)+5868	VMM(1)+58B6	SWAPPER
3	0	0	0	0	PAGERONLY
4	0	0	0	0	PAGERONLY
5	VMM(1)+5670	0	VMM(1)+5868	VMM(1)+58B6	SWAPPER
6	0	0	0	0	PAGERONLY
7	0	0	0	0	PAGERONLY
8	VMM(1)+5670	0	VMM(1)+5868	VMM(1)+58B6	SWAPPER
9	0	0	0	0	PAGERONLY
10	VWIN32(1)+FB6	0	0	0	PAGERONLY
11	VWIN32(1)+FB6	0	0	0	PAGERONLY
12	VMM(1)+5670	0	VMM(1)+5868	VMM(1)+58B6	SWAPPER
13	_DirtyOut	_VirginFree	_TaintedFree	_Dirty	SWAPPER

Figure 10-4. Second half of pagers output

ofs, where *Device* is the virtual device, *obj* is the object or segment number, and *ofs* the offset from the beginning of the segment. A zero indicates that the action function is not implemented for that pager. In a few cases, a linear address is given, e.g., bff7b4b6. This is an address in KERNEL32.

If you compare the pager type with the number of functions it has implemented you will note that SWAPPER type pagers provide the most functionality. This is understandable, since these pagers support the movement of data to and from the paging file. PAGERONLY type pagers do not use the system paging file, either because the pages are fixed or because they use a different backing file.

Another item of interest is that a pager can "inherit" functions from another pager. For instance, under the columns TaintedFree and Dirty, all pagers use the same implementation provided by VMM.

Ignore the descriptions column for a moment and just look at the addresses of the action functions. Handles 8 through 12 are unique in that the action functions are in KERNEL32's address range. Handles 5, 6, 7, 10, and 11 have action functions that reside in VWIN32. If the description strings weren't available, this KERNEL32/ VWIN32 association would be enough to suspect that these pagers are used by Win32.

The descriptions for the pagers with handles 5 through 12 were found by using the **.M** debugging command which is built-in to VMM for both the retail and debug versions. This command can be invoked in either WinIce or WDEB386; it has many options and reveals a wealth of information about the internal workings of the memory manager. The subcommand which displays the pager descriptors is **.MG**.

The last pager displayed in the output, the one with handle 13, is registered by *qpagers.vxd*, the helper VxD which PAGERS uses to collect the information it displays. We will be using this pager to get a closer look at when and why the pager action functions are called.

The Pager Action Functions

The pager action functions are given names like "virgin-in" and "tainted-free." Are these just cute phrases or do they have some significance? There is a special signficance attached to the words *virgin, tainted, clean,* and *dirty* as they apply to a pager's pages. A dirty page is one that has been modified by a write. It will revert to a clean page when the page has been paged-out to the paging file. Thus, a page may toggle back and forth between clean and dirty states during its lifetime. Pages start out as clean and virgin. Once a page has entered the dirty state, it is thereafter a tainted page—it can not reclaim its virginity, although it can re-enter the clean state. Thus a virgin page must remain clean.

VMM will call the various pager functions in the PD structure, to control the life of a page. The function **pd_virginin** is called to move a page into memory, if the page is clean and has never been modified. This could involve reading a portion from the original file on disk into the page or just initializing the page contents to zero. The function **pd_taintedin** is also used to move a page into memory, but for pages which have undergone some change. VMM also has two functions for moving pages out of memory. The first is called **pd_cleanout**, which is used to move out a page which has not been dirtied since the last time it was paged out. The function **pd_dirtyout** does the same, but for pages which have not been paged out since they were dirtied. The destination for a page out could be the paging file or the backing file for a memory-mapped file.

When a page is decommitted, either explicitly with **_PageDecommit** or implicitly with **_PageFree**, the function **pd_virginfree** or **pd_taintedfree** is called. If the page has never been modified, **pd_virginfree** is used, otherwise **pd_taintedfree** is called. Finally, the **pd_dirty** function is called by VMM to inform the pager that a page has been written to. This is not an immediate notification. If a page is dirtied in more than one memory context, this function will be called once for each context.

The Life of a Page

It is more interesting to see pager functions at work. You can trace through a couple of test routines from PAGERS (see Figure 10-4) by selecting either **Test1** or **Test2** from the **Test** menu. These test routines do not send their output to the Win32 application; rather, you need to run them in conjunction with a kernel debugger like WinIce or WDEB386, since the output is sent to a debugger console. The complete source code for *pagers.exe* and *qpagers.vxd* can be found on the companion diskette.

The first test routine is shown in Example 10-5. The sequence that this routine follows is very simple. It first reserves three pages of memory and then commits the pages. It then reads a byte and writes a byte to each page. The pages are then decommitted and then freed. Interspersed with these steps are printouts to the debug console of several data structures. *qpagers.vxd* installs its own pager which is a wrapper around calls to VMM's Swappable Zero-Init pager. As the **Test1** routine executes, the calls to the pager's action functions are also logged to the debug console. This output is shown in Example 10-6.

Example 10-5. Test1 Function From qpagers.vxd

```
void Test1( void ) {
   PBYTE pBase, p;
   DWORD linPageNum, i, cpg = 3;
   BYTE  abyte;
   int line=1;

   TestNum = 1;
   CheckPageRange( 0, 0 );

   pBase = _PageReserve( PR_PRIVATE, cpg, 0 );
   linPageNum = LinAddr_to_PageNum(pBase);

   Debug_Printf( "\nTEST1(%d):_PageReserve: reserve %d pages at
               linear addr = %lx\n", line++, cpg, pBase );
   for ( i=0, p=pBase; i<cpg; i++, p+=0x1000 )
      Dump_PTE( LinAddr_to_PageNum(p), 3 );

   Debug_Printf( "\nTEST1(%d): _PageCommit: linear addr = %lx,"
               "page number = %lx\n", line++, pBase, linPageNum );
```

Example 10-5. Test1 Function From qpagers.vxd (continued)

```
    _PageCommit( linPageNum, cpg, hMyPager, linPageNum,
                PC_WRITEABLE|PC_USER|PC_INCR );

    for ( i=0, p=pBase; i<cpg; i++, p+=0x1000 )
       Dump_PTE( LinAddr_to_PageNum(p), 3 );

    for ( i=0, p=pBase; i<cpg; i++, p+=0x1000 ) {
       Debug_Printf( "\nTEST1(%d): Read and write page at %lx\n",
                     line++, p );

       // This will call pd_virginin for pager,
       //  to load initial contents of page
       abyte = *p;
       Dump_PTE( LinAddr_to_PageNum(p), 3 );
       // This will call pd_dirty for pager,
       //  to flag that page has been modified
       *p = 'a';
       Dump_PTE( LinAddr_to_PageNum(p), 3 );
       }
    Debug_Printf( "\nTEST1(%d): _PageDecommit: linear addr = %lx\n",
                  line++, pBase );

    _PageDecommit( linPageNum, cpg, 0 );
    for ( i=0, p=pBase; i<cpg; i++, p+=0x1000 )
       Dump_PTE( LinAddr_to_PageNum(p), 3 );

    Debug_Printf( "\nTEST1(%d): _PageFree: linear addr = %lx\n",
                  line++, pBase );
    _PageFree( pBase, 0 );
    for ( i=0, p=pBase; i<cpg; i++, p+=0x1000 )
       Dump_PTE( LinAddr_to_PageNum(p), 3 );

    TestNum = 0;
    }
```

Example 10-6. Pager Function Trace—Test1

```
TEST1(1):_PageReserve: reserve 3 pages at linear addr = 760000
   pPTE=FF801D80 reserved PTE=00181000 iAR=0181
   pPTE=FF801D84 reserved PTE=00181000 iAR=0181
   pPTE=FF801D88 reserved PTE=00181000 iAR=0181

TEST1(2): _PageCommit: linear addr = 760000, page number = 760
   pPTE=FF801D80 iVP  =0000064A PTE=0064A206:.. cun r/w usr com
   pPTE=FF801D84 iVP  =00001932 PTE=01932206:.. cun r/w usr com
   pPTE=FF801D88 iVP  =0000153F PTE=0153F206:.. cun r/w usr com

TEST1(3): Read and write page at 760000
   _VirginIn(C0411F06[760],C135F000,760)
       pVP=C0411F00 cRef=0001 hPD=0D iAR=0181 data=760 ......B.
       pPTE=FF801D80 iVP  =0000064A PTE=0064A206:.. cun r/w usr com
   pPTE=FF801D80 Frame=000008D3 PTE=008D3227:.. cAP r/w usr com
```

Example 10-6. Pager Function Trace—Test1 (continued)

```
    pPTE=FF801D80 Frame=000008D3 PTE=008D3267:.. DAP r/w usr com

TEST1(4): Read and write page at 761000
    _VirginIn(C041DC16[761],C135F000,761)
        pVP=C041DC10 cRef=0001 hPD=0D iAR=0181 data=761 ......B.
        pPTE=FF801D84 iVP  =00001932 PTE=01932206:.. cun r/w usr com
    pPTE=FF801D84 Frame=0000063F PTE=0063F227:.. cAP r/w usr com
    pPTE=FF801D84 Frame=0000063F PTE=0063F267:.. DAP r/w usr com

TEST1(5): Read and write page at 762000
    _VirginIn(C041B498[762],C135F000,762)
        pVP=C041B492 cRef=0001 hPD=0D iAR=0181 data=762 ......B.
        pPTE=FF801D88 iVP  =0000153F PTE=0153F206:.. cun r/w usr com
    pPTE=FF801D88 Frame=00000244 PTE=00244227:.. cAP r/w usr com
    pPTE=FF801D88 Frame=00000244 PTE=00244267:.. DAP r/w usr com

TEST1(6): _PageDecommit: linear addr = 760000
    _Dirty(C04072BB[760],0,0)
        pPF=C04072B7 pVP=C0411F00 data=760 cLock=0000 cRef=0001 st=00
        pVP=C0411F00 cRef=0000 hPD=0D iAR=0181 pPF=C04072B7 TD.P..B.
        pPTE=FF801D80 Frame=000008D3 PTE=008D3267:.. DAP r/w usr com
    _TaintedFree(C0411F06[760],0,0)
        pVP=C0411F00 cRef=0000 hPD=0D iAR=0181 pPF=760 TD.P..B.
        pPTE=FF801D80 reserved PTE=00181000 iAR=0181
    _Dirty(C0405137[761],0,0)
        pPF=C0405133 pVP=C041DC10 data=761 cLock=0000 cRef=0001 st=00
        pVP=C041DC10 cRef=0000 hPD=0D iAR=0181 pPF=C0405133 TD.P..B.
        pPTE=FF801D84 Frame=0000063F PTE=0063F267:.. DAP r/w usr com
    _TaintedFree(C041DC16[761],0,0)
        pVP=C041DC10 cRef=0000 hPD=0D iAR=0181 pPF=761 TD.P..B.
        pPTE=FF801D84 reserved PTE=00181000 iAR=0181
    _Dirty(C0401D78[762],0,0)
        pPF=C0401D74 pVP=C041B492 data=762 cLock=0000 cRef=0001 st=00
        pVP=C041B492 cRef=0000 hPD=0D iAR=0181 pPF=C0401D74 TD.P..B.
        pPTE=FF801D88 Frame=00000244 PTE=00244267:.. DAP r/w usr com
    _TaintedFree(C041B498[762],0,0)
        pVP=C041B492 cRef=0000 hPD=0D iAR=0181 pPF=762 TD.P..B.
        pPTE=FF801D88 reserved PTE=00181000 iAR=0181
    pPTE=FF801D80 reserved PTE=00181000 iAR=0181
    pPTE=FF801D84 reserved PTE=00181000 iAR=0181
    pPTE=FF801D88 reserved PTE=00181000 iAR=0181

TEST1(7): _PageFree: linear addr = 760000
    pPTE=FF801D80 free
    pPTE=FF801D84 free
    pPTE=FF801D88 free
```

The first group of lines starts at **TEST1(1)**. These show the page table entries for the three pages reserved in the private arena (*PR_PRIVATE*). The linear address for the first page is at 760000h, the second is at 761000h, and the third is at

762000h. The corresponding addresses of the page table entries (*pPTE*) are
FF801D80h, FF801D84h, and FF801D88h. These are computed using the formula:

```
ff800000h + 4 * [linear page number] = pPTE
```

At this stage, the page table entries (PTE) at these locations are non-zero but the
flags in the lower 12-bits are all cleared. The number which is stored in page
frame address is an index to an *Arena Record* (iAR).

After committing the pages, the PTE contents are displayed again at `TEST1(2)`.
The lower 12 bits of flags in the PTE now have the value 206h. This corresponds
to the attributes: committed, clean, unaccessed, user, read/write, and not present.
Bits 9, 10, and 11 are not predefined by the x86 chip, and are used by the
memory manager to indicate whether the page is committed (Bit 9) and whether
the page is physically mapped (Bit 11). The number which is now stored in the
page frame address is an index to a Virtual Page (iVP). At this point, we haven't
actually made the pages physically present. We could have done that by specifying the *PR_PRESENT* flag in our **_PageCommit** call. What we have done is first,
reserve a swath of the linear address space which is private to our memory
context, and second, commit some pages of virtual memory.

At `TEST1(3)`, `TEST1(4)`, and `TEST1(5)`, a byte of memory gets "touched" in
each of the committed pages. In response, VMM brings these pages into physical
memory, and calls the pager function **pd_virginin** (here called **_VirginIn**). The
arguments to this function follow the **FUNPAGE** prototype given earlier. The first
argument is a pointer to *pagerdata*, one of the arguments passed to **_Page-
Commit**. If you refer back to the source, in Example 10-5, you'll see that we are
passing *linPageNum* as *pagerdata* and have specified *PC_INCR* in the *flags* argument. This means that the first argument to *pd_virginin* will be a pointer to the
linear page number of the page which needs to be loaded. The second argument
is the linear address of the page's contents (only valid during the pager function
callback). In this particular pager implementation, the page's contents, all 4096
bytes, are blasted with zeros.

Indented under **_VirginIn...** is a line starting with pVP=.... This shows the
contents of a *Virtual Page* structure. It includes such things as the handle to the
pager, the *pagerdata* passed in to *pd_virginin*, the index to the Arena Record,
and a flags byte describing the state of the page.

In the mid-section of the Test1 routine in Example 10-5, you will notice a **for** loop
where the page "touching" and "dirtying" is done. A touch occurs when a
memory location in the page is read (`abyte = *p`), while we make the page
dirty by writing a byte to it (`*p = 'a'`). Examination of the PTEs immediately
following each of these program statements reveals the changes that the page is
undergoing. The dump of the PTE immediately following a touch shows that the

lower 12 bits now have the value 227h, and indicate these attributes: commited, clean, accessed, user, read/write, and present. After a page has been dirtied, the lower 12 bits of the PTE have the value 267h, indicating that a single attribute has changed: it has gone from clean to dirty. Also note that since the present bit is set, the page frame address now refers to the physical address of a page of some system memory (it is no longer an iAR or iVP).

Since we dirtied some pages, we would expect to see some **pd_dirty** pager function calls (here called **_Dirty**). VMM's memory manager does not guarantee timely delivery of these notifications, in fact, we don't see them until we are decommitting the pages under TEST1(6). The **pd_dirty** function receives a pointer to the *pVP->pagerdata* for the page, but the other arguments do not appear to be valid. VMM's PD_ZEROINIT pager handles this call by freeing the corresponding swap file page if one has been allocated in the paging file.

As we leave the Test1 routine, we call **_PageDecommit** and **_PageFree** for the pages which we have been using. As each page is decommitted, the pager function, **pd_taintedfree** (here named **_TaintedFree**), is called. This call informs the pager that this is the last reference to the Virtual Page (pVP) before the page is decommitted. The **pd_taintedfree** function receives a pointer to *pVP->pagerdata* but the other arguments are not valid. VMM's PD_ZEROINIT pager handles this call by freeing the corresponding swap file page if one has been allocated in the paging file.

After **_PageDecommit** returns, a dump of each page's PTE shows that it has been reverted to its reserved state. **_PageFree** goes a step further by setting the PTEs to zero.

The output from the **Test2** routine is shown in Example 10-7; the source code for this routine is similar to that for **Test1** so it isn't shown here. Like **Test1**, **Test2** reserves and commits two pages, reads from one page and writes to the other, and then decommits and frees the pages. The additional twist added here is that **Test2** forces these two pages to get written out to the paging file.

Example 10-7. Pager Function Trace Showing Page-Outs & Page-Ins

```
TEST2(1):_PageReserve: reserve 2 pages at linear addr = 760000

TEST2(2):_PageCommit: linear addr = 760000, page number = 760

TEST2(3): Write page at 760000

TEST2(4): Read page at 761000

TEST2(5): Page table entries before _PageDiscardPages
    pPTE=FF801D80 Frame=000007EE PTE=007EE267:.. DAP r/w usr com
    pPTE=FF801D84 Frame=00000830 PTE=00830227:.. cAP r/w usr com
```

Example 10-7. Pager Function Trace Showing Page-Outs & Page-Ins (continued)

```
TEST2(6): _PageDiscardPages:  mark pages as page-out candidates

TEST2(7): Page table entries after _PageDiscardPages
   pPTE=FF801D80 Frame=000007EE PTE=007EE247:.. DuP r/w usr com
   pPTE=FF801D84 Frame=00000830 PTE=00830207:.. cuP r/w usr com

TEST2(8):_GetFreePageCount: FreePages = 4F3

TEST2(9): commit a lot of pages until, we get a Dirty-Out ..
 4F3 pages
   _Dirty(C040671A[760],0,0)
      pPF=C0406716 pVP=C04133FA data=760 cLock=0000 cRef=0001 st=00
      pVP=C04133FA cRef=0001 hPD=0D iAR=01C8 pPF=C0406716 TD.P....
      pPTE=FF801D80 Frame=000007EE PTE=007EE247:.. DuP r/w usr com
 5F3 pages
   _DirtyOut(C040671A[760],C135F000,FFFFFFFF)
      pPF=C0406716 pVP=C04133FA data=760 cLock=0830 cRef=0010 st=00
      pVP=C04133FA cRef=0001 hPD=0D iAR=01C8 pPF=C0406716 TD.PI.B.
      pPTE=FF801D80 iVP =00000863 PTE=00863206:.. cun r/w usr com
   _CleanOut(C0406A74[761],C135F000,FFFFFFFF)
      pPF=C0406A70 pVP=C041EE8A data=761 cLock=0E4E cRef=0010 st=00
      pVP=C041EE8A cRef=0001 hPD=0D iAR=01C8 pPF=C0406A70 ...PI.B.
      pPTE=FF801D84 iVP =00001B0B PTE=01B0B206:.. cun r/w usr com

TEST2(10): Original pages are no-longer present ..
   pPTE=FF801D80 iVP =00000863 PTE=00863206:.. cun r/w usr com
   pPTE=FF801D84 iVP =00001B0B PTE=01B0B206:.. cun r/w usr com

TEST2(11): Read from each page to force Virgin-in and Tainted-In ..
   _TaintedIn(C0413400[9F],C135F000,760)
      pVP=C04133FA cRef=0001 hPD=0D iAR=01C8 SF=9F T.S...B.
      pPTE=FF801D80 iVP =00000863 PTE=00863206:.. cun r/w usr com
   _VirginIn(C041EE90[761],C135F000,761)
      pVP=C041EE8A cRef=0001 hPD=0D iAR=01C8 data=761 ......B.
      pPTE=FF801D84 iVP =00001B0B PTE=01B0B206:.. cun r/w usr com

TEST2(12): Original pages are now present ...
   pPTE=FF801D80 Frame=00000337 PTE=00337227:.. cAP r/w usr com
   pPTE=FF801D84 Frame=00000C29 PTE=00C29227:.. cAP r/w usr com

TEST2(13):_PageFree: linear addr = 760000
   _TaintedFree(C0413400[760],0,0)
      pVP=C04133FA cRef=0000 hPD=0D iAR=01C8 pPF=760 T.SP..B.
      pPTE=FF801D80 free
   _VirginFree(C041EE90[761],0,0)
      pVP=C041EE8A cRef=0000 hPD=0D iAR=01C8 pPF=761 ...P..B.
      pPTE=FF801D84 free
```

Test2 does a couple of things to nudge these pages out. First, it makes use of the VMM service **_PageDiscardPages** to mark these pages as unaccessed. An unaccessed page will get paged out before an accessed one. You can see the

difference in the PTEs before and after the call to **_PageDiscardPages**, at
TEST2(5) and TEST2(7). Also note that one page is dirty and the other is clean.

Next, Test2 needs to overcommit pages to force the memory manager to start
moving some pages from memory to the paging file. As a starting point for determining the minimum number of pages to commit, the VMM service
_GetFreePageCount is used to determine the number of free pages in the system.
These pages are then reserved, committed, and touched to force them to be
present. Once **pd_dirtyout** has been called, signaling that one of our pages has
been moved to the paging file, a flag is set. If Test2 sees that this flag has been
set, it assumes it has succeeded; if it is not set, this group of pages is freed, and
the process is repeated with the same amount plus 256. At TEST2(9) in Example
10-7, you see that 4f3h pages were committed and touched, but that amount was
not sufficient, so they were freed and then 5f3h pages were tried, this time with
success. The pager functions **pd_dirtyout** (here named **_DirtyOut**) and **pd_
cleanout** (here named **_CleanOut**) were called to page out the dirty page and
then the clean page. Only two arguments to these functions are used. The first is
a pointer to *pagerdata* and the second is the linear address of the page's contents.
The third argument is always –1. This is the primary pager function where
PageFile_Read_Or_Write is called to write the contents of a dirtied page to the
paging file. While a swappable page is in memory, the Virtual Page structure
holds the address of the page's Page Frame structure. When the page is swapped
to the paging file, the Virtual Page structure holds the Swap Frame for the page,
i.e., the offset into the paging file to find the page's contents. You can see this
under TEST2(11) at the line starting pVP=.... Here, the SF=9F entry in the VP structure tells us that frame 9fh in the paging file contains this page.

VMM's PD_ZEROINIT pager has no implementation for **pd_cleanout**. This is
because a clean zero-initialized page can also be created by **pd_virginin**.

At TEST2(10), the contents of the page's PTEs are shown after both of the pages
have been paged out. Both pages have the same attributes: committed, clean,
unaccessed, user, read/write, and not present. The page frame field of the PTE
holds the index to the page's Virtual Page structure.

At TEST2(11), the two pages are accessed by reading a byte from each of them.
For the page which had been earlier modified, the pager function **pd_taintedin**
(here named **_TaintedIn**) is called by the memory manager, requesting that the
page's contents be restored. The pager function receives a pointer to *pagerdata*,
which now contains the swap frame in the paging file; a pointer to a buffer where
the page can be written; and the original linear page number where this page was
committed. This pager function is the counterpart to **pd_dirtyout**, because this is
the primary pager function where **PageFile_Read_Or_Write** is used to *read* the
contents of a tainted page from the paging file. Since the other page was never

---

Page Tables and Page Directories

At the very top of the linear address space, 4 megabytes are set aside for the system page tables. Recall that to map all linear addresses to physical pages, 2^{20} ($2^{32}/4096$) entries are needed. With each entry occupying a doubleword, the total space needed works out to 2^{22} bytes or 4 megabytes. Since the top of the linear address space is at *MAXSYSTEMLADDR* (FFBFFFFFh), the base address of the page table is FF800000h.

Within this linear address range, a single page is set aside for a page directory. It starts at FFBFE000h. This page is always present and has a physical address given by the contents of the CR3 register. Each entry in the page directory corresponds to a page in the page table, which may or may not be present. While Windows 95's layout for its page tables makes it possible to convert a linear address directly to a page table entry, there is no guarantee that the page containing that entry is present. So, the prudent thing to do is first check the page directory to see if the page containing that entry is present, and only then do a direct lookup of the page table entry.

Two portions of a linear address are used for referencing these tables. The most significant 10 bits of a linear address (*linaddr* >> 22) form an index to the page directory entries (PDEs). The linear page number consisting of the most significant 20 bits of the linear address (*linaddr* >> 12) provide an index to the page table entries (PTEs).

---

modified, **pd_virginin** (here named **_VirginIn**) only needs to create it from scratch by zero-initializing the page's contents.

At TEST2(12) the PTEs for these two pages are displayed. Both pages have the same attributes: committed, clean, accessed, user, read/write, and present. The fact that one of the pages is tainted is stored in the Virtual Page structure flags.

Finally, at TEST2(13), we decommit and free the two pages. The page which was tainted has the **pd_taintedfree** (here named **_TaintedFree**) function called for it whereas the unmodified page has the **pd_virginfree** (here named **_VirginFree**) function called for it. Both functions receive a pointer to the *pVP->pagerdata* member of the Virtual Page structure; the other arguments are zero. As noted in Test1, VMM's PD_ZEROINIT pager handles the **pd_taintedfree** call by freeing the corresponding swap file page if one has been allocated in the paging file. VMM's PS_ZEROINIT pager does not implement the **pd_virginfree** function.

Demand Page Loading

For a process to execute, the kernel needs to load its program image from disk. Rather than load the entire image all at once, it loads the image a page at a time—as the pages are needed. Windows 95 has several pagers which load executables or data on demand.

The Kernel32 Loader

Looking back at Figures 10-3 and 10-4, one might wonder how Windows 95 makes use of pagers. The first three pagers that we'll look at are given the descriptive names "Win32 Sys DLL Data" (5), "Win32 Sys DLL Code" (6), and "Win32 Zero-Init Sys DLL Data" (7). These pagers are registered by VWIN32 when it receives the "Begin PM App" control message during system initialization. Recall that this message arrives when KRNL386 gets loaded into the System VM. At this point KERNEL32 has not yet been loaded into memory.

After VWIN32 has registered its three pagers, it proceeds to reserve and commit pages for KERNEL32. To reserve the linear address range needed by KERNEL32, it issues the service call _**PageReserve**(0xbff70, 0x8f, PR_STATIC). This will reserve the address range BFF70000h to BFFFEFFFh.

Next, VWIN32 commits the first page of the file image using the service call _**Page-Commit**(0xbff70, 1, 6, 0, *PC_INCR|PC_STATIC|PC_USER*). This page contains the file's DOS header and PE (portable executeable) header. From these, the layout of the remainder of the file can be determined. In fact, the rest of the file gets loaded based upon the contents of the PE header's section table.*

KERNEL32 contains six sections; their names, sizes, and characteristics are summarized in Table 10-2. The VWIN32 loader looks at two characteristics of a PE section to decide which pager to commit it with. If it is loading a read-only section without initialized data, then pager 6 is used. If it is loading a read-only section with initialized data, then pager 7 is used. If it is loading a writeable section, then pager 5 is used. Here are the actual service calls which commit KERNEL32's sections:

```
_FREQASM (code)
_PageCommit(0xbff71,6,6,40000000h,PC_INCR|PC_STATIC|PC_USER)
_PageCommit(0xbff77,1,6,40010006h,PC_INCR|PC_STATIC|PC_USER)

.text (code)
_PageCommit(bff78h,41h,6,20000007h,PC_INCR|PC_STATIC|PC_USER)
_PageCommit(bffb9h,1,6,20070048,PC_INCR|PC_STATIC|PC_USER)
```

---

* See Chapter 8 of *Windows 95 System Programming Secrets*, by Matt Pietrek, for details of the PE file format.

```
_INIT (code)
_PageCommit(bffbah,1,6,40000048h,PC_INCR|PC_STATIC|PC_USER)
_PageCommit(bffbbh,1,6,40040049h,PC_INCR|PC_STATIC|PC_USER)

.data (data initialized at compile time)
_PageCommit(bffbch,3,5,c0000049h, PC_INCR|PC_STATIC|PC_USER|PC_
WRITEABLE)
_PageCommit(bffbfh,1,5,c001004ch, PC_INCR|PC_STATIC|PC_USER|PC_
WRITEABLE)

.edata (exports)
_PageCommit(bffc0h,4,6,a000004dh,PC_INCR|PC_STATIC|PC_USER)
_PageCommit(bffc4h,1,6,a0040051h,PC_INCR|PC_STATIC|PC_USER)

.rsrc (resources)
_PageCommit(bffc5h,12h,6,20000052h,PC_INCR|PC_STATIC|PC_USER)
_PageCommit(bffd7h,1,6,20060064,PC_INCR|PC_STATIC|PC_USER)
```

There are two **_PageCommit** calls for each section because VWIN32's algorithm commits the whole pages first and then, if it finds a remainder—a fraction of a page—it commits one more page for it. The **.data** section, which is the only section which is writeable, uses pager 5; all other sections use pager 6.

Table 10-2. PE Sections of KERNEL32

Name	Type	Linear Address	Size in Bytes	Characteristics
_FREQASM	code	BFF71000h	6D70h	Executeable, Read-only
.text		BFF78000h	41070h	Executeable, Read-only
_INIT	code	BFFBA000h	176Bh	Executeable, Read-only
.data	data	BFFBC000h	3CC0h	Read-write, shared
.edata	data	BFFC0000h	47E1h	Read-only
.rsrc	data	BFFC5000h	123CCh	Read-only

The pagerdata value supplied to these **_PageCommit** calls may look a little strange. The doubleword has two fields. The most significant 10 bits hold an index which is used to lookup a file handle. The lower 22 bits hold the file offset to the raw data to be read into a page; this is the byte offset divided by 512. Now take that value and rotate it to the right by 3 bits. This last twist has the magic effect of aligning bit 0 on the page digit. Since the PC_INCR flag is set for these pages, the pagerdata values will be incremented for each page in the set. This rotation makes sure the increment actually increases the file offset by 1000h bytes.

Referring once again to Figures 10-3 and 10-4, you can see that pager 5 is the same as VMM's Swappable Zero-Init pager, except that **pd_virginin** has been replaced with an action function in VWIN32. This same action function is used by pager 6 for handling both **pd_virginin** and **pd_taintedin**. This action function switches to KERNEL32's PSP, extracts the file handle index and file offset from the pagerdata, and then proceeds to seek to that location and read the page. The current PSP is restored and the function returns. The seek and read are executed using **_ExecVxDIntMustComplete**.

It is interesting that pager 5 uses the system paging file for backing up changes to KERNEL32's **.data** section. Except for the fact the section's initial contents are loaded directly from the KERNEL32 image, the life of pages in this section will be the same as those controlled by the PD_ZEROINIT pager.

The three pagers we just examined are only used with KERNEL32. It appears that at one time, files other than KERNEL32 were demand-paged using this code, since there is a file index built into the pagerdata value. Perhaps this pager is separate because it can be put to use before the Win32 subsystem is up and running, and thus serves as sort of a bootstrap pager.

The Win32 Loader

The next two pagers that we'll look at are given the descriptive names "Win32 EXE/DLL Data" (8) and "Win32 EXE/DLL Code" (9). These pagers are registered by KERNEL32 during its initialization. Unlike the pagers we have been looking at, these ones are more a part of KERNEL32 than of VMM. Of course, VMM services are used but via the Win32 **VxDCall** interface. Rather than drill down into KERNEL32's code, I'm going to spy on the **VxDCall**s for **PageReserve** and **Page-Commit**. We can use MultiMon to do this by loading the WIN32CB and FSHook drivers and enabling the filters for VMM Win32 Services (**PageReserve** and **Page-Commit**) and IFSMgr Filehook (**FS_OpenFile**). To capture the trace that we'll be looking at, press the **Start** button, launch the Notepad application, terminate Notepad, and then press the **Stop** button.

After you hit the **Show** button, scroll through the output until you find the point where *notepad.exe* is being opened (**FS_OpenFile**); you should see something similar to the output in Figure 10-5. What we see is a trace of the Win32 loader as it assigns pages and pagers to the sections of Notepad.

Right after the **FS_OpenFile** line, a **PageReserve** call is made with these arguments: linear page number = 400h, number of pages = 0ch, and flags = 10h (*PR_STATIC*). This call is reserving 48Kbytes for the file image of Notepad starting at linear address 400000h. We can use a tool like the Explorer's QuikView to determine Notepad's PE file sections. With this information we can interpret the sequence of **PageCommit** calls as follows:

```
PE header
_PageCommit(0x400,1,9,00f20000h,PC_INCR|PC_STATIC|PC_USER)

.text (code, 3953h bytes, read-only)
_PageCommit(401h,3,9,40f00000h,PC_INCR|PC_STATIC|PC_USER)
```

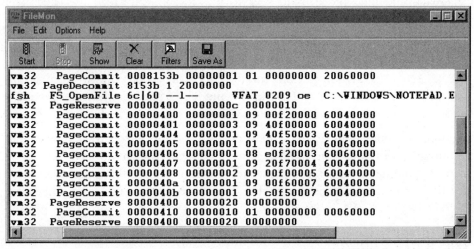

Figure 10-5. MultiMon output showing page commits when loading Notepad

```
_PageCommit(404h,1,9,40f50003h,PC_INCR|PC_STATIC|PC_USER)

.bss (data, 43ah bytes, uninitialized data, read-write)
_PageCommit(405h,1,1,00f30000h,
PC_INCR|PC_STATIC|PC_USER|PC_WRITEABLE)

.data (data initialized at compile time, 212h bytes, read-write)
_PageCommit(406h,1,8,e0f20003h,
PC_INCR|PC_STATIC|PC_USER|PC_WRITEABLE)

.idata (import table, c9ah bytes)
_PageCommit(407h,1,9,20f70004h,PC_INCR|PC_STATIC|PC_USER)

.rsrc (resources, 2b70h bytes)
_PageCommit(408h,2h,9,00f00005h,PC_INCR|PC_STATIC|PC_USER)
_PageCommit(40ah,1h,9,00f60007h,PC_INCR|PC_STATIC|PC_USER)

.reloc (relocation table, 91eh bytes)
_PageCommit(40bh,1,9,c0f50007h,PC_INCR|PC_STATIC|PC_USER).
```

This output appears to be generated by the same algorithm that is used by the KERNEL32 loader, only different pagers are used. Pager 9, which is used to load read-only sections of code or data, only implements **pd_virginin**. Pager 8, which is used to load read-write, initialized data sections, uses the same implementation of **pd_virginin**, but in other respects is a clone of PD_ZEROINIT. For uninitialized data sections, VMM's PD_ZEROINIT pager is used. Pages which are under control of pagers 1 or 8 are backed up by the system paging file.

Memory Mapped Files

Of the 12 system pagers we started out with, we are now down to the last three. These three are responsible for implementing memory-mapped files. They were given the descriptive names "Win32 Safe Mapped File" (10), "Win32 Unsafe Mapped File" (11), and "Win32 Copy-On-Write Mapped File" (12). Pagers 10 and 11 are identical except that the **pd_type** of the "unsafe" pager has the *PD_NEST-EXEC* bit set. The only information on this flag comes from a comment in *vmm.h*: "PD_NESTEXEC—must be specified if either the **pd_cleanout** or **pd_dirtyout** functions perform nested excecution or block using the BLOCK_SVC_INTS flag. To be safe, this flag should always be specified if the pager does any sort of file I/O to anything other than the default paging file." Pagers 10 and 11 implement **pd_virginin**, **pd_taintedin**, and **pd_dirtyout**. They have a *pd_type* of *PD_PAGERONLY*, so they do not swap to the system paging file.

Standard Win32 code for creating and accessing a mapped file is shown in Example 10-8. You can launch this test code from *pagers.exe* by selecting the **Test** menu, sub-item **MemMapped R/O**. The output shown in Figure 10-6 was collected by MultiMon while this code executed. MultiMon had WIN32CB and FSHook drivers loaded and the filters for VMM Win32 Services (**PageReserve**, **PageCommit**, and **PageFree**) and IFSMgr Filehook (**FS_OpenFile**, **FS_ReadFile**, **FS_WriteFile**, **FS_FileSeek**, and **FS_CloseFile**).

Example 10-8. MemMapped R/O Test

```
hFile = CreateFile( szFileName,GENERIC_READ, FILE_SHARE_READ,
                    NULL,OPEN_EXISTING,0,NULL);
if ( hFile != INVALID_HANDLE_VALUE ) {
  hMapFile = CreateFileMapping(hFile,NULL,PAGE_READONLY,0,0,NULL);
  if ( hMapFile != NULL ) {
    pMapImage = MapViewOfFile( hMapFile, FILE_MAP_READ,0,0,0);
      if ( pMapImage != NULL ) {
        for( i=0, p=pMapImage; i<16; i++, p+=0x1000 ) a[i] = *p;
        UnmapViewOfFile( pMapImage );
        }
    CloseHandle( hMapFile );
    }
  CloseHandle( hFile );
  }
```

The first line of output is from an attempt to create a new copy of *mapfile.tst*, a test file 64 Kbytes in length. In this case, the file had already been created, so the create call fails, but the subsequent open of the existing file succeeds, and returns a file handle of 264h. There are three intervening seeks, perhaps to determine the file size, before the **FS_ReadFile** call. This read corresponds to the **Win32 CreateFileMapping** call. It is a special case where *ir_length* is 0 and the *RO_MM_READ_WRITE* flag is set in *ir_options*. This combination indicates that a memory-

```
FileMon                                                                _ □ ×
File  Edit  Options  Help

  ▣      ▣      ▣      ✕      ▤      ▣
 Start   Stop   Show   Clear  Filters Save As

fsh    FS_OpenFile 6c|60 e-1--    VFAT -----  cn  E:\IFSBOOK\PAGERS\MAPFILE.TST ▲
fsh    FS_OpenFile 6c|60 --1--    VFAT 0264   oe  E:\IFSBOOK\PAGERS\MAPFILE.TST
fsh    FS_FileSeek 42|20 --1--    VFAT 0264
fsh    FS_FileSeek 42|20 --1--    VFAT 0264
fsh    FS_FileSeek 42|20 --1--    VFAT 0264
fsh    FS_ReadFile 00|00 --1--    VFAT 026b ■--  0H@0H
vm32   PageReserve 80060000 00000010 00000010
vm32     PageCommit 00002869 00000010 0a 00640000 60040000
fsh    FS_ReadFile d6|50 --1--    VFAT 026b ■--  1000H@0H
fsh    FS_ReadFile d6|50 --1--    VFAT 026b ■--  1000H@1000H
fsh    FS_ReadFile d6|50 --1--    VFAT 026b ■--  1000H@2000H
fsh    FS_ReadFile d6|50 --1--    VFAT 026b ■--  1000H@3000H
fsh    FS_ReadFile d6|50 --1--    VFAT 026b ■--  1000H@4000H
fsh    FS_ReadFile d6|50 --1--    VFAT 026b ■--  1000H@5000H
fsh    FS_ReadFile d6|50 --1--    VFAT 026b ■--  1000H@6000H
fsh    FS_ReadFile d6|50 --1--    VFAT 026b ■--  1000H@7000H
fsh    FS_ReadFile d6|50 --1--    VFAT 026b ■--  1000H@8000H
fsh    FS_ReadFile d6|50 --1--    VFAT 026b ■--  1000H@9000H
fsh    FS_ReadFile d6|50 --1--    VFAT 026b ■--  1000H@a000H
fsh    FS_ReadFile d6|50 --1--    VFAT 026b ■--  1000H@b000H
fsh    FS_ReadFile d6|50 --1--    VFAT 026b ■--  1000H@c000H
fsh    FS_ReadFile d6|50 --1--    VFAT 026b ■--  1000H@d000H
fsh    FS_ReadFile d6|50 --1--    VFAT 026b ■--  1000H@e000H
fsh    FS_ReadFile d6|50 --1--    VFAT 026b ■--  1000H@f000H
vm32     PageFree 82869000 10
fsh    FS_CloseFile d7|50 --1--   VFAT 026b p
fsh    FS_CloseFile 3e|20 --1--   VFAT 0264 f
```

Figure 10-6. Accessing a read-only memory mapped file

mapping is being created to an existing open file. This special call originates from **IFSMgr_Win32DupHandle** when it is called with the *DUP_MEMORY_MAPPED* flag. This service duplicates the handle 264h to 26bh before making the **FS_ReadFile** call on the duplicated handle.

When the Win32 API **MapViewOfFile** is called, virtual memory is reserved for the file image. Since we specified that the entire file be mapped, an equivalent number of pages are reserved. The **_PageReserve** request is for 10h pages in the shared memory area at 80060000h with the *PR_STATIC* flag. The subsequent commit passes in 82869h as the linear page number, so **_PageReserve** must have returned 82869000h as the base linear address of the mapping. **_PageCommit** commits all 10h pages using pager 10 with *PC_INCR*, *PC_STATIC*, and *PC_USER* flags. Since we requested *FILE_MAP_READ*, we are not given the *PC_WRITEABLE* attribute and the mapping is read-only.

Next, we proceed to read the first byte of each page of the mapping. Each read forces a **pd_virginin** call for a page which results in the series of **FS_ReadFile** calls on the duped handle 26bh. These reads also are marked with the *RO_MM_READ_ WRITE* flag. Note that if a page out occurs for one of mapped pages, it is essentially a discard since the pages can not enter the dirty state. A subsequent access would restore the page using **pd_virginin**. At the bottom of trace, we see the pages being freed in response to the **UnmapViewOfFile**, and then the **Close-Handle** calls for *hMapFile* and *hFile*.

Very similar Win32 code for creating and accessing a mapped file is shown in Example 10-9. You can launch this test code from *pagers.exe* by selecting the **Test** menu, sub-item **MemMapped R/W**. The output shown in Figure 10-7 was collected by MultiMon while this code executed. The difference between this example and the previous one is in granting the mapping read-write access and writing to it.

Example 10-9. MemMapped R/W Test

```
hFile = CreateFile( szFileName,GENERIC_READ|GENERIC_WRITE,
                    FILE_SHARE_READ,NULL,OPEN_EXISTING,0,NULL);
if ( hFile != INVALID_HANDLE_VALUE ) {
  hMapFile=CreateFileMapping(hFile,NULL,PAGE_READWRITE,0,0,NULL);
  if ( hMapFile != NULL ) {
    pMapImage = MapViewOfFile( hMapFile, FILE_MAP_WRITE,0,0,0);
    if ( pMapImage != NULL ) {
      for( i=0, p=pMapImage; i<16; i++, p+=0x1000 ) *p = 'A';
      UnmapViewOfFile( pMapImage );
      }
    CloseHandle( hMapFile );
    }
  CloseHandle( hFile );
  }
```

Zeroing in on just those areas which are different in Figure 10-7, we see that **_PageCommit** uses the *PC_WRITEABLE* attribute since we passed *FILE_MAP_WRITE* to **MapViewOfFile**. Although we are writing a byte to each page of the mapping, each write forces a **pd_virginin** call for a page which results in the series of **FS_ReadFile** calls on the duped handle. Eventually, when **UnmapViewOfFile** is called, we see **pd_dirtyout** in action as each page which has been dirtied written out to *mapfile.tst*.

Example 10-10 again illustrates very similar Win32 code for creating and accessing a mapped file. You can launch this test code from *pagers.exe* by selecting the **Test** menu, sub-item **MemMapped WriteCopy**. The output shown in Figure 10-8 was collected by MultiMon while this code executed. The difference between this example and the previous one is that write access is granted only to a copy of the mapping file. This difference in behavior is brought about by subtle changes in the flags to **CreateFileMapping**, which uses *PAGE_WRITECOPY*, and **MapViewOfFile**, which here uses *FILE_MAP_COPY*.

Underneath the Win32 code, we can see what is going on by looking at the MultiMon trace in Figure 10-8. When **MapViewOfFile** commits memory to match *mapfile.tst*'s file size, it uses pager 12, the one described as Win32 Copy-On-Write Mapped File. We see this in the **_PageCommit** call:

```
_PageCommit( 82869h, 10h, 12, 00700000h,
            PC_INCR|PC_STATIC|PC_USER|PCWRITEABLE)
```

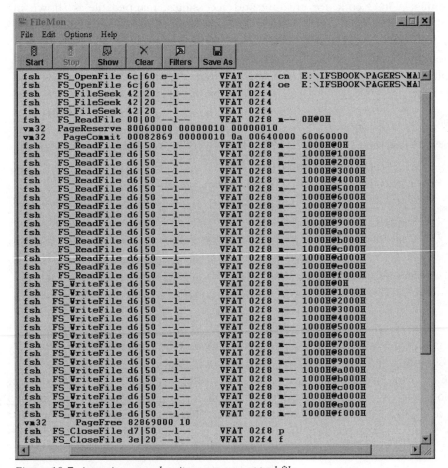

Figure 10-7. Accessing a read-write memory mapped file

Example 10-10. MemMapped WriteCopy Test

```
hFile = CreateFile( szFileName,GENERIC_READ|GENERIC_WRITE,
FILE_SHARE_READ,NULL,OPEN_EXISTING,0,NULL);
if ( hFile != INVALID_HANDLE_VALUE ) {
hMapFile=CreateFileMapping(hFile,NULL,PAGE_WRITECOPY,0,0,NULL);
if ( hMapFile != NULL ) {
   pMapImage = MapViewOfFile( hMapFile, FILE_MAP_COPY,0,0,0);
       if ( pMapImage != NULL ) {
       for( i=0, p=pMapImage; i<16; i++, p+=0x1000 ) *p = 'A';
          UnmapViewOfFile( pMapImage );
          }
       CloseHandle( hMapFile );
       }
   CloseHandle( hFile );
   }
```

The significance of this is that pager 12 has a *pd_type* of *PD_SWAPPER*, meaning that it uses the system paging file as a backing file, not the mapped file. The mapped file is accessed only on **pd_virginin** calls using **FS_ReadFile**, as we see in Figure 10-8. Writes to the mapped file only go as far as the memory page. A dirty page is paged out to the system paging file, not the mapped file.

```
FileMon                                                              _ □ ×
File  Edit  Options  Help

  █       █       ▦       ✕       ▣       ▦
 Start   Stop    Show    Clear  Filters  Save As

 fsh     FS_OpenFile 6c|60  e-1---      VFAT  ------ cn   E:\IFSBOOK\PAGERS
 fsh     FS_OpenFile 6c|60  ---1---      VFAT  021e   oe   E:\IFSBOOK\PAGERS
 fsh     FS_FileSeek 42|20  ---1---      VFAT  021e
 fsh     FS_FileSeek 42|20  ---1---      VFAT  021e
 fsh     FS_FileSeek 42|20  ---1---      VFAT  021e
 fsh     FS_ReadFile 00|00  ---1---      VFAT  0228  ■--  0H@0H
 vm32    PageReserve 80060000 00000010 00000010
 vm32    PageCommit  00082869 00000010  0c 00700000 60060000
 fsh     FS_ReadFile d6|50  ---1---      VFAT  0228  ■--  1000H@0H
 fsh     FS_ReadFile d6|50  ---1---      VFAT  0228  ■--  1000H@1000H
 fsh     FS_ReadFile d6|50  ---1---      VFAT  0228  ■--  1000H@2000H
 fsh     FS_ReadFile d6|50  ---1---      VFAT  0228  ■--  1000H@3000H
 fsh     FS_ReadFile d6|50  ---1---      VFAT  0228  ■--  1000H@4000H
 fsh     FS_ReadFile d6|50  ---1---      VFAT  0228  ■--  1000H@5000H
 fsh     FS_ReadFile d6|50  ---1---      VFAT  0228  ■--  1000H@6000H
 fsh     FS_ReadFile d6|50  ---1---      VFAT  0228  ■--  1000H@7000H
 fsh     FS_ReadFile d6|50  ---1---      VFAT  0228  ■--  1000H@8000H
 fsh     FS_ReadFile d6|50  ---1---      VFAT  0228  ■--  1000H@9000H
 fsh     FS_ReadFile d6|50  ---1---      VFAT  0228  ■--  1000H@a000H
 fsh     FS_ReadFile d6|50  ---1---      VFAT  0228  ■--  1000H@b000H
 fsh     FS_ReadFile d6|50  ---1---      VFAT  0228  ■--  1000H@c000H
 fsh     FS_ReadFile d6|50  ---1---      VFAT  0228  ■--  1000H@d000H
 fsh     FS_ReadFile d6|50  ---1---      VFAT  0228  ■--  1000H@e000H
 fsh     FS_ReadFile d6|50  ---1---      VFAT  0228  ■--  1000H@f000H
 vm32    PageFree    82869000 10
 fsh     FS_CloseFile d7|50  ---1---     VFAT  0228  p
 fsh     FS_CloseFile 3e|20  ---1---     VFAT  021e  f
```

Figure 10-8. Accessing a write-copy memory mapped file

Paging aims to minimize disk access and resource usage by bringing the disk imae into memory only as needed. In the next chapter we'll look at caching, which reduces disk access by keeping frequently used portions of the disk image in main memory.

11

VCACHE: Caches Big and Small

The idea of a cache was motivated by the need to reduce costly I/O processing. It is much faster to read a block of data from memory than it is to read the same data from a physical disk. The cache keeps some subset of a larger collection of data within local memory. Often, the items in the cache are determined by usage. The most recently used items are kept in the cache, and once the cache is full, the least recently used items are discarded to make room for new additions. This algorithm is referred to as least recently used, or LRU.

Windows 95 supplies *vcache.vxd* to provide two kinds of LRU caches to VxD writers. The first type of cache, the *block* cache, deals with 4096 byte memory pages; the size of the allocation is fixed. A separate data structure, represented by a cache block handle, is used to track each page. It contains information such as ownership, lookup keys, lock counts, and usage counts. This is the cache used by VFAT when accessing the system's disk drives. The second type of cache, the *lookup* cache, is suitable for small items; these items may be of variable and arbitrary size. This cache is the in-memory image of a section of the system registry. A lookup cache is created as a key with some maximum number of elements. The elements are just values under the key. The LRU algorithm kicks in when the number of values added under the key exceeds the maximum number of elements. The registry file serves as persistent storage for a lookup cache.

The official documentation for VCACHE's services is in the DDK document file *stdvxd.doc*. Unfortunately, the information presented there is incomplete. This chapter will help fill in what's missing and supply additional background information.

Where Does Block Cache Memory Come From?

Since the unit of allocation is a page, it should come as no surprise that the block cache is created using the sparse memory allocator. As we saw in the last chapter, using this allocator is a two-stage procedure where memory is first reserved and then committed. The actual call used to reserve the range of memory used for the block cache looks like this:

```
linBase =_PageReserve(PR_SYSTEM,maxCache,PR_FIXED)
```

where *PR_SYSTEM* requests that the pages be reserved anywhere in the system arena (C0000000h-FFBFFFFFh) and *PR_FIXED* says do not move the pages on a **_PageReAllocate**. The subsequent call, which commits some of this range to form the initial cache, takes this form:

```
_PageCommit(linBase>>12,initCache,PD_FIXEDZERO,0,PC_FIXED)
```

Note that these pages are *PC_FIXED*, meaning that the memory is permanently locked. Not all of the pages initially reserved are committed. Instead the following algorithm is used to determine the initial cache size:

```
minInitial = (minCache>=64) ? 64 : minCache;
initCache = maxCache - 1024;
if ( initCache <= minInitial ) initCache = minInitial;
if ( initCache > maxCache )    initCache = maxCache;
if ( initCache > 2304 )        initCache = 2304;
```

Put simply, the initial cache size will be 1024 less than the number of reserved pages but will not exceed 2304.

In somewhat the same way that DYNAPAGE and PAGESWAP use legacy entries in the *system.ini* file to set various parameters controlling the paging file, VCache uses entries in the [**vcache**] section of the *system.ini* file to set parameters controlling the block cache. The keys which VCache retrieves during initialization are *minfilecache*, *maxfilecache*, and *CacheBufRRT*. The *minfilecache* and *maxfilecache* entries are in units of kilobytes; if a value is not specified in the *system.ini* file, a default of 0 is used.

The values of minfilecache and maxfilecache, in turn, determine the values of *minCache* and *maxCache*; *maxCache* sets the number pages which are reserved for the block cache; *minCache* and *maxCache*, together determine the value of *initCache*, the subset of reserved pages which are initially committed for use. To get from *minfilecache* and *maxfilecache* to the final values of *minCache* and *maxCache*, the following algorithm is used:

```
max = Get_Profile_Decimal_Int( "vcache", "maxfilecache", 0 ); // kbytes
min = Get_Profile_Decimal_Int( "vcache", "minfilecache", 0 );
maxCache = (max + 3)/4;                          // round up to nearest page
minCache = (min + 3)/4;
numFreeLockablePages = _GetFreePageCount(0);        // returned in EDX
if (minCache == 0)                                  // using defaults?
   minCache = (numFreeLockablePages < 1280) ? numFreeLockablePages/40:
                                     numFreeLockablePages/24;
avail = (numFreeLockablePages >= 392) ? numFreeLockablePages-384 : 8;
if (minCache > avail) minCache = avail;
if (minCache <= 8) minCache = 8;
if (maxCache > avail) maxCache = avail;
if (maxCache > 204800) maxCache = 204800;
if (maxCache < minCache) minCache = maxCache;
```

Summarizing, if your system is using defaults for its cache size, VCache will determine these values at Device Init time from the number of lockable free pages returned by **_GetFreePageCount**. If this function reports 1280 pages or more, the minimum cache size is the number of free lockable pages divided by 40; if more than 1280 pages are free, this amount is divided by 24 to arrive at the minimum size. In no case will the minimum be less than 8 pages. The default setting for the maximum cache size is the number of free lockable pages minus 384. In no case will the cache size exceed 204800 pages. Table 11-1 shows default initial cache sizes for several PC configurations.

Table 11-1. Default Block Cache Sizes for Some Typical Systems

System Description	Free Lockable Pages	Minimum Cache Pages	Maximum Cache Pages	Initial Cache Pages
486DX-66 Desktop, 12 MB	2074	86	1690	666
Pentium-60 Desktop, 16 MB	2962	123	2578	1554
486DX-75 Notebook, 20MB	4199	174	3815	2304

What we have described so far is the initial configuration of the cache if you were to take a snap shot after VCache has finished its initialization. Like the swap file, cache size is dynamic. Let's take a look at how the memory manager can make the cache shrink or allow it to grow.

How Does the Memory Manager Control Block Cache Size?

VCache has two services which are used to add or remove a page from those committed to the cache. The service which is called by the memory manager to reclaim a page is **VCache_RelinquishPage**, and to add a page, it calls **VCache_UseThisPage**.

A call to **VCache_RelinquishPage** may be traced back to numerous locations in VMM: the page fault handler; the various memory manager functions such as **_PageCommit**, **_LinPageLock**, etc.; a callback installed by **Call_When_Idle**; or the ongoing one-second timeout procedure installed by **Set_Async_Time_Out**. The memory manager actually calls **VCache_RelinquishPage** through a wrapper function that I've named **Take_VCache_Page**. VMM will call this function to attempt to reclaim some of VCache's memory only if there are no free pages available and other appropriate conditions are met. Here is the pseudocode for **Take_VCache_Page**:

```
DWORD Take_VCache_Page() {
    DWORD linPage, numPage, iCachePage;
    if (amtShrinkCache==0 || curCachePages<=minCachePages) return 0;
    amtGrowCache = 0;
    linPage = VCache_RelinquishPage();          // request a page
    if (linPage == 0 ) goto not_taken;
    numPage = linPage>>12;                       // convert linear addr
                                                 // to page number
    if (numPage < pgnumCacheStart) goto not_taken;   // less than
                                                     // cache?
    iCachePage = numPage - pgnumCacheStart;      // page index
    if (iCachePage >= maxCachePages) goto not_taken;  // greater than
                                                      // cache?
    _FreeUsedPage(pBitMap_VCachePages, ++iCachePage); // mark page
                                                      // unused
    amtShrinkCache--;     // shrunk by one page
    curCachePages--;      // current cache size is one less
    return linPage;       // return linear address of page
not_taken:
    amtShrinkCache = 0;   // shrink failed, turn off further attempts
    return 0;             // no linear address returned
    }
```

On entry this function checks several global VMM variables before proceeding. First, *amtShrinkCache* should be set to a non-zero value by the memory manager, to indicate the number of pages to reclaim. Secondly, the current number of pages in the cache should not drop below *minCachePages*; if it does then the request is ignored. If these conditions are met, **VCache_RelinquishPage** is called to get the linear address of a page within the cache. In response to this request, VCache will first give up pages which are on its free list. Once those are exhausted it will start searching for candidates on its LRU list. Only those which are not held or dirty, and which have aged sufficiently, will be sacrificed.

If a linear page address is returned by **VCache_RelinquishPage**, then **Take_VCache_Page** verifies that its page number lies in the range which has been reserved for the cache. VMM maintains a bit array of used cache pages (*pBitMap_VCachePages*). When a page is reclaimed from the cache, its corresponding bit is cleared by the function **_FreeUsedPage**. VMM's internal counters (*amtShrinkCache* and *curCachePages*) are updated and the linear address of the page is returned. The *caller* of **Take_VCache_Page** then uncommits the physical page corresponding to the linear address. This makes the page free to be used for other needs and at the same time changes the status of the linear address from committed to reserved.

The opposite of shrinking the cache is growing the cache, and VMM has a global variable, *amtGrowCache*, which indicates how many pages to give back to VCache. This variable is updated at one-second intervals by a timeout procedure installed by **Set_Async_Time_Out**. The decision to grow the cache is based on two statistics returned by **VCache_GetStats** at these one-second intervals: the number of cache blocks which have been discarded and the number of cache hits to the last 26 LRU cache blocks. When conditions are appropriate for growing the cache, VMM sets up an event callback that will invoke **VCache_UseThisPage**. Rather than call this function directly, VMM schedules a wrapper function, **Give_VCache_Page** (my name), as an event using the **Call_Restricted_Event** service. The pseudocode for **Give_VCache_Page** follows:

```
void Give_VCache_Page( void ) {
    DWORD iCachePage, numPage;
    if (amtGrowCache == 0) return;            // is VCache getting pages?
    while(TRUE) {
        iCachePage = _GetUnusedPage(pBitMap_VCachePages,maxCachePages);
        if (iCachePage == 0) return;
        numPage = pgnumVCacheStart + iCachePage - 1;        // new page
        if (_PageCommit(numPage,1,PD_FIXED,0,PC_FIXED|PC_WRITEABLE)==0)
            _FreeUsedPage(pBitMap_VCachePages,iCachePage);
            return;
            }
        Flush_TLB();
        DecCounter(); /* D1_F7E4 */
        VCache_UseThisPage(numPage<<12);                // give page to VCache
        curCachePages++;
        if (amtGrowCache == 0) break;
        amtGrowCache--;
        }
    }
```

This routine first checks that *amtGrowCache* is non-zero, i.e., there is something to do. If so, it enters a loop where it attempts to grow the cache a page at a time until the requested number of pages has been added. To add a page to the cache it needs to know the linear address of a page in the cache's address range which is currently uncommitted. By scanning the bitmap of unused cache pages, *pBitMap_VCachePages*, the index of an unused page is returned by **_GetUnusedPage**. This index is converted into a page number and passed to **_PageCommit** to map a physical page to a linear address in the cache. That linear address is then passed to **VCache_UseThisPage**, to inform VCache that it is available.

To be complete, I should mention one other method by which the cache can be made to grow. VMM's Win32 service number 0x28 checks if the current cache size is at least 128 pages. If it is not, *amtGrowCache* is set by the following expression:

```
if ( 128 <= maxCachePages ) amtGrowCache = 128 - curCachePages;
else  amtGrowCache = maxCachePages - curCachePages;
```

and then **Give_VCache_Page** is scheduled to run by **Call_Restricted_Event**.

Block Cache Data Structures

The pages which belong to the block cache are either in use or placed on a free list. The pages on the free list form a one-way linked list. The head of the free list is stored in a VCache global variable *pFreePageList*; each page in the free list contains a link at byte offset 0x100 from the beginning of the page. A page which is in use can either contain cache data or cache blocks. The cache block data structure is 64 bytes in length, so a page can store 64 cache blocks.

Pages which are used to store cache blocks are tracked by an array (*pCBPagesList*) of the page linear addresses. The size of this array is determined by the maximum cache size; it is given by the formula: ((*maxCachePages* + 63)/64)*4 bytes. This array is allocated from the heap at Device Init time. Initially it is zero-filled, but as each page is removed from the free list to create new cache blocks, the page's linear address is added to the first available slot in the array. Once a page is allocated for creating cache blocks, it is never reclaimed to the free page pool.

Pages which are used to contain data are referenced by the linear address stored in the *BufPtr* member of the cache block data structure (shown below). These pages come from the same pool of free pages. There is a one-to-one correspondence between cache blocks and data pages.

This brings us to the cache block, the central data structure used by block cache services. Here is the layout of this structure:

```
typedef struct {
    struct cb* cb_next;     /* 00 - head of free list/collision list */
```

```
    struct cb* cb_prev;      /* 04 - tail of free list/collision list */
    DWORD      FSKey1;       /* 08 - hash key 1 */
    DWORD      FSKey2;       /* 0C - hash key 2 */
    void*      BufPtr;       /* 10 - page containing cache data */
    DWORD      FSDData[7];   /* 14 - area reserved for FSD use */
    WORD       HoldCnt;      /* 30 - lock to prevent discard/reclaim */
    BYTE       Dirty;        /* 32 - cache data is modified */
    BYTE       FSD_ID;       /* 33 - ID of FSD which owns page */
    DWORD      AgeCnt;       /* 34 - relative age of block */
    struct cb* lru_next;     /* 38 - MRU end of list */
    struct cb* lru_prev;     /* 3C - LRU end of list */
    } CB, *PCB;
```

Cache blocks which are not in use are placed on a free list whose head is given by a VCache global variable (*pCBFreeList*). In these cache blocks, the members *cb_next* and *cb_prev* provide linkage for members in the list.

Cache blocks which are in use are strung together on a different list, the LRU list. The head of this list is a pseudo-cache block in VCache's locked data area. Only two members of this cache block are used, *lru_next* and *lru_prev*. These point to the head and the tail of the list. The most recently used cache block is at the head of this list, while the least recently used cache block is at the tail of this list. The *lru_next* and *lru_prev* members provide the linkage for this doubly-linked list.

Each cache block is uniquely identified by two keys, *FSKey1* and *FSKey2*, and a one-byte ownership ID, *FSD_ID*. The *FSKey1* and *FSKey2* values are allowed any values other than 0. For example, VFAT uses *FSKey1* as the logical sector number and *FSKey2* as the volume resource handle. These two keys are used in conjunction with a hash table. Each bucket or entry in the hash table consists of two pointers. If the bucket is empty, the pointers reference the address of their bucket. If the bucket contains one cache block, then both bucket pointers point to the same cache block. Both of the cache block's *cb_next* and *cb_prev* pointers refer back to the hash table bucket. If the bucket contains more than one cache block, the first bucket pointer refers to the first cache block and the second bucket pointer refers to the last cache block. The intervening cache blocks that belong to the bucket are linked by the *cb_next* and *cb_prev* members. The *cb_prev* pointer of the first cache block and the *cb_next* pointer of the last cache block refer back to the hash table bucket. The cache blocks in a bucket have *FSKey1* and *FSKey2* values which hash to the same value. This hash value serves as an index into the hash table.

To calculate a hash value VCache uses a simple hash function which is represented here as C pseudocode:

```
i = (FSKey1 & 0xffff0000)>>16;
i ^= FSKey1;
i ^= FSKey2;
i &= LookupMask;
```

The value *i* which results from these statements is used to directly index the hash table. The value *i* is constrained to the hash table range by the last step where it is ANDed with the *LookupMask*. The *LookupMask* depends upon the hash table size. If the hash table has 2047 (7ffh) buckets, then the mask will be (7ffh)<<3 or 3ff8h. Before a match is returned by a search, the cache blocks in the bucket are compared with *FSKey1*, *FSKey2*, and *FSD_ID*, to verify it is exact.

VCACHE may have up to 10 clients. Each client registers with VCache at Device Init time and if successful receives a unique identifier. This is the value that will be stored in the FSD_ID member of this client's cache blocks. Internally, VCache keeps track of its clients using a structure like this:

```
struct { DWORD BlksInUse;
        DWORD BlksReserved;
        void (*DiscardFunc)();
        DWORD reserved;
        } reg_data[10];
```

The index to **reg_data[]** is *FSD_ID*—0x64. The *BlksReserved* and *DiscardFunc* members are supplied by the client when it registers. *BlksReserved* specifies the minimum number of cache block pages which this client can not drop below (this value can be 0). *DiscardFunc* is the address of a function which VCache will call when it is about to discard a cache block and its data page. This allows an FSD to update its data structures when a page is no longer in the cache.

An FSD should set the *Dirty* byte in the cache block structure, to a non-zero value if the contents of a page have been modified. This flag is controlled by the FSD and is used to prevent VCache from discarding a page. It is the responsibility of the FSD to write a dirty page to disk and clear the flag. Another flag which the FSD can use to prevent a page from being discarded is *HoldCnt*. This word value is an unsigned count of locks which have been requested on the page. As long as at least one lock is outstanding, the page will not be discarded. An FSD may use the 28 bytes in **FSDData[]** for any information it may wish to store along with a page. This area is free format, so it is up to the FSD to define how it will be used.

When a new cache block is created, its age, the member *AgeCnt*, is initialized to the current value of VCache's global variable *nAgeCount*, and then *nAgeCount* is incremented. This is equivalent to making the cache block most recently used. This also implies that the block is placed at the head of the MRU list.

Block Cache Services

Table 11-2 summarizes the services which VCache provides to use the block cache. The first step to using the block cache services is to register with VCache at Device Init time using **VCache_Register**. Registration can be undone at a later time with the service **VCache_Deregister**. When registering you supply a buffer discard callback function.

Table 11-2. VCache's Block Cache Services

Service	Function
VCache_AdjustMinimum	Adjusts the number of reserved blocks for a FSD
VCache_CheckAvail	Verifies that enough cache blocks are available
VCache_Deregister	Frees cache resources owned by a FSD
VCache_Enum	Calls enumeration function for all blocks owned by FSD
VCache_FindBlock	Finds or creates a cache block
VCache_FreeBlock	Places a cache block and its data page on free lists
VCache_GetSize	Returns number of blocks in cache
VCache_GetStats	Returns statistics for use by memory manager
VCache_Get_Version	Gets Vcache's version number
VCache_Hold	Increments cache block's *HoldCnt*
VCache_MakeMRU	Moves cache block to head of MRU list
VCache_RecalcSums	Debugs only (not available in retail release)
VCache_Register	Installs discard function and returns FSD ID
VCache_SwapBuffers	Swaps data pages between two cache blocks
VCache_TestHandle	Validates a cache block handle
VCache_TestHold	Tests cache block's *HoldCnt*
VCache_Unhold	Decrements cache block's *HoldCnt*
VCache_VerifySums	Debugs only (not available in retail release)

This buffer discard function will receive the address of the cache block which is being discarded, in the ESI register. Cache block discards may occur in response to **VCache_RelinquishPage** and **VCache_FindBlock** (with the *VFCB_Create* flag) calls. A cache block is a candidate for discarding if it has its *Dirty* flag clear, its *HoldCnt* is zero, and its *AgeCnt* is such that: ($nAgeCount - cb.AgeCnt$) > *AgeDelta*. At initialization time, the global variable *AgeDelta* is set to *initCache* / 8 (where *initCache* is the initial cache size) or 16, whichever is smaller. As the cache is dynamically sized, *AgeDelta* is not adjusted unless the cache size drops below 128 pages, in which case it is recalculated as *curTotalCachePages* / 8.

The real workhorse of the cache block interface is **VCache_FindBlock**. It is really several functions rolled into one. In addition to finding blocks, it can also create new cache blocks and change the LRU order of blocks. It receives four arguments: AH contains the FSD ID, AL contains option flags, EBX contains hash *key1*, and EDI contains hash *key2*. If AL is zero, a search is performed for a cache block matching the other three parameters. A successful search is indicated by a *carry* clear return. In this case, ESI contains the cache block handle (the address of the cache block) and EAX contains the address of the buffer (the *BufPtr* member). If the AL has the VCFB_Create flag set, and a matching cache block is not found, a new cache block will be created. In this case, the return values refer to the newly created cache block and buffer. Other flags can be used in AL, such as *VCFB_Hold* to increment the *HoldCnt* of a find, and *VCFB_MakeMRU* to move a find to the head of the MRU list. The service **VCache_MakeMRU** provides a more efficient way to move a cache block to the head of the MRU list. It takes a cache block handle in ESI as its single argument.

Before allocating some cache blocks, you can verify that the number of cache blocks you need are available using the service **VCache_CheckAvail**. Before calling, the AH register is loaded with the FSD ID and ECX is loaded with the desired number of blocks. The result of this call is given by the state of the *carry* flag. If the *carry* flag is set, not enough buffers are available; otherwise the request can be granted and the number of buffers available is returned in EAX.

The services **VCache_Hold**, **VCache_Unhold**, and **VCache_TestHold** all take a cache block address in ESI as arguments. The only thing these functions do is manipulate or test the *HoldCnt* member of the specified cache block. **VCache_Hold** increments *HoldCnt*, **VCache_Unhold** decrements *HoldCnt*, and **VCache_TestHold** returns *HoldCnt* in EAX and the zero flag is set if *HoldCnt* is 0.

VCache_FreeBlock removes a cache block specified by the ESI register and its associated buffer from the MRU list. The cache block and the buffer page are placed on their respective free lists.

Monitoring VCache

MultiMon includes a monitor for VCache services. Using it in conjunction with the file system hook adds some additional detail to our understanding of VFAT's FSD functions. As an example, I'll execute the DISKDUMP program from Chapter 9 with three monitors: VCHook, FSHook, and TAGMON. Example 11-1 is a small portion of the trace output.

Note that for **vch** lines, the **dev** column contains the FSD ID and the handle column contains the cache block handle. If the handle is marked with an asterisk, it represents a newly created cache block.

In this trace, *DISKDUMP* performs three **FS_DirectDiskIO** reads. The first read is of the volume's boot sector, the second is of the first sector of the first FAT, the third is of the first sector of the second FAT, and at the end of the trace we see the beginning of a read of the root directory sectors. The **fsh** entries in the trace are highlighted; these lines of the trace are added on completion of the **FS_DirectDiskIO** calls. The **vch** entries of the trace record VFAT's calls into VCache's services.

Example 11-1. Sample Output of Three Trace Monitors

```
Mon      Function                 Flags1          Dev    Handle      Args
---    ----------------------   --------------   ---    --------    --------------
tag ==== diskdump (D) ====
tag == Lock Logical Vol
tag == Read Boot Sector (0)
vch  VCache_FindBlock                           FSD(64h)            Key1: fffffffd
                                                                    Key2: c1636614
                             Ret Carry
vch    VCache_FindBlock        Creat MkMRU      FSD(64h)            Key1: fffffffd
                                                                    Key2: c1636614
                             Ret Carry           c3f60fc0* Buf: c3fb4000
vch    VCache_Hold                               c3f60fc0
vch    VCache_Unhold                             c3f60fc0
vch    VCache_Hold                               c3f60fc0
vch    VCache_Unhold                             c3f60fc0
fsh    FS_DirectDiskIO (dd) Rd                   VFAT               cnt=1H sec=0H
tag == Start Read First FAT (1H)
vch    VCache_FindBlock                         FSD(64h)            Key1: fffffffd
                                                                    Key2: c1636614
                             Ret                 c3f60fc0  Buf: c3fb4000
vch    VCache_MakeMRU                            c3f60fc0
vch    VCache_Hold                               c3f60fc0
vch    VCache_Unhold                             c3f60fc0
fsh    FS_DirectDiskIO (dd) Rd                   VFAT               cnt=1H sec=1H
tag == Start Read Second FAT (83H)
vch    VCache_FindBlock                         FSD(64h)            Key1: 0000007d
                                                                    Key2: c1636614
                             Ret Carry
vch    VCache_FindBlock                         FSD(64h)            Key1: 0000007d
                                                                    Key2: c1636614
                             Ret Carry
vch    VCache_FindBlock                         FSD(64h)            Key1: 0000007d
                                                                    Key2: c1636614
                             Ret Carry
vch    VCache_FindBlock        Creat Hld MkMRU FSD(64h)             Key1: 0000007d
                                                                    Key2: c1636614
vch    VCache_Hold                               c3f1f000
                             Ret Carry Locked    c3f1f000* Buf: c3faf000
vch    VCache_Unhold                             c3f1f000
vch    VCache_FindBlock        Creat MkMRU      FSD(64h)            Key1: 0000007d
                                                                    Key2: c1636614
vch    VCache_MakeMRU                            c3f1f000
                             Ret Locked          c3f1f000  Buf: c3faf000
vch    VCache_Hold                               c3f1f000
vch    VCache_Unhold                             c3f1f000
fsh    FS_DirectDiskIO (dd) Rd                   VFAT               cnt=1H sec=83H
tag == Start Read Root DIR (105H)
vch    VCache_FindBlock                         FSD(64h)            Key1: 00000105
                                                                    Key2: c1636614
                             Ret                 c3f1ffc0  Buf: c3ff0000
```

For instance, the following sequence is associated with the read of boot sector 0:

VCache_FindBlock (find fails)
VCache_FindBlock (create and make MRU)
VCache_Hold (lock buffer for read)
VCache_Unhold (unlock)
VCache_Hold (lock buffer for transfer)
VCache_Unhold (unlock)
FS_DirectDiskIO (VFAT returns)

From this sequence we see that VFAT first searches for a cache block for the needed sector and volume, and only if that fails does it create a new cache block. We can also infer that VFAT doesn't just read in a single sector; rather, it reads an entire page. This is revealed by the following sequence for the subsequent read of the first sector of the first FAT (sector 1):

VCache_FindBlock (find succeeds)
VCache_MakeMRU (make MRU)
VCache_Hold (lock buffer for transfer)
VCache_Unhold (unlock)
FS_DirectDiskIO (VFAT returns)

In this case the search for the cache block succeeds because it is already in memory, having been loaded along with the boot sector.

The keys which are passed to **VCache_FindBlock** require some explanation. The second key is the simply the address of the volume's resource block structure (see Chapter 9, *VFAT: The Virtual FAT File System Driver*) which is owned by VFAT. The first key represents the sector on the volume. But how does sector 0 become 0xfffffffd? Why do both sector 0 and sector 1 use this same hash key?

To understand this, you need to look at the disk layout. The sectors in a volume either lie in the system area (boot sector, FATs, root directory entries) or in clusters which are assigned to files and subdirectories through the FAT. The line between these regions is drawn at the first sector of the first available cluster. Cache blocks are also aligned at this boundary. In our DISKDUMP example, volume D has the first sector of the first cluster at sector 125h. This value serves as a key for sectors 125h, 126h, ... 12Ch, since the volume's sector size allows 8 sectors to be stored in a cache page. Since this alignment boundary lies on a sector which is not an even multiple of 8, the key for the first cache block will start at (125h mod 8)–8 or –3 (0xfffffffd), and this value will serve as the key for sectors –3, –2, –1, 0, 1, 2, 3, and 4.

The Lookup Cache Data Structures

The lookup cache is an in-memory image of the keys and values under the system registry section: *HKLM\System\CurrentControlSet\Services\VxD\VCache\ Lookup*. Figure 11-1 shows this registry section for a typical system which is attached to a LAN. On this system two caches have been created: *ServerName-Cache* by IFSMgr and *VREDIR_Names* by VREDIR. The cache keys consist of the registry values Key0000, Key0001, and Key0002; the corresponding cache data items are the registry values Data0000, Data0001, and Data0002. As shown, *Server-NameCache* contains 3 items and the *NumElements* value reflects this. The *MaxElements* value, 0x1e, indicates that the cache will hold 30 elements in memory. If the number of elements exceeds this amount, the excess items which are least recently used are retained in the system registry file. The *Flags* value does not appear to be used.

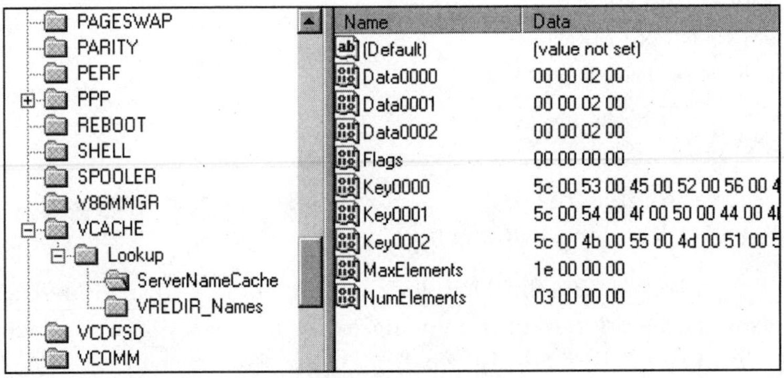

Figure 11-1. Registry editor display of the lookup cache

Internally, VCache uses the **IFSMgr_GetHeap** service to allocate storage for data structures and the memory-image of each lookup cache. IFSMgr's heap allocator disburses blocks from locked pages. Each cache is represented by a single **LOOKUP_KEY** data structure and one or more **LOOKUP_VAL** structures, one for each cache item. The **LOOKUP_KEY** structures are strung together in a linked list to facilitate the validation of lookup cache handles (*HLOOKUP*), to determine whether a cache name is already in use. Here is the layout for a **LOOKUP_KEY**:

```
typedef struct {
    void* next;       /* head of list of LOOKUP_VAL structures (mru) */
    void* prev;       /* tail of list of LOOKUP_VAL structures (lru) */
    PLOOKUP_KEY next_cache;    /* next lookup cache */
    char* pszCacheName; /* name of the cache */
    DWORD refcnt;       /* number of cache users */
    DWORD numElements;  /* current number of elements */
    DWORD maxElements;  /* max number of elements retained in memory */
    DWORD Flags;        /* determines type of background processing */
```

```
    HKEY hKey;           /* registry key handle */
} LOOKUP_KEY, *PLOOKUP_KEY;
```

Each cache item is represented by a **LOOKUP_VAL** structure; it has this declaration:

```
typedef struct {
    void* next;           /* next LOOKUP_VAL structure */
    void* prev;           /* previous LOOKUP_VAL structure */
    PLOOKUP_KEY cache;    /* back pointer to lookup cache */
    DWORD KeySum;         /* checksum of the Key value */
    DWORD dwKeyLen;       /* length of the Key value */
    DWORD dwDataLen;      /* length of the Data value */
    DWORD iElement;       /* zero-based index of element */
    DWORD Flags;          /* determines type of background processing */
    void* pKey;           /* pointer to buffer containing Key */
    void* pData;          /* pointer to buffer containing Data */
} LOOKUP_VAL, *PLOOKUP_VAL;
```

These two types of structures are what the lookup cache is built from.

Whenever new items are added to a cache, or when the value of a cache item changes, or when a lookup occurs which moves an item to the head of the MRU list, this change needs to be written to the corresponding registry key. These updates to the registry are deferred until an **Appy Time** callback is executed. This callback is scheduled each time a cache change occurs, unless a callback is already pending; a callback will occur after a 300 second time-out expires. Prior to scheduling the callback, the *Flags* members of the affected **LOOKUP_KEY** and **LOOKUP_VAL** structures are set to indicate the kind of processing which is required. When it is called, the callback handler starts at the head of the **LOOKUP_KEY** list and examines the *Flags* member of each structure. For those structures needing attention, it first clears the *Flags* member and then completes the registry update. While this background processing is taking place, calls to the lookup services will return with an error code of 1.

Lookup Cache Services

Table 11-3 summarizes the services which VCache provides to use the lookup cache.

Table 11-3. VCache's Lookup Cache Services

Service	Description
_VCache_CloseLookupCache	Closes registry key and releases storage
_VCache_CreateLookupCache	Creates or opens a lookup cache
_VCache_DeleteLookupCache	Not implemented, just returns 0
_VCache_Lookup	Looks up a cache key and return its data
_Vcache_UpdateLookup	Adds or updates elements in the cache

Unlike the block cache services which use processor registers for passing arguments, the lookup cache services all use a C calling convention. Also, unlike a block cache which must be registered at Device Init time, a lookup cache can be created after initialization.

The service **_VCache_CreateLookupCache** is called to create a lookup cache. This function's prototype has this form:

```
int _VCache_CreateLookupCache(char* psz, DWORD max, DWORD flags,
                              HLOOKUP* ph)
```

It receives four arguments. The first is the name of the cache which will become the name of the registry key which will hold the cache's contents. Additional arguments include the maximum number of elements the cache will hold in memory, a DWORD of *flags* (initialized to 0), and the address of a doubleword in which a handle to the lookup structure will be returned. VCache searches through the list of LOOKUP_KEY structures to see if the named cache already exists. If the LOOKUP_KEY does not exist, then an attempt is made to open the registry key. If the registry key is found, then the values under the key are enumerated; a LOOKUP_KEY and one or more LOOKUP_VAL structures are allocated from IFSMgr's heap and initialized with the results of this enumeration. The address of the LOOKUP_KEY is then inserted at the head of list.

If this is a brand new cache without an entry in the registry, then only a LOOKUP_KEY structure is allocated from IFSMgr's heap, and its address is inserted at the head of the LOOKUP_KEY list. The registry key is not created until an entry is added to the cache using **_VCache_UpdateLookup**.

A bug is revealed if **_VCache_CreateLookupCache** is called with the name of a key which is already opened. The function will fail in an unexpected way. An error code is returned which is the content of an uninitialized stack variable. To work around this, initialize the contents of the *ph* argument to zero before invoking this function and check the contents of *ph* for a non-zero value to verify that the function has succeeded.

Closing a lookup cache should be accomplished with **_VCache_Close-LookupCache**. This service takes a single argument, the *HLOOKUP* handle. This function validates the *HLOOKUP* handle, decrements the LOOKUP_KEY *refcnt* member if it is non-zero, sets the close-bit in the *Flags* member, then schedules an **Appy Time** callback in 300 seconds. What the **Appy Time** handler is supposed to do, is remove the LOOKUP_KEY from the list, close the associated registry key, and release the storage held by the LOOKUP_KEY and any LOOKUP_VALs. However, yet another bug lurks in **_VCache_CloseLookupCache**. When the **Appy Time** handler is walking the list of LOOKUP_VALs and reclaiming memory, it enters an infinite loop! Perhaps this is why IFSMgr and VREDIR call this function only at system shutdown, so the **Appy Time** callback never gets called.

_VCache_UpdateLookup is the service used for adding or updating key/data pairs in a cache. This function's prototype has this form:

```
int _VCache_UpdateLookup(HLOOKUP h, DWORD keylen, void* pKey,
                         DWORD datalen, void* pData)
```

It calculates a checksum value for the specified key's value (pointed to by *pKey*) and compares this checksum with the *KeySum* member of any LOOKUP_VALs in the cache. If a match is found, the contents of the existing LOOKUP_VAL structure are modified to hold the new values. If no match is found, a new LOOKUP_VAL structure is allocated and initialized with the *pKey* and *pData* values provided as arguments. In either case, appropriate *Flags* bits are set and then an **Appy Time** callback is scheduled in 300 seconds. The **Appy Time** handler will refresh or create keys and values in the registry to reflect the current set of LOOKUP_VAL structures. Note that if a new value is being added to the cache, its LOOKUP_VAL moves to the head of the cache's MRU list. Also, once the number of elements in the cache exceeds *maxElements*, each addition of an element requires that the LOOKUP_VAL at the LRU end of the list be removed.

_VCache_Lookup is the service used for retrieving data for a specified cache key. This function's prototype has this form:

```
int _VCache_Lookup(HLOOKUP h, DWORD keylen, void* pKey,
                   DWORD* pdatalen, void* pData)
```

It calculates a checksum value for the specified key's value (pointed to by *pKey*) and compares this checksum with the *KeySum* member of any LOOKUP_VALs in the cache. If a match is found, the data associated with the key is copied to the buffer at *pData*. One side effect of this function is that it moves the accessed cache element to the head of the MRU list.

An Example: IFSMgr's ServerNameCache

IFSMgr uses the lookup cache to store server names. A connection is made to a server by calling the **FS_ConnectNetResource** entry point of its network FSD. To find the correct entry point, IFSMgr needs to know the provider ID for the network. (For a review of provider IDs, see the section "FSD Registration" in Chapter 8, *Anatomy of a File System Driver*.) Sometimes the provider ID is known and the required function can be found by a table lookup: **Mount-VolTable[*provider ID*]**. In other cases, only the server name is known, so each remote FSD is tried in turn until a connect succeeds.

To minimize these trial-and-error connections, IFSMgr maintains a lookup cache which maps server names to network IDs. Network IDs are manifest constants enumerated in the Win32 SDK file *winnetwk.h*. This file includes entries such as:

```
#define     WNNC_NET_MSNET       0x00010000
#define     WNNC_NET_LANMAN      0x00020000
#define     WNNC_NET_NETWARE     0x00030000
```

These network IDs are easily mapped to the provider IDs.

The primary service in which the *ServerNameCache* is put to use is **IFSMgr_SetupConnection**. Each time this service successfully completes a connection it updates the cache by calling the following function:

```
int UpdateServerNameCache(ParsedPath* pp, BYTE proid) {
    DWORD Data, datalen=sizeof(DWORD);
    unsigned short* pUniPath;
    DWORD keylen;

    if (hServerNameCache == 0) return;
    Data = NetIDs[proid];
    pUniPath = pp->pp_elements[0]->pe_unichars;
    keylen = pp->pp_elements[0]->pe_length - sizeof(short);
    return _VCache_UpdateLookup(hServerNameCache, keylen,
                        pUniPath, datalen, &Data );
    }
```

The `ParsedPath` argument to this function comes from the *ir_ppath* member of the `ioreq` structure. This contains the canonicalized UNC path, starting with the server name and share name. (For a review of the `ParsedPath` structure see Chapter 6, *Dispatching File System Requests*.) The first element of the `ParsedPath` structure, the Unicode server name, is used as the key for the cache. The second argument to this function is the provider ID for the FSD which performed the connection. This value is converted to a NetID and it becomes the data associated with the key.

When **IFSMgr_SetupConnection** gets a request without an explicit provider ID, then another function is utilized to perform a cache lookup:

```
int ServerNameToNetID( ParsedPath* pp ) {
    DWORD Data, datalen=sizeof(DWORD);
    unsigned short* pUniPath;
    DWORD keylen, retc;

    if (hServerNameCache == 0) return 0;
    pUniPath = pp->pp_elements[0]->pe_unichars;
    keylen = pp->pp_elements[0]->pe_length - sizeof(short);
    retc = _VCache_Lookup( hServerNameCache, keylen,
                        pUniPath, &datalen, &Data );
    if ( retc != 0 ) return 0;
    return Data;
    }
```

This function takes a single `ParsedPath` argument which contains the server name as its first `PathElement`. This is used to perform a cache lookup and if successful, the variable *Data* will contain the matching NetID. IFSMgr uses another internal function to convert the NetID into a provider ID.

12

A Survey of IFSMgr Services

I promised myself that if I ever wrote a book about VxDs, I wouldn't fill it up with warmed-over API descriptions. The DDK's IFS document and online help file should be your basic references for API descriptions. But in some cases, the information these resources contain is inadequate to effectively use IFSMgr's services. In this chapter, I'll address some of these shortcomings. I'm going to single out several categories of services and provide more complete documentation for them. However, all IFSMgr services are summarized in a series of tables.

The summary tables use the following conventions. The Ordinal column contains the service ordinal number starting with 0. In a few cases the value in this column will have a subscript; this is the ordinal for the equivalent service in Windows 3.11. The column headings 16, 22, and 22+ refer to the three different versions of IFSMgr: Windows 3.11, Windows 95 build 950, and build 950B (OEM 2). The trend is toward providing more services, starting with 61 in Windows 3.11, to 117 in Windows 95 build 950, to 121 in build 950B. These counts include a number of services which have no implementation, i.e., in the retail builds, at least, the service returns 0 or perhaps sets the *carry* flag. In the table, these "unimplemented" services are marked with a *u*, debug services are marked with a *d*, and services which are only available at initialization are indicated by an *i*. An *h* indicates that a service is meant to be hooked, and not called directly. The Segment column indicates whether the function resides in locked or pageable code. Note that just because a service entry point is in locked code doesn't preclude it from taking a path through pageable code. The Ref column gives chapter numbers where a service is used or described.

The descriptions presented here apply to the Windows 95 versions of IFSMgr. However, the services provided by Windows 3.11 are also tabulated. The companion disk contains the library *ifswraps.clb*, a C library of wrapper functions for all of the IFSMgr services. For more information on the library, see Appendix D, *IFS Development Aids*.

IFSMgr Versions

Your first line of attack to determine which version of IFSMgr a system is using should be to call **IFSMgr_Get_Version**. For Windows 3.11 this will return 0x16, and for Windows 95 it will return 0x22. Currently, two versions of Windows 95 exist; the retail build 950 and OEM service release 2, which is referred to as build 950B. The IFSMgr VxDs which accompany these two Windows 95 versions are somewhat different. If you examine the file properties of these drivers using Explorer, the file versions reported are 4.00.950 and 4.00.1111. One way to distinguish these drivers at runtime is to examine the Device Descriptor Block to see how many services are in the service table. For file version 4.00.950 this value is 117 and version 4.00.1111 it is 121.

FSD Registration

Table 12-1 lists IFSMgr's registration services. For a detailed discussion of these functions see Chapter 8, *Anatomy of a File System Driver*.

Table 12-1. IFSMgr FSD Registration Services

Ord	Service Name	16	22	22+	Segment	Ref
1	IFSMgr_RegisterMount	x	x	x	locked	8
2	IFSMgr_RegisterNet	x	x	x	locked	8
3	IFSMgr_RegisterMailSlot	x	x	x	locked	13
80	IFSMgr_FSDUnmountCFSD		x	x	pageable	8
98	IFSMgr_RegisterCFSD		x	x	locked	8
117	IFSMgr_Service_117 (Deregister FSD)			x	locked	
118	IFSMgr_Service_118 (Register FSD)			x	locked	

Services 117 and 118 are new to build 950B. Although these services are not yet documented, it is clear that they provide FSDs with the capability of registering and deregistering with IFSMgr.

Heap Management

Given the extensive set of VMM services for memory allocation, you might wonder why IFSMgr has to offer yet another set of services (see Table 12-2). It is because FSDs and filehooks can't touch pageable memory and can't invoke memory allocation services which might cause paging when handling the swap file and memory-mapped files. The reasons for these requirements are discussed in Chapter 7, *Monitoring File Activity*. To work around these restrictions, IFSMgr allocates some fixed system pages and then disburses blocks from these pages using the service **IFSMgr_GetHeap**. The blocks are returned to the heap by the service **IFSMgr_RetHeap**. Beyond these basic functions, there are additional services for special needs, such as assuring memory is available under critical conditions. To begin, let's look at how the heap gets initialized and how it is organized.

Table 12-2. IFSMgr Heap Management Services

Ord	Service Name	16	22	22+	Segment	Ref
12	IFSMgr_RegisterHeap	x	x	x	locked	12
13	IFSMgr_GetHeap	x	x	x	locked	12
14	IFSMgr_RetHeap	x	x	x	locked	12
15	IFSMgr_CheckHeap	d	d	d	locked	
16	IFSMgr_CheckHeapItem	d	d	d	locked	
17	IFSMgr_FillHeapSpare	x	x	x	locked	12

Heap Initialization and Data Structures

IFSMgr's heap management services become available after it completes the System Critical initialization phase. At the end of this initialization, one page of fixed system memory is allocated to the main heap and another one to the spare heap.

The main and spare heaps are separate one-way linked lists of heap blocks. A heap block consists of one or more pages of fixed system memory. At the beginning of each heap block, a 32-byte structure is used to manage the heap block's allocations. This structure has the following layout:

```
typedef struct tagMemHdr {
    void* pBlk;                 /* address of this heap block */
    DWORD signature;            /* IFSMgr's signature, 'IFSH' */
```

```
    struct tagMemHdr* next;    /* address of next heap block */
    DWORD blksize;             /* size of heap block */
    void* pEnd;                /* offset to last DWORD in block */
    void* pAvail;              /* available allocation area */
    WORD amtFree;              /* max allocation size available */
    WORD cnt;                  /* number of allocs in this block */
    int alloc[0];              /* size of first allocation */
    } MEMHDR, *PMEMHDR;
```

Allocations are made from the block's memory range starting at alloc and extending to pEnd. The first available (free) allocation address in the block is at pAvail. The following diagram illustrates a heap block containing three allocations, A, B, and C.

20	Aaaaaaaaaaaaaaaaaaaaaaaaaaaaaaaaaaaaaaaaaaaaaaa
-20	Bbbbbbbbbbbbbbbbbbbbbbbbbbbbbbbbbbbbbbbbbbbbbbb
10	Cccccccccccccccccc
00	<< end of block

The four bytes preceding each allocation holds its length. For example, allocation A is specified by the address of its first byte (represented by the uppercase A); the length of this allocation is given by the doubleword at address A-4 and is 20 bytes long. Allocation B has a negative length; this signifies that the 20 byte allocation is free. It is followed by allocation C with a length of 10 bytes. The length of a heap block's first allocation is given by `alloc[0]`. Starting with this first allocation, all allocations in a heap block can be walked using these length fields. The very last doubleword in the heap block contains a 0, and marks an allocation of length 0.

IFSMgr's allocator uses a "first-fit" algorithm. The *amtFree* member of the header structure indicates the maximum block size that might be allocated from the heap block. If the *amtFree* value is large enough to satisfy the requested allocation size, the first available allocation in the heap block, given by the address *pAvail*, is combined with any adjoining free allocations to create a single free allocation. If this allocation is large enough to satisfy the request, it is used, possibly splitting the allocation into a used portion and a new free allocation. If the size of the allocation is insufficient, this process is repeated for the next free allocation in the block. If the request is not satisifed in one block, the next block in the heap is tried. For each successful allocation from a heap block, the *cnt* member is incremented.

IFSMgr_GetHeap

IFSMgr_GetHeap receives a single argument, the requested size of the allocation, in bytes. If successful it returns the address of the allocation; if it fails it returns NULL. The actual size of the allocation is adjusted by the formula (*req_amt* + 7) &

0xfffffffc. This rounds the allocation size up to the nearest multiple of 4 and adds 4 bytes for the doubleword which holds the size of the allocation.

Heap blocks are searched in order for one which will satisfy this allocation request. When all of the main heap blocks have been searched and none can satisfy the request, some other storage possibilities are tried. First, the registered heap reclamation functions are called to see if any user can free an allocation of at least the requested size. If that does not succeed, the blocks on the spare heap are searched to see if they can satisfy the request. If a block on the spare list can supply the required allocation, the block is moved from the spare list to the main heap, and the allocation succeeds. Finally, if the spare heap can not meet the request, the allocation will fail if it is less than or equal to 4096 bytes but will succeed if it is greater than this amount and the required pages can be allocated.

This distinction between "small" and "large" allocations is important. There are situations in which you would rather fail an allocation than have the service attempt to grow the heap by allocating more pages. As long as you stick to allocations of 4096 bytes or less, you will get this behavior. However, if you call **IFSMgr_GetHeap** at a time when it is safe to perform page allocations, then you can make multiple page allocations from this service. Then, instead of failing, a new heap block containing the needed pages will be added to the main heap.

The DDK documentation states that the largest allocation that may be made by this function is 32 Kbytes or 8 pages. It would seem that the upper limit on allocation size is determined by the *amtFree* member of the heap block. This member is an unsigned short so 64 Kbytes or 16 pages appears to be the actual upper limit. Note that this is a limit imposed by the maximum size of a heap block.

IFSMgr_RegisterHeap

In the description of **IFSMgr_GetHeap**, I referred to a heap reclamation function. This function is registered by **IFSMgr_RegisterHeap**. Registering a function simply places it at the current front of a linked list. When reclamation functions are called by **IFSMgr_GetHeap**, the function at the head of the list is called first, then the next function, and so forth until the tail of the list is reached. The tail of the list holds IFSMgr's heap reclamation function; it returns without doing anything.

When a reclamation function is called it receives the requested size of the allocation on the stack in the doubleword at location EBP+0Ch. If the function returns zero in EAX, then it is saying that it can not supply the needed memory. However, if the function returns a non-zero value in EAX, then the doubleword stored at location EBP+8 is interpreted as the address of a heap block. **IFSMgr_GetHeap** will examine the available allocation given by the *pAvail* member of the heap block. If this allocation can not satisfy the request, then **IFSMgr_GetHeap** will fail; otherwise it will be used to satisfy the request.

IFSMgr_FillHeapSpare

Each call to this service adds a one-page block of fixed memory from the system arena to the spare heap list. As we have seen, **IFSMgr_GetHeap** uses the blocks on the spare list as a reserve when an allocation can not be met by the main heap. Once a block on the spare list is used, it is removed from the spare list and added to the main heap.

IFSMgr calls this service before dispatching protected mode and V86 mode Int 21h requests.

IFSMgr_RetHeap

This function receives the address of an allocation made via **IFSMgr_GetHeap**. In response the function searches the main heap blocks to find one for which the allocation's address lies between *alloc* and *pEnd*. The allocation being freed is combined with any free allocations which may follow it. This free allocation is then marked with a negative value equal to its total size. The *cnt* member of the heap block is then decremented and if the *cnt* has reached 0, this heap block is moved to the spare heap list.

Reclaiming the Spare Heap

When the heap is initialized during System Critical initialization, a recurring 30-second event is started which monitors the spare heap list. When this event function is called, any blocks found on the spare heap list are freed back to the system. This event is scheduled using the service **IFSMgr_SchedEvent** and the *EVF_NOTCRIT* flag, so that it is safe to use VMM's **_PageFree** service.

Time Management

The time management services deal with three different time representations: DOS, Net, and Win32. A *DOS* time represents a local time; it is stored in a `dostime_t` structure which consists of three components:

- Packed 16-bit word containing, year, month, and day: bits 0-4, day (1-31); bits 5-8, month (1-Jan, 2-Feb, etc.); bits 9-15, year offset from 1980.

- Packed 16-bit word containing hour, minute, and second: bits 0-4, seconds divided by 2; bits 5-10, minute (0-59); and bits 11-15, hour (0-23).

- A byte containing the number of 10 millisecond intervals in 2 seconds to add to the time (0-199).

A *Net* time is a 32-bit unsigned value which is the number of seconds which have elapsed since January 1, 1970. This time is in UTC (Coordinated Universal Time) which used to be known as Greenwich Mean Time (GMT), i.e., the local time at the Greenwich meridian. A remainder component preserves the number of milliseconds in a fractional 1 second interval.

A *Win32* time is a 64-bit value specifying the number of 100-nanosecond intervals that have elapsed since 12:00 am, January 1, 1601. A Win32 time is stored in a **_FILETIME** structure which stores the 64-bit value as high and low doublewords. This time is is also in UTC.

Table 12-3 enumerates the time management services which IFSMgr provides. The services **IFSMgr_Get_NetTime** and **IFSMgr_Get_DOSTime** retrieve the current date and time as Net time or DOS time, respectively. The next six functions are pairs of functions which convert a given time representation to one of the other possible representations, e.g., **IFSMgr_NetToDosTime** converts a Net time to a DOS time and **IFSMgr_NetToWin32Time** converts a Net time to a Win32 time. Note that a Win32 time can not be retrieved directly—it must be derived from either a Net time or DOS time.

Table 12-3. IFSMgr Time Management Services

Ord	Service Name	16	22	22+	Segment	Ref
6	IFSMgr_Get_NetTime	x	x	x	locked	12
7	IFSMgr_Get_DOSTime	x	x	x	pageable	12
55	IFSMgr_NetToDosTime		x	x	pageable	12
56	IFSMgr_DosToNetTime		x	x	pageable	12
57	IFSMgr_DosToWin32Time		x	x	pageable	12
58	IFSMgr_Win32ToDosTime		x	x	pageable	12
59	IFSMgr_NetToWin32Time		x	x	pageable	12
60	IFSMgr_Win32ToNetTime		x	x	pageable	12
96	IFSMgr_GetTimeZoneBias		x	x	pageable	12
119	IFSMgr_Service_119			x	pageable	

The next-to-last function in this group, **IFSMgr_GetTimeZoneBias**, retrieves the offset in minutes which is applied to the local time to convert it to UTC. This value is stored in the registry under the key *HKLM\System\CurrentControlSet\Control\-TimeZoneInformation* in the variable *ActiveTimeBias*. The **Time Zone** tab under the Control Panel's **Date/Time** properties is used to change this value. IFSMgr is notified of any changes to the *ActiveTimeBias* by hooking VWIN32's service, **VWIN32_ActiveTimeBiasSet**.

Network Management

Table 12-4 lists IFSMgr's network management services. Many of these services are discussed in Chapters 8 and 13. The services in this group can be divided into server and client categories. The server functions include **IFSMgr_ServerDOSCall**, **IFSMgr_SetLoopBack**, and **IFSMgr_ClearLoopBack**. **IFSMgr_ServerDOSCall** is the means that a server uses to execute a local file system request on the behalf of some network client. How IFSMgr dispatches these requests is described in Chapter 6, *Dispatching File System Requests*. A server will also use **IFSMgr_SetLoopBack** and **IFSMgr_ClearLoopBack** to maintain loopback paths. A loopback path refers to a shared network resource on the local machine. For instance, if a system's server name is TOPDOG and it is sharing a directory *C:\BIN* as DEV, then one of the system's loopback paths is the UNC path *\\TOPDOG\DEV*. The function **IFSMgr_SetLoopBack** receives pairs of UNC paths and local paths which allow mapping of local UNC paths to a local drive and directory, e.g., *\\TOPDOG\DEV* maps to *C:\BIN*. **IFSMgr_ParsePath** checks the UNC paths it receives against this loopback list and for matches, it substitutes the local path.

Table 12-4. IFSMgr Network Management Services

Ord	Service Name	16	22	'22+	Segment	Ref
8	IFSMgr_SetupConnection	x	x	x	pageable	8
9	IFSMgr_DerefConnection	x	x	x	locked	8
10	IFSMgr_ServerDOSCall	x	x	x	pageable	6, 8
25	IFSMgr_MakeMailSlot	x	x	x	pageable	13
26	IFSMgr_DeleteMailSlot	u	x	x	pageable	13
27	IFSMgr_WriteMailSlot	x	x	x	pageable	13
36_{38}	IFSMgr_NetFunction	h	h	h	pageable	7
37_{39}	IFSMgr_DoDelAllUses	x	x	x	pageable	
40_{42}	IFSMgr_SetReqHook	i	i	i	init	5
41_{43}	IFSMgr_SetPathHook	i	i	i	init	7
42_{44}	IFSMgr_UseAdd	x	x	x	pageable	8
43_{45}	IFSMgr_UseDel	x	x	x	pageable	8
44_{46}	IFSMgr_InitUseAdd	i	i	i	init	8
46_{48}	IFSMgr_DelAllUses	x	x	x	pageable	
93	IFSMgr_FSDMapFHtoIOREQ		x	x	pageable	
106	IFSMgr_CheckDelResource		x	x	pageable	
108	IFSMgr_SetupFailedConnection		h	h	pageable	8

Table 12-4. IFSMgr Network Management Services (continued)

Ord	Service Name	16	22	22+	Segment	Ref
113	IFSMgr_SetLoopback		x	x	pageable	12
114	IFSMgr_ClearLoopback		x	x	pageable	12

Event Management

Table 12-5 lists IFSMgr's event management services.

Table 12-5. IFSMgr Event Mangement Services

Ord	Service Name	16	22	22+	Segment	Ref
18	IFSMgr_Block	x	x	x	locked	
19	IFSMgr_Wakeup	x	x	x	locked	
20	IFSMgr_Yield	x	x	x	pageable	12
21	IFSMgr_SchedEvent	x	x	x	locked	12
22	IFSMgr_QueueEvent	x	x	x	locked	12
23	IFSMgr_KillEvent	x	x	x	locked	12
24	IFSMgr_FreeIOReq	x	x	x	locked	12
54	IFSMgr_BlockNoEvents		x	x	locked	12
105	IFSMgr_RunScheduledEvents		x	x	locked	12

The event management services in several cases are simply wrappers for VMM services. Important exceptions are **IFSMgr_SchedEvent**, **IFSMgr_QueueEvent**, and **IFSMgr_FreeIoreq**. These allow creation of a special kind of IFSMgr event that is accompanied with an initialized `ifsreq` structure. Considerable detail is provided for these functions, since the DDK documentation is incomplete.

IFSMgr_SchedEvent and IFSMgr_QueueEvent

The prototypes for these functions are given by:

```
void IFSMgr_SchedEvent( pevent pev, unsigned long time )
void IFSMgr_QueueEvent( pevent pev )
```

The only difference between these functions is that **IFSMgr_SchedEvent** specifies a timeout which must elapse before the event is scheduled. An event is described by the following data structure:

```
typedef struct tagEvent {
    DWORD ev_reserv1;
    DWORD ev_handle;      /* handle returned by Set_Global_Time_Out,
                             Call_Priority_VM_Event, or
                             Call_Restricted_Event */
    DWORD ev_VMHand;      /* VM Handle for EVF_VMEVENT */
```

```
      DWORD ev_func;          /* event callback function */
      DWORD ev_func_data;     /* data ptr for use by event callback
                                 function */
      BYTE  ev_flags;         /* flags which define the event type (see
                                 below) */
      BYTE  ev_reserv2[3];
      } event, *pevent;
```

The type of event which is scheduled depends on the options which are set in the *ev_flags* member. The following flags are defined: *EVF_NOTNESTEDEXEC* (0x08), *EVF_TASKTIME* (0x10), *EVF_VMEVENT* (0x20), and *EVF_NOTCRIT* (0x40). There are several combinations which are permitted; these are shown in Table 12-6. Most of these flags restrict when the event is scheduled. The one exception is *EVF_TASKTIME*, which determines whether an `ifsreq` structure is initialized and passed to the callback.

Table 12-6. Permissible Event Types for IFSMgr_SchedEvent

ev_flags	event type	event restrictions	boost
0 (default)	global, Call_Priority_VM_Event	PEF_Wait_For_STI, PEF_Always_Sched, PEF_Wait_Crit	0x400000
EVF_NOTNESTEDEXEC EVF_VMEVENT:	VM (passed in EBX) Call_Restricted_Event	PEF_Wait_For_STI, PEF_Always_Sched, PEF_Wait_Not_Crit, PEF_Wait_Not_Nested	0
EVF_NOTNESTEDEXEC	global, Call_Restricted_Event	PEF_Wait_For_STI, PEF_Always_Sched, PEF_Wait_Not_Crit, PEF_Wait_Not_Nested	0
EVF_NOTCRIT	global, Call_Prioirty_VM_Event	PEF_Wait_For_STI, PEF_Always_Sched, PEF_Wait_Not_Crit	0
EVF_VMEVENT	VM (passed in VMHand) Call_Priority_VM_Event	PEF_Wait_For_STI, PEF_Always_Sched	0x1000

Note that the callback routine is not the event procedure. A single event procedure is used for all of the event types. The function **ev_func** is called from the common event procedure. The callback function has the following prototype:

```
      void EventCallback( pevent pev, pioreq pir )
```

The *ev_func_data* member may be used to pass a pointer to a data structure or a doubleword data item to the callback. If the event which scheduled the callback is not *EVF_TASKTIME*, then *pir* will be NULL. According to the DDK documentation, *EVF_TASKTIME* can be used in conjunction with *EVF_NOTCRIT* and *EVF_NOTNESTEDEXEC*.

This service may also be used to create initialized `ifsreq` blocks for calling into an FSD or IFSMgr. The ifsreq blocks created in this way set the *ir_pev* member to the address of the event structure associated with it; *ir_user, ir_error, ifs_ VMHandle,* and *ifs_PV* are the only other members which are initialized. Although the documentation refers to the allocated structure as `ioreq`, a full `ifsreq` structure is actually allocated (including space for the client register structure). Once the callback procedure has completed its event processing, it must return the `ifsreq` block to IFSMgr using the service **IFSMgr_FreeIoreq**.

IFSMgr_KillEvent

This service can be used to cancel an event which has been scheduled by either **IFSMgr_SchedEvent** or **IFSMgr_QueueEvent**. It receives the address of the event structure and, depending on the state of the event and type of event, it may issue **Cancel_Time_Out**, Cancel_Priority_VM_Event, or **Cancel_Restricted_Event**.

Wrapped VMM Services

Several of the services in this group are essentially thin wrappers around VMM synchronization services. **IFSMgr_Block**, **IFSMgr_BlockNoEvents**, and **IFSMgr_Wakeup** utilize the **_BlockOnID** and **_SignalID** services from VMM. The implementations are as follows:

```
void IFSMgr_Block( unsigned long BlockID ) {
    push BLOCK_ENABLE_INTS|BLOCK_SVC_INTS
    push BlockID
    VMMCall( _BlockOnID );
    _asm cld
    }

void IFSMgr_BlockNoEvents( unsigned long BlockID ) {
    push 0
    push BlockID
    VMMCall( _BlockOnID );
    _asm cld
    }

void IFSMgr_Wakeup( unsigned long BlockID ) {
    push BlockID
    VMMCall( _SignalID );
    }
```

The Windows 3.11 versions of these functions use **Wait_Semaphore** and **Signal_Semaphore** since the thread services are new to Windows 95.

Two other services are provided which allow events to run in a nested execution block. The main difference between these is that **IFSMgr_Yield** enables interrupts in the VM before running events. Here are the implementations of these functions:

```
void IFSMgr_Yield() {
   VMMCall( Begin_Nest_Exec );
   VMMCall( Enable_VM_Ints );
   VMMCall( Resume_Exec );
   VMMCall( End_Nest_Exec );
   _asm cld
   }

void IFSMgr_RunScheduledEvents() {
   if ( bPendingGlobalEvents ) {
      VMMCall( Begin_Nest_Exec );
      VMMCall( Resume_Exec );
      VMMCall( End_Nest_Exec );
      _asm clc
      }
   }
```

The global variable *bPendingGlobalEvents* is set by a call to **Schedule_Global_Events** and cleared by a call to **Resume_Exec**. IFSMgr hooks these two functions in order to maintain this flag.

Codepage and Unicode Conversion

Windows 95 is a mixed environment, using both BCS and Unicode character encodings. BCS encodings (single-byte or double-byte character sets) are used primarily by applications, although some subsystems, such as OLE, do use Unicode. IFSMgr uses Unicode encodings for file, network, and device names.

BCS encodings are represented by codepages. Two codepages are available for an application to use: an ANSI codepage and an OEM codepage. The OEM codepage is associated with MS-DOS applications and includes the line-drawing characters. Win32 console applications also use the OEM codepage by default. The ANSI codepage is used by Windows 95 applications (Win16 and Win32). The specific codepages a Windows 95 system uses depends on the locale; for the United States, the defaults are MS-DOS US codepage 437 for OEM, and US codepage 1252 (Latin 1) for ANSI.

While it is always possible to convert non-Unicode data to Unicode, the reverse is not always possible. When it isn't possible to convert a Unicode character to a character of the current codepage, a default character is used (the underscore character, "_" (0x5f)).

When IFSMgr initializes, it loads conversion tables that map between its local codepages (OEM and ANSI) and the corresponding subset of Unicode. Addresses of these tables are returned by **IFSMgr_GetConversionTablePtrs**.

Each of the conversion services shown in Table 12-7 that contain BCS requires an argument specifying one of the manifest constants *BCS_OEM* or *BCS_WANSI* to select a codepage for the conversion. The services **BCSToBCS** and **BCSToBCS-Upper** require two such arguments, since these functions convert a string from OEM to ANSI codepage or vice versa (the "Upper" version also uppercases the destination string). The services **UniToBCS** and **BCSToUni** convert from Unicode to BCS or vice versa. **UniToBCSPath** takes a `ParsedPath` structure representing a canonicalized Unicode pathname and converts it to BCS. **UniCharToOEM** converts a Unicode character to a character of the OEM codepage. **UniToUpper** converts a Unicode string to upper case.

Table 12-7. IFSMgr Codepage and Unicode Conversion Services

Ord	Service Name	16	22	22+	Segment	Ref
29[1]	IFSMgr16_Service_29 (get translation table)	x			locked	
30[1]	IFSMgr16_Service_30 (translate string)	x			locked	
64	UniToBCS		x	x	pageable	12
65	UniToBCSPath		x	x	pageable	12
66	BCSToUni		x	x	pageable	12
67	UniToUpper		x	x	pageable	12
68	UniCharToOEM		x	x	pageable	12
81	IFSMgr_GetConversionTablePtrs		x	x	pageable	12
112	BcsToBcs		x	x	pageable	12
116	BcsToBcsUpper		x	x	pageable	12

[1] Services 29 and 30 are specific to Windows 3.11.

Filename Manipulation

There are three fundamental filename types which IFSMgr uses: *Unicode FCB Name, Unicode 8.3 Name*, and *Unicode Long Name*. The FCB is an ancient MS-DOS structure known as the *file control block* which contains a drive identifier, filename, extension, file size, record size, various file pointers, and date and time stamps. The filename is limited to 8 characters and padded with spaces; similarly, the extension is limited to 3 characters and also padded with spaces. The Unicode version of this name format is the same except that each character occupies 16 bits. So instead of being an 11-byte name it becomes a 22-byte name.

A Unicode 8.3 Name is also limited to an 8-character filename and 3-character extension. However, the name and extension are separated by a dot character and the name and extension are not padded with spaces. If the filename does not have an extension, then there is no trailing dot. This filename type is also referred to as "short."

A Unicode Long Name is just a Unicode string. The dot character assumes no special significance and is treated like any other character. A Unicode 8.3 Name is a special case of a Unicode Long Name.

The services which IFSMgr supplies for manipulating these types of names are shown in Table 12-8.

Table 12-8. IFSMgr Filename Manipulation Services

Ord	Service Name	16	22	22+	Segment	Ref
69	CreateBasis		x	x	pageable	12
71	AppendBasisTail		x	x	pageable	12
72	FcbToShort		x	x	pageable	12
73	ShortToFcb		x	x	pageable	12
110	ShortToLossyFcb		x	x	pageable	12
120	IFSMgr_Service_120			x	pageable	

IFSMgr provides several services for converting one name type to another. **Create-Basis** takes a Unicode Long Name and converts it into a Unicode FCB Name (the "basis") according to a set of truncation and translation rules. **FCBToShort** converts a Unicode FCB Name to a Unicode 8.3 Name, whereas **ShortToFCB** does just the opposite. The service **ShortToLossyFCB** also translates a Unicode 8.3 Name to a Unicode FCB Name but uses only Unicode characters which are also available in the OEM codepage. The **AppendBasisTail** service adds a "numeric tail" to the 8 character filename portion of a Unicode FCB Name created by **Create-Basis**. This function assures that after appending the numeric tail, the filename will not exceed 8 bytes if it is converted to BCS. This service is used to create short name aliases for long filenames. One thing that the short to FCB conversion services fail to do is convert "*" into a sequence of "?" characters. You can detect the presence of this wildcard character by examining the parsing flags; it will be indicated with the *FILE_FLAG_HAS_STAR* bit. This becomes an issue with the meta-matching services when short name matching semantics are being used. In this matching mode, only the "?" character is treated as a wildcard ("*" is a literal character).

Filename Matching

Table 12-9 lists the filename matching services which IFSMgr provides.

When an FSD needs to search media for a matching filename or a set of filenames that match a wildcard string, **IFSMgr_MetaMatch** is the service to use. This service takes a pattern string, a filename to test, and flags which control the matching semantics. If the pattern string and the filename to be tested are in Unicode FCB format, then DOS matching semantics are specified. If the pattern string and filename are Unicode Long or Unicode 8.3, then NT matching semantics are specified. When matching a Unicode Long Name pattern against Unicode 8.3 Names, it may be necessary to append a trailing dot to the short name to get DOS compatible match behavior.

Table 12-9. IFSMgr Filename Matching Services

Ord	Service Name	16	22	22+	Segment	Ref
61	IFSMgr_MetaMatch		x	x	pageable	12
62	IFSMgr_TransMatch		x	x	pageable	12
70	MatchBasisName		x	x	pageable	12

MatchBasisName is a specialized match service which serves as an aid in generating unique numeric tails for long filename aliases. This service takes two Unicode FCB Names. One is generated by **CreateBasis** from a Unicode Long Name, and the other comes from a directory entry on the media and may contain a numeric tail as part of its 8-character filename. The return value from **MatchBasisName** will fall into one of three categories: no match (0), match on directory entry without numeric tail (–1), or match on directory entry with a numeric tail (value of numeric tail). After testing the entries in a directory for matches with a basis name, a list of numeric values already in use will be obtained. A new unique alias can be generated by calling **AppendBasisTail** with a value which isn't in use.

IFSMgr_TransMatch translates a DOS search structure (`srch_entry`) into a Win32 find structure (`_WIN32_FIND_DATA`). On entry, the ASCIIZ 8.3 filename returned by the FSD search is in the *se_name* member of `srch_entry`. This name is converted to Unicode by **BCSToUni** and deposited in the *cFileName* member of `_WIN32_FIND_DATA`. If the 8.3 matching semantics bit in the *ifs_nflags* member of the `ifsreq` structure is set, then both *cFileName* and the Unicode search pattern strings are converted to Unicode FCB Names. They are compared by **IFSMgr_MetaMatch** using short name semantics (*UFLG_DOS*). If the above mentioned *ifs_nflags* bit is not set, then Unicode pattern string is compared with *cFileName* using longname matching semantics (*UFLG_NT*). If **IFSMgr_MetaMatch** reports a match, file attributes, date/time, and file size are translated and copied from `srch_entry` to `_WIN32_FIND_DATA`.

Path Parsing

IFSMgr's path parsing services are listed in Table 12-10. The primary path parsing service is **IFSMgr_ParsePath**. **IFSMgr_FSDParsePath** is a wrapper around **IFSMgr_**

ParsePath and is intended to be used by FSDs. These services take an `ifsreq` structure as their only input.

Table 12-10. IFSMgr Path Parsing Services

Ord	Service Name	16	22	22+	Segment	Ref
74	IFSMgr_ParsePath		x	x	pageable	7, 8, 12
94	IFSMgr_FSDParsePath		x	x	pageable	12
115	IFSMgr_ParseOneElement		x	x	pageable	12

The *ir_data* member of `ifsreq` holds the input path string which is to be parsed. This string can be encoded as either BCS or Unicode. The *ifs_nflags* member contains two bits which indicate the string type. If bit 0 is set, it contains characters which are in the current OEM codepage, whereas if it is clear, characters come from the current ANSI codepage. If bit 1 is clear, the string uses BCS encoding, but if it is set, Unicode is used.

The parsing routines require some buffers for working space and to return the `ParsedPath` data structure. If the *ir_ppath* member of `ifsreq` is initialized to 0xfffffbbb, then IFSMgr will assign the caller a buffer from its pool of parse buffers. These buffers are reclaimed by IFSMgr when it performs cleanup after a command is dispatched. You shouldn't use this facility if you are performing your own cleanup since the internal functions which are needed are not available to FSDs. The alternative is to pass in a pointer to your own buffer. You do this by creating a 1820-byte allocation and assigning its address to both *ir_ppath* and *ifs_pbuffer*.

The main result of a parsing operation is a canonicalized path stored in a `ParsedPath` structure at *ir_ppath*. For a review of the `ParsedPath` data structure see Chapter 6. Other members which will be filled in include *ir_uFName* (case-preserved base filename in Unicode), *ir_upath* (unparsed pathname in Unicode), and *ifs_drv* (the local volume referenced in the pathname or 0xff if the path is remote).

The return value of **IFSMgr_ParsePath** also contains information about the path; the format of the doubleword which is returned is described by Table 12-11. The DDK documentation only gives descriptions of the parsing flag values; it does not mention the value returned in the low byte. This value classifies the path type.

Table 12-11. IFSMgr_ParsePath Return Value

Parsing Flag/Path Name Type	High Byte	Mid Word	Low Byte
Parsing flags:			
FILE_FLAG_WILDCARDS	80h	x	x
FILE_FLAG_HAS_STAR	40h	x	x

Table 12-11. IFSMgr_ParsePath Return Value (continued)

Parsing Flag/Path Name Type	High Byte	Mid Word	Low Byte
FILE_FLAG_LONG_PATH	20h	x	x
FILE_FLAG_KEEP_CASE	10h	x	x
FILE_FLAG_HAS_DOT	08h	x	x
FILE_FLAG_IS_LFN	04h	x	x
Path name types:			
Standard path	x	x	0
?	x	x	1
UNC Path	x	x	2
Invalid Pathname[1]	x	x	3
Path is Hooked	x	x	4
Network Printer[1]	x	x	5
Invalid Resource[1]	x	x	6
Character FSD Device Name	x	x	7
DOS Device Name	x	x	8

[1] Thanks to Geoff Chappell for supplying these entries.

IFSMgr_ParsePath also performs some substitutions for path componenets. It will replace **subst** drives with their alias drives and directories. It will also detect UNC paths which are in the loopback list and replace them with their local drive and directory. A path check routine may also be installed and called by **IFSMgr_Parse-Path** using the service **IFSMgr_SetPathHook**; see Chapter 7 for details.

IFSMgr calls **IFSMgr_ParsePath** to prepare an `ifsreq` packet before passing it to an FSD. Chapter 8 describes how this function is indirectly responsible for mounting drives and devices and establishing connections to network resources.

IFSMgr_ParseOneElement takes the `PathElement` member of a `ParsedPath` structure as argument. It simply returns the parsing flags for the single `PathElement`. These are the same flag values returned by **IFSMgr_ParsePath**, but in that case they refer to the entire path.

File Sharing

Table 12-12 lists IFSMgr's file sharing services.

Table 12-12. IFSMgr File Sharing Services

Ord	Service Name	16	22	22+	Segment	Ref
82	IFSMgr_CheckAccessConflict		x	x	locked	8
83	IFSMgr_LockFile		x	x	locked	12

Table 12-12. IFSMgr File Sharing Services (continued)

Ord	Service Name	16	22	22+	Segment	Ref
84	IFSMgr_UnlockFile		x	x	locked	12
85	IFSMgr_RemoveLocks		x	x	locked	12
86	IFSMgr_CheckLocks		x	x	locked	12
87	IFSMgr_CountLocks		x	x	locked	12
88	IFSMgr_ReassignLockFileInst		x	x	locked	12
89	IFSMgr_UnassignLockList		x	x	locked	12

These services fall into two categories. The first group is used by an FSD to maintain a lock list for a file handle. IFSMgr is the actual keeper of the active lock list for a file. To add a lock to a file, **IFSMgr_LockFile** is called like this:

```
IFSMgr_LockFile( &pFSDLockList, pir->ir_pos, pir->ir_locklen,
                 pir->ir_pid, pir->ir_fh, pir->ir_options )
```

This call is shown as it might be made from an FSD's **FS_LockFile** function, which receives a pointer to the **ioreq** structure in *pir*. As you can see, in addition to the lock's starting position and length, the process, file open instance, and lock options are recorded as well. The variable *pFSDLockList* holds the return value, the head of the lock list for this file. Typically, this would be stored as part of a data structure that is associated with the open file instance. **IFSMgr_UnlockFile** removes a single lock; it must be called with the same parameters that were used in the **IFSMgr_LockFile** call. There are occasions when all locks must be removed from a single file open instance or all file open instances, such as closing a file or deleting a file. To handle this situation, use **IFSMgr_RemoveLocks**. Before touching a locked region of a file, an FSD should call **IFSMgr_CheckLocks** to see if a read or write operation would violate any active locks. Finally, **IFSMgr_Count-Locks** gives an FSD a means of counting the number of active locks on an open file instance.

The services **IFSMgr_UnassignLockList** and **IFSMgr_ReassignLockList** are used for saving and restoring locks for files which are temporarily closed during a level 3 volume lock. A level 3 lock prevents all processes except the lock owner from reading or writing to the disk. In preparation for entering this mode, the files on the volume are closed with a special *ir_options* flag (*FILE_CLOSE_FOR_LEVEL3_LOCK*). On a normal close, the FSD would call **IFSMgr_RemoveLocks**, but when it receives this flag it should save the lock list for each file by calling **IFSMgr_Unas-signLockList**. Later, when the level 3 volume lock is relinquished, a special *ir_options* flag (*OPEN_FLAGS_REOPEN*) is specified for each file as it is reopened. As part of opening the file, the FSD needs to restore any locks that previously existed; **IFSMgr_ReassignLockList** retrieves the necessary information.

See Chapter 8 for details on using **IFSMgr_CheckAccessConflict**.

Plug-and-Play

Table 12-13 lists IFSMgr's plug-and-play services.

Table 12-13. IFSMgr Plug-and-Play Services

Ord	Service Name	16	22	22+	Segment	Ref
76	_VolFlush		x	x	pageable	12
77	NotifyVolumeArrival		x	x	pageable	12
78	NotifyVolumeRemoval		x	x	pageable	12
79	QueryVolumeRemoval		x	x	pageable	12
97	IFSMgr_PNPEvent		x	x	pageable	8

Three of these functions are called by IOS (I/O Supervisor) to query or report a change in state of a plug-and-play drive. **NotifyVolumeArrival** reports the appearance of a new drive to IFSMgr, **NotifyVolumeRemoval** reports the removal of a drive, and **QueryVolumeRemoval** checks the status of a drive prior to removing it. **_VolFlush** is also included under plug-and-play services, since it is usually necessary to flush dirty buffers to a volume before removing it from the system. This service takes a volume number and an optional flag which forces any cached data to be discarded. This service ultimately results in a **FS_FlushVolume** call to the volume's FSD.

IFSMgr_PNPEvent is a frontend to the Configuration Manager service **CONFIGMG_Broadcast_Device_Change_Message**. **IFSMgr_PNPEvent** constructs and broadcasts several types of messages which report the arrival and removal of network resources, plug-and-play drives, and network transports. Drivers that register with the Configuration Manager through **CONFIGMG_Register_Device_Driver** supply a callback entry point that receives these PNP broadcasts. These broadcasts are also sent to applications via the *WM_DEVICECHANGE* message.*

Win32 Support

Table 12-14 lists IFSMgr's Win32 support services.

The Win32 Support services all carry the warning: "This service is intended solely for the purpose of the Win32 subsystem. It should not be used by any other VxD in the system." OK, you've been warned.

---

* For an excellent discussion of plug-and-play and the configuration manager, see Chapters 11 and 12 of *Systems Programming for Windows 95* by Walter Oney. His book also includes a useful spy utility which monitors *WM_DEVICECHANGE* messages.

Table 12-14. IFSMgr Win32 Support Services

Ord	Service Name	16	22	22+	Segment	Ref
49	IFSMgr_Win32DupHandle		x	x	pageable	10
51	IFSMgr_Win32_Get_Ring0_Handle		x	x	pageable	6
99	IFSMgr_Win32MapExtendedHandleToSFT		x	x	pageable	12
101	IFSMgr_Win32MapSFTToExtendedHandle		x	x	pageable	12
107	IFSMgr_Win32GetVMCurdir		x	x	pageable	12

We already encountered **IFSMgr_Win32DupHandle** when we examined the creation of memory-mapped files in Chapter 10, *Virtual Memory, the Paging File, and Pagers*. This function is called in response to the Win32 API **CreateFileMapping** and the duplicated handle is used to refer to the memory-mapping. This service is also used to create "normal" handle duplicates via the Win32 API, **DuplicateHandle**.

IFSMgr_Win32_Get_Ring0_Handle was discussed in Chapter 6 when we looked at how IFSMgr tracks open files. This function takes an extended file handle (or system file number, 200h or greater) and converts it into the address of an fhandle structure. The latter, of course, is the same as a ring-0 file handle as used by **IFSMgr_Ring0_FileIO**.

IFSMgr_Win32MapSFTToExtendedHandle and its counterpart, **IFSMgr_Win32MapExtendedHandleToSFT**, are used to map extended file handles to DOS handles, and vice versa. These services must be called in the context of the DOS VM.

IFSMgr_Win32GetVMCurdir returns the current directory for the specified drive in the context of the current VM. The current directory is stored for a drive as "per-VM" data in the *pv_curdir[]* member of the VM's **pervm** structure (see Appendix C, *IFSMgr Data Structures*).

Ring-0 File I/O

The service **IFSMgr_Ring0_FileIO** (see Table 12-15) has become very popular among VxD writers. Finally, there is an easy way to access the file system from ring-0. This service supplies a subset of the Int 21h interface, including some commonly used functions. The mechanism IFSMgr uses to dispatch ring-0 file system requests was described in Chapter 6.

Table 12-15. IFSMgr ring-0 File I/O Services

Ord	Service Name	16	22	22+	Segment	Ref
50	IFSMgr_Ring0_FileIO		x	x	locked	

IFSMgr_Ring0_FileIO is essentially a ring-0 interrupt 21h interface. You load the EAX, EBX, ECX, EDX, and ESI registers with parameters, invoke the function, and get the results in the EAX and ECX registers and in buffers referred to by the input registers. As in the Int 21h interface, the AH portion of EAX input register holds the function number. Only 15 major functions are supported, some of which have subfunctions; these are listed in Table 12-16. See the DDK documentation for details on register usage for each function.

Table 12-16. IFSMgr_Ring0_FileIO Functions

Function Name	Value	Preamble	Dispatch	Segment
R0_OPENCREATFILE	D500h	R0_MapPath	dR0_OpenCreate	locked
R0_OPENCREATEFILE_IN_ CONTEXT	D501h	R0_MapPath	dR0_OpenCreate	locked
R0_READFILE	D600h	R0_Default	dR0_ReadWrite	locked
R0_WRITEFILE	D601h	R0_Default	dR0_ReadWrite	locked
R0_READFILE_IN_CONTEXT	D602h	R0_Default	dR0_ReadWrite	locked
R0_WRITEFILE_IN_CONTEXT	D603h	R0_Default	dR0_ReadWrite	locked
R0_CLOSEFILE	D700h	R0_Default	dR0_Close	locked
R0_GETFILESIZE	D800h	R0_Default	dR0_FileSize	locked
R0_FINDFIRSTFILE	4E00h	R0_MapPath	dFindFile	pageable
R0_FINDNEXTFILE	4F00h	None	dFindFile	pageable
R0_FINDCLOSEFILE	DC00h	R0_Default	dFindClose	pageable
R0_FILEATTRIBUTES I GET_ATTRIBUTES	4300h	R0_MapPath	dAttribs	pageable
R0_FILEATTRIBUTES I SET_ATTRIBUTES	4301h	R0_MapPath	dAttribs	pageable
R0_RENAMEFILE	5600h	R0_MapPath	dRename	pageable
R0_DELETEFILE	4100h	R0_MapPath	dDelete	pageable
R0_LOCKFILE	5C00h	R0_Default	dLock	pageable
R0_GETDISKFREESPACE	3600h	R0_DriveChk1	dDriveData	pageable
R0_READABSOLUTEDISK	DD00h	R0_DriveChk2	dAbsReadWrite	pageable
R0_WRITEABSOLUTEDISK	DE00h	R0_DriveChk2	dAbsReadWrite	pageable
Ring0 Ioctl	DFxxh	R0_Default	dR0_Ioctl	locked

As with the protected-mode and virtual-86 mode Int 21h handler, a preamble is called on each ring-0 Int 21h function. If the preamble returns with carry set, the function is not dispatched. Note that the preamble functions for the ring-0 interface can *not* be modified using **IFSMgr_SetReqHook**. For many of the functions, the **R0_Default** preamble is used, which simply clears the carry flag and returns, allowing the function to be dispatched. Functions which receive a pathname as an argument call **R0_MapPath**, which in turn calls an Int 21h preamble which uses

Map_Flat to convert DS:DX into linear addresses and possibly run the path through **IFSMgr_ParsePath**. When this preamble is called from the ring-0 interface, however, it does nothing. The only preambles which actually test the input parameters are **R0_DriveChk1** and **R0_DriveChk2**, and they only validate the zero-based drive number. So you need to heed the DDK warning: "Users of this service should be very careful to check that they are passing in valid parameters."

Table 12-16 also enumerates the dispatch routines which are invoked for each ring-0 function. For most of the functions, a common dispatch routine is shared by the ring-0 interface and the PM/V86 mode Int 21h handler. The dispatch routines which are unique to the ring-0 interface have names which begin with dR0. These routines reside in locked code.

Miscellaneous

Table 12-17 lists IFSMgr's services which don't fall into one of the other categories.

Table 12-17. IFSMgr Miscellaneous Services

Ord	Service Name	16	22	22+	Segment	Ref
0	IFSMgr_Get_Version	x	x	x	locked	12
4	IFSMgr_Attach	u	u	u	locked	
5	IFSMgr_Detach	u	u	u	locked	
11	IFSMgr_CompleteAsync	x	x	x	pageable	
38_{40}	IFSMgr_SetErrString	x	x	x	pageable	
39_{41}	IFSMgr_GetErrString	x	x	x	pageable	
45_{47}	IFSMgr_ChangeDir	x	x	x	pageable	
47	IFSMgr_CDROM_Attach		x	x	pageable	
48	IFSMgr_CDROM_Detach		x	x	pageable	
52_{58}	IFSMgr_Get_Drive_Info	x	u	u	locked	
53	IFSMgr_Ring0GetDriveInfo		x	x	locked	
63	IFSMgr_CallProvider		u	u	locked	
75	Query_PhysLock		x	x	locked	
90	IFSMgr_MountChildVolume		x	x	pageable	
91	IFSMgr_UnmountChildVolume		x	x	pageable	
92	IFSMgr_SwapDrives		x	x	pageable	
95	IFSMgr_FSDAttachSFT		u	u	pageable	
102	IFSMgr_FSDGetCurrentDrive		x	x	pageable	
103	IFSMgr_InstallFileSystemApiHook		x	x	locked	7
104	IFSMgr_RemoveFileSystemApiHook		x	x	locked	7

Table 12-17. IFSMgr Miscellaneous Services (continued)

Ord	Service Name	16	22	22+	Segment	Ref
109	_GetMappedErr		x	x	locked	
111	IFSMgr_GetLockState		x	x	locked	

Debugging

Table 12-18 lists IFSMgr's debugging services.

Table 12-18. IFSMgr Debugging Services

Ord	Service Name	16	22	22+	Segment	Ref
28	IFSMgr_PopUp	u	u	u	pageable	
29	IFSMgr_printf		d	d	locked	
30	IFSMgr_AssertFailed		d	d	locked	
31	IFSMgr_LogEntry	d	d	d	locked	
32	IFSMgr_DebugMenu	d	d	d	locked	
33	IFSMgr_DebugVars	d	d	d	locked	
34	IFSMgr_GetDebugString	d	d	d	locked	
35	IFSMgr_GetDebugHexNum	d	d	d	locked	
100	IFSMgr_DbgSetFileHandleLimit		d	d	locked	

13

VREDIR: The Microsoft Networks Client

The client side of Microsoft Networks file and printer sharing services is brought to you by VREDIR, the virtual redirector. It is an example of the network redirector type of FSD. Microsoft Networks is based upon the Server Message Block (SMB) file sharing protocol. This protocol was introduced with the original IBM PC Network. Today it is the protocol that is used to network the PC world, including MS-DOS, Windows for Workgroups, Windows NT, and OS/2 (not to mention Windows 95). In August 1996, Microsoft launched an initiative to move this protocol to the Internet under the name Common Internet File System, or CIFS.

To aid our exploration of VREDIR, two new monitors for MultiMon are introduced. The first is a NetBIOS monitor that displays all calls through VNETBIOS; the second is a monitor that displays the types of SMB packets passing through NetBIOS. While they aren't a substitute for a LAN protocol analyzer or "packet sniffer," they have the advantage of integrating well with our IFSMgr Filehook monitor so we can relate file system requests to the resultant network activity.

VREDIR is just one stratum in a sequence of protocols. Let's begin by looking at VREDIR's place amongst the network components.

VREDIR and Other Network Components

Figure 13-1 shows IFSMgr at the top of a protocol stack. IFSMgr passes `ifsreq` packets to VREDIR for any file system requests that are resolved to a remote Microsoft Networks server. VREDIR, in turn, generates one or more NetBIOS calls which send requests to a remote computer using the Server Message Block (SMB) file sharing protocol. The NetBIOS request may be sent using one of the three transport protocols: NetBEUI, TCP/IP, or IPX/SPX (or any transport that supports NetBIOS). The last two require shims to convert the NetBIOS request into a form amenable to TCP/IP or IPX/SPX. These protocols frame the SMB packet or transferred data with appropriate headers and trailers before passing it to the NDIS driver. Incoming packets wend their way up to VNETBIOS which notifies clients of completed requests and the receipt of data. Since VREDIR is the Microsoft Networks *client*, it does not accept requests from other systems; VSERVER fulfills that role.

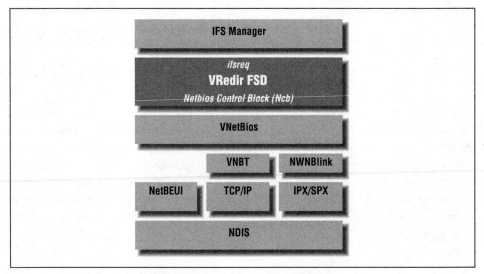

Figure 13-1. VREDIR's protocol stack

The two interfaces in Figure 13-1 which we are most interested in are the IFSMgr/ VREDIR and VREDIR/VNETBIOS boundaries. IFSMgr and VREDIR use the standard FSD linkage which we explored in Chapter 8, *Anatomy of a File System Driver*. For VREDIR to establish a connection to a remote "share," there must be a server on a remote computer which is sharing it. Although peer-to-peer Windows 95 networks would rely on VSERVER to provide these shares, many other SMB server possibilities exist, including Windows for Workgroups, LAN Manager, Windows NT, OS/2, and UNIX/Linux workstations running SAMBA. To represent a connection, IFSMgr creates a shell resource on the client computer. For instance, suppose a single server exposes two different directories as shares with UNC names *SERVER**DESKTOP* (local directory: *c:\windows\Desktop*) and *SERVER**PGMS* (local directory: *c:\Program Files*). If a file is opened in each directory from a remote computer using full UNC paths, two shell resources will be created, one for each shared resource connection. On the other hand, if we were to open two files in the remote directory *SERVER**DESKTOP* only a single shell resource would be required. In either case, two file handles are needed.

This mapping of connections represented by *server**share* names to shell resources distinguishes network FSDs from local FSDs which map shell resources to logical volumes.

Our examination of FSDs has emphasized the IFSMgr-to-FSD interface, since this is a consistent and common interface for all types of FSDs. It is the lower interface of an FSD that is unique to each driver; for example with VFAT, the interface is to IOS; with MONOCFSD the interface is to a monochrome display adapter; with FSINFILE the interface is to a ring-0 file. In the case of VREDIR, the lower interface is with NetBIOS. NetBIOS is sometimes confused with NetBEUI. NetBIOS is a programming interface whereas NetBEUI is a transport protocol.

VREDIR Interfaces

The upper side of VREDIR communicates with IFSMgr via the function table interface. Network FSDs populate their function tables with somewhat different routines than a local FSD. Since shared resources may be of several different types, open operations on these resources may return addresses to one of several handle-based function tables. The lower side of VREDIR needs to communicate with the local area network. There are two levels at which this is done. The first is concerned with the mechanics of sending and receiving packets to specific servers on the net—this is taken care of by the NetBIOS interface, which we examine here. The second level concerns the content of these packets, i.e., formatting the packets according to the protocol expected by the server. This is taken care of by the SMB file sharing protocol which we'll examine in the next section.

The FSD Interface

As we saw in Chapter 8, a shell resource is matched with a volume-based function table in the FSD which owns it. In the case of a network FSD, the volume-based table of functions might be thought of as the UNC path-based table of functions. Each UNC path corresponds to a specific connection. VREDIR uses a single volume-based function table which contains the 15 entries shown below:

FS_DeleteFile	FS_Dir	FS_FileAttributes	FS_Search	FS_GetDiskInfo
FS_OpenFile	FS_Rename	FS_Ioctl16Drive	FS_QueryInfo	FS_Disconnect
FS_NamedPipe-UNCRequest	FS_Flush	FS_GetDiskParms	FS_FindOpen	FS_DASDIO

The functions which are listed in bold characters are implemented by VREDIR. Note that **FS_Ioctl16Drive**, **FS_GetDiskParms**, and **FS_DASDIO** are not implemented in a network FSD but **FS_NamedPipeUNCPipeRequest** is. This is in contrast to a local FSD. **FS_NamedPipeUNCRequest** is added to provide support for named pipes.

VREDIR is more complex when it comes to supplying a handle-based function table via **FS_OpenFile**. Shell resources for a network FSD can be of several types: *RESTYPE_DISK* for a network drive-mapping, *RESTYPE_SPOOL* for a remote spooled printer, *RESTYPE_CHARDEV* for a remote character device, *RESTYPE_IPC* for a named pipe to a remote system, and *RESTYPE_WILD* for a catch-all group. (The manifest constants *RESTYPE_DISK*, etc., are defined in the DDK header file *ifs.h* and are passed into several IFSMgr services as well as **FS_ConnectNet-Resource**.)

Table 13-1 shows the handle-based functions (in bold) for each resource type. The **FS_ReadFile** and **FS_WriteFile** functions at the top use different routines depending on the open access mode. A "deny" entry means that the function both sets *ir_error* to *ERROR_ACCESS_DENIED* and returns that error code. A "zero" entry means that the function sets *ir_length* to zero and it returns success.

Table 13-1. VREDIR's Handle-Based Function Table

Function	WILD	DISK	SPOOL	CHARDEV	IPC
FS_ReadFile					
ReadOnly	deny	**read1**	zero	deny	**read2**
WriteOnly	deny	deny	deny	deny	deny
Read/Write	deny	**read1**	zero	deny	**read2**
Execute	deny	**read1**	zero	deny	deny
FS_WriteFile					
ReadOnly	deny	deny	deny	deny	deny
WriteOnly	deny	**write1**	**write1**	deny	**write2**
Read/Write	deny	**write1**	**write1**	deny	**write2**
Execute	deny	deny	deny	deny	deny
FS_SeekFile	deny	**seek1**	**seek1**	deny	zero
FS_CloseFile	**close1**	**close1**	**close1**	**close1**	**close1**
FS_CommitFile	deny	**commit1**	**commit1**	deny	zero
FS_FileLocks	deny	**lock1**	**lock1**	deny	deny
FS_FileDateTime	deny	**times1**	**times1**	deny	deny
FS_NamedPipeRequest	deny	deny	deny	deny	**pipe1**
FS_NamedPipeHandleInfo	deny	deny	deny	deny	**nethdl1**
FS_EnumerateHandle	deny	**enum1**	**enum1**	deny	deny

We can see from the table that all resource types use a common **FS_CloseFile** function, **close1**. For *RESTYPE_WILD* and *RESTYPE_CHARDEV* resources, **FS_CloseFile** is the only function implemented. *RESTYPE_DISK* and *RESTYPE_SPOOL* resources use the same set of functions, except that the spooler doesn't return any data when a read is attempted. *RESTYPE_IPC* uses a separate set of read and write routines. It is the only resource type to implement **FS_NamedPipeRequest** and **FS_NamedPipeHandleInfo**. In VREDIR's implementation, the volume-based function **FS_NamedPipeUNCRequest** and the handle-based function **FS_Named-PipeRequest** use a common routine. One additional handle-based function table exists for the function **FS_FindFirstFile**. It returns **FS_FindNextFile** as the read function and **FS_FindClose** as its **FS_CloseFile** function. The remaining functions are all assigned the deny routine.

The NetBIOS Interface

The NetBIOS interface is supplied by the VxD VNETBIOS. A NetBIOS command is issued by filling a Network Control Block (NCB) structure with command parameters and then passing it to the NetBIOS entry point. In MS-DOS and Win16 programs, this is accomplished by pointing ES:BX at the NCB and invoking software Int 5Ch. Win32 programs may call the C library function **Netbios** with a pointer to the NCB. The way that VxDs use NetBIOS is to load the linear address of the NCB in EBX and call the service **VNETBIOS_Submit**.

The Network Control Block which is used to request NetBIOS services has the following layout:

```
typedef struct _NCB {
    UCHAR  ncb_command;              /* 00 command code */
    UCHAR  ncb_retcode;             /* 01 return code */
    UCHAR  ncb_lsn;                 /* 02 local session number */
    UCHAR  ncb_num;                 /* 03 number of our network name */
    PUCHAR ncb_buffer;              /* 04 address of message buffer */
    WORD   ncb_length;              /* 08 size of message buffer */
    UCHAR  ncb_callname[NCBNAMSZ];  /* 0A blank-padded name of remote */
    UCHAR  ncb_name[NCBNAMSZ];      /* 1A our blank-padded netname */
    UCHAR  ncb_rto;                 /* 2A rcv timeout/retry count */
    UCHAR  ncb_sto;                 /* 2B send timeout/sys timeout */
    void (*ncb_post)(struct _NCB*); /* 2C POST routine address */
    UCHAR  ncb_lana_num;            /* 30 lana (adapter) number */
    UCHAR  ncb_cmd_cplt;            /* 31 0xff => commmand pending */
    UCHAR  ncb_reserve[10];         /* 32 reserved, used by BIOS */
    HANDLE ncb_event;               /* 3C HANDLE to Win32 event which */
                                    /* will be set to the signalled */
                                    /* state when an ASYNCH command */
                                    /* completes */
} NCB, *PNCB;
```

This definition comes from the Win32 SDK header file *nb30.h*; an equivalent header is not provided in the DDK. Several fields in this structure are used in every NetBIOS command; others are only needed for certain commands. The member *ncb_command* holds the command code. By default, a command does not return until it completes. Most commands can be issued in asynchronous fashion by setting the high bit in the command code. This means that the command returns before completion and the initial return code in ncb_retcode indicates that the command is pending. When the command does complete, the routine specified by *ncb_post* is called with the address of the completing NCB. The member *ncb_lana_num* originally was used to specify the network adapter number, with the first adapter having a value of zero, the second adapter a value of one, and so forth. The use of *ncb_lana_num* has since been extended to also enumerate available protocols. For instance, if a system has two network adapters and both NetBEUI and IPX/SPX protocols installed, the system would have four LANA numbers. Each number would correspond to one of the combinations of adapter and protocol. Windows 95 does not allow the user to control this mapping except that a default protocol may be selected under the **Network** properties from Control Panel. The protocol which is selected as the default will have a LANA number of 0.[*]

NetBIOS commands are grouped into four broad categories: name support, datagram support, session support, and utility. The manifest constants which are used here to refer to NetBIOS commands are defined in the header file *nb30.h*. The name commands add and remove names from the local name table. The first name in this table is the local node name or MAC address and cannot be deleted. A name is added to the table with the command **NCBADDNAME** but only if it is verified to be unique on the LAN. Each name is subsequently referred to by its index in the local name table. A name is removed from the local name table with **NCBDELNAME**. A non-unique group name may also be added to the local name table using the command **NCBADDGRNAME**. In order for this command to succeed, the group name must not have already been claimed as a unique name on the LAN. Group names are intended to be registered by more than one network node.

Datagrams are used for non-guaranteed connectionless message transfers. The send (**NCBDGSEND**) and receive (**NCBDGRECV**) datagram commands are used to send messages to a unique name or a group name on the LAN. To broadcast a message to all stations on a LAN, the send broadcast datagram (**NCBDGSENDBC**) and receive broadcast datagram (**NCBDGRECVBC**) commands are used.

A session establishes a connection between a server and client station. On the server side a station will execute a **NCBLISTEN** command to await a client request. A client connects to the server by issuing a **NCBCALL** command. If the

---

[*] For more information see *How to Use LANA Numbers in a 32-bit Environment*, Microsoft Knowledge Base article Q138037. See *http://www.microsoft.com/kb/articles/q138/0/37.htm*.

connection succeeds, NetBIOS assigns it an LSN (local session number). The client and server exchange data over the connection using the **NCBSEND** and **NCBRECV** commands. A session is closed by issuing the **NCBHANGUP** command with the corresponding LSN.

The NetBIOS utility commands include **NCBRESET**, which resets the NetBIOS name and session tables and aborts any existing sessions; **NCBCANCEL**, which cancels a specified NetBIOS command; **NCBASTAT**, which requests status of a local or remote adapter. NCBASTAT can be used to retrieve the MAC address of an adapter.[*]

MultiMon's NetBIOS monitor only sees commands which are issued through **VNETBIOS_Submit**. The driver name for this monitor is *nbhook.vxd*. We will be using this monitor in a following section to trace VREDIR's operation.

This has been a condensed overview of NetBIOS. For more, see *C Programmer's Guide to NetBIOS*, by W. David Schwaderer (Howard Sams & Co., 1988).

The SMB File Sharing Protocol

SMB has been with us since the introduction of the IBM PC LAN. It has evolved since then to become the native file-sharing protocol for LAN Manager, Windows NT, OS/2, and Windows 95. UNIX and Linux platforms can also become SMB servers and clients by installing the SAMBA suite. SAMBA is available via FTP from *samba.anu.edu.au* and comes bundled with many Linux distributions.

Message Block Format

As I mentioned earlier, SMB stands for Server Message Block file-sharing protocol. It provides a command structure for allowing remote computers to access a server's resources. The client computer issues commands to a server using a message block and the server responds with a matching reply. Each message block has a common header and an area which is specific to a command. Here is the declaration of the SMB header structure:[†]

```
typedef struct {
    UCHAR Protocol[4];              // 00 Contains 0xFF,'SMB'
    UCHAR Command;                  // 04 Command code
    union {
        struct {
            UCHAR ErrorClass;       // 05 Error class
```

---

[*] See *Getting the MAC Address for an Ethernet Adapter*, Microsoft Knowledge Base Article Q118623. See *http://www.microsoft.com/kb/articles/q118/6/23.htm*.

[†] From the draft document *Microsoft Networks SMB File Sharing Protocol*, Document Version 6.0p, Jan. 1, 1996, Microsoft Corp.

```
            UCHAR Reserved;              // 06 Reserved for future use
            USHORT Error;                // 07 Error code
            } DosError;
        ULONG NtStatus;                  // 05 NT-style 32bit error code
        } Status;
    UCHAR Flags;                         // 09 Flags
    USHORT Flags2;                       // 0A More flags
    union {
        USHORT Pad[6];                   // 0C Ensure this section
                                         // is 12 bytes

        struct {
            USHORT PidHigh;              // 0C High part of PID
                                         // (NT Create And X)

            struct {
                ULONG  HdrReserved;      // 0E Not used
                USHORT Sid;              // 12 Session ID
                USHORT SequenceNumber;   // 14 Sequence number
                } Connectionless;        // IPX
            }
        };
    USHORT Tid;                          // 18 Tree identifier
    USHORT Pid;                          // 1A Caller's process id
    USHORT Uid;                          // 1C Unauthenticated user id
    USHORT Mid;                          // 1E multiplex id
    UCHAR  WordCount;                    // 20 Count of parameter words
    // The remaining fields depend upon command type
    USHORT ParameterWords[ WordCount ];  // The parameter words
    USHORT ByteCount;                    // Count of bytes
    UCHAR  Buffer[ ByteCount ];          // The bytes
    } SMB_HEADER;
```

In this declaration; UCHAR is unsigned char, USHORT is unsigned short, and ULONG is unsigned long. Note that the first 33 bytes of every message block have a common definition. The member *WordCount* determines the length of the following parameter section. The member *ByteCount* determines the length of the following buffer. The interpretation of the parameter and buffer sections are specific to each command.

The *Command* member specifies the operation which the message block refers to. The same operation code is used whether it is in the message block sent by the client or in the response message block returned by the server. The *Status* member is filled by a server in a response message block; depending on the capablities of the client, it may return a 32-bit error code in NtStatus or fill in the *ErrorClass* and *Error* members of DosError. The *Flags* and *Flags2* members use bits to indicate various client capablities, e.g., strings are represented in ASCII or Unicode. The ConnectionLess structure is needed only if the underlying transport is connectionless, such as UDP or IPX. The *Tid*, *Pid*, *Uid*, and *Mid* fields are various IDs. A *Tid* refers to a resource on the server to which the client has successfully connected. The client uses the *Tid* in subsequent requests on that resource. A *Pid* is a unique identifier generated by the client to correspond to the calling process. A client uses the *Pid* value in a response message block to sort out which process the server is responding to. A *Mid* would be used by a multi-threaded client to identify a thread within a process. It allows for multiplexing multiple message blocks on the same connection. A *Uid* is returned in a server response message block as an identifier representing a validated account name and password. *Uids* are only returned by *user level* servers but not by *share level* servers. A share level server simply makes a resource available on the network to any client which knows its name; password protection is optional. The last fixed member in the header is *WordCount*. It tells us the number of intervening words between it and the member *ByteCount*. *ByteCount* tells us the number of bytes until the end of the message block.

Commands and Dialects

Table 13-2 lists all of the SMB commands which are currently documented. SMB clients support varying levels of functionality. When they establish a connection with a server, the first command which is exchanged is **SMB_COM_NEGOTIATE**. In this command the client tells the server which versions or dialects of the SMB protocol it can understand. For instance, when VREDIR in Windows 95 sends this message, it lists the following dialects that it can support:

> PC NETWORK PROGRAM 1.0
> MICROSOFT NETWORKS 3.0
> DOS LM1.2X002
> DOS LANMAN 2.1
> Windows for Workgroups 3.1a
> NT LM 0.12.

There are something like 10 different dialects of the SMB protocol. When a client claims compatibility with a certain dialect, it is also claiming compatibility with that dialect's precursors. Table 13-2 indicates the major dialect in which a command was introduced.

Table 13-2. SMB File Sharing Protocol Commands

Command Name	Code	Dialect
SMB_COM_CREATE_DIRECTORY	0x00	PCNET PROGRAM 1.0
SMB_COM_DELETE_DIRECTORY	0x01	PCNET PROGRAM 1.0
SMB_COM_OPEN	0x02	PCNET PROGRAM 1.0
SMB_COM_CREATE	0x03	PCNET PROGRAM 1.0
SMB_COM_CLOSE	0x04	PCNET PROGRAM 1.0
SMB_COM_FLUSH	0x05	PCNET PROGRAM 1.0
SMB_COM_DELETE	0x06	PCNET PROGRAM 1.0

Table 13-2. SMB File Sharing Protocol Commands (continued)

Command Name	Code	Dialect
SMB_COM_RENAME	0x07	PCNET PROGRAM 1.0
SMB_COM_QUERY_INFORMATION	0x08	PCNET PROGRAM 1.0
SMB_COM_SET_INFORMATION	0x09	PCNET PROGRAM 1.0
SMB_COM_READ	0x0A	PCNET PROGRAM 1.0
SMB_COM_WRITE	0x0B	PCNET PROGRAM 1.0
SMB_COM_LOCK_BYTE_RANGE	0x0C	PCNET PROGRAM 1.0
SMB_COM_UNLOCK_BYTE_RANGE	0x0D	PCNET PROGRAM 1.0
SMB_COM_CREATE_TEMPORARY	0x0E	PCNET PROGRAM 1.0
SMB_COM_CREATE_NEW	0x0F	PCNET PROGRAM 1.0
SMB_COM_CHECK_DIRECTORY	0x10	PCNET PROGRAM 1.0
SMB_COM_PROCESS_EXIT	0x11	PCNET PROGRAM 1.0
SMB_COM_SEEK	0x12	PCNET PROGRAM 1.0
SMB_COM_LOCK_AND_READ	0x13	LANMAN 1.0
SMB_COM_WRITE_AND_UNLOCK	0x14	LANMAN 1.0
SMB_COM_READ_RAW	0x1A	LANMAN 1.0
SMB_COM_READ_MPX	0x1B	LANMAN 1.0
SMB_COM_READ_MPX_SECONDARY	0x1C	LANMAN 1.0
SMB_COM_WRITE_RAW	0x1D	LANMAN 1.0
SMB_COM_WRITE_MPX	0x1E	LANMAN 1.0
SMB_COM_WRITE_COMPLETE	0x20	LANMAN 1.0
SMB_COM_SET_INFORMATION2	0x22	LANMAN 1.0
SMB_COM_QUERY_INFORMATION2	0x23	LANMAN 1.0
SMB_COM_LOCKING_ANDX	0x24	LANMAN 1.0
SMB_COM_TRANSACTION	0x25	LANMAN 1.0
SMB_COM_TRANSACTION_SECONDARY	0x26	LANMAN 1.0
SMB_COM_IOCTL	0x27	LANMAN 1.0
SMB_COM_IOCTL_SECONDARY	0x28	LANMAN 1.0
SMB_COM_COPY	0x29	LANMAN 1.0
SMB_COM_MOVE	0x2A	LANMAN 1.0
SMB_COM_ECHO	0x2B	LANMAN 1.0
SMB_COM_WRITE_AND_CLOSE	0x2C	LANMAN 1.0
SMB_COM_OPEN_ANDX	0x2D	LANMAN 1.0
SMB_COM_READ_ANDX	0x2E	LANMAN 1.0
SMB_COM_WRITE_ANDX	0x2F	LANMAN 1.0
SMB_COM_CLOSE_AND_TREE_DISC	0x31	?
SMB_COM_TRANSACTION2	0x32	LM1.2X002

Table 13-2. SMB File Sharing Protocol Commands (continued)

Command Name	Code	Dialect
SMB_COM_TRANSACTION2_SECONDARY	0x33	LM1.2X002
SMB_COM_FIND_CLOSE2	0x34	LM1.2X002
SMB_COM_FIND_NOTIFY_CLOSE	0x35	?
SMB_COM_TREE_CONNECT	0x70	PCNET PROGRAM 1.0
SMB_COM_TREE_DISCONNECT	0x71	PCNET PROGRAM 1.0
SMB_COM_NEGOTIATE	0x72	PCNET PROGRAM 1.0
SMB_COM_SESSION_SETUP_ANDX	0x73	LANMAN 1.0
SMB_COM_LOGOFF_ANDX	0x74	LM1.2X002
SMB_COM_TREE_CONNECT_ANDX	0x75	LANMAN 1.0
SMB_COM_QUERY_INFORMATION_DISK	0x80	PCNET PROGRAM 1.0
SMB_COM_SEARCH	0x81	PCNET PROGRAM 1.0
SMB_COM_FIND	0x82	LANMAN 1.0
SMB_COM_FIND_UNIQUE	0x83	LANMAN 1.0
SMB_COM_NT_TRANSACT	0xA0	NT LM 0.12
SMB_COM_NT_TRANSACT_SECONDARY	0xA1	NT LM 0.12
SMB_COM_NT_CREATE_ANDX	0xA2	NT LM 0.12
SMB_COM_NT_CANCEL	0xA4	NT LM 0.12
SMB_COM_OPEN_PRINT_FILE	0xC0	PCNET PROGRAM 1.0
SMB_COM_WRITE_PRINT_FILE	0xC1	PCNET PROGRAM 1.0
SMB_COM_CLOSE_PRINT_FILE	0xC2	PCNET PROGRAM 1.0
SMB_COM_GET_PRINT_QUEUE	0xC3	PCNET PROGRAM 1.0

The most basic dialect is that named PCNET PROGRAM 1.0. This is also called the "core protocol" because it is the minimum SMB implementation. The next significant expansion of the protocol occurred with LANMAN 1.0. The other dialects listed in Table 13-2 are LM1.2X002 for Lan Manager 2.0 and NT LM 0.12, Lan Manager 2.0 for Windows NT. Windows 95 supports this "highest" dialect.

The names of the commands provide some hint as to what they do. For instance, **SMB_COM_OPEN** opens a file on the server, **SMB_COM_QUERY_INFORMATION**, gets file attributes for a file on a server, and **SMB_COM_TREE_CONNECT** establishes a connection to a shared directory (or "tree") on the server. You'll notice many commands have the suffix "ANDX". These commands support a form of command batching in which a single message block contains more than one command. For instance, **SMB_COM_OPEN_ANDX** will open a file and possibly do commands "X", where additional commands are defined by fields in the parameter section of the message block.

Message Flow

To get a feel for how the SMB protocol is used, let's follow the steps taken in response to a simple Win32 program that performs these statements:

```
hFile = CreateFile( "\\\\WETSUIT\\DESKTOP\\Notes.doc",
                    GENERIC_READ, 0, NULL, OPEN_EXISTING, 0, NULL);
size = GetFileSize( hFile, NULL );
ReadFile( hFile, pBuf, size, &actual, NULL );
CloseHandle( hFile );
```

Table 13-3 shows the exchange of messages between client and server when this code executes. The first six lines in the table correspond to the single Win32 **CreateFile** call. If a connection does not already exist with the specified server (WETSUIT) then a session is established using **SMB_COM_NEGOTIATE** and **SMC_COM_SESSION_SETUP_ANDX**. If these commands succeed then a connection is made to the share named DESKTOP by the command **SMB_COM_TREE_CONNECT_ANDX**. Note that these ANDX commands are batched together into a single message block. Once the connection is made, the file open executes and finally **CreateFile** returns. We don't see any evidence of the **GetFileSize** call being sent to the server. The next SMB commands we see correspond to the file read and file close. After the file close completes the connection remains set up. If the shared resource is not accessed for some period of time, then a **SMB_COM_TREE_DISCONNECT** command is sent to the server on the *Tid* which was returned by **SMB_COM_TREE_CONNECT_ANDX**.

Table 13-3. Sample SMB Client/Server Exchange

Client Sends:	Server (WETSUIT) Replies:
SMB_COM_NEGOTIATE	
	SMB_COM_NEGOTIATE—specify dialect to use
SMB_COM_SESSION_SETUP_ANDX and **SMB_COM_TREE_CONNECT_ANDX** specify subdirectory to connect to (*WETSUIT**DESKTOP*)	
	SMB_COM_SESSION_SETUP_ANDX and **SMB_COM_TREE_CONNECT_ANDX**— returns Tid for connected resource, and resource type
SMB_COM_OPEN_ANDX specify access and open modes and filename relative to "virtual root" ("*notes.doc*") given by *Tid*	
	SMB_COM_OPEN_ANDX returns *Fid* (file ID), filesize, attributes, and granted access
SMB_COM_READ_RAW specify the *Tid* and *Fid* that read is on as well as *ByteCount*	

Table 13-3. Sample SMB Client/Server Exchange (continued)

Client Sends:	Server (WETSUIT) Replies:
	Raw data returned in one or more packets
SMB_COM_CLOSE close the specified *Fid* (relative to the *Tid*)	
	SMB_COM_CLOSE server acknowledges close
Timeout elapses on the shared resource without any accesses occurring to it	
SMB_COM_TREE_DISCONNECT tell server that the resource referenced by the *Tid* is no longer needed	
	SMB_COM_TREE_DISCONNECT server acknowledges disconnect

CIFS: The Common Internet File System

In August 1996, Microsoft proposed a new file sharing protocol for the Internet called CIFS: Common Internet File System Protocol. The two most common protocols used on the Internet today are the Hypertext Transport Protocol (HTTP) and the File Transfer Protocol (FTP). HTTP is a read-only protocol and FTP is for transferring complete files. CIFS would provide file sharing with read-write access and thus support collaborative work on files across the Internet. The SMB protocol, upon which CIFS is based, already implements a variety of locking and security features which give clients more optimized access to server files than HTTP or FTP. CIFS is also intended to given all applications access to files on the Internet, not just web browsers.

The full specification for CIFS/1.0 has been submitted to the Internet Engineering Task Force (IETF) as an Internet draft document and is available via FTP from *ftp:// ietf.cnri.reston.va.us/internet-drafts/draft-heizer-cifs-v1-spec-00.txt*. More recent revisions can be found at links from Microsoft's CIFS home page at *http:// www.microsoft.com/intdev/cifs*. For an interesting counterpoint, see David Farber's article "CIFS Considered Harmful," at *http://avian.org/avian/papers/cifs.txt*.

Although the CIFS specification does not address the issue of how filenames are mapped to servers and shares, its does give three examples of how this might be done. Its first example is the URL, *file://fs.megacorp.com/users/fred/stuff.txt*. In this case, the server name is delimited by the leading double slashes and the next slash, and everything after that is the relative name, i.e., *fs.megacorp.com* and *users/fred/stuff.txt*, respectively. As we saw in Chapter 2, *Where Do Filenames Go?* URLs do not make up a part of the operating system's namespace (at least not at this time)—a web browser is required to interpret them. The second example the specification gives is an UNC name, such as *corpserver**public**policy.doc*. Here again, the server name is delimited by the leading double slashes and the next slash, and everything after that is the relative name, i.e., *corpserver* and *public**policy.doc*, respectively. In the specification's final example, a drive letter is mapped to a server and relative name, through a lookup table. For instance, if drive *x:* is mapped to the server, *corpserver*, and the relative name is *public*, then the name *x:**policy.doc* is equivalent to our previous example.

Once a server name is extracted from a client URL or UNC name, it needs to be converted to a server transport address. Again, this is not a part of the CIFS specification. Traditionally, the SMB protocol is implemented using the NetBIOS API and so a server name would be limited by NetBIOS naming conventions (i.e., up to 15 characters and uppercase). However, CIFS is really targeted at servers out on the Internet and server names should be resolved using DNS (the Domain Name System). The CIFS specification also notes that a server name may be given using dotted decimal notation, as in 157.33.135.101. In this case, the server transport address is simply its 32-bit IP address.

A connection is established with session service TCP port 139 of the server by sending a session request packet. This packet contains a *calling* name and *called* name. The calling name is used to distinguish clients using the same transport address. The called name is the invalid NetBIOS name *SMBSERVER padded with spaces to 15 characters. A CIFS server should accept a session request with this called name. Note that CIFS is using NetBIOS on top of TCP as detailed in RFC 1001/1002.*

Once the connection is established with the server, the flow of SMB commands would follow the same pattern as we saw in the previous section, "Message Flow."†

Tracing VREDIR Operations

Now that you have a grasp of the FSD interface, NetBIOS, and SMB, we can take a look at how these are used together. We'll use the same example from the previous section. This time we'll execute it and collect a trace with MultiMon. The

---

* See Karl Auerbach, *Protocol Standard for a Netbios Service on a Tcp/Udp Transport: Concepts and Methods*, RFC 1001, March 1987; and *Protocol Standard for a Netbios Service on a Tcp/Udp Transport: Detailed Specifications*, RFC 1002, March 1987.

† For a readable account of the CIFS/SMB protocol's various types of locks (opportunistic locks, exclusive locks, batch oplocks, and level II oplocks) see the article by Paul Leach and Dan Perry, *CIFS: A Common Internet File System*, in Microsoft Interactive Developer, November, 1996 (this article can be viewed online at *http://www.microsoft.com/mind*).

monitors that were used to collect this trace were Int21 Win32 Service (**w21**), IFSMgr Filehook (**fsh**), NetBIOS Calls (**ncb**), and SMB Packets (**smb**):

Monitor	Function	Status	Device	Handle	Parameters
	CreateFile				
w21	LFN(71)Extended Open(6c)				
					\\WETSUIT\DESKTOP\Notes.doc
ncb	Call	async	Lana=07	c16b7640	Callname:WETSUIT
ncb	Call	post(00)		c16b7640	LSN:07*
ncb	Send	async	Lana=07	c16b7640	LSN:07
					Buffer:c3a743e4(009a)
smb	NEGOTIATE	request		c16b7640	
ncb	Send	post(00)		c16b7640	
ncb	Send	async	Lana=07	c16b7640	LSN:07
					Buffer:c3a743e4(008e)
smb	SESSION_SETUP_ANDX				
	TREE_CONNECT_ANDX	request		c16b7640	\\WETSUIT\DESKTOP
ncb	Send	post(00)		c16b7640	
ncb	Send	async	Lana=07	c16b7640	LSN:07
					Buffer:c3a743e4(004c)
smb	OPEN_ANDX	request		c16b7640	Notes.doc
ncb	Send	post(00)		c16b7640	
fsh	FS_OpenFile (6c)		VREDIR	2f2*	\NOTES.DOC oe
	GetFileSize				
w21	Seek(42)			2f2	(1) offs=0
fsh	FS_FileSeek (42)		VREDIR	2f2	ofs=0H b
w21	Seek(42)			2f2	(2) offs=0
fsh	FS_FileSeek (42)		VREDIR	2f2	ofs=0H e
w21	Seek(42)			2f2	(0) offs=0
fsh	FS_FileSeek (42)		VREDIR	2f2	ofs=0H b
	ReadFile				
w21	Read(3f)			2f2	cnt=4800
					buf=13f:d934
ncb	Receive	async	Lana=07	c16b7640	LSN:07
					Buffer:c3ab7934(4800)
ncb	Send	async	Lana=07	c16b76e0	LSN:07
					Buffer:c3a743e4(0033)
smb	READ_RAW	request		c16b76e0	
ncb	Send	post(00)		c16b76e0	
ncb	Receive	post(00)		c16b7640	
fsh	FS_ReadFile (d6)		VREDIR	2f2	cnt=4800H ofs=0H
	ptr=65d934H				
	CloseHandle				
w21	Close(3e)			2f2	
ncb	Send	async	Lana=07	c16b7640	LSN:07
					Buffer:c3a743e4(0029)
smb	CLOSE	request		c16b7640	
fsh	FS_CloseFile (3e)		VREDIR	2f2	f
ncb	Send	post(00)		c16b7640	

The output has been grouped into four sections, one section for each Win32 function call.

Beginning with the **CreateFile** call, we see that it gets passed to VWIN32 where it becomes dispatched as a protected-mode Int 21h function 716ch. This function will enter IFSMgr through the dispatch function which we named **dOpenCreate** (see Chapter 6, *Dispatching File System Requests*). As **dOpenCreate** prepares an ifsreq structure, it generates a canonicalized pathname by a call to **IFSMgr_ParsePath**. As we saw in Chapter 7, *Monitoring File Activity*, this service will establish a connection to a server and share using **IFSMgr_SetupConnection**, if it is passed an UNC path. VREDIR is called at this point through its **FS_ConnectNetResource** entry point, but this doesn't show up in our trace because the call is made directly through the table of registered FSDs (**ConnectNetTable**) and not through the system filehooks.

The first action that we see VREDIR take is to make a NetBIOS **Call** to the specified server, in this case WETSUIT. The line in the trace indicates that this function call was made asynchronously to LANA 7 using an NCB at address c16b7640h. The next line of the trace shows that this command has completed successfully (`post(0)`) and a Local Session Number of 7 has been assigned to this connection with WETSUIT.

Now that a session has been established, VREDIR does a NetBIOS **Send**, reusing the same NCB at c16b7640h. This NCB contains a pointer to a buffer at c3a743e4h which is 9ah bytes in size. This buffer contains the message block for the **SMB_COM_NEGOTIATE** command which is sent to the session partner of LSN 7 (WETSUIT). Again this is an asynchronous command, and we see it complete two lines down where its matching `post(0)` is recorded. At this stage, we have notified WETSUIT about the dialects of SMB which we support. The next NetBIOS Send command transfers a message block containing a batched command consisting of **SMB_COM_SESSION_SETUP_ANDX** and **SMB_COM_TREE_CONNECT_ANDX**. The latter command creates a connection to the subdirectory *\\WETSUIT\DESKTOP* and returns a *Tid* which is used in subsequent commands which reference this server and share. When this command completes, we have seen the last action taken on behalf of **FS_ConnectNetResource**. From this we see that VREDIR needs to keep at least two pieces of information about this connection, its LSN and its *Tid*. The resource handle (*ir_rh*) which VREDIR returns to IFSMgr retains this and other state information. IFSMgr in turn builds its own shell resource structure (`shres`) to represent the connection.

The last NetBIOS **Send**, under the **CreateFile** section, transfers a message block containing a **SMB_COM_OPEN_ANDX** command. This requests that the server WETSUIT open the file named *Notes.doc* on the *Tid* for this connection. This action is taken in response to a call to VREDIR's **FS_OpenFile** entry point. The trace output line for this call occurs after the NetBIOS activity, because the file-hook reports function calls after they complete. Just as the resource handle retains VREDIR's information about a connection, VREDIR's returned file handle (*ir_fh*) retains information about this open file. This would include things such as the *Fid* (file identifier) returned by the **SMB_COM_OPEN_ANDX** command, its open mode, and various file attributes. When VREDIR returns, IFSMgr builds its own file handle structure (**fhandle**) and assigns it an extended handle of 2f2h.

GetFileSize is implemented as three Int 21h function 42xxh calls via VWIN32. The first seek moves the file pointer from its current position to offset 0. Then a seek is performed to the end of the file to determine its maximum byte position; then the file pointer is restored to the beginning of the file. Although VREDIR's **FS_FileSeek** entry point is called on each of these seeks, VREDIR refers to information stored in its file handle structure to satisfy the requests.

ReadFile becomes an Int 21h function 3fh call passed to IFSMgr via VWIN32. This call then gets passed to the **FS_ReadFile** entry point of VREDIR. The first action we see taken is to initiate an asynchronous NetBIOS **Receive** command for 4800h bytes on LSN 7. While this **Receive** is pending, a NetBIOS **Send** transfers a message block containing a **SMB_COM_READ_RAW** command to the server. We see the read command finish first, followed by the receive. The underlying protocol handles the assembly of incoming data packets into the 4800h byte buffer.

Finally, at the end, **CloseHandle** becomes an Int 21h function 3eh call passed to IFSMgr via VWIN32. This call then gets passed to the **FS_CloseFile** entry point of VREDIR. The NetBIOS **Send** transfers a message block containing a **SMB_COM_CLOSE** command for the *Fid* returned by the earlier **SMB_COM_OPEN_ANDX** command.

As noted in Table 13-3, a matching **SMB_COM_TREE_DISCONNECT** will not occur for a few minutes, so the connection remains alive. This allows other files in this subdirectory or its subdirectories to be opened using the same LSN and *Tid*.

IPC for Network FSDs

Some implementation details are unique to network file system drivers. One of these involves handling inter-process communication (IPC). With Microsoft Networks, two IPC mechanisms are provided, *mailslots* and *named pipes*. These peer-to-peer communication services are implemented by using commands from the SMB protocol.

Mailslots

The simplest type of interprocess communication (IPC) which VREDIR and IFSMgr support is the *mailslot*. A mailslot user plays one of two roles. The mailslot server creates the mailslot and only reads from it. The mailslot client opens the mailslot and only writes to it. A single process may be both a mailslot client and server. Data is transferred as datagrams and thus its arrival is not guaranteed.

Registering a mailslot

In order for mailslot services to be made available to a system, an FSD registers with IFSMgr using **IFSMgr_RegisterMailSlot**. Up to four FSDs may register as mailslot providers. Each registrant passes in a **FS_ConnectNetResource** function. The contents of the `ifsreq` structure on entry to **FS_ConnectNetResource** carry unique interpretations for a mailslot:

ir_flags
> 0, create mailslot; 1, delete mailslot; 2, write mailslot

ir_options
> 1, first mailslot create; >1, subsequent create

ir_ppath
> canonicalized UNC mailslot name without the leading *MAILSLOT*\\ component

ir_data
> supplies address of function to be used for mailslot reads

ir_aux1
> IFSMgr's mailslot handle (address of mailslot block)

ir_pos
> TRUE, call originated in an FSD; FALSE, call originated in User API

ir_hfunc
> pointer to handle function table

ifs_psr
> pointer to IFSMgr's mailslot shell resource

ir_aux1
> on return, contains mailslot handle created by IFSMgr

ir_error
> on return, contains error code (0 if successful)

In Chapter 8 we examined the mounting and connecting functions used by local, network, and character FSDs. In these cases, the **FS_MountVolume** or **FS_Connect-NetResource** functions always returned a volume-based function table. We don't see that with mailslots; furthermore, the shell resource structure for mailslots sets *sr_func* to NULL. Mailslots which are created using Win32 and MS-DOS APIs are represented by an SFT-backed DOS file handle. The `fhandle` structure associated with this file handle holds the handle-based function table in the member *fh_hf*. The functions which a mailslot implements are **FS_ReadFile**, **FS_WriteFile**, **FS_CloseFile**, **FS_FileDateTime**, and **FS_NetHandleInfo**.

Server-side

The **FS_ConnectNetResource** function is not called until a mailslot is created. There are three ways to do this: use the Win32 API **CreateMailslot**, use the MS-DOS function 5f4dh (**DosMakeMailslot**), or use the IFSMgr service **IFSMgr_MakeMailslot**. The Win32 API encapsulates the mailslot in a KERNEL32 object. It utilizes MS-DOS function 5f4dh to create a DOS file handle to the mailslot. **IFSMgr_MakeMailslot** works at a lower level. It returns a handle to a memory block which contains a definition of the mailslot. For requests which originate at the user level, the handle to this memory block is stored in a `fhandle` structure in the *fh_fh* member.

When a mailslot is created, it is given a UNC name of the form \\.*MAILSLOT**testslot*. The leading characters, "\\.\", indicate that a mailslot can only be created on a local machine. The actual name of the mailslot is the portion that follows "\\.*MAILSLOT*\". Also note that mailslot names follow the 8.3 naming convention.*

To see if the mailslot contains something to be read, the Win32 API **GetMailslotInfo** or the MS-DOS function 5f4fh (**DosMailslotInfo**) is called. One of the pieces of information it returns is a pointer to a buffer containing the size of the next waiting message. If no message is waiting, this buffer contains the value MAILSLOT_NO_MESSAGE.

If a mailslot message is present to be read, the Win32 API **ReadFile** or one of the MS-DOS functions 3fh (**Read File**) or 5f50h (**DosReadMailslot**) is called. Ultimately, these functions utilize **FS_ReadFile** in the handle-based function table which was setup when the mailslot provider registered itself. The *fh_fh* member of the file's `fhandle` structure tells us where the mailslot block is located. The read operation is completed by transferring the requested amount of data from the mailslot's buffers into the caller's buffer and adjusting pointers and counts.

The actual reception of datagrams for a mailslot is pretty involved. Briefly, a mailslot server issues a NetBIOS Receive Datagram command on a specific local name number. These commands will be pending until a datagram arrives for the

---

* This is documented in the Microsoft Knowledge Base article Q139716, *BUG: Windows 95 Limits Mailslot Names to 8.3 Naming Convention*. See *http://www.microsoft.com/kb/articles/q139/7/16.htm*.

name. When a datagram does come in, a **Receive Datagram** completes and the post routine is called. The post routine stores an appropriate handler address in the NCB, and then calls **Call_Priority_VM_Event** with an event procedure and the NCB as reference data. In the event handler, a **Receive Datagram** command is re-issued for the same local name number and the post handler function is called. The handler processes the NCB and input buffer. It verifies that the buffer contains a SMB message block with a **SMB_COM_TRANSACTION** command (sub-command 1). If everything is in order, then a **IFSMgr_WriteMailslot** command is issued using the contents of the NCB and associated buffer. This service gets an asynchronous `ifsreq` packet from IFSMgr, fills it with the service's arguments, and then calls into the mailslot **FS_WriteFile**. When **FS_WriteFile** returns, the `ifsreq` packet is released by calling **IFSMgr_FreeIOReq**.

Removing a mailslot requires calling the matching close function. For a handle returned by **CreateMailslot** use **CloseHandle**; for a handle returned by MS-DOS function 5f4dh (**DosMakeMailslot**), call either MS-DOS function 3eh (**Close**) or function 5f4eh (**DosDeleteMailslot**); for a handle returned by **IFSMgr_MakeMailslot** call **IFSMgr_DeleteMailslot**.[*]

Client-side

Writing to a mailslot first requires obtaining a mailslot handle. A write-only mailslot handle is obtained via the Win32 API **CreateFile**. This only creates a KERNEL32 mailslot object in which a pointer is stored to the mailslot name. For the write to be a broadcast to all processes in the local workgroup, a name of the form **MAILSLOT**testslot* is used. To target a specific machine, use its computername, as in *COMPUTERNAME**MAILSLOT**testslot*. When the mailslot handle is no longer needed, it is closed by a Win32 **CloseHandle** call.

A message is actually written to a mailslot when the Win32 **WriteFile** API is called. This function, in turn, invokes the MS-DOS function 5f52h (**DosWriteMailslot**). If the write originates in an MS-DOS application or a Win16 program, then only MS-DOS function 5f52h need be called, since the Win32 **CreateFile** and **CloseHandle** calls are only for KERNEL32 object housekeeping. Ultimately the way the write operation is completed depends on whether the write is to the local machine or a remote machine. A write to a remote machine invokes **FS_ConnectNetResource**, with *ir_flags* set to 2, whereas a write to a local machine invokes the mailslot **FS_WriteFile** function. **FS_WriteFile** looks up the mailslot name which is passed in *ir_ppath* to see if it exists. If it does, the address of the mailslot memory block is consulted to see if a read function was supplied when the mailslot was created. If

---

[*] Partial documentation for the MS-DOS variants of the mailslot functions can be found in Chapter 19 (LAN Manager) of *Uninterrupted Interrupts* by Ralf Brown and Jim Kyle (Addison-Wesley).

so, then that function is called, otherwise IFSMgr's implementation is called which writes to the local mailslot buffer. On the other hand, if **FS_ConnectNetResource** (*ir_flag* = 2) is called, it will generate a NetBIOS **Send Datagram** command. The datagram is a message block containing a **SMB_COM_TRANSACTION** command, subcommand type 1. This message block holds the mailslot name as well as the data of the mailslot message.

Named Pipes

Unlike mailslots, named pipes fit nicely into the remote FSD model. Windows 95 only supports client-side named pipes. A client connects to a known named pipe by calling the Win32 API **CreateFile** using a UNC name of the form *\\SERVER\PIPE\testpipe*. As with other UNC names, a connection is first attempted to the specified server using the service **IFSMgr_SetupConnection**. A call to VREDIR's **FS_ConnectNetResource** entry point attempts to establish the connection. If the connection succeeds, then a shell resource structure is constructed for the connection, and, in this case, it is marked with *sr_type* of 4 for IPC (interprocess communication). The shell resource structure also will receive *sr_func*, the address of VREDIR's UNC path-based function table. To finish the **CreateFile** call, the **FS_OpenFile** entry point in this table is called to connect to the server's named pipe. A successful return results in a `fhandle` structure for the extended file handle which is used to refer to this named pipe in subsequent API calls. This `fhandle` structure will hold the **FS_ReadFile**, **FS_WriteFile**, and a pointer to the miscellaneous handle-based functions in VREDIR.

VREDIR uses a common handler for both **FS_NamedPipeUNCRequest** (from the UNC path-based function table) and **FS_NamedPipeRequest** (from the handle-based function table). This works because both functions use the *ir_flags* member of `ifsreq` to specify a command code. The *ir_flags* value is used as a subcommand to a **SMB_COM_TRANSACTION** command, i.e., each of the named pipe functions is represented by a corresponding SMB message block. One exception to this rule is **FS_NetHandleInfo** (**FS_NamedPipeHandleInfo**); it has its own handle-based function for setting and returning a handle's buffering characteristics.

14

Looking Ahead

During the media blitz that accompanied the rollout of Windows 95 in the summer of 1995, Microsoft kept asking us "Where do you want to go today?" Now, Microsoft is at work on our destination for tomorrow. Although the Internet phenomenon caught them off guard, Microsoft is positioning the Windows platform as the platform of choice for Internet browsing and establishing personal intranets. Even if the Internet dominates the future, it will require an infrastructure to support it on both client and server.

Since the release of Windows 95, we have seen some indications as to what direction these infrastructure changes will take. As of the close of 1996, Microsoft has completed or announced two enhancements to Windows 95 that are relevant to the file system. The first is the shipment of OEM Service Release 2, which included support for FAT32. The second is the WDM (Win32 Driver Model) initiative. We looked at FAT32 in Chapter 9, *VFAT: The Virtual FAT File System Driver*, but we haven't discussed WDM yet.

What is significant about WDM is that the Windows NT driver model is becoming the model for future Windows 95 drivers. To better understand WDM, we need to look at the Windows NT architecture, especially as it applies to the file system. It is also important to contrast these systems so that you'll have some idea of how a Windows 95 file system design would be ported to Windows NT.

IFSMgr vs. NT's Object Manager

Just as Windows 95 distinguishes code executing at ring-3 and ring-0 privilege levels, Windows NT distinguishes user-mode and kernel-mode execution. In user mode several subsystems coexist which support the execution of Win32, Windows 3.x/MS-DOS, OS/2, and POSIX applications. Each of these subsystems is a separate process acting as a server of a particular API, and their clients are applications written to those APIs. In theory, when a client application calls an API the application makes a request of the server through an inter-process communication mechanism known as LPC (a local variant of RPC). To improve performance, requests which don't use or modify the subsystem's global data are serviced within client-side DLLs.

Ultimately, all subsystems are implemented using a common set of primitive kernel-mode functions, supplied by the NT Executive. In Windows 95, these kernel-mode functions would be comparable to the Win32 services supplied by VMM, VWIN32, and a few other VxDs. The NT Executive is compartmentalized into several system service groupings such as the object manager, the process manager, the virtual memory manager, and the I/O manager. Of these, the object manager and the I/O manager play significant roles in the implementation of Windows NT file systems.

The *object manager* is the NT Executive's means of managing system resources. Each object type corresponds to a shareable system resource. Some of these object types include process, thread, file, device, driver, object directory, and symbolic link. As in the object-oriented use of the term, an NT object has attributes and methods. The attributes describe the state of the object, such as name or access mode, and the methods provide ways of performing operations on the objects, such as open, close, or query. Except perhaps for KERNEL32 objects (see Chapter 4, *File System API Mapping*), there is nothing comparable in Windows 95.

Objects need to be located, retrieved, and shared. This is made possible by giving them unique names. These names are global to a single computer. An object of type object directory may contain other objects and object directories. This allows object names to be structured in a hierarchical fashion, much like pathnames. As with pathnames, the component object names are separated by backslashes. For example, *\Device\HardDisk0\Partition1* refers to an object directory named *Device* which contains a variety of device objects including *Floppy0*, *Serial0*, *Serial1*, and *Parallel0*, to name a few. It also contains *HardDisk0*, which is an object directory that, in turn, contains the device objects *Partition0* and *Partition1*.

To minimize name searching, objects are opened by name and returned a unique handle. Thereafter, other object methods are invoked using the handle. When a thread is done using the object, it closes the object's handle and thereby relinquishes its use of the resource.

Symbolic link objects can be used to assign an alias to another object name. When a lookup is performed for a name, if a symbolic link object is encountered, the lookup continues with the name which the link references. A special type of symbolic link is used to represent the system's drive letters. For example, when the object manager is asked to lookup *DosDevices\C:*, it finds that *DosDevices* is a symbolic link to the object directory named *??*. The search is continued in the object directory *??* for *C:*. There, the object *C:* is located and is found to be a symbolic link to *Device\HardDisk0\Partition1*. The object manager uses this technique to associate a specific device with a drive letter or volume. Symbolic links are also used to associate devices with other names, like LPT1, NUL, PRN, COM1, PIPE, etc.

We can now begin to see the mechanism that the object manager uses to associate names in the Windows NT namespace with devices. But does the object manager know about names that are used by a file system? For example, how is the name *c:/winnt/notepad.exe* treated by the object manager? We know from the discussion above that *c:* is a symbolic link which after expansion will leave us with the complete name, *Device\HardDisk0\Partition1\winnt\notepad.exe*. As the object manager performs a name search, for each object in a name, it looks to see if the object has a parse method. This is a method that is unique to some objects; it is registered with the object manager when these objects are created. If a parse method is found, then the remainder of the name is passed to the parse method to locate the object. Thus, a parse method allows an object to extend the namespace beyond that which object manager is aware of. In the example above, the device object *Partition1* defines a parse method which is responsible for the namespace on a partition of the hard disk. Depending on whether the partition is FAT, HPFS, or NTFS, a different parse method will be used to locate members of the namespace.

If we look at Windows 95 to find similar functionality to what we have described in the object manager, we would have to select the IFSMgr service, **IFSMgr_Parse-Path**. Recall that this service takes a name and converts it into canonicalized form and also determines its associated shell resource. The shell resource provides the link to the file system driver. The file system driver may also supply a path check routine which is called by **IFSMgr_ParsePath** to customize parsing.

IFSMgr vs. NT's I/O Manager

The object manager is able to use a drive letter to link a filename to a device object, but how is I/O performed on that device and how is a particular file system associated with a device? To answer these questions we need to turn our attention to the I/O manager.

The *I/O manager* is concerned with three types of NT Executive objects: file, device, and driver. A file object is an in-memory representation of some physical device. It could be a text file on a floppy disk, a tape drive, or a serial communications port, so don't let the word "file" make you think it applies only to disk subsystems. File objects are different than other objects that are handled by the object manager. Most objects are manipulated directly because the object *is* a memory resource. A file object, however, is an intermediary between some physical resource and the object manager. The object manager doesn't know about the peculiarities of the hardware to which the file object refers. Instead, the object manager calls the I/O manager to assist with accesses to the device.

When a user-mode program opens a file handle, a new file object is created to represent the underlying physical resource. More than one process may open a file handle to a single physical resource and each is represented by a separate file object. Since multiple processes are accessing a shared resource, they must synchronize their access using locks or by opening the file object with exclusive write access.

A file object exposes a number of services to user-mode applications. These include create, open, read, write, query file information, set file information, get attributes, set attributes, lock byte range, unlock byte range, etc. These services are provided with the assistance of the I/O manager.

When an application opens a file, it supplies a filename. This name contains an implicit reference to a device object where the file object resides. For example, *c:\autoexec.bat* refers to the device *\Device\HardDisk0\Partition1*. This device object has a parse method and so the object manager gives the remainder of the name to the device. The open then completes with the help of the I/O manager, which creates a file object in which it stores a pointer to the device object. Ultimately, the application is returned a file handle.

The device object refers to one of three types of NT device drivers. There is the *low-level driver,* which corresponds to a device object; a *file system driver,* which corresponds to a particular file system such as FAT, HPFS, or NTFS, and is represented by a driver object; and an *intermediate driver,* which situates itself between the other two, e.g., a network transport driver would be above the MAC layer NDIS driver but below the file system redirector driver. Although these drivers provide drastically different functionality, they all use a common structure. At a minimum, a device driver has routines which load and unload it from the system plus a set of dispatch routines for each operation which it supports.

As I noted above, file objects carry around pointers to the device objects which contain them. Device objects contain pointers which refer back to the driver object which is layered above them. Driver objects contain the dispatch routines which the I/O manager calls when it needs to satisfy an I/O request. The driver object will need to call upon the dispatch routines in the device object to fulfill these requests. This linkage up and down the driver chain is very flexible and allows for the insertion of auxiliary drivers to achieve special needs, such as providing filtering.

What we have been examining is the linkage used to tie filenames to specific file system drivers. In Windows 95, linkage ties a filename or file handle to a shell resource which contains a pointer to the dispatch routines of the responsible file system driver. Although KERNEL32 creates file objects for Win32 applications, the actual tracking of file handles occurs within IFSMgr, by its use of `fhandle` structures.

One of the most dramatic differences between Windows 95 and Windows NT is NT's use of the file object to model all system I/O. In Windows 95, each class of devices has its own peculiar interfaces and driver construction. By contrast, the Windows Driver Model (or Windows NT uniform driver model) structures file system drivers the same way as it structures a driver for a SCSI host adapter.

Just as IFSMgr creates `ifsreq` packets to route I/O requests to file system drivers, the NT I/O manager creates IRPs (I/O request packets) in response to I/O requests and routes them through the various driver layers. Unlike the packets which IFSMgr uses, IRPs contain separate stack locations for each driver which it will be sent to. For instance, when the I/O manager receives a disk file read request, it would create an IRP and fill in the first stack location with parameters describing the operation from the file system driver's point of view. On receiving the IRP, the file system driver would convert the request into a form that the disk device driver will understand, and place those parameters in the second stack location. On return, the I/O manager sends the same IRP to the disk device driver which then uses the parameters in the second stack locations to perform the operation.

This has been a very brief look at the file system in Windows NT. Here are some references for additional information: Helen Custer, 1993, *Inside the Windows NT File System* (Microsoft Press, 1993); the online help documents which accompany the *NT Device Driver Kit*; Mark Russinovich and Bryce Cogswell, "Examining the Windows NT File System," *Dr. Dobb's Journal* (1997); Art Baker, *The Windows NT Device Driver Book: A Guide for Programmers* (Prentice-Hall, 1997); Rajeev Nagar, *Windows NT File System Internals* (O'Reilly & Associates, Inc., 1997).

NT Kernel Mode Drivers vs. VxDs

With this thumbnail sketch of the Windows NT file system architecture, it should be apparent that Windows 95 and Windows NT are drastically different. Although we have been comparing pieces of two operating systems that execute at ring-0 on x86 microprocessors, the manner in which these systems provide support for privileged operations is also worlds apart. Windows 95 uses VxDs to provide ring-0 support, whereas Windows NT uses kernel-mode drivers.

In terms of its file structure, a kernel-mode driver is like a Win32 dynamic-link library, i.e. it is a Portable Executable or PE file. A VxD, on the other hand, is a Linear Executable or LE file. Unlike PE files, LE files have an optional real-mode initialization section, which is executed before the processor switches into protected-mode. Windows 95 relies upon this capability when it starts up to learn about the configuration of and to communicate with its DOS substrate.

The way that these two driver types expose their interfaces is also very different. A VxD exports the address of its Device Descriptor Block, which contains the address of its control procedure, optional service table, optional PM and V86 APIs, and optional Win32 service table. On the other hand, a kernel-mode driver exports the names of its entry points, in the same way you would export functions in a Win32 DLL. To call ring-0 operating system functions in the NT Executive, you link a kernel-mode driver with the import library NTOSKRNL and simply call the functions by name (or ordinal). Contrast this with the mechanism used by a VxD to call a service in another VxD using Int 20h dynalinks.

As you know, writing a VxD requires selecting appropriate services from the hundreds which are provided by VMM, IFSMgr, VWIN32, etc. Similarly, writing a kernel-mode driver requires selecting appropriate functions from the hundreds which are provided by NTOSKRNL. Add to this the fundamental architectural differences which we examined in the last two sections, and you should have a pretty clear picture of the chasm that separates these two worlds.

Despite the obvious difficulties, Microsoft is building a bridge from Windows 95 to Windows NT by providing support for kernel-mode drivers in Windows 95. Note that this is a one-way bridge; there has been no announced support for VxDs in Windows NT. The building of this bridge has been called the Win32 Driver Model (WDM) initiative. See the WDM homepage on Microsoft's site at *http://www.microsoft.com/hwdev/pcfuture/wdm.htm*.

WDM

WDM was officially unveiled at the Windows Hardware Engineering Conference (WinHEC) in April 1996. Although it impacts Windows 95 developers most by making them prepare for a new driver infrastructure, it also impacts Windows NT developers by introducing common drivers for plug-and-play, power management, and the Universal Serial Bus (USB). The presentations emphasized that the initial focus of WDM would be on device drivers and *not* file system drivers. Furthermore, although Windows NT will not support VxDs, VxDs can peacefully coexist with WDM on Windows platforms. WDM will also coexist with existing class-specific driver models such as mass storage and networking.

Even though the stated focus of WDM will be on new buses and device types, the changes should impact a lot of system components. This is because drivers written to this standard require a new and extensive API. Most of this API is declared in the header file *ntddk.h*. Services from the I/O manager, the virtual memory manager, the kernel, etc. are represented here.

At the time this book is being completed, WDM is still under development. At WinHEC-97, in April 1997, a WDM beta was distributed as well as a Developer's Release of Memphis. In addition to FAT32, and WDM support for USB, 1394, Plug-and-Play, and Power Management, the next release of Windows (code-named Memphis) will incorporate WDM streaming-class drivers for audio and video. This is inline with the Microsoft goal of making the PC the "Entertainment PC" in 1998. To support this effort, Memphis will ship with DVD drivers, including a new file system driver called *udf.vxd* for the Universal Disk Format used by the DVD-ROM.

Is WDM on Windows in your future? Probably not any time soon, if you are working on file system drivers or file system hooks. When I put this question to one of the Microsoft speakers at the WinHEC-96 conference, their response was that the Windows platform would probably be phased out before they got around to converting the mass storage, network, and file system drivers to WDM.

However, WDM *is* in your future if you plan to do any Windows NT file system development. As Windows NT continues to build momentum, there may be more pressure to extend WDM on Windows to a wider array of drivers.

MultiMon: Setup, Usage, and Extensions

MultiMon is used throughout this book as a multi-purpose spy program. By installing this tool you can perform the experiments described in the text and do exploration on your own. To help you get up to speed with MultiMon, this appendix will describe what it is, how it works, and how to set it up and use it. I've also included some background information on its design and implementation. For the more adventurous, I'll show how to extend its capabilities for your own purposes.

What Is MultiMon?

Monitor or spy programs are very popular among PC programmers. They afford the user an opportunity to examine the inner workings of living and breathing systems and applications. This is a valuable capability because seeing code in action speaks louder than words. Spy programs also have the annoying habit of revealing undocumented or incompletely documented APIs and data structures. You will encounter a fair share of undocumented features in this way.

The predecessor to MultiMon was called *FileMon*. It was the basis for my article "Monitoring Windows 95 File Activity in Ring 0," in *Windows/DOS Developer's Journal*, July 1995. FileMon is a monitoring tool which displays the calls made by IFSMgr into the underlying file system drivers. It was used to demonstrate how to write a Windows 95 file system hook using IFSMgr services. FileMon also illustrated a simple technique for exchanging information between a Win32 application and a VxD which allowed the VxD to display its output in a console application window. MultiMon includes and extends the capabilities that FileMon had.

MultiMon, which you get on the companion diskette, was designed as a general purpose tool to use in exploring Windows 95 internals. MultiMon provides a general framework for collecting and reporting on events of interest. An event could be the occurrence of a software interrupt, a call to a hooked VxD service, or even a direct application call. These events are reported by *monitors*. A monitor detects a certain kind of event, encapsulates a description of it in a generic data structure, and then sends that structure to an *event manager*. The event manager acts as a funnel. It receives events from a variety of monitors and serializes these events in a large queue. The event manager also supplies monitors with chunks of memory in which events are recorded. The event manager is also busy writing portions of the queue to a *log file*.

Two types of event managers are supplied: a session manager and a boot manager. The boot manager allows monitoring of events during system startup, and the session manager is a dynamic VxD loaded by the Win32 *reporter* application. The reporter application formats and displays the events so they can be scrolled or saved to a text file. The reporter is also responsible for displaying the drivers which are available for installation, the APIs which will be monitored for each driver, and whether the APIs are to be monitored during system startup.

Some benefits of the MultiMon design are:

- By placing the event manager in a VxD, we are able to report on events from ring-0 as well as ring-3.

- By supporting multiple monitors we are able to add an additional dimension to event traces; for example, we can view events in multiple operating system modes: ring-0, virtual-86, and Win16/ring-3 (by hooking services which support these various modes).

- Supporting multiple monitors also allows us to monitor multiple API types at the same time.

This approach is inherently extensible and configurable. Simply add and remove monitors to get the mix that provides the picture you want.

Using MultiMon

We have included MultiMon on the companion disk. This section explains how to install, configure, and use MultiMon.

Installation

The installation diskette contains a Setup program for installing MultiMon as well as other utilities and source code. Simply launch *setup.exe* from the floppy diskette using the standard Windows 95 installation procedure (from Control Panel select **Add/Remove Programs**) and follow the steps of the installation wizard. The installation program will prompt you for a destination directory. Use any location that is convenient. All of the files transferred to your system end up in this directory or its subdirectories.

New entries are also added to the system registry. For this reason, MultiMon and other components are removed by running *uninstal.exe* using the standard Windows 95 uninstall procedure (from Control Panel select **Add/Remove Programs**) and following the steps of the uninstall wizard.

Selecting Drivers and Monitors

A monitor is supplied in a monitor driver in the form of a VxD. Monitors could also be implemented as DLLs, TSRs, or DOS device drivers, but we will only use VxDs here. MultiMon distinguishes two types of monitors based on how they are loaded. A static monitor is already present in memory before the MultiMon application is executed. A dynamic monitor is loaded by MultiMon before data collection begins. A static monitor is a static VxD whereas a dynamic monitor is a dynamic VxD. The advantage of using a static monitor is that it can report events during system startup. In the current version, MultiMon only supports static monitors.

MultiMon maintains entries of known static and dynamic monitors in the system registry. Candidates for inclusion in the registry are VxDs in the directory from which MultiMon is launched. Only VxDs which have a *VersionInfo* resource with a File Description containing a "MultiMon" string are included. During initialization, MultiMon determines which of these monitors are present and displays them in the **Add/Remove Driver** dialog box. Dynamic monitors are distinguished from static monitors by having the string "Dynamic" somewhere in their File Description string.

MultiMon setup is the initial step where the user selects a set of drivers to be used for event collection (using the **Add/Remove Driver** dialog). After a set of drivers has been selected, it may be necessary to restart the system if the selection includes static components which are not currently in memory. Figure A-1 shows the **Add/Remove Driver** dialog which is reached via the **Options** menu. A driver is added by selecting it in the uninstalled column and then clicking the **Add** button. A driver is removed by selecting it in the installed column and then clicking the **Remove** button. A driver with a ",s" suffix it is a static driver; if it has a ",d" suffix it is a dynamic driver.

Once MultiMon detects installed drivers, the **Filters** dialog will display all available monitors for those drivers. A driver may contain more than one monitor; each

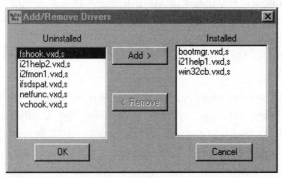

Figure A-1. MultiMon dialog for installing drivers

monitor is independently enabled and disabled. You enable those which are of
interest and disable the others. Table A-1 shows the list of drivers and supported
monitors which are included on the companion diskette. Each of these monitors
is used in this book.

Table A-1. MultiMon Drivers and Monitors

Driver	Monitor Description
fshook	IFSMgr file system hook
netfunc	IFSMgr_NetFunction hook
ifsdspat	IFSMgr dispatcher
vchook	VCACHE services
vectors	Interrupts and Callbacks
nbhook	0 NetBIOS calls
"	1 SMB packets
win32cb	0 VWIN32 Int 21h Dispatch
"	1 VWIN32 Win32 Services
"	2 VWIN32 DeviceIoControl
"	3 VMM Win32 Services
i21help1	0 Protect-Mode Int 21h hook (pre IFSMgr)
"	1 Virtual-86 Mode Int 21h hook (pre IFSMgr)
i21help2	0 Protect-Mode Int 21h hook (post IFSMgr)
"	1 Virtual-86 Mode Int 21h hook (post IFSMgr)
i2fmon1	0 Protect-Mode Int 2fh hook (pre IFSMgr)
"	1 Virtual-86 Mode Int 2fh hook (pre IFSMgr)
bootmgr	Event manager during system startup
sessmgr	Event manager after startup

Filtering Output

In addition to being able to turn monitors on and off, individual APIs may also be selectable. For instance, you may enable notifications of Int 21h Function 4ch but disable notifications of Int 21h Function 2ah. Not all monitors have API selections. Figure A-2 shows the **Filters** dialog which is reached via the **Filters** toolbar button or the **Options** menu. It shows two panes. On the left all available monitors are displayed. If the checkbox in front of the monitor name is checked, that monitor is enabled. The right pane displays a list of API functions for that monitor. If an API is checked, it will generate notifications. Two buttons at the bottom of the dialog provide shortcuts for either selecting all APIs or deselecting all APIs.

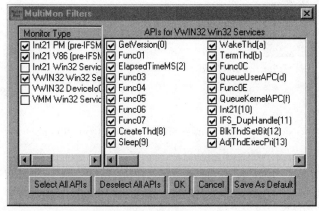

Figure A-2. MultiMon Filters dialog

Saving a Configuration

The registry is used to save one default configuration for each monitor. A configuration is defined as the enabled/disabled state for a monitor and its map of enabled/disabled APIs. The configuration for the currently selected monitor is saved by pressing the **Save As Default** button. In addition to the convenience of saving a commonly used configuration, the default configuration is the configuration used by BOOTMGR.

Toolbar and Menu Commands

MultiMon consists of a single window with a toolbar with buttons (see Figure A-3) for convenient access to the common menu commands. Only a handful of commands are used frequently: **Start** and **Stop** for starting and stopping data collection, **Show** for displaying a captured log file, **Clear** for clearing the current display buffer, **Filters** for setting up data collection monitors and API filters, and **SaveAs** for writing the buffer to a text file.

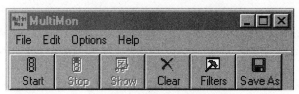

Figure A-3. MultiMon's menubar and toolbar

The **Options** menu under the main menu provides access to the **Filters** and the **Add/Remove Drivers** dialogs, as shown in Figure A-4.

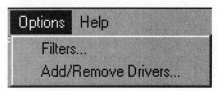

Figure A-4. Accessing MultiMon's configuration dialogs

A Sample Session

Here are the steps to follow to get a quick sample of the output from the FSHook monitor.

1. In the **Add/Remove Drivers** dialog: remove all drivers from the installed column; add only FSHook. You may be prompted to restart your system to load the static FSHook driver.

2. In the **Filters** dialog: under the monitor type column, check "IFSMgr File-Hook"; in the window entitled "APIs for IFSMgr FileHook" check all boxes by pressing the **Select All APIs** button.

3. Press the **Start** button to begin capturing events.

4. Perform some activity you wish to monitor, e.g., pop the **Properties** dialog for the desktop window.

5. Press the **Stop** button to end capturing events.

6. Press the **Show** button to display the contents of the log file.

Two lines of output from the log file are shown in Figure A-5. This view of the data is the same as the "Details" view used by the Windows 95 Explorer. A column can be resized by dragging the right boundary of the column header. If the current column size truncates data, the display shows an elipsis (...) to indicate there is more to see.

All monitors use the same column headers for their output. The columns and their contents are described in Table A-2. These are general guidelines about what to

Module	Type	Function	Flags1	Device	Handle	Args	Flags2	▲
Rundll32	fsh	FS_ReadFile (d6)	e_cLnu_sLXRmwoa	VFAT	02eb	1e8H@80H	---	
Rundll32	fsh	FS_Dir (60)	e_cLnu_sLXrmwoa	VFAT			83	
						C:\WINDOWS\...		▼

Figure A-5. MultiMon Sample Output

expect in each column; for specifics about usage for a particular monitor, see Appendix B, *MultiMon: Monitor Reference.*

Table A-2. MultiMon Output Format

Column Name	Contents
Module	Module owning the thread which generated the event
Type	A code which identifies the monitor that reported the event
Function	An API name or description
Flags1	Generic flags
Device	Target device name for the call
Handle	File or other handle value
Args	Arguments passed in or return values from the API call
Flags2	Additional flags specific to the API

Using the Boot Monitor

Normally, MultiMon does not capture events until a session is initiated by the user. However, sometimes it is desirable to monitor the events occurring during system startup. This is made possible by using the saved configurations for active monitors (the active/inactive state of a monitor is stored as part of its default configuration). This configuration information is stored in the registry under keys for each driver. When the driver loads, it consults its registry entries to determine whether it should be active and which APIs to monitor.

At system startup, the file system is not ready to receive writes to a log file. To circumvent this, an additional driver is used, called *bootmgr.vxd*. It allocates some pages of memory in which to temporarily store captured events. Events are captured until either the buffer fills up or the user launches MultiMon after system initialization completes. When MultiMon starts, it writes BOOTMGR's buffer to a *boot.log* file and then frees the allocated pages. The size of the capture buffer defaults to 10 pages but a user-defined value can be specified through the registry value *cpgInBuf* (a DWORD type) under the key *HKLM\System\CurrentControlSet\Services\VxD\MultiMon_bootmgr.*

When MultiMon is initially started after collecting a trace using *BOOTMGR*, the user receives a prompt advising him of the captured log and asks if he would like to view it.

MultiMon's Use of the Registry

MultiMon uses two different areas of the registry. First, it uses a typical application entry under HKEY_LOCAL_MACHINE given by *Software\OReilly\MultiMon*. The *LogDir* value found here gives the directory where session and boot log files are stored. If any dynamic monitors are installed, each driver would have a subkey under this application key. The subkey would contain the same entries as for a static monitor which we will describe below.

The second area of the registry which MultiMon utilizes is also under HKEY_LOCAL_MACHINE, in the section which defines the system's static VxDs: *System\CurrentControlSet\Services\VxD*. The Windows 95 loader enumerates the subkeys in this section. The loader attempts to load each VxD driver name given by the *StaticVxD* value in each subkey. The value of *StaticVxD* is a string which may contain a fully-qualified path.

MultiMon creates a subkey for each static driver which is displayed in the **Add/ Remove Dialog**. To prevent name collisions, the key name is formed by prepending *MultiMon_* to the driver or device name. For example, the entry for *fshook.vxd* would be *MultiMon_fshook*. The *StaticVxD* value is defined to point to the launch directory for MultiMon, where all monitor drivers are kept.

Underneath the *MultiMon_* driver key, one key will be defined for each monitor that the driver supports. Monitor keys start at 0 and increment by one for each additional monitor. For example, if the driver has two monitors, then the keys 0 and 1 will be defined. Within each monitor key several values will be defined which are used to record its default configuration. These include the values *Enabled*, *NumApi*, *Index*, and *ApiStates*.

MultiMon's Design and Implementation

When I started thinking about what MultiMon should be, I envisioned a framework which could support many different kinds of "snooping tools." I knew that as work on this book continued the need would arise for several small applets that would demonstrate or prove assertions made here. These applets would differ in how they insinuate themselves into the system and the kind of data they would generate but from that point on they were the same: they needed a conduit to deliver the data to a frontend where it could be formated and displayed. So rather than write these as several separate utilities, they are implemented as different monitor drivers for MultiMon.

Win32 Frontend

The frontend or reporter portion of MultiMon is a respectable Win32 application written in C. The user interface is based upon a dialog box which contains a list-view control and status control, so no window creation code is needed for these parts. A dialog procedure handles the requisite windows messages, like WM_INIT-DIALOG, WM_SIZE, WM_COMMAND, etc.

As far as possible, the Windows 95 common controls were leveraged to increase functionality without adding a lot of custom code. The listview control is used for output display. It has several advantages: essentially unlimited buffer size, column headers for labeling output, and easy column resizing.

At one point, I had output from the monitors being displayed directly to listview. However, this had a major drawback. Since much of the window drawing code relies heavily on 16-bit USER and GDI, it is acquiring the Win16Mutex. This created a severe bottleneck at times. To alleviate this, output is written to a log file by a separate thread, independently of the user interface thread. This creates much smoother operation and significantly reduces the impact of monitoring on system performance.

The main thread handles the message pump and responds to user input. A secondary thread is dedicated to the interface with the event manager, *sessmgr.vxd*. When events are being captured with *bootmgr.vxd*, the MultiMon application is *not* loaded.

VxD/Win32 Interface

When MultiMon initializes it looks to see if *bootmgr.vxd* is loaded. If it is found, a **DeviceIoControl** command is sent to it, requesting that it shut down any active monitors and save its capture buffer to *boot.log*. Then *sessmgr.vxd* is loaded and a secondary thread is created to interface with it.

SESSMGR also receives a list of drivers, their active monitors, and selected APIs before event capture begins. SESSMGR uses this list to initialize the monitors.

MultiMon's secondary thread also uses the **DeviceIoControl** interface to communicate with SESSMGR. As part of initialization a Win32 event object is passed to SESSMGR for synchronization with MultiMon. The secondary thread calls into SESSMGR using **DeviceIoControl** and it blocks. After an event or group of events are written to the log file, SESSMGR signals the blocked thread and it resumes execution by returning from **DeviceIoControl**. MultiMon then checks the return value from **DeviceIoControl**. An error return indicates that data collection has stopped, otherwise the **DeviceIoControl** call is repeated and the thread blocks again. This loop exits with an error when MultiMon sends SESSMGR a **DeviceIo-Control** command to stop.

During this loop SESSMGR is writing the collected events to a binary log file named *session.log*, using IFSMgr's ring-0 file I/O functions. When event collection is stopped, MultiMon reads, formats, and displays the contents of this file into the listview control.

VxD Monitors

SESSMGR creates a pool of event blocks from an area of locked memory. Event blocks hold an EBLOCK structure in which a monitor describes an event. Monitors request an event block, record the event, and then send it back to the event manager. The event manager then writes one or more event blocks to the log file and then frees the event blocks for reuse.

Communication between the event manager and the monitors is by means of private messages using VMM's **Directed_Sys_Control** API. The following messages are used:

- REQUEST_EVENT_BLK is sent by monitors to SESSMGR or BOOTMGR to request an event block.

- EVENT_NOTIFY is sent by monitors to SESSMGR or BOOTMGR to report an event.

- PRIVATE_ARM_MONITOR is sent by SESSMGR to all known monitors, to place the each monitor into an "armed" state; the monitor receives a list of APIs which are to be watched.

- PRIVATE_INIT is sent by SESSMGR to all armed monitors, to start event capture.

- PRIVATE_SHUTDOWN is sent by SESSMGR or BOOTMGR to all active monitors, to stop event capture.

- REGISTER_MONITOR is sent by a static monitor to BOOTMGR to be placed on a list to receive PRIVATE_SHUTDOWN messages.

A monitor is just a VxD which adds handlers for PRIVATE_ARM_MONITOR, PRIVATE_INIT, and PRIVATE_SHUTDOWN, and which sends REQUEST_EVENT_BLK, EVENT_NOTIFY, and perhaps REGISTER_MONITOR messages to SESSMGR or BOOTMGR.

Extending MultiMon

Extending MultiMon with a new monitor requires additions in two areas. First an existing VxD needs to be modified or a new VxD must be written, to collect the desired data. Secondly, the Win32 application has to add a new report routine for the new type of data.

Writing a Monitor

Writing a monitor involves writing a VxD. VxDs can be written in assembly language, but it is more common today to use either the C wrappers that accompany the Windows 95 DDK or a third party package called VToolsD from Vireo Software. The examples in the book use C and the DDK.

I won't attempt to review the mechanics of VxD construction here. Appendix D, *IFS Development Aids*, describes some extensions that I have added to the DDK to make the process more palatable. *Systems Programming for Windows 95* by Walter Oney, 1996, Microsoft Press, is a good book to consult for further information.

I'd like to give you a feel for how easy it is to write a monitor. To illustrate, I've come up with an example that is both simple and useful. It is sometimes handy to output strings to the trace log file to mark various execution points or perhaps print out a function's return values. This requires that you have the source to the application you are monitoring so that **DeviceIoControl** calls can be inserted. We'll only consider Win32 applications, although the idea could be extended to Win16 and DOS applications.

The implementation of the entire monitor VxD is in a single source file, *tagmon.c*, which you can find on the companion diskette. It starts off with a `Declare_DDB` macro which defines the Device Descriptor Block for the VxD. This specifies the VxD's name, initialization order, etc. so the loader will install it properly. The DDB also gives the address of the VxD's control procedure, **CtrlMsgDispatch**, which is the heart of our monitor (see Example A-1).

Example A-1. Tagmon's Control Procedure

```
void __declspec( naked ) CtrlMsgDispatch( void ) {
    BEGIN_DISPATCH_MAP
        ON_DEVICE_INIT( CtrlMsg_Device_Init )
        ON_SYS_VM_TERMINATE( CtrlMsg_Sys_VM_Terminate )
        ON_W32_DEVICEIOCONTROL( CtrlMsg_W32DeviceIoControl )
        ON_DIRECTED1( PRIVATE_ARM_MONITOR, CtrlMsg_Arm_Monitor )
        ON_DIRECTED1( PRIVATE_INIT, CtrlMsg_Private_Init )
        ON_DIRECTED0( PRIVATE_SHUTDOWN, CtrlMsg_Private_Shutdown )
        ON_DEFAULT( )
```

Example A-1. Tagmon's Control Procedure (continued)

```
END_DISPATCH_MAP
}
```

The system sends messages to each VxD's control procedure to notify it of system-wide events which it may need to respond to. The control procedure only needs to respond to messages in which it is interested.

Each line between the macros **BEGIN_DISPATCH_MAP** and **END_DISPATCH_MAP** is like a "case" statement. For example, you might read the first line as "on receiving a DEVICE_INIT message call the function **CtrlMsg_Device_Init**." From this listing you see that there are handlers for the three messages which are private to SESSMGR and our monitor. These are PRIVATE_ARM_MONITOR, PRIVATE_INIT, and PRIVATE_SHUTDOWN. The handlers for these are responsible for enabling and disabling the monitor.

The event which our monitor is going to report is actually a **DeviceIoControl** call into the VxD. This is handled by the third line, which can be read "on receiving a W32_DEVICEIOCONTROL message call the function **CtrlMsg_W32DeviceIo-Control**." The code for this handler is shown in Example A-2.

Example A-2. Tagmon's Handler for DeviceIoControl

```
int SYSCTRL_CALLBACK CtrlMsg_W32DeviceIoControl( int service,
                        PDIOCPARAMETERS pDIOCParams ) {
    switch( service ) {
        case DIOC_OPEN:
        case DIOC_CLOSEHANDLE:
            return 0;

        case DIOC_TAG_STRING:
            if ( pDIOCParams->cbInBuffer == 0 )
                return ERROR_NOT_SUPPORTED;

            MessageOut( (char*)pDIOCParams->lpvInBuffer );
            return 0L;

        default:
            return ERROR_NOT_SUPPORTED;
    }
}
```

The value of the input variable *service* can be a system-defined value such as *DIOC_OPEN* or *DIOC_CLOSEHANDLE*, or it can be a programmer-defined value like *DIOC_TAG_STRING*. When the *DIOC_TAG_STRING* service is requested, we expect the input structure **DIOCParams** to contain specific values; the member *lpvInBuffer* should point to a buffer containing a string and *cbInBuffer* should contain a non-zero count of the length of the string. When set up in this way, the Win32 application could insert a tag using a call like this:

```
    char szTagStr[80]; // string to insert in Trace Log
    DWORD cb;          // count of bytes returned
    wsprintf( szTagStr, "Calling from XXX - %d", somevar );
    DeviceIoControl( hTagmon, DIOC_TAG_STRING, szTagStr,
                     lstrlen(szTagStr), NULL, 0, &cb, 0 );
```

The function **MessageOut** is where the monitor's unique functionality resides; everything else is either part of a standard VxD framework or the handlers for private messages between TAGMON and SESSMGR.

The implementation of MessageOut is shown in Example A-3. It uses two private messages to communicate with SESSMGR's control procedure: REQUEST_EVENT_ BLK to get an EBLOCK to report an event, and EVENT_NOTIFY to report the event. REQUEST_EVENT_BLK returns TRUE and an EBLOCK's address in *pb* if it is successful; it returns FALSE and a non-NULL value in *pb* if this is the last EBLOCK; it returns FALSE and a NULL value in *pb* when the buffer is exhausted. This arrangement gives the caller a chance to report an OVR_ERROR event when the last EBLOCK is returned.

Example A-3. Inserting a Tag into a Trace Log

```
void MessageOut( char* pstr ) {
    PEBLOCK pb;
    if (Directed_Sys_Control1(pSessMgr, REQUEST_EVENT_BLK, &pb)) {
        // We allocate the block zero initialized
        pb->type = TAG_STRING;
        memcpy( pb->szModName, TAGMON_DDB.DDB_Name, 8 );
        memcpy( pb->onestr, pstr, 31 );
        Directed_Sys_Control1( pSessMgr, EVENT_NOTIFY, pb );
        }
    else if ( pb != NULL ) {
        pb->type = OVR_ERROR;
        Directed_Sys_Control1( pSessMgr, EVENT_NOTIFY, pb );
        }
    }
```

Adding to the Reporter

Let's continue this example by making the necessary additions to MultiMon to support tag strings. The first place to start is with the header file *monitor.h*. You need to make entries for a new monitor in three tables in this header file: **Monitors[]**, **DisplayHandler[]**, and **FilterFuncs[]**. **Monitors[]** is an array of **MONDEF** structures, one structure per monitor. A **MONDEF** has the definition given in Example A-4. To add a new entry to **Monitors[]** you only need to worry about a few of **MONDEF**'s members. First you need to give it a *name* that will be used in the **Filter** dialog, e.g., "Tag Strings". Then you should determine a value for *numApis*, i.e., how many different APIs you need to distinguish. For instance, the API monitor for VCACHE has the value 25 which corresponds to the number of services which VCACHE exports. Since TAGMON does not have any APIs, we use 0. Next, insert the device name of the driver which is to contain the monitor in the member *szDevName*. The rest of the members are initialized to 0 or NULL, as appropriate. If you have more than one monitor in your driver, you need to bump *iMon* by 1 for each additional monitor.

Example A-4. MONDEF Structure

```
typedef struct {
    UINT flags;          // bit0:installed, bit1:enabled
    BOOL bChecked;       // monitor checked in Filters dialog
    int iMon;            // 0-based index for monitor in this driver
    char* name;          // User-friendly monitor name
    int numApis;         // number of APIs monitored
    UINT* pApiState;     // array of enabled/disabled states
    char szDevName[9];// device name for Monitor
    } MONDEF, *PMONDEF;
```

To finish up our additions to *monitor.h*, add a display handler function to `DisplayHandler[]` and a filter function to `FilterFuncs[]`. Precede these tables with "extern" declarations for these new functions.

The common index to these three data structures is defined by a unqiue manifest constant which is added to *multimon.h*. For TAGMON, we will use the constant *TAG_STRING*. This index is used as the type in the EBLOCK structure.

With the data structures taken care of, we need to now write some code—the display handler and filter function. The display handler function is called to return a string for each column of the listview display. The prototype for the function has this form:

```
    void  Display_Handler(int iSubItem,PEBLOCK pb,char* pszText)
```

where *iSubItem* is the zero-based index to the listview column, *pb* is a pointer to a data structure describing the event, and *pszText* is a pointer to a buffer in which to insert the string. The contents of an EBLOCK consists of some predefined header information followed by an area that is free-format. A monitor will typically define a structure to fill this area. The display handler for our TAGMON monitor is shown in Example A-5.

Example A-5. Display Handler for TAGMON

```
void Display_Handler_Tagmon( int iSubItem, PEBLOCK pb,
char* pszText ) {
    *pszText = '\0';
    switch( iSubItem ) {
        case 0 :            // Module - Module Name
            strcpy( pszText, pb->szModName );
            break;
        case 1 :            // Type - Type of Monitor
```

Example A-5. Display Handler for TAGMON

```
            strcpy( pszText, "tag" );
            break;
        case 2 :                // Function - Function Name
            strcpy( pszText, pb->onestr );
            break;
        case 3 :                // Flags1 - flags common to all functions
        case 4 :                // Device - Device Name
        case 5 :                // Handle - System File Number (SFN)
        case 6 :                // Args - arguments specific to this function
        case 7 :                // Flags2 - flags specific to this function
        default:
            break;
        }
    }
```

The filter function is called to return a string which describes an API. This is used to populate the listview control in the **Filter** dialog. The prototype for the function has this form:

```
    char* Filter_Func(int index)
```

It returns a pointer to a static string.

The display handler and filter function along with static string tables are placed in a separate C file and added to the build. Some additional examples of extension files can be found on the companion diskette: *hookmon.c, vcmon.c, int2fmon.c,* etc.

B

MultiMon: Monitor Reference

MultiMon comes with the monitors listed in Table A-1 of Appendix A, *MultiMon: Setup, Usage, and Extensions.* The kind of output produced by each of these monitors is quite varied and yet MultiMon presents this information using the same view. This appendix describes in detail the information displayed by each monitor and thus serves as a reference.

Generally, a single line of output describes a single event. However, in some instances, the information will not conveniently fit in a single line, and so a second line of output is reported for the same event. You will see this approach with the file system hook, FSHook. When displaying traces of services, it is sometimes useful to show the entry values on one line and then the return values on a separate line. Another thing to keep in mind when examining traces is that some monitors report an event when an API completes, and other monitors report an event on entry into an API.

In the descriptions that follow, a C `printf` format is used to define output strings. These format strings are enclosed in double quotes, while arguments are represented by suggestive variable names, e.g., `"drive=%c"`, `drive_letter`.

Interrupt 21h

Driver	Monitor	Type
I21Help1	PM Int21 hook (pre IFSMgr)	p21
I21Help1	V86 Int21 hook (pre IFSMgr)	v21
I21Help2	PM Int21 hook (post IFSMgr)	p21-
I21Help2	V86 Int21 hook (post IFSMgr)	v21-
Win32cb	VWIN32 Int21 Dispatch	w21

ListView Column Usage

Module:

Module owning execution thread

Function:

Int 21h function name

Flags1:

Not used

Device:

Not used

Handle:

DOS (SFT) or extended (SFN) file handle

Args by function:

39h, 3ah, 3bh, 3ch, 3dh, 41h, 43h, 4bh, 4eh, 5ah, 5bh, 6ch, 7139h, 713ah, 713bh, 7141h, 7143h, 714eh, 7160h, 716ch	"%s", szPathname
36h, 47h, 7147h, 4404h, 4405h, 4408h, 4409h, 440dh, 440eh, 440fh, 4411h	"drive=%c", drive_letter
3fh, 40h	"cnt=%x buf=%x:%04x", byte_count, buffer_segment, buffer_offset
42h	"(%d) offs=%08lx", seek_mode, seek_offset
50h	"seg=%04x", PSP_segment

Flags2 by function:

7143h	Gt(GET_ATTRIBUTES) St(SET_ATTRIBUTES) Gs(GET_ATTRIB_COMP_FILESIZE) Sm(SET_ATTRIB_MODIFY_DATETIME) Gm(GET_ATTRIB_MODIFY_DATETIME) Sa(SET_ATTRIB_LAST_ACCESS_DATETIME) Ga(GET_ATTRIB_LAST_ACCESS_DATETIME) Sc(SET_ATTRIB_CREATION_DATE_TIME) Gc(GET_ATTRIB_CREATION_DATE_TIME) Gu(GET_ATTRIB_FIRST_CLUST)

Interrupt 2Fh

Driver	Monitor	Type
I2fmon1	PM Int2f hook (pre IFSMgr)	p2f
I2fmon1	V86 Int2f hook (pre IFSMgr)	v2f

ListView Column Usage

Module:
Module owning execution thread

Function:
Int 2fh function name

Flags1:
Not used

Device:
For function 1684 only, "%s(%xh)", device_name, device_id

Handle:
Not used

Args:
Not used

Flags2:
Not used

IFSMgr Dispatcher

Driver	Monitor	Type
ifsdspat	IFSMgr dispatcher	dsp

ListView Column Usage

Module:
Module owning execution thread

Function:
"Func=%08lx", register_ECX

Flags1:
Not used

Device:
Not used

Handle:
Not used

Args:
"EDX=%08lx ESI=%08lx", register_EDX, provider

Flags2:
Not used

IFSMgr File System Hook

Driver	Monitor	Type
fshook	IFSMgr file system hook	fsh

ListView Column Usage

Module:

Module owning execution thread

Function:

FS_xxx function name

Flags1:

Flags common to all functions represented by string of characters: *e_clnu_ slxrmwoa*

e   command failure

c   character resource

l   local resource

n   network resource

u   UNC resource

s   IFSMgr_ServerDOSCall

l   LFN call

x   uses extended handles

r   IFSMgr_Ring0_FileIO

m   8.3 match semantics

w   Win32 caller

o   Unicode/BCS string

a   ANSI/OEM

Device:

Name of FSD being called

Handle:

System File Number (SFN) asterisk indicates newly created or opened handle

Args (line 1):

Arguments specific to a function

IFSFN_READ, IFSFN_WRITE	cnt=%lxH ofs=%lxH ptr=%lxH, byte_count, file_position, linear_buf_address
IFSFN_SEEK	ofs=%lxH, file_position

IFSFN_GETDISKINFO	"drive: %c free: %08lx", drive_letter, free_space
IFSFN_QUERY(level 2)	"Level2 drive: %c", drive_letter
IFSFN_QUERY(level 1)	"Level1 drive: %c", drive_letter
IFSFN_CONNECT(local disk volume)	"drive: %c", drive_letter
IFSFN_IOCTL16DRIVE, IFSFN_GETDIS-KPARMS, IFSFN_FLUSH	"drive: %c", drive_letter
IFSFN_DASDIO (DIO_ABS_READ_SECTORS)-(DIO_ABS_WRITE_SECTORS)	"cnt=%lxH sector=%lxH ptr=%lxH", byte_count, absolute_sector, linear_buf_address
IFSFN_DASDIO (DIO_SET_LOCK_CACHE_STATE)	"Level 0 taken" or "Level 0 released", or "Level 3 taken" or "Level 3 released"

Args (line 2):

Pathname or filename argument

Flags2:

Flags specific to a function

IFSFN_READ, IFSFN_WRITE	flags "msn": **m**— memory-mapped R0 I/O; **s**—called by swapper; **n**—no caching of read/write
IFSFN_SEEK	flag character: **b**—seek relative to beginning of file; **e**—seek relative to end of file
IFSFN_CLOSE, IFSFN_FINDCLOSE, IFSFN_FCNCLOSE	flag: **f**—CLOSE_FINAL, **p**—CLOSE_FOR_PROCESS, **h**—CLOSE_HANDLE
IFSFN_COMMIT	flag: **a**—FILE_COMMIT_ASYNC, **n**—FILE_NO_LAST_ACCESS_DATE
IFSFN_FILELOCKS	flag: **L**—LOCK_REGION, **U**—UNLOCK_REGION
IFSFN_FILETIMES	**Gm**(GET_MODIFY_DATETIME) **Sm**(SET_MODIFY_DATETIME) **Ga**(GET_LAST_ACCESS_DATETIME) **Sa**(SET_LAST_ACCESS_DATETIME) **Gc**(GET_CREATION_DATE_TIME) **Sc**(SET_CREATION_DATE_TIME)
IFSFN_ENUMHANDLE	**fi** ENUMH_GETFILEINFO *get file info by handle* **fn** ENUMH_GETFILENAME *get filename associated with handle* **ir**ENUMH_GETFINDINFO *get info for resuming* **rf** ENUMH_RESUMEFIND *resume find operation* **rd** ENUMH_RESYNCFILEDIR *resync dir entry info for file*

IFSFN_CONNECT(Network)	flags "x y", where x is: **r**(RESOPT_UNCREQUEST) **e**(RESOPT_DEVATTACH) **c**(RESOPT_UNCCONNECT) **d**(RESOPT_DISCONNECTED) **n**(RESOPT_NO_CREATE) **s**(RESOPT_STATIC) and where y is: *****(RESTYPE_WILD) **d**(RESTYPE_DISK) **s**(RESTYPE_SPOOL) **c**(RESTYPE_CHARDEV) **i**(RESTYPE_IPC)
IFSFN_CONNECT(Local)	flag character: **m**(IR_FSD_MOUNT) **v**(IR_FSD_VERIFY) **g**(IR_FSD_UNLOAD) **c**(IR_FSD_MOUNT_CHILD) **p**(IR_FSD_MAP_DRIVE) **u**(IR_FSD_UNMAP_DRIVE)
IFSFN_DIR	option string: **mk**(CREATE_DIR), **rm**(DELETE_DIR), **ck**(CHECK_DIR), **83**(QUERY83_DIR), **lf**(QUERYLONG_DIR)
IFSFN_FILEATTRIB	option string: **Gt**(GET_ATTRIBUTES) **St**(SET_ATTRIBUTES) **Gs**(GET_ATTRIB_COMP_FILESIZE) **Sm**(SET_ATTRIB_MODIFY_DATETIME) **Gm**(GET_ATTRIB_MODIFY_DATETIME) **Sa**(SET_ATTRIB_LAST_ACCESS_DATETIME) **Ga**(GET_ATTRIB_LAST_ACCESS_DATETIME) **Sc**(SET_ATTRIB_CREATION_DATE_TIME)
IFSFN_FILEATTRIB (cont.)	**Gc**(GET_ATTRIB_CREATION_DATE_TIME), **Gu**(GET_ATTRIB_FIRST_CLUST)
IFSFN_FLUSH	flag character: **d**(VOL_DISCARD_CACHE) **r**(VOL_REMOUNT)
IFSFN_SEARCH	flag character: **f**(SEARCH_FIRST) **n**(SEARCH_NEXT)
IFSFN_DISCONNECT	flag character: **n**(DISCONNECT_NORMAL) **i**(DISCONNECT_NO_IO) **s**(DISCONNECT_SINGLE)

IFSFN_OPEN	option string, "x y" where x is (open action value): **cn**(ACTION_CREATENEW (10h)) **ca**(ACTION_CREATEALWAYS (12h)) **oe**(ACTION_OPENEXISTING (01h)) **oa**(ACTION_OPENALWAYS (11h)) **re**(ACTION_REPLACEEXISTING (02h)) and y, is (special option): **m**(MM_READ_WRITE (8000h)) **c**(OPEN_FLAGS_COMMIT (4000h)) **e**(OPEN_FLAGS_NO_CRITERR (2000h)) **s**(R0_SWAPPER_CALL (1000h)) **r**(OPEN_FLAGS_REOPEN (0800h)) **a**(OPEN_FLAGS_ALIAS_HINT (0400h)) **p**(OPEN_FLAGS_NO_COMPRESS (0200h)) **n**(OPEN_FLAGS_NO_CACHE (0100h)) **i**(OPEN_FLAGS_NOINHERIT (0080h))
IFSFN_DASDIO -DIO_ABS_READ_SECTORS	option string "Read"
IFSFN_DASDIO -DIO_ABS_WRITE_SECTORS	option string "Write"
IFSFN_DASDIO -DIO_SET_LOCK_CACHE_STATE	option string "Volume Lock"

IFSMgr_NetFunction Hook

Driver	Monitor	Type
netfunc	IFSMgr_NetFunction hook	nfh

ListView Column Usage

Module:

Module owning execution thread

Function:

Func=%08lx, Client_AX, where Client_AX contains the following values for IFS Manager broadcasts:

NF_PROCEXIT (111Dh)	NF_PRINTERUSE (0004h)
NF_DRIVEUSE (0001h)	NF_PRINTERUNUSE (0005h)
NF_DRIVEUNUSE (0002h)	NF_NetSetUserName (1181h)
NF_GETPRINTJOBID (0003h)	

or Client_AX contains the function number for **Upper8E_Preambles** installed using **IFSMgr_SetReqHook**.

Flags1:

Not used

Device:

Not used

Handle:

Not used

Args:

"EDX=%08lx ESI=%08lx", ifsreq.ifs_func, provider

Flags2:

Not used

Interrupts and Callbacks

Driver	Monitor	Type
vectors	Interrupts and Callbacks	vec

ListView Column Usage

Module:

Module owning execution thread

Function:

VMM Service Names, including:

Install_V86_Break_Point	Allocate_V86_Call_Back
Allocate_PM_Call_Back	Hook_V86_Int_Chain
Get_V86_Int_Vector	Set_V86_Int_Vector
Get_PM_Int_Vector	Set_PM_Int_Vector

Flags1:

"Entry" or "Return" depending on which side of the service the display line was generated.

Device:

Not used

Handle:

On entry, interrupt number as a string "Int %x"

Args by service:

On entry:

Install_V86_Break_Point	"V86 BrkPt=%X:%04X Ring0 Function=%08lx (%s)", brk_segment, brk_offset, func_addr, VxD_Name
Allocate_V86_Call_Back	"Ring0 Function=%08lx (%s)", func_addr, Vxd_Name
Allocate_PM_Call_Back	"Ring0 Function=%08lx (%s)", func_addr, Vxd_Name
Hook_V86_Int_Chain	"Ring0 Hook=%08lx (%s)", func_addr, Vxd_Name
Get_V86_Int_Vector, Set_V86_Int_Vector	"V86 Vector=%X:%04X", V86_segment, V86_offset
Get_PM_Int_Vector, Set_PM_Int_Vector	"PM Vector=%X:%lX", PM_selector, PM_offset

On return:

Allocate_V86_Call_Back	"V86 App Callback: %x:%04x", V86_callback_segment, V86_callback_offset
Allocate_PM_Call_Back	"PM App Callback: %x:%04x", PM_callback_selector, PM_callback_offset

Flags2:

Not used

VCACHE Services

Driver	Monitor	Type
vchook	VCache services	vch

ListView Column Usage

Module:

Module owning execution thread

Function:

Entry: VCACHE service name

Return: Return, except for **VCache_FindBlock**, which displays the string "Return [Carry] [Locked]"

Flags1:

Options on entry to **VCache_FindBlock**:

Create	Hold	MakeMRU
LowPri	MustCreate	RemoveFromLRU

Device:

FSD cache ID

Handle:

Cache block handle

Args by function:

VCache_Get_Version(Return)	Ver: %04x, version_number
VCache_Register(Return)	"DiscardFunc: %08lx MinReserv: %lx", buffer_discard_func, min_reserved_blocks
VCache_GetSize(Return)	*For a specific FSD ID:* "MaxFSDBlks: %lx MaxCacheBlks: %lx", max_blocks_for_fsd, max_num_cache_blocks *For any FSD (id=0):* "CurCacheSize: %lx MaxCacheBlks: %lx", num_blocks_in_cache, max_num_cache_blocks
VCache_CheckAvail(Entry)	"Needed: %lx", num_blocks_needed
VCache_CheckAvail(Return)	"Avail: %lx", num_avail_blocks
VCache_FindBlock(Entry)	"Key1: %08lx Key2: %08lx", key1_value, key2_value
VCache_FindBlock(Return)	"Buffer: %08lx", addr_of_buffer (if non-zero handle)
VCache_Enum	"EnumFunc: %08lx", enum_function_addr
VCache_VerifySums VCache_RecalcSums	"SectorSize: %lx", sector_size_in_bytes
VCache_TestHold(Return)	"HoldCnt: %d", block_hold_count
VCache_GetStats	"Misses: %d Hits: %d Discards: %d VCache: %08lx", misses_to_last26_discards, hits_to_last26_lru, num_discards_since_last_call, linear_base_addr
VCache_AdjustMinimum	"New Quota: %08lx", new_quota_size
VCache_SwapBuffers	"BlockHdl1: %08lx BlockHdl2: %08lx", cache_block1, cache_block2
VCache_RelinquishPage	"RelPage: %08lx", linear_addr_of_page
VCache_UseThisPage	"AddPage: %08lx", linear_addr_of_page

_VCache_CreateLookupCache	"CacheName: %s MaxElems: %d Flags: %08lx", lookup_name, max_elements, ptr_cache_handle
_VCache_DeleteLookupCache	"CacheName: %s", cache_name
_VCache_Lookup _VCache_UpdateLookup	"Key: \%s\ Data len: %d", lookup_name, data_len

Flags2:

Not used

VWIN32 Win32 Services

Driver	Monitor	Type
win32cb	VWIN32 Win32 Services	vw32

ListView Column Usage

Module:

Module owning execution thread

Function:

VWin32 Win32 service name

Flags1:

Not used

Device:

Not used

Handle:

Not used

Args:

Not used

Flags2:

Not used

VWIN32 DeviceIoControl (IFSMgr, VWIN32, WSOCK)

Driver	Monitor	Type
win32cb	VWIN32 DeviceIoControl	dev

ListView Column Usage

Module:

Module owning execution thread

Function:

Func=%08lx, Client_AX

Function:

Open Device, Close Device, or **dwIoControlCode**

Control codes for IFSMgr, VWIN32, and WSOCK are labeled

Flags1:

Not used

Device:

VxD device name

Handle:

For WSOCK calls, handle context address

Args:

For WSOCK calls, arguments to functions

Flags2:

Not used

VMM Win32 Services

Driver	Monitor	Type
win32cb	VMM Win32 services	vm32

ListView Column Usage

Module:

Module owning execution thread

Function:

VMM Win32 service name

Flags1:

Not used

Device:

Not used

Handle:

Not used

Args:

Arguments specific to a function as array of unlabeled doubleword values

Flags2:

Not used

NetBIOS Calls

Driver	Monitor	Type
nbhook	NetBIOS calls	ncb

ListView Column Usage

Module:

Module owning execution thread

Function:

NetBIOS service name

Flags1:

Entry: if call is asynchronous, "async" will appear here

Return: if call was asynchronous, "post(%02x)", ncb_returncode, will appear here

Device:

Lana=%02x, lana_number

Handle:

Address of NCB (Network Control Block)

Args:

Entry arguments specific to a function

NCBCALL, NCBLISTEN, NCBADDNAME, NCBDELNAME, NCBADDGRNAME	"Callname: %s", ncb_callname
NCBHANGUP, NCBRESET	"LSN: %02x", ncb_lsn
NCBSEND, NCBRECV, NCBSENDNA	"LSN: %02x Buffer: %08lx(%04x)", ncb_lsn, ncb_buffer, ncb_length
NCBRECVANY, NCBDGRECV, NCBDGSENDBC, NCBDGRECVBC, NCBSSTAT, NCBACTION, NCBENUM, NCBFINDNAME	"Buffer: %08lx(%04x)", ncb_buffer, ncb_length
NCBCANCEL	"Canceled NCB: %08lx", addr_of_ncb
NCBDGSEND, NCBASTAT	"Buffer: %08lx(%04x) Callname: %s", ncb_buffer, ncb_length, ncb_callname

0x48 (Send-Receive)	"LSN: %02x SendBuf: %08lx(%04x) RecvBuf: %08lx(%04x)", ncb_lsn, ncb_buffer, ncb_length, buffer_dword, buffer_word
NCBCHAINSEND, NCBCHAINSENDNA:	"LSN: %02x Buffer1: %08lx(%04x) Buffer2: %08lx(%04x)", ncb_lsn, ncb_buffer, ncb_length, buffer_dword, buffer_word
NCBTRACE, NCBLANSTALERT, NCBUNLINK:	Nothing displayed
Default	"Buffer: %08lx(%04x) Callname: %s", ncb_buffer, ncb_length, ncb_callname

Args:

Return values specific to a function

NCBCALL	"LSN: %02x*", ncb_lsn
0x48 (Send-Receive)	"RecvBuf: %08lx(%04x)", ncb_buffer, ncb_length
NCBRECVANY:	"LSN: %02x Length: %04x", ncb_lsn, ncb_length

Flags2:

Flags specific to a function

NCBRECVANY, NCBDGSEND, NCBDGRECV, NCBDGSENDBC, NCBDGRECVBC, NCBRESET, 0x48(Send-Receive)	"NAME#: %02x", ncb_num

SMB Packets

Driver	Monitor	Type
nbhook	SMB packets	smb

ListView Column Usage

Module:

Module owning execution thread

Function:

SMB command name; up to three batched commands may be listed

Flags1:

Entry: request

Return: reply

Device:

Not used

Handle:

Address of NCB (Network Control Block) whose buffer references the SMB command

Args:

Arguments specific to a function

SMB_COM_OPEN	"%s", pathname_or_domain
SMB_COM_OPEN_ANDX	
SMB_COM_TREE_CONNECT	
SMB_COM_SESSION_SETUP_ANDX	
SMB_COM_TREE_CONNECT_ANDX	
SMB_COM_TRANSACTION	"%s SubCommand:%02x", mailslot_or_namedpipe, subcommand_code
SMB_COM_TRANSACTION2	Subcommands 0 through 0x0e: "%s", trans2_subcommand_name

Flags2:

Not used

C

IFSMgr Data Structures

Knowing the layout of IFSMgr's key data structures is fundamental to reaching an understanding of IFSMgr's operation. In this appendix, various undocumented data structures utilized by IFSMgr are defined. These structures are also available in the header file *ifsmgrex.h* on the companion diskette. These data strucutes are valid for IFSMgr version 22h. Your driver or file hook should verify this version number before using these structures.

Several of the undocumented structures are displayed by a debug command in the IFSMgr version which accompanies OSR2. This version of IFSMgr has a so-called "dot" command which is invoked by typing **.ifsmgr** from the WDEB386 or WinIce prompt. This command will display the contents (and member names) for structures such as **ifsreq**, **shres**, and **fhandle**.

The ioreq Structure

This data structure is defined in *ifs.h* and described in detail in the DDK documentation. Many IFSMgr APIs and interfaces are passed a pointer to an **ioreq** structure, which in reality is an **ioreq** structure embedded in an **ifsreq** structure. The reason the **ioreq** structure is emphasized by the DDK is that it is the only portion of an **ifsreq** structure which an FSD should know or care about; the other portions of the **ifsreq** structure are for IFSMgr's eyes only. The **ioreq** structure is discussed at length in Chapter 6, *Dispatching File System Requests*.

```
typedef struct {
    DWORD    ir_length;   /* 00 - length of user buffer (eCX) */
    BYTE     ir_flags;    /* 04 - misc. status flags (AL) */
    BYTE     ir_user;     /* 05 - user ID for this request */
    WORD     ir_sfn;      /* 06 - System File Number of file handle */
    DWORD    ir_pid;      /* 08 - process ID of requesting task */
    DWORD    ir_ppath;    /* 0C - pointer to unicode pathname */
```

```
    DWORD      ir_aux1;    /* 10 - secondary user data buffer (CurDTA) */
    DWORD      ir_data;    /* 14 - ptr to user data buffer (DS:eDX) */
    WORD       ir_options; /* 18 - request handling options */
    WORD       ir_error;   /* 1A - error code (0 if OK) */
    DWORD      ir_rh;      /* 1C - resource handle OWNED by FSD */
    DWORD      ir_fh;      /* 20 - file (or find) handle OWNED by FSD */
    DWORD      ir_pos;     /* 24 - file position for request */
    DWORD      ir_aux2;    /* 28 - misc. extra API parameters */
    DWORD      ir_aux3;    /* 2C - misc. extra API parameters */
    DWORD      ir_pev;     /* 30 - ptr to IFSMgr event for async
                                   requests */
    DWORD      ir_fsd[16]; /* 34 - Provider work space */
    } ioreq;
```

The ifsreq Structure

When an IFSMgr API calls for a pointer to an **ioreq** structure, it actually receives an **ifsreq** structure. This works because the first member of **ifsreq** is a nested **ioreq** structure. This structure is discussed at length in Chapter 6. Member names are based on output from OSR2's **.ifsmgr** command.

```
    typedef struct {
      ioreq        ifs_ir;        /* 0   embedded ioreq structure */
      /* These members are known only to IFSMgr */
      fhandle*     ifs_pfh;       /* 74  pointer to fhandle structure */
      DWORD        ifs_psft;      /* 78  pointer to SFT */
      shres*       ifs_psr;       /* 7C  pointer to shell resource */
      DWORD        ifs_pdb;       /* 80  linear base of owner PSP */
      DWORD        ifs_proid;     /* 84  provider id */
      BYTE         ifs_func;      /* 88  function of dispatched command */
      BYTE         ifs_drv;       /* 89  drive from dispatched command */
      BYTE         ifs_hflag;     /* 8A  flag */
      BYTE         ifs_nflags;    /* 8B  flags, see Table C-1 */
      void*        ifs_pbuffer;   /* 8C  pointer to parse buffer */
      HVM          ifs_VMHandle;  /* 90  VM of request */
      void*        ifs_PV;        /* 94  pointer to "per VM data" area */

      union {
        Client_Register  ifs_crs;            /* 98  client registers for
                                                     dispatch */
        Ring0_Register   ifs_ring0_frame;    /* 98  client registers for
                                                     ring0 file i/o */
        ServerDos_Register ifs_server_frame; /* 98  client registers for
                                                     server DosCall */
      }
    } ifsreq;
```

Volume Information (volinfo)

The **volinfo** structures are referenced by pointers in the **SysVolTable** array (see Chapter 6, Figure 6-2). The **volinfo** structure is used to support **subst** drives (see

Table C-1. Bit Usage for ifs_nflags

Bit Number	Meaning
7	**IFSMgr_ServerDosCall**
6	LFN
5	Uses extended handles
4	**IFSMgr_Ring0_FileIO**
3	8.3 match semantics
2	Win32 API
1	Unicode/BCS
0	OEM/ANSI

Chapter 8, Figure 8-1); it also holds references to the CDS structure and the shell resource structure.

```
typedef struct {
    shres*   vi_psr;         /* 00 ptr shell resource for volume */
    char*    vi_pszRootDir;  /* 04 path following drive & colon in CDS */
    WORD     vi_Client_CX;   /* 08 */
    BYTE     vi_unk1;        /* 0A */
    BYTE     vi_flags;       /* 0B  Volume is subst drive 0x10
                                    ?                      0x08
                                    ?                      0x04
                                    Static connection      0x02
                                    ?                      0x01 */
    WORD     vi_leng;        /* 0C length of Unicode subst path */
    BYTE     vi_unk2;        /* 0E */
    BYTE     vi_drv;         /* 0F one-based volume */
    string_t vi_subst_path;  /* 10 Unicode Subst path */
    void*    vi_CDS_copy;    /* 14 Copy of CDS */
} volinfo;
```

Shell Resource (shres)

The shell resource is the key data structure used by IFSMgr to represent volumes, connections to network shares, and character devices. Chapter 6 and Chapter 8 give numerous examples of the creation and use of shell resources. Member names are based on output from OSR2's **.ifsmgr** command.

```
typedef struct {
    WORD         sr_sig;      /* 00 signature 'Sr' */
    BYTE         sr_serial;   /* 02 */
    BYTE         sr_idx;      /* 03 offset of entry in psr list */
    struct shres *sr_next;    /* 04 next link in one-way linked
                                    list */
    DWORD        sr_rh;       /* 08 FSD's volume handle */
    struct volfunc *sr_func;  /* 0C FSD's volume function table */
    DWORD        sr_inUse;    /* 10 reference count */
    WORD         sr_uword;    /* 14 zero-based volume number */
```

```
        WORD        sr_HndCnt;          /* 16 count of open handles on
                                             volume */
        BYTE        sr_UNCCnt;          /* 18 */
        BYTE        sr_DrvCnt;          /* 19 number of volinfo structures
                                             referencing this sr*/
        BYTE        sr_rtype;           /* 1A 0 - wild
                                             1 - local disk
                                             2 - spooled printer
                                             3 - character device
                                             4 - IPC (named pipe) */
        BYTE        sr_flags;           /* 1B IFSFH_RES_CFSD -    0x80
                                             IFSFH_RES_LOCAL -   0x10
                                             IFSFH_RES_NETWORK, 0x08
                                             IFSFH_RES_UNC,     0x01 */
        DWORD       sr_ProID;           /* 1C index to MountVolTable[] */
        void*       sr_VolInfo;         /* 20 pointer to VRP (only local
                                             drive) */
        fhandle*    sr_fhandleHead;     /* 24 pointer to one-way linked list
                                             of open files */
        DWORD       sr_LockPid;         /* 28 pid of lock owner */
        DWORD       sr_LockSavFunc;     /* 2C */
        BYTE        sr_LockType;        /* 30 type of volume lock in place:
                                             0 - no lock in effect
                                             1 - level 0 lock in effect
                                             2 - level 1 lock in effect
                                             3 - level 2 lock in effect
                                             4 - level 3 lock in effect */
        BYTE        sr_PhysUnit;        /* 31 */
        WORD        sr_LockFlags;       /* 32 flags related to volume lock
                                             state */
        DWORD       sr_LockOwner;       /* 34 ring 0 thread ID of lock
                                             owner */
        WORD        sr_LockWaitCnt;     /* 38 */
        WORD        sr_LockReadCnt;     /* 3A */
        WORD        sr_LockWriteCnt;    /* 3C */
        BYTE        sr_flags2;          /* 3E */
        BYTE        sr_reserved;        /* 3F */
        void*       sr_pnv;             /* 40 */
        } shres;
```

The fhandle Structure

The fhandle is the key data structure used by IFSMgr to represent handles to
files and character devices. Chapter 6 gives examples of the use of file handles.
Member names are based on output from OSR2's **.ifsmgr** command.

```
    typedef struct {
        struct hndlfunc fh_hf;          /* 00 ptr to FSD's handle-based
                                             function table */
        fh_t        fh_fh;              /* 0C FSD's file handle */
        shres*      fh_psr;             /* 10 ptr to shell resource which
                                             contains object */
        void*       fh_pSFT;            /* 14 ptr to DOS SFT structure */
```

```
    DWORD           fh_position;    /* 18 */
    WORD            fh_devflags;    /* 1C */
    BYTE            fh_hflag;       /* 1E */
    BYTE            fh_type;        /* 1F */
    WORD            fh_ref_count;   /* 20 */
    WORD            fh_mode;        /* 22 */
    hlockinfo*      fh_hlockinfo;   /* 24 ptr to hlockinfo structure */
    void*           fh_prev;        /* 28 ptr to previous fhandle in
                                          linked-list */
    void*           fh_next;        /* 2C ptr to next fhandle in
                                          linked-list */
    WORD            fh_sfn;         /* 30 system file number for
                                          handle */
    WORD            fh_mmsfn;       /* 32 SFN for memory-mapped file
                                          dup */
    DWORD           fh_pid;         /* 34 */
    DWORD           fh_ntid;        /* 38 */
    WORD            fh_fhFlags;     /* 3C */
    WORD            fh_InCloseCnt;  /* 3E */
    } fhandle;
```

The hlockinfo Structure

This structure is used to defined a file lock:

```
typedef struct {
    struct hndlfunc hl;             /* 00 */
    DWORD           hl_lock;        /* 0C */
    DWORD           hl_flags;       /* 10 */
    DWORD           hl_pathlen;     /* 14 */
    unsigned short  hl_pathname[0]; /* 18 */
    } hlockinfo;
```

The SFT Structure

The SFT (System File Tables) is a legacy MS-DOS structure. The following layout is for DOS 4.0 or newer and is based on *Undocumented DOS*, Second Edition, by Andrew Schulman and others (see pages 709-710).

```
typedef struct {
    WORD        sft_numhandles;
    WORD        sft_openmode;
    BYTE        sft_attrib;
    WORD        sft_devinfo;
    void*       sft_devheader;
    WORD        sft_start_cluster;
    WORD        sft_file_time;
    WORD        sft_file_date;
    DWORD       sft_file_size;
    DWORD       sft_cur_offset;
    WORD        sft_rel_cluster;
    DWORD       sft_sector_direntry;
```

```
    BYTE        sft_num_direntry;
    char        sft_fcbname[11];
    void*       sft_prev;
    WORD        sft_vmid;
    WORD        sft_psp_segment;
    WORD        sft_offset;
    WORD        sft_abs_cluster;
    DWORD       sft_dos_driver;
    } sft;
```

The CDS Structure

The CDS (Current Directory Structure) is a legacy MS-DOS structure. The following layout is for DOS 4.0 or newer and is also based on *Undocumented DOS* (see pages 710-711).

```
    typedef struct {
        char    cds_root_pathname[67];       /* 00 ASCIIZ root directory */
        WORD    cds_attrib;                  /*    Drive attributes */
        BYTE    cds_physdrv;
        BYTE    cds_flag;
        WORD    cds_cluster_parent_dir;
        WORD    cds_entry_num;
        WORD    cds_cluster_current_dir;
        WORD    cds_media_change;
        WORD    cds_ofs_visible_dir;
        } cds;
```

Per-VM Data

During Device Init, IFSMgr allocates per-VM data using the service **Allocate_ Device_CB_Area**. The size of this area is determined by the following formula:

```
    cb_area_size = sizeof(pervm) + ((256 + NumDosFCBs) * sizeof(void*) * 2)
```

What is returned by this service is the offset to IFSMgr's per-VM data from the address given by the VM handle. It is the sum of these two values which is stored in *ifsreq.ifs_PV*.

The layout of IFSMgr's per-VM data is divided into three areas. At the beginning of the area is the **pervm** structure given below. It is followed by two additional tables of equal size which will hold pointers for up to 256 SFT entries plus pointers for FCB's inherited from MSDOS before Windows 95 started. The second of these two tables is pointed at by the **pervm** member *pv_ppsft*.

```
    typedef struct {
        void*   pv_next;        /* 00 */
        void*   pv_prev;        /* 04 */
        BYTE    pv_flags;       /* 08  bit 0 */
                                /*     bit 1 */
```

```
                                    /*      bit 2 */
                                    /*      bit 3 */
                                    /*      bit 4  Local Int21 hooker*/
                                    /*      bit 5  Control-C check */
                                    /*      bit 6 */
                                    /*      bit 7 */
    BYTE        pv_cnt;             /* 09 */
    BYTE        pv_curdrv;          /* 0A */
    BYTE        pv_unk2;            /* 0B */
    void*       pv_dispfunc;        /* 0C  address of dispatch function */
    ifsreq*     pv_pifs;            /* 10  active ifsreq */
    pevent      pv_pev_vm;          /* 14  VM tasktime event */
    DWORD       pv_Client_DS;       /* 18  DS:DX or DS:EDX */
    DWORD       pv_Client_EDX;      /* 1C  address of Disk Transfer Area */
    HEVENT      pv_hev;             /* 20 */
    fhandle*    pv_pfh[32];         /* 24 */
    pevent      pv_pev_vm2;         /* 48 */
    void*       pv_ppsft;           /* 4C  pointer to second SFT table */
    void*       pv_curdir[32];      /* 50  current directory for this VM */
    WORD        pv_flags2;          /* D0 */
    WORD        pv_unk2;            /* D2 */
    } pervm;
```

Per-Thread Data

IFSMgr piggybacks a doubleword onto every thread. It does this by allocating a thread data slot (using VMM service **_AllocateThreadDataSlot**) at Device Init time. Unlike some other devices which use this doubleword to store a pointer to a more substantial data structure, IFSMgr is content with using just the data slot. The data slot is located by an offset from the address of a thread's control block—which is the same as the ring-0 thread handle. The layout of IFSMgr's thread doubleword is as follows:

Bit	31	30	29	28-16	15-0
Use	Marked	Blocked	NoBlock	Not used	Count

If this doubleword is non-zero, then the coresponding thread is "in" IFSMgr. When a thread enters IFSMgr its count is incremented; when leaving it is decremented. The top three bits are used as flags for the state of threads which have entered IFSMgr.

Geoff Chappell shared his insights regarding the use of these bit flags in a recent email:

> The bit flags are concerned with the status of one thread with respect to threads that propose to work or have started to work on a volume lock.

> Working on a volume lock—for instance, to apply a lock or release one—has a potentially wide-ranging and even brutal effect on IFS operations that are already under way (say, in other threads). If a thread wants to work on a volume lock,

then it will have to wait until nobody else is working on the same volume lock—but even after then, it will have to wait until no thread is doing anything that might be affected by the change in the volume's lock state.

At the time that a thread is to start working on a volume lock, there is not much status information to go on. IFSMgr assumes that just about any thread that is in an IFS operation is liable to be affected. The *general* scheme is to set the *Marked* flag in each of them.

Some threads will already have the *NoBlock* flag set because it was deduced at an earlier stage that their IFS operation could not be affected by work on a volume lock. For instance, these threads do not get "marked."

Some threads will already have the *Blocked* flag set because they are blocked at places in their IFS operations where it is known not to matter if a volume lock gets worked on. For instance, if a thread has to wait for a parse buffer to become available, then it is not very far into its IFS operation and certainly a long way from being worried whether some volume is locked. Threads that have blocked at safe places do not get "marked" either.

The thread that wants to work on the volume lock blocks on a special key. As the other threads execute, some may finish their IFS operations. That's good: it makes one less thread to worry about. The general scheme when the IFSMgr decides a thread can't be affected by work on a volume lock is that if the thread has its "Marked" flag set, then the flag is cleared and the thread is deemed to no longer contribute to the count of threads that could be affected. When there are no longer any threads that could be affected, all threads waiting to work on volume locks are signalled.

Another good outcome, handled the same way, is that a "marked" thread blocks at a place known to be safe.

Some threads that were blocked at safe places may wake up. These and other threads (with or without the *Marked* flag) may eventually reach far enough into their IFS operation that they want access to a volume whose lock is to be worked on by some waiting thread. For some operations (such as on the paging file and on memory-mapped files and on pages opened as immovable), this won't matter, but in general, a thread that wants to access the volume will have to block until the work on that particular volume's lock is done. Again, the IFSMgr knows that the thread cannot now be affected by work on the volume's lock and so again, it may signal the threads that are waiting to work on volume locks.

In summary, *Marked* means that the thread is thought (possibly only cautiously) to prevent proceeding immediately with proposed work on a volume lock, *Blocked* means that the thread is blocked at a stage where it can't be affected by proposed work on a volume lock and *NoBlock* means that if work on a volume lock is proposed, then this thread is not to be regarded as preventing the work.

D

IFS Development Aids

This appendix describes some aids that were used in developing the sample code which accompanies the book. Since I have adopted the DDK's approach to writing VxDs in C (see *What's New in Windows 95 for VxD Writers?* by Ruediger Asche, April 24, 1994, MSDN CD), these aids fill in a few gaps where I felt there were some deficiencies.

chentry.exe: No Assembly Required

Usually, a VxD's device descriptor block (DDB) and control message dispatch procedure are placed in a small assembly language module. This is linked with the C object modules to build the final VxD. The reason this assembly language module is needed is that the Microsoft compiler only generates decorated public names. The least amount of decoration you can achieve is a leading underscore. Why is this a problem?

A VxD has a single exported symbol which is its device name with the suffix "_DDB" appended. This points to the device descriptor block and is used by the loader to find the segments in a VxD when bringing the module into memory. The C compiler only allows names like _FSHOOK_DDB, where FSHOOK_DDB is what is really desired. Using the decorated name would require clients of the VxD to use the name _FSHOOK when referring to it. Clearly this is not desirable.

The *chentry.exe* utility lets you go ahead and use decorated names by removing the underscore from the exported name *after* the VxD is built. If the exported DDB name does not have a leading underscore, CHENTRY does nothing. To use CHENTRY, you simply add the command **chentry VxdName** following the link step in your makefiles.

vxd.h: Some Basic Macros

If you use CHENTRY in your build process, then what you used to maintain in a separate assembly language module can now be incorporated in your C source file. This makes single source file VxDs easy to construct.

Every VxD requires two basic structures, a device descriptor block and a control message dispatch procedure. The primary purpose of *vxd.h* is to provide macros for setting up these two constructs.

Setting up a VxD's device descriptor block requires two steps. First, before the include statement for *vxd.h*, define the name for your device descriptor block. For example, these statements set up a device descriptor block for the VECTORS VxD:

```
#define  DDB  VECTORS_DDB
#include "vxd.h"
```

Inside *vxd.h* the following macro is defined which will be used from our C source file to initialize the contents of VECTORS_DDB:

```
// Declare Device Descriptor Block
#define Declare_DDB( name, major, minor, dispatch, devID, init,
                     v86proc, pmproc, refdata, svctbl, numsvcs )
    struct VxD_Desc_Block
        DDB = {  0, DDK_VERSION, devID, major, minor, 0, name, init,
                (DWORD)dispatch, (DWORD)v86proc, (DWORD)v86proc,
                0, 0, refdata, svctbl, numsvcs, 0, 'Prev',
                sizeof( struct VxD_Desc_Block ), 'Rsv1', 'Rsv2',
                'Rsv3' };
```

Then from the C source file, within a locked data segment, a global instance of the DDB is defined like this:

```
Declare_DDB( "VECTORS ",1,0,CtrlMsgDispatch,
            UNDEFINED_DEVICE_ID, VMM_INIT_ORDER,
            0, 0, 0, 0, 0 );
```

The control message dispatch procedure is constructed from macros that make it resemble a message map. Here is a typical dispatch procedure for a MultiMon monitor:

```
void __declspec( naked ) CtrlMsgDispatch( void ) {
    BEGIN_DISPATCH_MAP
        ON_SYS_CRITICAL_INIT    ( CtrlMsg_Sys_Crit_Init )
        ON_DEVICE_INIT          ( CtrlMsg_Device_Init )
        ON_INIT_COMPLETE        ( CtrlMsg_Init_Complete )
        ON_SYS_VM_TERMINATE     ( CtrlMsg_Sys_VM_Terminate )

        ON_DIRECTED1    ( PRIVATE_ARM_MONITOR, CtrlMsg_Arm_Monitor )
        ON_DIRECTED1    ( PRIVATE_INIT, CtrlMsg_Private_Init )
        ON_DIRECTED0    ( PRIVATE_SHUTDOWN, CtrlMsg_Private_Shutdown )
        ON_DEFAULT      ( )
```

```
END_DISPATCH_MAP
}
```

Between the `BEGIN_DISPATCH_MAP` and `END_DISPATCH_MAP` macros, one line is specified for each control message which is to have a handler. The macro `ON_DEFAULT` must be the last message handler macro; it returns properly for any message which does not have a handler. Each message handler macro specifies a function which is called for a particular control message. For instance, `ON_DEVICE_INIT` specifies that **CtrlMsg_Device_Init** will be called on receipt of a Device Init message. This function has a prototype defined in *vxd.h* as follows:

```
int SYSCTRL_CALLBACK CtrlMsg_Device_Init( HVM hSysVM, PCHAR pCmdTail );
```

These prototypes are required so that the proper arguments are pushed on the stack prior to calling the handler. The header file *vxd.h* contains macros and message handler prototypes for known control messages.

The dispatch macros also handle directed system control messages, those control messages which are private to a set of cooperating VxDs. The macros `ON_DIRECTED0` and `ON_DIRECTED1` take two arguments, the handler function and a message number (e.g. *PRIVATE_INIT*). The message number is private to the cooperating VxDs but is required to be in the range 0x70000000 to 0x7FFFFFFF. The reason that two `ON_DIRECTED` macros are used here is that `ON_DIRECTED0` calls a handler that takes no arguments whereas `ON_DIRECTED1` calls a handler which takes one argument which is passed in the EBX register.

One more fundamental macro that is included helps when creating a stack frame for a "hooked procedure." This is used when declaring a hook procedure for VMM's **Hook_Device_Service**. New with Windows 95 is the ability to unhook these services. To do so requires creating a proper function preamble and this is done by declaring the function with the `HOOK_PREAMBLE` macro:

```
// These two jumps make up the hook preamble
// These are needed to support Unhook_Device_Service
// The real hook procedure begins after these at "real_entry"
#define    HOOK_PREAMBLE(prev)            \
           _asm    jmp short real_entry   \
           _asm    jmp dword ptr prev     \
           _asm    real_entry:
```

The *prev* argument to this macro is a doubleword storage location which holds the original service's address. This location is filled in automatically by the **Hook_Device_Service** function. Here is an example of how this macro would be used:

```
// Win95 Hook_Device_Service fills this in!
PFN pPrev_Allocate_PM_Call_Back;

void __declspec( naked ) My_Allocate_PM_Call_Back( void ) {
  HOOK_PREAMBLE(pPrev_Allocate_PM_Call_Back)
  /* body of hook procedure */
```

```
  _asm      ret
  }
// This call installs the hook procedure
Hook_Device_Service( GetVxDServiceOrdinal(Allocate_PM_Call_Back),
                     My_Allocate_PM_Call_Back );
// This call removes the hook procedure
Unhook_Device_Service( GetVxDServiceOrdinal(Allocate_PM_Call_Back),
                       My_Allocate_PM_Call_Back );
```

vxd.h contains a variety of other simple macros which I leave to you to explore.

IFSWRAPS

IFSWRAPS is a static library, included on the companion diskette, which provides C callable functions for all IFSMgr services as well as a few VWIN32 and VMM services. This library was constructed in the same way as VXDWRAPS which accompanies the DDK. The header file *ifswraps.h* is included in source files where you call the library functions.

Most of the services supplied by IFSMgr use the C calling convention. This makes it almost trivial to make wrappers for these functions since no coding is required. For these functions, the calling parameters and return values are as described in the DDK. There are a handful of functions which use registers to pass arguments and receive return values; only these functions require some special treatment. These exceptions are described below:

unsigned long IFSMgr_Win32_Get_Ring0_Handle(sfn_t fhext,DWORD pFilePos)*
   On entry, **fhext** contains the extended file handle to be converted. If successful, the return value is the ring-0 file handle and *pFilePos* will contain the current file position for the handle passed in. If the conversion fails, the function returns 0.

int IFSMgr_Ring0_FileIO(EREGS pRegs)*
   The *pRegs* argument points to an EREGS structure containing the input values of registers:

```
    typedef struct eregs { DWORD r_eax;
                           DWORD r_ebx;
                           DWORD r_ecx;
                           DWORD r_edx;
                           DWORD r_esi;
                           DWORD r_edi;    } EREGS;
```

If the return value is 0, the call was successful and the EREGS structure contains the return values in registers; if the return value is non-zero, it is an error code. See the DDK for register assignments for each call.

int IFSMgr_Ring0GetDriveInfo(DWORD unit)

The unit argument is zero-based drive number. Returns −1 if the drive is not an IFS drive, otherwise returns *flags* describing the drive (see DDK for flag bits).

int IFSMgr_ServerDOSCall(HVM hvm,unsigned int fcn,PDPL32 dpl, PCRS pCRegs)

The calling arguments include *hvm*, the handle of the current VM; *fcn*, the requested function number; *dpl*, a pointer to the extended 32-bit DPL (see DDK for definition); and *pCRegs*, a pointer to the client register structure. Returns −1 if the request is not accepted, 0 if request is accepted.

int IFSMgr_Get_Version(VOID)

If 0 is returned, no IFSMgr is loaded; otherwise the return value is the version number.

BOOL Query_PhysLock(DWORD unit)

The unit argument is the Int 13h unit number for the disk which is being queried; if TRUE is returned, the current process owns the volume lock.

The following services are also wrapped by IFSWRAPS:

```
DWORD VWIN32_GetCurrentProcessHandle(VOID)
VOID Simulate_Far_Jmp(DWORD selector, DWORD offset)
BOOL Get_PM_Int_Vector(DWORD intnum, PWORD pSel, PDWORD pOfs)
BOOL Hook_PM_Interrupt(DWORD intnum, PWORD pSel, PDWORD pOfs,
     PVOID handler, DWORD refdata)
BOOL Hook_V86_Int_Chain(DWORD intnum, PVOID handler)
BOOL Test_Sys_VM_Handle(HVM hvm)
PVOID Map_Flat(DWORD segofs, DWORD offof)
BOOL Directed_Sys_Control0(PVMMDDB pDDB, DWORD SysControl)
BOOL Directed_Sys_Control1(PVMMDDB pDDB, DWORD SysControl,
     PVOID arg1)
BOOL Directed_Sys_Control2(PVMMDDB pDDB, DWORD SysControl,
     PVOID arg1, PVOID arg2)
PVOID Hook_Device_Service(DWORD svcnum, PVOID handler)
BOOL Unhook_Device_Service(DWORD svcnum, PVOID handler)
```

DEBIFS

DEBIFS is the name of a VxD, included on the companion diskette, which contains a *dot command*. By dot command I mean a command which you enter in your debugger, like **.vmm b**. The commands which DEBIFS provides dump out useful information about IFSMgr's data structures. The available commands are:

.debifs i address

Dumps an `ifsreq` structure at specified address

.debifs s address

Dumps a `shres` structure at specified address

.debifs f address

Dumps a `fhandle` structure at specified address

Here is a sample dump of an `ifsreq` structure:

```
:.debifs i esi
ifsreq at C1581D38:
 ir_length(0)=00710000 ir_flags(4)=C0 ir_user(5)=01 ir_sfn(6)=00FF
 ir_pid(8)=00012437   ir_ppath(C)=FFFFFBBB ir_data(14)=81A30001
 ir_aux1(10)=FFFFFFFF ir_aux2(28)=00000000 ir_aux3(2C)=00000000
 ir_options(18)=0000  ir_rh(1C)=00000000   ir_fh(20)=00000000
 ir_pos(24)=00000000  ir_pev(30)=00000000  ir_error(1A)=0000
 ir_fsd[](34)=00000000,(38)=00000000,(3C)=00000000,(40)=00000000,...
 ifs_pfh(74)=00000000 ifs_psft(78)=00000000 ifs_psr(7C)=00000000
 ifs_proid(84)=FFFFFFFF ifs_pdb(80)=00024360
 ifs_func(88)=6C ifs_drv(89)=03 ifs_hflag(8A)=00
 ifs_nflags(8B)=60 { LFN ExtH OEM }
 ifs_pbuffer(8C)=FFFFFBBB  ifs_VMHandle(90)=C3D20154  ifs_PV(94)=C3D203EC
 Client registers:
  EAX(B4)=00006CC0  EBX(A8)=000000C0  ECX(B0)=00710000  EDX(AC)=81A30001
  EDI(98)=00000003  ESI(9C)=0071F68C  DS(D4)=013F       ES(D0)=013F
```

This dump was created from SoftIce for Windows 95. Note that a register name may be passed as an address; in actuality, any valid debugger expression may be used for an address. The hexadecimal value in parentheses following each member name is the offset of the member from the beginning of the structure.

Bibliography

Arun, Russ. 1994. "Chicago File System Features—Tips & Issues," Microsoft Corp. White Paper, April 22, 1994.

Asche, Ruediger. 1994. "What's New in Windows 95 for VxD Writers?," Microsoft Developer's Network CD-ROM, April 1994.

Auerbach, Karl. 1987. "Protocol Standard for a Netbios Service on a Tcp/Udp Transport: Concepts and Methods," RFC 1001.

Auerbach, Karl. 1987. "Protocol Standard for a Netbios Service on a Tcp/Udp Transport: Detailed Specifications," RFC 1002.

Baker, Art. 1997. *The Windows NT Device Driver Book: A Guide for Programmers.* Prentice-Hall, Inc.

Brown, Ralf and Kyle, Jim. 1994. *Uninterrupted Interrupts. (A Programmer's CD-ROM Reference to Network APIs and to BIOS, DOS, and Third-Party Calls).* Addison-Wesley Publishing Co.

Crawford, John and Gelsinger, Patrick. 1987. *Programming the 80386.* SYBEX, Inc.

Custer, Helen. 1993. *Inside Windows NT.* Microsoft Press.

DiLascia, Paul and Stone, Victor. 1996. "Sweeper," *Microsoft Interactive Developer*, vol.1, no.1 (Spring 1996), p.16

Microsoft Corp. 1993. *Microsoft MS-DOS Programmer's Reference (Version 6).* Microsoft Press.

Microsoft Corp. 1995. *Windows 95 Device Driver Kit.* A component of the Microsoft Developer's Network (MSDN) subscription.

Microsoft Corp. 1995. *Programmer's Guide to Microsoft Windows 95*. Microsoft Press.

Microsoft Corp. 1995. *Microsoft Windows 95 Resource Kit*. Microsoft Press.

Microsoft Corp. 1996. "Microsoft Networks SMB File Sharing Protocol," Document Version 6.0p.

Mitchell, Stan. 1995. "Monitoring Windows 95 File Activity in Ring 0," *Windows/DOS Developer's Journal*, vol.6, no.7 (July 1995), p.6

Oney, Walter. 1996. *Systems Programming for Windows 95*. Microsoft Press.

Perry, Dan. 1996. "CIFS: A Common Internet File System," *Microsoft Interactive Developer*, vol.1, no.5 (November 1996), p.56

Pietrek, Matt. 1996. *Windows 95 System Programming Secrets*. IDG Books Worldwide.

Russinovich, Mark and Cogswell, Bryce. 1997. "Examining the Windows NT File System," *Dr. Dobb's Journal*, vol.21, no.2 (February 1997).

Schulman, Andrew. 1992. "Exploring Demand-Paged Virtual Memory in Windows Enhanced Mode," *Microsoft Systems Journal*, vol.7, no.8 (December 1992), p.17.

Schulman, Andrew. 1994. *Undocumented DOS*, Second Edition. Addison-Wesley Publishing Co.

Schulman, Andrew. 1994. *Unauthorized Windows 95*. IDG Books Worldwide.

Schwaderer, W. David. 1988. *C Programmer's Guide to NetBIOS*. Howard Sams & Co.

Silberschatz, Abraham and Galvin, Peter. 1994. *Operating Systems Concepts*. Addison-Wesley Publishing Co., Fourth Edition.

Internet Resources

Windows 95 File System / VxDs

O'Reilly Windows Center	*http://www.ora.com/centers/windows/*
Author Page: "Inside Win95 File System"	*http://www.sourcequest.com/win95ifs/*
Device Driver Development Home Page	*http://www.albany.net/~danorton/ddk*
Vireo Software Home Page	*http://www.vireo.com*
UseNet Newsgroup	*comp.os.ms-windows.programmer.vxd*

CIFS/SMB

CIFS and SMB specifications	*ftp://ftp.microsoft.com/developr/drg/CIFS*
CIFS Home Page	*http://www.microsoft.com/intdev/cifs/cifs.htm*
SAMBA download	*ftp://samba.anu.edu.au/pub/samba*
UseNet Newsgroup	*comp.protocols.smb*

WDM/Kernel-Mode Drivers

WDM Home Page	*http://www.microsoft.com/hwdev/pcfuture/wdm.htm*
WDM for Windows & Windows NT	*http://www.microsoft.com/hwdev/pcfuture/wdmview.htm*
NT Internal Home Page	*http://www.ntinternals.com*
Microsoft Interactive Developer	*http://www.microsoft.com/mind*
UseNet Newsgroup	*comp.os.ms-windows.programmer.nt.kernel-mode*

Index

About the Author

Stan Mitchell is a consulting software engineer in Silicon Valley. He specializes in driver and system level programming on the Wintel platform. Stan earned a Bachelor of Science degree from Wayne State University in 1970 and a Master of Science from University of Waterloo in 1976.

He entered the microcomputer field in 1979. His early projects emphasized logic design of single-board microcomputers and micro-controllers. The most memorable project during this period was the design of a full-SCSI host adapter with 8048 firmware at Adaptec, Inc.

After the introduction of the IBM-PC, Stan shifted his focus to MS-DOS system software and then to MS-Windows. His recent projects have included developing a NetBIOS layer over TCP/IP for NetManage and a Windows 95 file system monitor for Xerox/XSoft.

Stan and his wife Maggie, make Milpitas, CA, their home. In his spare time, he likes to romp with his dogs (Yanni and Munchkin), play a serious game of table tennis, and browse the shelves of nearby bookstores.

Colophon

The animal featured on the cover of *Inside the Windows 95 File System* is a representative of one of the more than 65,000 species of mollusks. There are six classes of mollusk. The largest of these classes is the gastropod. The coiled shell on the animal on the cover of this book is typical of many, but not all, gastropods. This mollusk may be an Astraea Heliotropium, a native of the waters surrounding New Zealand. The Astraea Heliotropium grows to a size of three to four inches, and has a lovely iridescent purplish-pink shell.

No species shows as much diversity of shape and size as the mollusk. Despite this diversity, most mollusks have the same basic body plan. The word mollusk means "soft bodied." The soft mollusk body is composed of a combined head-foot containing the central nervous system and a layer of tissue called the mantle that covers the internal organs. The mantle also secretes the shell that covers the mollusk's body. The shell is part of the animal and grows with it.

Edie Freedman designed the cover of this book, using a 19th-century engraving from the Dover Pictorial Archive. The cover layout was produced with Quark XPress 3.3 using the ITC Garamond font.

The inside layout was designed by Edie Freedman and Nancy Priest and implemented in FrameMaker 5.0 by Mike Sierra. The text and heading fonts are ITC Garamond Light and Garamond Book. The illustrations that appear in the book were created in Macromedia Freehand 5.0 by Chris Reilley. This colophon was written by Clairemarie Fisher O'Leary.

 **More Titles from O'Reilly**

Windows

Inside the Windows 95 Registry

By Ron Petrusha
1st Edition August1996
594 pages, includes diskette
ISBN 1-56592-170-4

This book covers remote registry access, differences between the Win95 and NT registries, and registry backup. You'll also find a thorough examination of the role that the registry plays in OLE, coverage of undocumented registry services, and more. Petrusha shows programmers how to access the Win95 registry from Win32, Win16, and DOS programs, in C and Visual Basic. VxD sample code is also included. The book includes a diskette with registry tools such as REGSPY, a program that shows exactly how Windows applications, libraries, and drivers use settings in the registry.

Windows NT in a Nutshell

By Eric Pearce
1st Edition June 1997 (est.)
342 pages, ISBN 1-56592-251-4

Anybody who installs Windows NT, creates a user, or adds a printer is an NT system administrator (whether they realize it or not). This book organizes NT's complex 4.0 GUI interface, dialog boxes, and multitude of DOS-shell commands into an easy-to-use quick reference for anybody who uses or manages an NT system. It features a new tagged callout approach to documenting the GUI as well as real-life examples of command usage and strategies for problem solving, with an emphasis on networking. Windows NT in a Nutshell will be as useful to the single-system home user as it will be to the administrator of a 1,000-node corporate network.

Inside the Windows 95 File System

By Stan Mitchell
1st Edition May 1997
400 pages, ISBN 1-56592-200-X

This book details the Windows 95 File System, as well as the new opportunities and challenges it brings developers. Over the course of the book, the author progressively strips away the layers of the Win95 File System, which reside in a component named Installable File System Manager or IFSMgr, providing the reader with information crucial for effective File System development. Its "hands-on" approach will help developers become better equipped to make design decisions using the new Win95 File System features.

Windows Annoyances

By David A. Karp
1st Edition June 1997
300 pages (est.), ISBN 1-56592-266-2

Windows Annoyances, a comprehensive resource for intermediate to advanced users of Windows 95 and NT 4.0, details step-by-step how to customize your Win95/NT operating system through an extensive collection of tips, tricks, and workarounds.

You'll learn how to customize every aspect of these systems, far beyond the intentions of Microsoft. An entire chapter on the registry explains how to back up, repair, compress, and transfer portions of the registry for personal customization. Win95 users will discover how Plug and Play, the technology that makes Win95 so hardware-compatible, can save time and improve the way you interact with your computer. You'll also learn how to benefit from the new 32-bit software and hardware drivers that support such features as improved multitasking and long filenames.

C and C++

C++: The Core Language

By Gregory Satir & Doug Brown
1st Edition October 1995
230 pages, ISBN 1-56592-116-X

C++: The Core Language is a first book for C programmers transitioning to C++, an object-oriented enhancement of the C programming language. Designed to get readers up to speed quickly, this book thoroughly explains the important concepts and features and gives brief overviews of the rest of the language. Covers features common to all C++ compilers, including those on UNIX, Windows NT, Windows, DOS, and Macintosh.

Practical C++ Programming

By Steve Oualline

1st Edition September 1995
584 pages, ISBN 1-56592-139-9

Fast becoming the standard language of commercial software development, C++ is an update of the C programming language, adding object-oriented features that are very helpful for today's larger graphical applications.

Practical C++ Programming is a complete introduction to the C++ language for the beginning programmer, and also for C programmers transitioning to C++. Topics covered include good programming style, C++ syntax (what to use and what not to use), C++ class design, debugging and optimization, and common programming mistakes. At the end of each chapter are a number of exercises you can use to make sure you've grasped the concepts. Solutions to most are provided.

Practical C Programming

By Steve Oualline
3rd Edition July 1997 (est.)
475 pages, ISBN 1-56592-306-5

There are lots of introductory C books, but this new edition of *Practical C Programming* is the one that has the no-nonsense, practical approach that has made Nutshell Handbooks® so popular. C programming is more than just getting the syntax right. Style and debugging also play a tremendous part in creating programs that run well and are easy to maintain.

The third edition of *Practical C Programming* teaches how to create programs that are easyto read, debug, and maintain. It features more extensive examples, offers an introduction to graphical development environments, describes Electronic Archaeology (the art of going through someone else's code), and stresses practical rules. The book covers several Windows compilers, in addition to UNIX compilers. Program examples conform to ANSI C.

Checking C Programs with lint

By Ian F. Darwin
1st Edition October 1988
82 pages, ISBN 0-937175-30-7

The lint program checker has proven time and again to be one of the best tools for finding portability problems and certain types of coding errors in C programs. Lint verifies a program or program segments against standard libraries, checks the code for common portability errors, and tests the programming against some tried and true guidelines. Linting your code is a necessary (though not sufficient) step in writing clean, portable, effective programs. This book introduces you to lint, guides you through running it on your programs, and helps you interpret lint's output.

Perl

Programming Perl, Second Edition

By Larry Wall, Tom Christiansen,
& Randal L. Schwartz
2nd Edition September 1996
676 pages, ISBN 1-56592-149-6

Programming Perl, Second Edition, is coauthored by Larry Wall, the creator of Perl. Perl is a language for easily manipulating text, files, and processes. It provides a more concise and readable way to do many jobs that were formerly accomplished (with difficulty) by programming with C or one of the shells. This heavily revised second edition contains a full explanation of Perl version 5.003.

Learning Perl, Second Edition

By Randal L. Schwartz
Foreword by Larry Wall
2nd Edition July 1997
400 pages, ISBN 1-56592-284-0

This second edition of *Learning Perl*, with a foreword by Perl author Larry Wall, fully covers Perl, Version 5. In this new edition, program examples and exercise answers have been radically updated to reflect typical usage under Perl 5, and numerous details have been added or modified. In addition, you'll find new sections introducing Perl references and CGI programming.

Learning Perl, Second Edition is ideal for system administrators, programmers, and anyone else wanting a down-to-earth introduction to this useful language. Written by a Perl trainer, its aim is to make a competent, hands-on Perl programmer out of the reader as quickly as possible. The book takes a tutorial approach and includes hundreds of short code examples, along with some lengthy ones. The relatively inexperienced programmer will find *Learning Perl* easily accessible. For a comprehensive and detailed guide to advanced programming with Perl, read O'Reilly's companion book, *Programming Perl, Second Edition*.

CGI Programming on the World Wide Web

By Shishir Gundavaram
1st Edition March 1996
450 pages, ISBN 1-56592-168-2

This book offers a comprehensive explanation of CGI and related techniques for people who hold on to the dream of providing their own information servers on the Web. It starts at the beginning, explaining the value of CGI and how it works, then moves swiftly into the subtle details of programming.

Perl 5 Desktop Reference

By Johan Vromans
1st Edition February 1996
44 pages, ISBN 1-56592-187-9

This is the standard quick-reference guide for the Perl programming language. It provides a complete overview of the language, from variables to input and output, from flow control to regular expressions, from functions to document formats—all packed into a convenient, carry-around booklet. Updated to cover Perl version 5.003.

Mastering Regular Expressions

By Jeffrey E. F. Friedl
1st Edition January 1997
368 pages, ISBN 1-56592-257-3

Regular expressions, a powerful tool for manipulating text and data, are found in scripting languages, editors, programming environments, and specialized tools. In this book, author Jeffrey Friedl leads you through the steps of crafting a regular expression that gets the job done. He examines a variety of tools and uses them in an extensive array of examples, dedicating an entire chapter to Perl.

How to stay in touch with O'Reilly

1. Visit Our Award-Winning Web Site

http://www.ora.com/

★ "Top 100 Sites on the Web" —*PC Magazine*
★ "Top 5% Web sites" —*Point Communications*
★ "3-Star site" —*The McKinley Group*

Our web site contains a library of comprehensive product information (including book excerpts and tables of contents), downloadable software, background articles, interviews with technology leaders, links to relevant sites, book cover art, and more. File us in your Bookmarks or Hotlist!

2. Join Our Email Mailing Lists

New Product Releases

To receive automatic email with brief descriptions of all new O'Reilly products as they are released, send email to:
listproc@online.ora.com
Put the following information in the first line of your message (*not* in the Subject field):
subscribe ora-news "Your Name" of "Your Organization" (for example: subscribe ora-news Kris Webber of Fine Enterprises)

O'Reilly Events

If you'd also like us to send information about trade show events, special promotions, and other O'Reilly events, send email to: **listproc@online.ora.com**
Put the following information in the first line of your message (*not* in the Subject field):
subscribe ora-events "Your Name" of "Your Organization"

3. Get Examples from Our Books via FTP

There are two ways to access an archive of example files from our books:

Regular FTP

- ftp to:
  ftp.ora.com
  (login: anonymous
  password: your email address)
- Point your web browser to:
  ftp://ftp.ora.com/

FTPMAIL

- Send an email message to:
  ftpmail@online.ora.com
  (Write "help" in the message body)

4. Visit Our Gopher Site

- Connect your gopher to:
  gopher.ora.com

- Point your web browser to:
  gopher://gopher.ora.com/

- Telnet to:
  gopher.ora.com
  login: gopher

5. Contact Us via Email

order@ora.com
To place a book or software order online. Good for North American and international customers.

subscriptions@ora.com
To place an order for any of our newsletters or periodicals.

books@ora.com
General questions about any of our books.

software@ora.com
For general questions and product information about our software. Check out O'Reilly Software Online at **http://software.ora.com/** for software and technical support information. Registered O'Reilly software users send your questions to: **website-support@ora.com**

cs@ora.com
For answers to problems regarding your order or our products.

booktech@ora.com
For book content technical questions or corrections.

proposals@ora.com
To submit new book or software proposals to our editors and product managers.

international@ora.com
For information about our international distributors or translation queries. For a list of our distributors outside of North America check out:
http://www.ora.com/www/order/country.html

O'Reilly & Associates, Inc.
101 Morris Street, Sebastopol, CA 95472 USA
TEL   707-829-0515 or 800-998-9938
          (6am to 5pm PST)
FAX   707-829-0104

Titles from O'Reilly

Please note that upcoming titles are displayed in italic.

WEBPROGRAMMING

Apache: The Definitive Guide
Building Your Own Web
 Conferences
Building Your Own Website
*Building Your Own Win-CGI
 Programs*
CGI Programming for the World
 Wide Web
Designing for the Web
HTML: The Definitive Guide,
 2nd Ed.
JavaScript: The Definitive Guide,
 2nd Ed.
Learning Perl
Programming Perl, 2nd Ed.
Mastering Regular Expressions
WebMaster in a Nutshell
Web Security & Commerce
*Web Client Programming with
 Perl*
World Wide Web Journal

USING THE INTERNET

Smileys
The Future Does Not Compute
The Whole Internet User's Guide
 & Catalog
The Whole Internet for Win 95
Using Email Effectively
Bandits on the Information
 Superhighway

JAVA SERIES

Exploring Java
Java AWT Reference
*Java Fundamental Classes
 Reference*
Java in a Nutshell
Java Language Reference
Java Network Programming
Java Threads
Java Virtual Machine

SOFTWARE

WebSite™ 1.1
WebSite Professional™
Building Your Own Web
 Conferences
WebBoard™
PolyForm™
Statisphere™

SONGLINE GUIDES

NetActivism   NetResearch
Net Law   NetSuccess
NetLearning   NetTravel
Net Lessons

SYSTEM ADMINISTRATION

Building Internet Firewalls
Computer Crime: A
 Crimefighter's Handbook
Computer Security Basics
DNS and BIND, 2nd Ed.
Essential System Administration,
 2nd Ed.
Getting Connected: The Internet
 at 56K and Up
Linux Network Administrator's
 Guide
Managing Internet Information
 Services
Managing NFS and NIS
Networking Personal Computers
 with TCP/IP
Practical UNIX & Internet
 Security, 2nd Ed.
PGP: Pretty Good Privacy
sendmail, 2nd Ed.
sendmail Desktop Reference
System Performance Tuning
TCP/IP Network Administration
termcap & terminfo
Using & Managing UUCP
Volume 8: X Window System
 Administrator's Guide
Web Security & Commerce

UNIX

Exploring Expect
Learning VBScript
Learning GNU Emacs, 2nd Ed.
Learning the bash Shell
Learning the Korn Shell
Learning the UNIX Operating
 System
Learning the vi Editor
Linux in a Nutshell
Making TeX Work
Linux Multimedia Guide
Running Linux, 2nd Ed.
SCO UNIX in a Nutshell
sed & awk, 2nd Edition
Tcl/Tk Tools
UNIX in a Nutshell: System V
 Edition
UNIX Power Tools
Using csh & tsch
When You Can't Find Your UNIX
 System Administrator
Writing GNU Emacs Extensions

WEB REVIEW STUDIO SERIES

Gif Animation Studio
Shockwave Studio

WINDOWS

Dictionary of PC Hardware and
 Data Communications Terms
Inside the Windows 95 Registry
Inside the Windows 95 File
 System
Windows Annoyances
*Windows NT File System
 Internals*
Windows NT in a Nutshell

PROGRAMMING

Advanced Oracle PL/SQL
 Programming
Applying RCS and SCCS
C++: The Core Language
Checking C Programs with lint
DCE Security Programming
Distributing Applications Across
 DCE & Windows NT
Encyclopedia of Graphics File
 Formats, 2nd Ed.
Guide to Writing DCE
 Applications
lex & yacc
Managing Projects with make
Mastering Oracle Power Objects
Oracle Design: The Definitive
 Guide
Oracle Performance Tuning, 2nd
 Ed.
Oracle PL/SQL Programming
Porting UNIX Software
POSIX Programmer's Guide
POSIX.4: Programming for the
 Real World
Power Programming with RPC
Practical C Programming
Practical C++ Programming
Programming Python
Programming with curses
Programming with GNU Software
Pthreads Programming
Software Portability with imake,
 2nd Ed.
Understanding DCE
Understanding Japanese
 Information Processing
UNIX Systems Programming for
 SVR4

BERKELEY 4.4 SOFTWARE DISTRIBUTION

4.4BSD System Manager's
 Manual
4.4BSD User's Reference Manual
4.4BSD User's Supplementary
 Documents
4.4BSD Programmer's Reference
 Manual
4.4BSD Programmer's
 Supplementary Documents
X Programming
Vol. 0: X Protocol Reference
 Manual
Vol. 1: Xlib Programming Manual
Vol. 2: Xlib Reference Manual
Vol. 3M: X Window System User's
 Guide, Motif Edition
Vol. 4M: X Toolkit Intrinsics
 Programming Manual, Motif
 Edition
Vol. 5: X Toolkit Intrinsics
 Reference Manual
Vol. 6A: Motif Programming
 Manual
Vol. 6B: Motif Reference Manual
Vol. 6C: Motif Tools
Vol. 8 : X Window System
 Administrator's Guide
Programmer's Supplement for
 Release 6
X User Tools
The X Window System in a
 Nutshell

CAREER & BUSINESS

Building a Successful Software
 Business
The Computer User's Survival
 Guide
Love Your Job!
Electronic Publishing on CD-
 ROM

TRAVEL

Travelers' Tales: Brazil
Travelers' Tales: Food
Travelers' Tales: France
Travelers' Tales: Gutsy Women
Travelers' Tales: India
Travelers' Tales: Mexico
Travelers' Tales: Paris
Travelers' Tales: San Francisco
Travelers' Tales: Spain
Travelers' Tales: Thailand
Travelers' Tales: A Woman's
 World

O'REILLY™

TO ORDER: **800-998-9938** • *order@ora.com* • *http://www.ora.com/*
OUR PRODUCTS ARE AVAILABLE AT A BOOKSTORE OR SOFTWARE STORE NEAR YOU.
FOR INFORMATION: **800-998-9938** • **707-829-0515** • *info@ora.com*

International Distributors

UK, Europe, Middle East and Northern Africa (except France, Germany, Switzerland, & Austria)

INQUIRIES
International Thomson Publishing Europe
Berkshire House
168-173 High Holborn
London WC1V 7AA, United Kingdom
Telephone: 44-171-497-1422
Fax: 44-171-497-1426
Email: itpint@itps.co.uk

ORDERS
International Thomson Publishing Services, Ltd.
Cheriton House, North Way
Andover, Hampshire SP10 5BE, United Kingdom
Telephone: 44-264-342-832
  (UK orders)
Telephone: 44-264-342-806
  (outside UK)
Fax: 44-264-364418 (UK orders)
Fax: 44-264-342761 (outside UK)
UK & Eire orders: itpuk@itps.co.uk
International orders: itpint@itps.co.uk

France

Editions Eyrolles
61 bd Saint-Germain
75240 Paris Cedex 05
France
Fax: 33-01-44-41-11-44

FRENCH LANGUAGE BOOKS
All countries except Canada
Phone: 33-01-44-41-46-16
Email: geodif@eyrolles.com

ENGLISH LANGUAGE BOOKS
Phone: 33-01-44-41-11-87
Email: distribution@eyrolles.com

Australia

WoodsLane Pty. Ltd.
7/5 Vuko Place, Warriewood NSW 2102
P.O. Box 935, Mona Vale NSW 2103
Australia
Telephone: 61-2-9970-5111
Fax: 61-2-9970-5002
Email: info@woodslane.com.au

Germany, Switzerland, and Austria

INQUIRIES
O'Reilly Verlag
Balthasarstr. 81
D-50670 Köln
Germany
Telephone: 49-221-97-31-60-0
Fax: 49-221-97-31-60-8
Email: anfragen@oreilly.de

ORDERS
International Thomson Publishing
Königswinterer Straße 418
53227 Bonn, Germany
Telephone: 49-228-97024 0
Fax: 49-228-441342
Email: order@oreilly.de

Asia (except Japan & India)

INQUIRIES
International Thomson Publishing Asia
60 Albert Street #15-01
Albert Complex
Singapore 189969
Telephone: 65-336-6411
Fax: 65-336-7411

ORDERS
Telephone: 65-336-6411
Fax: 65-334-1617
thomson@signet.com.sg

New Zealand

WoodsLane New Zealand Ltd.
21 Cooks Street (P.O. Box 575)
Wanganui, New Zealand
Telephone: 64-6-347-6543
Fax: 64-6-345-4840
Email: info@woodslane.com.au

Japan

O'Reilly Japan, Inc.
Kiyoshige Building 2F
12-Banchi, Sanei-cho
Shinjuku-ku
Tokyo 160 Japan
Telephone: 81-3-3356-5227
Fax: 81-3-3356-5261
Email: kenji@ora.com

India

Computer Bookshop (India) PVT. LTD.
190 Dr. D.N. Road, Fort
Bombay 400 001
India
Telephone: 91-22-207-0989
Fax: 91-22-262-3551
Email: cbsbom@giasbm01.vsnl.net.in

The Americas

O'Reilly & Associates, Inc.
101 Morris Street
Sebastopol, CA 95472 U.S.A.
Telephone: 707-829-0515
Telephone: 800-998-9938 (U.S. & Canada)
Fax: 707-829-0104
Email: order@ora.com

Southern Africa

International Thomson Publishing Southern Africa
Building 18, Constantia Park
240 Old Pretoria Road
P.O. Box 2459
Halfway House, 1685 South Africa
Telephone: 27-11-805-4819
Fax: 27-11-805-3648

O'REILLY™

TO ORDER: **800-998-9938** • **order@ora.com** • **http://www.ora.com/**
OUR PRODUCTS ARE AVAILABLE AT A BOOKSTORE OR SOFTWARE STORE NEAR YOU.
FOR INFORMATION: **800-998-9938** • **707-829-0515** • **info@ora.com**

O'REILLY™

O'Reilly & Associates, Inc.
101 Morris Street
Sebastopol, CA 95472-9902
1-800-998-9938

Visit us online at:
http://www.ora.com/
orders@ora.com

O'REILLY WOULD LIKE TO HEAR FROM YOU

Which book did this card come from?

_____

Where did you buy this book?
- ❏ Bookstore
- ❏ Direct from O'Reilly
- ❏ Bundled with hardware/software
- ❏ Other _____

- ❏ Computer Store
- ❏ Class/seminar

What operating system do you use?
- ❏ UNIX
- ❏ Windows NT
- ❏ Other _____

- ❏ Macintosh
- ❏ PC(Windows/DOS)

What is your job description?
- ❏ System Administrator
- ❏ Network Administrator
- ❏ Web Developer
- ❏ Other _____

- ❏ Programmer
- ❏ Educator/Teacher

❏ Please send me O'Reilly's catalog, containing a complete listing of O'Reilly books and software.

Name _____ Company/Organization _____

Address _____

City _____ State _____ Zip/Postal Code _____ Country _____

Telephone _____ Internet or other email address (specify network) _____

Nineteenth century wood engraving
of a bear from the O'Reilly &
Associates Nutshell Handbook®
Using & Managing UUCP.

BUSINESS REPLY MAIL

FIRST CLASS MAIL   PERMIT NO. 80   SEBASTOPOL, CA

Postage will be paid by addressee

O'Reilly & Associates, Inc.
101 Morris Street
Sebastopol, CA 95472-9902